# Playing the Market

# Playing the Market

*Retail Investment and Speculation in Twentieth-Century Britain*

KIERAN HEINEMANN

OXFORD
UNIVERSITY PRESS

# OXFORD
## UNIVERSITY PRESS

Great Clarendon Street, Oxford, OX2 6DP,
United Kingdom

Oxford University Press is a department of the University of Oxford.
It furthers the University's objective of excellence in research, scholarship,
and education by publishing worldwide. Oxford is a registered trade mark of
Oxford University Press in the UK and in certain other countries

First Edition published in 2021

Impression: 1

Published in the United States of America by Oxford University Press
198 Madison Avenue, New York, NY 10016, United States of America

British Library Cataloguing in Publication Data
Data available

Library of Congress Control Number: 2021937520

ISBN 978–0–19–886425–7

DOI: 10.1093/oso/9780198864257.001.0001

Printed and bound by
CPI Group (UK) Ltd, Croydon, CR0 4YY

*For Millen*

# Acknowledgements

I am tremendously grateful to Emmanuel College, Cambridge for providing such a unique academic environment and for awarding me a Derek Brewer PhD studentship, without which I could not have carried out the doctoral research that forms the basis of this book. The German Academic Exchange Service kindly granted me a one-year PhD Scholarship, while the North American Conference on British Studies and the Royal Historical Society generously provided travel funding for research and conferences.

The foundation of this research was laid in Berlin and would not have made it to Cambridge without the support and encouragement of my friends Angelo D'Abundo, Can Atli, Hannes Bemm, Konstantin Bosch, Sören Brandes, Johannes Groß, Franzi Grun, Rafael Jakob, Julian Jürgenmeyer, Sebastian Kempkens, Nino Klingler, and Katharina Wendler. Thomas Mergel, Michael Wildt, and Heinrich August Winkler have been important academic mentors at Humboldt University and I am grateful for their support.

In London, the members of staff at the British Library and the German Historical Institute provided excellent working conditions. I am much indebted to Andrew Riley and Heidi Egginton at the Churchill Archives Centre in Cambridge for having pointed me towards valuable source material. Lord Howell, Sir Tim Lankester, Sir Patrick Sergeant, and Michael Walters kindly agreed to talk to me about their experiences with Mrs Thatcher and/or City journalism. Philip Lovelace of the London Stock Exchange Group kindly granted permission to use in this book data from the Financial Times All Share Index.

I owe a great deal to the following friends and colleagues for making the work on this book such an inspiring intellectual journey in all sorts of ways: Tom Arnold-Forster, Sarah Bendall, Owen Brittan, Alex Campsie, Laura Carter, Aled Davies, Lucy Delap, <acks verso>Freddy Foks, Rhys Jones, David Kynaston, Peter Mandler, Tiago Mata, Partha Moman, George Moore, Duncan Needham, Alexander Nützenadel, Kim Priemel, Dame Fiona Reynolds, Laura Rischbieter, Ben Slingo, Will Summers, and Zoë Thomas.

Jon Lawrence has been a wonderful PhD supervisor, who always guided me in the right direction, while at the same time granting me the necessary freedom to pursue my ideas. Martin Daunton encouraged me to turn the thesis into a book and has been an invaluable source of advice along the way. I am grateful to Katie Bishop, Samantha Downes, and Céline Louasli for giving the book a home at Oxford University Press.

I am grateful to my family, simply for being there for me. My Mum helped me understand why Thatcher came to power. My Dad taught me what it means to be a historian. And Patrick stood up for his little brother when he felt that radical economic historians were having a go at him.

By far the largest debt of gratitude, however, I owe to Millen Belay for making this wonderful journey possible. Before it came to an end, she gave birth to our children Theodor and Selma, and she put up with their dad spending quite a few sunny days at the library instead of in the playground. This book is for her.

*London,*
*July 2020*

# Table of Contents

# Introduction

## Writing the History of Capitalism from below

Early in 2019, at the height of the negotiations over the United Kingdom's departure from the European Union, diplomats and civil servants on the continent were shocked by Britain's level of political disintegration, lack of diplomatic skill, and the degree of delusion that seemed to have stricken members of the ruling Conservative Party and decision makers in Westminster. But in spite of the Brexit chaos, in one regard the European Commission genuinely thought that its member states could learn something from Britain and that there was a field in which the departing member was setting exemplary standards. As part of its ambitious initiative for a Capital Markets Union, the Commission had just published a report with proposals for 'fostering the participation of retail investors in the EU's capital markets'.[1] It found that continental European investors are historically risk-averse when it comes to investing in financial securities; and that in Britain investors have access to 'a broader range of low-cost investment products and services than in many other EU countries'. In Britain, the private investor plays a far bigger role in the stock market than in continental Europe. A total of 19 per cent of UK shares listed on the London Stock Exchange are held by individuals, while in France and Germany, for instance, this applies to only 8 per cent of listed domestic shares. More than ten years after the financial crash of 2008, which hit the United Kingdom harder than most of its continental counterparts, popular engagement with financial securities remains high and nowhere in Europe are people more likely to view the stock market as a national pastime than in Britain. Its fascination with the markets can be measured by millions of retail stockbroking accounts and by around 125,000 amateur traders who indulge in spread betting, a high-risk gambling format that allows retail punters to place bets on the price movements of stocks, currencies, or commodities without owning the actual financial securities. This peculiar melange of gambling and speculation was invented in Britain and is certainly not on the European Commission's list of proposals for widening participation in financial markets, but spread betting encapsulates the heightened risk appetite of British investors. In Europe, Britain

---

[1] European Securities and Markets Authority, Annual Statistical Report: Performance and costs of retail investment products in the EU, 10 January 2019. 'EU to probe where retail investors are getting a fair deal', *The Financial Times*, 17 March 2019.

*Playing the Market: Retail Investment and Speculation in Twentieth-Century Britain.* Kieran Heinemann,
Oxford University Press (2021). © Kieran Heinemann. DOI: 10.1093/oso/9780198864257.003.0001

stands out as a financial nation and a society of investors, not only because of the City of London's economic clout but because financial markets are deeply embedded in the United Kingdom's social fabric. How did the world of finance come to be so deeply embedded in British culture and how did investment and speculation develop into mass activities over time?

In search of an answer, many observers point to the 1980s, the decade when the City of London regained its status as a global financial capital, and Margaret Thatcher's 'popular capitalism' opened up the stock market to millions of people by privatizing nationalized industries in heavily advertised give-away flotations. While the 1980s were certainly a formative period for modern Britain and its financial landscape, this book argues that the origins of today's fascination with the markets run much deeper. It tells the story of how Britain set out during the interwar period to develop a unique stock market culture that gained further traction in the post-war 'age of affluence', and in many ways helped pave the way for Thatcher's agenda of economic individualism and market populism. After the Great War, traditional moral and cultural constraints about financial securities—which had still been powerful in the Victorian period—collapsed. Throughout the interwar and post-war decades, first bonds and then shares lost their stigma of being either immoral or suitable only for the upper classes. Promising higher than average returns and a similar thrill of risk and reward as gambling on horses or the football pools, the stock market became a popular pastime for millions of Britons—even at a time when Britain had nationalized industries and politicians of both major parties indulged in staunchly anti-finance rhetoric. This book discusses the social, cultural, political, and economic forces that brought about a seismic shift in the relationship between British finance and society. At the beginning of the century, there was a consensus among members of Britain's financial and political establishment that 'ordinary people' or 'amateurs' should stay away or even be barred from stock trading, an activity condemned by critics as an economically disguised form of gambling. As the century drew to a close, however, 'popular capitalism' had become an electorally successful slogan, Britain had more shareholders than union members, and to play the market had developed into a socially acceptable hobby practised by millions of people.

The prevailing top-down narrative by business and economic historians of twentieth-century British finance is that of 'shattered dominance'[2] and of a 'Great Reversal',[3] after the 'Golden Years'[4] of the late-Victorian and Edwardian investor capitalism. During the period 1850–1914 the City of London was the

[2] R. Michie, *The London Stock Exchange: A History* (Oxford: Oxford University Press, 2001), p. 143.

[3] L. Hannah, 'London as the Global Market for Corporate Securities before 1914', in Y. Cassis and L. Quennouëlle-Corre (eds), *Financial Centres and International Capital Flows in the Nineteenth and Twentieth Centuries* (Oxford: Oxford University Press, 2011), pp. 126–160.

[4] D. Kynaston, *The City of London: Golden Years, 1890–1914* (London: Pimlico, 1996), II.

financial nerve centre of the British Empire, and the London Stock Exchange the world's largest securities market. However, as a result of two world wars, government intervention, and restrictive practices in the City, British securities markets experienced a steep decline. Only after the Conservative governments' free-market revival of the 1980s, Britain again committed to 'the fortright promotion of the Anglo-Saxon system of capitalism' in which the stock market was the driving engine of the economy.[5] When highlighting Britain's 'commitment to equities', and more generally the 'advanced equity culture' of the Anglo-Saxon world, scholars often reference the ratio between stock market capitalization and gross domestic product (GDP).[6] Britain's 'Great Reversal' is reflected in this ratio dropping from an all-time high of 250 per cent in 1914, to 28 per cent in 1974.[7] Nevertheless, throughout the twentieth century, this ratio remained higher in Britain and the United States than in the largest Continental-European economies, where the stock market played a less prominent role in company finance. This book does not intend to refute these narratives, which are valid from a top-down macroeconomic level, and they form an important backdrop to my story. But a different story emerges when we explore financial capitalism during the twentieth century from below: not one of decline, but one in which the British people increasingly, yet gradually became more involved, fascinated by and dependent on the stock market, both directly and indirectly. Macroeconomic data are an important source of this study, but I argue that figures like market capitalization as percentage of GDP or even the numbers of individual shareholders do not tell the full story. For instance, while the British stock market shrank from its Edwardian record level as a result of two world wars, ever more middle- and lower-income households began to invest in stocks and shares. Total shareholder numbers, as several scholars have pointed out, are 'notoriously difficult to obtain'[8] in the first place. They are 'even harder to evaluate'[9] because they merely offer a cold snapshot of a given time and offer very little insight into the dynamics of investment behaviour. Neither does such data tell us anything about a stock market's place in society, about people's attitudes towards certain investment practices, or about their motivations for participating in the market— or for staying away from it.

This book is therefore not an economic history of the stock market. It argues that the popularization of investment in Britain had as much to do with changes in

---

[5] J. Littlewood, *The Stock Market: 50 Years of Capitalism at Work* (London, San Francisco, CA: Financial Times, Pitman Publishing, 1998), p. 424.

[6] Michie, *The London Stock Exchange*, p. 626.

[7] Hannah, 'London as the Global Market for Corporate Securities before 1914', p. 149.

[8] M. Hollow, 'A Nation of Investors or a Procession of Fools? Reevaluating the Behavior of Britain's Shareholding Population through the Prism of the Interwar Sharepushing Crime Wave', *Enterprise and Society* 20 (2019), p. 137.

[9] S. Fraser, *Every Man a Speculator: A History of Wall Street in American Life* (New York: HarperCollins, 2005), p. 391.

cultural habitus and social attitudes as with financial and economic forces. The liberalization of gambling laws, individualization, or religious decline played into this process as did the trend of rising incomes, inflation rates, or the development of new investment vehicles for retail investors. This book deliberately looks beyond the City of London, the epicentre of Britain's financial sector, and its institutions like the London Stock Exchange. In fact, the City was for a long time a major obstacle to and not driving force behind wider share ownership in Britain. We will see how, in the post-war decades at least, the Church of England did more to popularize investment among people of average means than the London Stock Exchange. The development of investment and speculation into mass activities is difficult to capture by means of conventional narratives of twentieth-century Britain that set out from a Victorian liberal capitalism, which transformed into a social democratic Welfare State in the course of two world wars, only to be swept away again by a 'neoliberal' revival of free markets in the Thatcher period. Thinking about the century in this way blocks our view on periods in which economic individualism developed a powerful appeal even though economic policy was becoming more corporatist. It also risks missing out on the ways in which ordinary people actively appropriated market knowledge and capitalist practices at a time when antisocialist commentators on the political right feared that the post-war Welfare State had eroded what they saw as middle-class values of thrift and readiness to defer gratification. In his opus magnum of twentieth-century Britain, David Edgerton has recently reminded us that '[t]he mere visibility of ideas and of things is no guide to their significance' and that, for instance, 'British capitalism was less visible than nationalized industries'.[10] In a similar vein I believe Britain's small investors and speculators have been rendered invisible by a historiography occupied with big ideas, ideologies, structures, and political language.

Explanations for what drove Britain's widespread fascination with the markets are not primarily found in the engine rooms of high finance or Westminster politics but by exploring the engagement with financial markets from the perspective of the private investor. Financial capitalism was not exclusively an elite phenomenon but gained legitimacy by including and indeed fascinating the masses. Accordingly, in its endeavour to examine the history of British capitalism 'from the bottom up, all the way to the top',[11] the study draws on a wide assortment of source material. Alongside 'official' papers of stockbrokers, policy-makers, and City journalists, we will hear the voices of small investors that uncover the experiences ordinary Britons made with the stock market. If we listen

---

[10] D. Edgerton, *The Rise and Fall of the British Nation: A Twentieth-Century History* (London: Allan Lane, 2018), p. xxix.

[11] S. Beckert, J. C. Ott, L. Hyman, et al., 'Interchange: The History of Capitalism', *Journal of American History* 101 (2014), pp. 503–536.

to their stories, the diversity of attitudes towards investment and speculation comes to the fore as well as the inherent difficulty of distinguishing between the two categories. Retail investors, however, have left behind very little archival traces. Hardly any collections of stockbroking firms who were known to cater for less affluent clients have survived the takeover waves of the 1980s. Those who have, mainly contain minutes of partner meetings, memorabilia, and ledgers that document trading activity—but no correspondence with clients.[12] However, with a little effort and serendipity, I was able to rescue some voices, experiences, and expectations of ordinary private investors. Private investors, for instance, provided written evidence to public bodies like the Wilson Committee and they frequently wrote letters to newspapers, engaging in debates or sharing anecdotes. These ego documents should not be taken as a representative depiction of the investing public and require careful analysis. But they complicate many prevailing stereotypes of private investment as a 'very serious business'. Instead, many investors enjoyed the excitement and thrill that could go along with taking an active interest in the markets. What some investors considered a perfectly legitimate way of making money, others may have viewed as immoral profiteering. The ensuing moral debates over the social value of buying and selling financial securities mattered profoundly for the legitimacy and popularity of capitalism.

Who and what constituted the investing public? The main focus of this book is on the stock market. But we will pay close attention to the ways in which investment and speculation in stocks and shares correlated with other markets, most notably the bond and the housing market. There has been much research lately on Britain's share- and bondholder population and investment behaviour during the nineteenth and twentieth centuries, which sought to determine investor numbers from company registrars and contemporary surveys.[13] However, the fundamental question of this book is not how many people held financial securities, and which type, over time. I wish to highlight some new insights about the social and cultural meaning of investment that can be gained from extending our scope beyond a numerical understanding of the investing public. This means exploring a wider set of questions: Where did the public gather information about the markets and how were financial securities represented in the media? Why did some 'investors' merely gamble on the price movements of

---

[12] At least this applies to collections of the following member firms of the London Stock Exchange, which I have consulted at the London Metropolitan Archives: James Capel & Co., Mullens & Co., Heseltine, Powell & Co., G. S. Herbert and Sons, T. T. Curwen and Sons, Holland and Balfour, Gordon L. Jacobs & Co., Galloway and Pearson. It may be that collections of regional stockbroking firms hold other material.

[13] J. Rutterford, 'The Evidence for "Democratization" of Share Ownership in Great Britain in the Early Twentieth Century', in D. R. Green and J. Rutterford (eds), *Men, Women, and Money: Perspectives on Gender, Wealth, and Investment 1850–1930* (Oxford, New York: Oxford University Press, 2011), pp. 184–206; J. Rutterford, 'The Shareholder Voice: British and American Accents, 1890–1965', *Enterprise and Society* 13 (2012), pp. 120–153.

financial securities, while others bought and sold them directly? What drove some investors out of financial securities and into collectibles like wine, art, and furniture—or old bond and share certificates? As we shall see, investment behaviour was not only affected by interest rates, inflation, and house prices—but also by attitudes towards gambling or by trends in collectibles. In other words, the investing public intersected with the gambling and the collecting public in ways that scholars have overlooked so far.

Debates over the contested relationship between stock market activity and gambling will prove particularly insightful. Take, for instance, today's measures to regulate the market in financial spread betting. In the United Kingdom, spread bets are a legal way of betting on the prices of stocks, bonds, commodities, or currencies, without owning the underlying financial security. Today's debate over tightening the regulatory framework of spread betting has some revealing historical parallels that will be a major theme in this book. Critics understandably argue that someone who merely gambles on the movement of prices without owning the underlying financial security should not be considered and treated as an investor. While outlawed under gambling laws in the US, in Britain spread bets are regulated as financial instruments by the Financial Conduct Authority although profits derived from these wagers—like winnings from gambling—are still exempt from capital gains tax. The historical progenitor of spread betting companies is the notorious 'bucket shop'. Bucket shops were bookmakers that mushroomed in financial districts like the City of London, where punters could wager bets on the movement of prices, also without ever owning the security which the bet was tied to. They were considered the 'poor man's stock exchange' because they allowed those to play the market who would otherwise not have the social or financial privilege to participate in the real exchanges. In the 1920s and 1930s, naturally, these shops operated in a far less regulated environment, which encouraged some 'bucketeers' to defraud their customers. Eventually this brought the regulator into the arena and the practice of share gambling was outlawed. These vicarious forms of market participation can be just as revelatory as *factual* ownership of securities. They allow us to understand how distinctions between financial speculation and gambling were drawn and redrawn over time and to make sense of the multiple ways in which the stock market captured the public imagination. A similar logic applies to the speculative practice of 'stagging'— applying for shares in new company issues in the hope of reselling them quickly for a profit. Stags are hyperactive market participants, but they do not appear in shareholder statistics and are technically not part of what is commonly referred to as the 'shareholder population'. However, their increased activity from the late 1950s prompted highly contentious debates over the morality of stagging that highlight the gradual waning of older constraints about financial speculation in the post-war period.

## Legacies: Britain's Stock Market in the Nineteenth Century

Over the course of the twentieth century, different actors redrew the lines between what was to be considered prudent investment, suitable for the many, and risky speculation, better left to experts. These ideas and concepts were carrying plenty of historical baggage from the previous century, at the end of which the stock exchange had become a key component in the institutional setting of Victorian capitalism. At the outset of the nineteenth century, however, most Britons viewed stock market transactions with moral suspicion or outright condemnation. Speculation was condemned on religious grounds and 'perceived as a sin committed in the ungodly pursuit of wealth' and was commonly associated with 'idleness, corruption and greed'.[14] Even staunch liberals and free-trade proponents like William Cobbett would condemn '[t]he talk about "speculations"; that is to say, adventurous dealings, or, rather, commercial gamblings' as 'the most miserable nonsense that ever was conceived in the heads of idiots'.[15] It was only towards the second half of the century that this perception began to change. In 1855, the Limited Liability Act legally confirmed the concept of the joint stock company, which had been contributing to enormous industrial growth and imperial expansion.[16] In the following decades, the number of investors grew from approximately 170,000 in 1855 to 640,000 in 1902.[17] Desperate to cast off their social stigma, financiers conceptualized their practices as a genuine economic and purposeful operation far removed from gambling. Paul Johnson has reconstructed how '[a]ctions that were pejoratively termed "gambling" in the 1810s were described as "speculation" by mid-century, and as "investment" by the century's end'.[18] The Royal Commission on the Stock Exchange in 1877–78 marks an important turning point towards a public perception of stock market operators as daring entrepreneurs and rational, calculating bearers of commercial risk. The commission exonerated the Stock Exchange of any gambling accusations and concluded that its bad reputation in this regard had in fact resulted from an intrusion of 'people of limited' means who had engaged in unbridled and ruinous speculation in the decades prior.[19] From an establishment's perspective, the problem was no longer speculation per se, but the question of *who* speculated.

---

[14] J. Taylor, *Creating Capitalism: Joint-Stock Enterprise in British Politics and Culture, 1800–1870* (London: Royal Historical Society, 2006), p. 56.

[15] W. Cobbett, *Rural Rides in the Counties of Surrey, Kent, Sussex* (London: W. Cobbett, 1830), p. 294.

[16] Taylor, *Creating Capitalism*.

[17] R. Michie, 'Gamblers, Fools, Victims, or Wizards? The British Investor in the Public Mind, 1850–1930', in D. R. Green (ed.), *Men, Women, and Money: Perspectives on Gender, Wealth and Investment 1850–1930* (Oxford: Oxford University Press, 2011), p. 161.

[18] P. Johnson, *Making the Market: Victorian Origins of Corporate Capitalism* (Cambridge: Cambridge University Press, 2010), p. 224.

[19] P. Johnson, 'In Pursuit of Prudence: Speculation, Risk, and Class in Victorian Britain', in C. Griffiths (ed.), *Classes, Cultures, and Politics: Essays on British History for Ross McKibbin* (Oxford:

The Royal Commission of 1878 'identified "people of limited means" as being key to the accusation of gambling' in stocks and shares, and condemned the 'social promiscuity' they observed when finding manual labourers next to wealthy financiers on the shareholder lists of public companies.[20] Indeed, as James Taylor reminds us, it 'was speculation among the lower orders that really pre-occupied commentators. What was so disturbing was the belief that in the maelstrom of speculative frenzies, society's hierarchies were dissolved and could be reformed in new, unusual shapes'.[21] Inclusion and exclusion from the market were largely decided along class lines, in London more than elsewhere. Here, the Stock Exchange viewed the prospect of speculation among the lower classes as a lose-lose situation. If plebeian investors happened to gain a windfall profit from successful trading, this would be a threat to social hierarchies and the Victorian class system. If, on the other hand, working- and lower middle-class investors lost money in unguided dealings, this could bring the Stock Exchange into disrepute. Therefore, clear distinctions between amateurs and professional operators were introduced to the debate during the 1870s, a decade that saw an increase in academic writing on financial affairs.

In 1874, the banker Arthur Crump wrote a *Theory of Stock Exchange Speculation*, laying out what became the classical economic argument in favour of the speculator as a pioneer of enterprise who anticipates future business trends and stabilizes prices, thereby benefiting markets and society.[22] Ironically he drew inspiration from the French anarchist thinker, Pierre-Joseph Proudhon, who had first articulated these theorems in 1853.[23] Like Proudhon, Crump argued that only the 'professional speculator, who has the right sort of head, sufficient capital, patience, perseverance, coolness, and a business-like aptitude for laying down the elaborate machinery that is necessary for mercantile success' should be allowed access to the market.[24] More than anything, what made a professional was access

Oxford University Press, 2011), pp. 59–69. Similar developments played out in the United States; see M. de Goede, *Virtue, Fortune, and Faith*, Borderlines (Minneapolis, MN: University of Minnesota Press, 2005). For Germany see A. Engel, 'Vom verdorbenen Spieler zum verdienstvollen Spekulanten: Ökonomisches Denken über Börsenspekulation im 19. Jahrhundert', *Jahrbuch für Wirtschaftsgeschichte* 54 (2013), pp. 49–70.

[20] Quote after Johnson, 'In Pursuit of Prudence', p. 66. On the Royal Commission see also G. Robb, *White-Collar Crime in Modern England: Financial Fraud and Business Morality, 1845–1929* (Cambridge: Cambridge University Press, 1992), pp. 82–83.

[21] Taylor, *Creating Capitalism*, p. 81.

[22] 'The undue inflation or depression of prices will be counteracted by speculative operations [ ... ] and in that sense speculation is directly of immense benefit.' A. Crump, *The Theory of Stock Exchange Speculation*, 2nd edn (London: Longmans, Green, and Co, 1874), p. 129. For this line of argument see also R. Giffen, *Stock Exchange Securities: An Essay on the General Causes of Fluctuations in their Price* (London: George Bell and Sons, 1877), pp. 14–26.

[23] P.-J. Proudhon, *Manuel du Spéculateur à la Bourse*, 4th edn (Paris: Librairie de Garnier Frères, 1857). On Proudhon's reception and his key position in the intellectual history of financial speculation see A. Preda, *Framing Finance: The Boundaries of Markets and Modern Capitalism* (Chicago, IL: University of Chicago Press, 2009), pp. 180–185.

[24] Crump, *The Theory of Stock Exchange Speculation*, p. 16.

to insider knowledge and the readiness to make the most out of this information asymmetry:

> The professional operator does not scruple to lay traps, and drive the public into them, by plying them with fictitious telegrams, if he can get them published, and by forming syndicates to 'rig' the markets. [ . . . ] He must systematically not only disregard the interest of other people, but deliberately calculate upon the weaknesses of human nature which characterize the crowd, in order to work upon them for his own ends.[25]

The counterpart of the scheming, ruthless professional was the 'haphazard' or 'amateur speculator'. This 'person of flabby character' with 'a taste for the excitement of dabbling in the markets [that] grows into a thirst, and from that into a mania' had to be excluded, in order for speculation to be beneficial and respectable.[26] In 1896, the Harvard economist Henry Emery Crosby wrote the first American treatise of organized speculation, arguing along lines very similar to Crump 'that the negative effects of speculation were not inherent in financial practices but were caused by amateur participation in the stock markets'.[27]

So by the end of the century, a distinction had been firmly established between the professional operator, who had sufficient capital and information to take on risk, and the amateur, who was framed as a gullible, reckless gambler that had to be kept at bay in order for speculation to unfold its economic benefits. Unlike in the US, where Wall Street pushed for universal share ownership after the Great War, the City of London with its ingrained paternalism deliberately sought to hamper the popularization of investment and harboured a deep-seated aversion against amateur involvement in its market. London had even gained a reputation for having organized its Stock Exchange strictly as 'the monopoly of the rich'[28] in comparison to the more open exchanges in New York, Paris, or Berlin, where 'Tom, Dick, and Harry can go to the public gallery and see their business done'.[29] Writing in 1894, the German sociologist Max Weber even called for 'an organization of the [European] exchanges more along the lines of the English'.[30] He

---

[25] Crump, *The Theory of Stock Exchange Speculation*, p. 47.
[26] Crump, *The Theory of Stock Exchange Speculation*, p. 50.
[27] Quote after de Goede, *Virtue, Fortune, and Faith*, pp. 78–79. On Emery see also C. B. Cowing, *Populists, Plungers, and Progressives: A Social History of Stock and Commodity Speculation* (Princeton, NJ: Princeton University Press, 1965), p. 49; Preda, *Framing Finance*, pp. 183–184.
[28] M. Weber, 'Stock and Commodity Exchanges [Die Börse (1894)]', translated by Steven Lestition, *Theory and Society* 29 (2000), p. 334. Original M. Weber, *Die Börse: Innerer Zweck und äussere Organisation der Börsen*, Göttinger Arbeiterbibliothek (Göttingen: Vandenhoeck und Ruprecht, 1894), Bd. 1, Heft 2–3.
[29] H. S. Muller, *Scientific Speculation*, The 'Money-Maker' Manuals for Investors (London: The Office of the Money-Maker, 1901), p. 26.
[30] Weber, 'Stock and Commodity Exchanges', 333. Weber's stock exchange writings occupy an awkward place in his oeuvre. He would later regard stock markets as 'very imperfect specimens of

praised the London Stock Exchange for being 'organized "plutocratically" in that a significant amount of wealth and security deposits are required as preconditions for admittance to business on the exchange'.[31] As we will see, up until the Thatcher years, decision makers in the City as well as in Westminster were uneasy with trusting ordinary people to make their own financial decisions.

But although the high Victorian era saw the Stock Exchange officially exonerated, it continued to face criticism from across the political spectrum. Bourgeois social and cultural mores condemned horse racing, card games, or lotteries for subverting 'the meritocratic principles of the Puritan work ethic, in which capital is earned by hard work, talent and deferred gratification'.[32] Likewise, because speculative dealings in company shares seemed to rely heavily on chance, famous Victorians like Thomas Carlyle or John Ruskin attacked speculators for 'discouraging honest enterprise and promoting gambling and the base pursuit of wealth'.[33] And then of course, from the second half of the century, there was the emerging labour movement that drew heavily on the socialist critique of capitalism playing into the hands of the 'rentier class' that lived comfortably off the 'unearned income' its investments generated while the proletariat toiled for its survival. It is worth noting, however, that the stock market even cast a spell on some of its fiercest critics. Take for instance the founding fathers of modern Socialism, Karl Marx and Friedrich Engels, who speculated in stocks and shares during their time in Victorian London.[34] While Engels, a factory owner and avid reader of *The Economist*, exemplified the typical affluent investor of the period, his impoverished friend Marx was a prime example of a plebeian speculator who was looked down upon by the gentlemanly elites of the City of London. Nevertheless, their critique of the rentier class did leave a mark on Britain's political economy, most notably in the Liberal Party's 1907 budget that introduced differential taxation between 'earned' and 'unearned' income—a differentiation that survived until 1984 when the Thatcher government abolished the surcharge on income derived from capital investments.

---

modern capitalism', which explains their almost complete absence from his magnum opus, the *Protestant Ethic and the Spirit of Capitalism*, which famously argued that Puritanism and Protestant morality abetted the advance of modern capitalism. Quote after P. Ghosh, *Max Weber and the Protestant Ethic: Twin Histories* (Oxford: Oxford University Press, 2014), p. 66.

[31] Weber, 'Stock and Commodity Exchanges', p. 334. On membership requirements see Michie, *The London Stock Exchange*, pp. 155–159.

[32] M. Clapson, *A Bit of a Flutter: Popular Gambling in England, c.1820–1961* (Manchester: Manchester University Press, 1992), pp. 19–20.

[33] Taylor, *Creating Capitalism*, p. 73.

[34] While Engels's career as an investor and factory owner is well known, Marx's dabbling in the stock market is less well documented. He claimed on 25 June 1864 towards his uncle that he gambled in US and British shares, but nine days later explained to Engels that 'if he had had the money, he would have made a killing in the stock market' (my translations). Marx Engels Gesamtausgabe², Abt. 3, Bd. 12, Briefwechsel: Januar 1862 bis September 1864, 584.

As the nineteenth century drew to a close, the stock market occupied an ambiguous place in Victorian society. On the one hand, the Crown and Parliament had labelled the Stock Exchange an institution of national importance, and stock market operators had become established members of Britain's economic elites. Furthermore, the infrastructure for a modern investing public was mostly in place: a popular financial press, an urban network of exchanges connected via telegraphy, and academic theories that presented speculation as a purposeful economic activity. On the other hand, dealing in financial securities, particularly among ill-informed and less affluent members of the public, continued to be condemned by conservative, religious, and socialist critics alike. This 'severe moral opprobrium'[35] that surrounded finance during the Victorian and Edwardian period forms an important backdrop against which the continued suspicion of finance as well as the relaxation in attitude towards investment during the twentieth century will be better understood.

Throughout this book, I will contrast Britain's case with developments in retail investment in the United States and in Continental Europe, especially Germany. Popular finance in the US has lately been studied extensively,[36] and comparisons between the US and Britain have often been made.[37] Comparisons with Germany, however, are sparse in this field, and therefore this perspective will offer fresh insights into unique aspects of Britain's equity culture.[38] Germany's case is particularly insightful because towards the end of the nineteenth century, the Berliner Börse had become the second largest stock exchange in Europe after London—a position Berlin competed over with the Paris Bourse. Whereas the London Stock Exchange was a private members' club, its Berlin equivalent was a quasi-public institution, and therefore far more accessible to the public—both in terms of visitors' access to the exchange building and with regards to dealing costs for retail investors. There is evidence that in the late nineteenth century, retail participation in the stock market was no less common in Germany than in Britain. Similar to the Royal Commission of 1878, German officials launched a public inquiry into the stock market in 1892, which found that share dealing had

[35] G. R. Searle, *Morality and the Market in Victorian Britain* (Oxford: Oxford University Press, 1998), p. 82.

[36] J. C. Ott, *When Wall Street Met Main Street: The Quest for an Investors' Democracy* (Cambridge, MA: Harvard University Press, 2011); U. Stäheli, *Spectacular Speculation: Thrills, the Economy, and Popular Discourse* (Stanford, CA: Stanford University Press, 2013); P. Knight, *Reading the Market: Genres of Financial Capitalism in Gilded Age America* (Baltimore, MD: Johns Hopkins University Press, 2016); Fraser, *Every Man a Speculator*.

[37] J. Rutterford and D. P. Sotiropoulos, 'The Rise of the Small Investor in the US and the UK, 1895 to 1970', *Enterprise and Society* (2017), pp. 485–535; R. Michie, *The London and New York Stock Exchanges 1850–1914* (London: Allen & Unwin, 1987).

[38] A recent exception is a German comparative study of the Berliner Börse and the London Stock Exchange: M. Buchner, *Die Spielregeln der Börse: Institutionen, Kultur und die Grundlagen des Wertpapierhandels in Berlin und London, ca.1860–1914* (Tübingen: Mohr Siebeck, 2019).

extended 'deep into the middle and lower ranks of society'.[39] One of the reasons why scholars have so far downplayed the extent of popular stock market engagement in twentieth-century Britain is that they have drawn parallels only to the US, where retail investment indeed was more vibrant. A different picture emerges when we compare Britain with Germany, and if we bear in mind that in both countries the stock market had captured the public imagination by the turn of the century. Why then, did Britain in the following decades develop such a more vibrant stock market culture?

## The Hazy Line between Investment, Speculation, and Gambling

The stock traders that formed the first securities markets in the early modern period hardly distinguished between dealing in financial securities and gambling.[40] It is important to bear in mind that gambling is not—as many financial professionals and economists would have us believe—something that is antithetical to the otherwise rational and prudent sphere of modern finance, but one of its constituent features. Historically, the striking resemblance between investment activity and gambling came to the fore in myriad ways and remains ever-present to this day.[41] For one, the language of the stock market is heavily influenced by the language of the casino and the turf. Investors are referred to as 'punters', a term originally reserved for clients of a betting shop. Speculators 'backed' mining, rubber, or railway shares like a gambler 'backed' horses. Relatively reliable and safe investments in large, established firms were referred to as 'blue chip stocks'— in analogy to the blue $25 chip in a poker game being that of the highest value. In his eminent study *Homo Ludens*, which argues that gamesmanship was a fundamental aspect of human evolution, the Dutch cultural historian Johan Huizinga made some perceptive observations on the kinship between gambling and modern finance:

> The hazy border-line between play and seriousness is illustrated very tellingly by the use of the words 'playing' or 'gambling' for the machinations on the Stock Exchange. The gambler at the roulette table will readily concede that he is playing; the stockjobber will not. He will maintain that buying and selling on the off-chance of prices rising or falling is part of the serious business of life, at least of business life, and that it is an economic function of society. In both cases

---

[39] *Bericht der Börsen-Enquete-Kommission* (Berlin: Reichsdruckerei), p. 130.
[40] Preda, *Framing Finance*.
[41] For a legal history of efforts to distinguish between speculation and gambling in the United States over the course of the nineteenth and twentieth centuries see S. Banner, *Speculation: A History of the Fine Line between Gambling and Investing* (New York, Oxford: Oxford University Press, 2017).

the operative factor is the hope of gain; but whereas in the former the pure fortuitousness of the thing is generally admitted (all 'systems' notwithstanding), in the latter the player deludes himself with the fancy that he can calculate the future trends of the market. At any rate the difference of mentality is exceedingly small.[42]

Indeed, the affinity between the two realms holds much explanatory power. As much as it explains right- as well as left-wing criticism of the stock market as an immoral casino, it allows us to understand how the stock market developed a mass appeal over time. Taking seriously the 'entertaining and spectacular surplus'[43] of the stock market allows us, for instance, to explain the allure of bucket shops in the interwar period or to demonstrate how the stock market game entered more and more British households during the post-war decades.

But we should not suggest that Britain's small investors were ever a culturally homogenous group. This book will address the diversity of attitudes, moral tensions, and social divisions *within* the investing public that we cannot capture if we look at shareholders as aggregated data. In this regard as a reaction to post-war permissiveness about speculation, traditional shareholders began to fashion themselves as 'genuine investors'. This concept took share *ownership* literally and claimed moral superiority over frequent buying and selling of shares. 'Genuine investors' framed their long-term commitment to companies as an exercise in self-styled middle-class virtues of thrift, responsibility, and deferred gratification. This discussion highlights the continuing duality of meaning surrounding stock market activity—using judgement to place funds with companies that generate long-term income, and buying and selling quickly to take advantage of short-term price movements in order to generate quick capital gains. The moral outrage expressed by the self-styled 'genuine investors' allows us to better understand the departure away from traditional notions of investment and the embracing of a more swashbuckling and speculative paradigm.

## Financialization, Declinism, and Neoliberalism

Exploring the history of financial capitalism from the bottom up does not mean to lose sight of structural changes. The challenge remains to mediate between the micro and the macro, the representative and the unrepresentative. Arguably the most important structural transformation that forms a backdrop to this story was the global expansion of finance that gained traction in the 1970s and is today

---

[42] J. Huizinga, *Homo Ludens: A Study of the Play Element in Culture* (London: Routledge & Kegan Paul, 1949), p. 52. The book was first published in 1938.
[43] Stäheli, *Spectacular Speculation*, p. 29.

referred to as 'financialization'. The term describes 'the increasing role of financial motives, financial markets, financial actors and financial institutions in the operation of the domestic and international economies'[44] and is used in a critical fashion, for instance by Rana Foroohar, who has identified financialization as the 'economic illness' of our time.[45] In Britain, financialization took the shape of a steady institutionalization of equity markets. Beginning in the 1950s, institutional investors like pension funds and insurance companies increasingly moved their capital from property and fixed-income securities—government and corporate bonds—into industrial shares. While in the early 1960s, private investors still held more than half of the shares listed on the London Stock Exchange their share of equity had declined to 20 per cent by 1990—although shareholder numbers had skyrocketed from 3 million to around 10 million during the Thatcher years.[46] From the 1950s increasingly, pensions and life insurances came to be managed by a new class of investment managers who released private investors of the burden to manage a portfolio of stocks and shares themselves for retirement planning. At the same time, a new investment vehicle arose that allowed investors of average and modest means to own shares indirectly. The unit trust industry shook up Britain's financial landscape by pooling ordinary investors' small sums of savings, and investing them in a professionally managed fund of equities and other asset classes. Yet, direct investment in the stocks and shares by retail investors continued to increase, suggesting that more and more investors were trying to beat the fund managers at their own game. The ambivalent implications of the institutionalization of British securities markets will be a recurring theme of this book.

Throughout the twentieth century, Britain's financial sector was the object of much public criticism, resulting in often heavy disputes between successive Westminster governments and the City. The Labour Party's critique of finance grew more powerful during the depression that followed the 1929 stock market crash and helped shift the political climate in favour of state intervention and stricter market regulation. After World War II (WWII), the Labour government's nationalization of public utilities, including the Bank of England, sent shockwaves across the City with institutions like the Stock Exchange fearing to likewise come under public ownership. But even with Conservatives in power, relationships between the City and the government were strained, and commentators on both the right and the left held the financial sector responsible for Britain's industrial

[44] G. A. Epstein, 'Introduction: Financialization and the World Economy', in G. A. Epstein (ed.), *Financialization and the World Economy* (Cheltenham: Edward Elgar, 2006), p. 3. The literature on 'financialization' has grown enormously in the past few years. For an overview see A. Engel, 'The Bang after the Boom: Understanding Financialization', *Zeithistorische Forschungen/Studies in Contemporary History* 12 (2015), pp. 500–510.

[45] Rana Foroohar, *Makers and Takers: How Wall Street Destroyed Main Street* (New York: Crown Business, 2017), p. 5.

[46] Office for National Statistics, Share Ownership: *A Report on the Ownership of Shares at 31st December 1997* (London: The Stationery Office, 1997), p. 8.

decline. In short, free-market advocates partly blamed the City's restrictive practices for decline, while Labour accused banks and investors of depriving domestic
industry by focusing its lending and investment activity overseas. Both points of
criticism became key tenets of the theory of 'gentlemanly capitalism', according to
which Britain's financial and political elites were taken in by a 'rejection of
industrial society' and a 'surrender to aristocratic values'.[47]

This book does not seek to settle such debates or to determine whether Britain
*was* in decline during the twentieth century or to what extent. It is worth pointing
out, however, that recent scholarship is casting more and more doubt on the
narrative of decline, for instance, by pointing out that 'even if the thesis [of
gentlemanly capitalism] were true in 1900, it was no longer true of 1950'.[48]
What is relevant for the wider context of this book is the sense of alarm that
characterized these contemporary debates, and the way in which perceived decline
was politicized, particularly by the New Right.[49] In this context, it is also worth
pointing out that many of Thatcher's precursors contrasted Britain's decline with
post-war Western Germany's simultaneous economic success—another factor
why the comparative perspective on Germany will prove insightful. This contentious debate is an important background to Britain's quest for wider share
ownership, advocates of which became obsessed with warnings of Britain's decline
from the late 1950s. Many right-wing politicians and journalists subscribed to the
belief that the post-war social democratic settlement had eroded the alleged
'industrial spirit' of the middle classes, and many of them became influential
advisers to Margaret Thatcher. With Jim Tomlinson, I speak of 'declinism' when
referring to this alarmist belief that Britain lagged behind the economic performance of its competitors—and the numerous ways in which this belief was exploited
for political purposes.[50] As such, wider share ownership was a project that sought
to remedy Britain's perceived over-consumption and lack of investment. The
resulting proposals increasingly framed the stock market as a site for the British
people to rediscover capitalist or 'Victorian' virtues of thrift and deferred gratification. To some extent these suggestions—some of which later inspired Margaret

[47] For a thorough criticism of the concept of 'gentlemanly capitalism' see M. Daunton,
'"Gentlemanly Capitalism" and British Industry 1820–1914', *Past and Present* 122 (1989), p. 133,
quotes.

[48] Edgerton, *The Rise and Fall of the British Nation*, p. 130. Edgerton points out that by 1950, Britain
had developed a 'strong national-industrial economy'.

[49] In Britain, the term 'New Right' denotes a post-war movement of politicians, journalists, and
intellectuals with close ties to the Conservative Party, who embraced economic liberalism and social
conservatism.

[50] J. Tomlinson, 'Thrice Denied: "Declinism" as a Recurrent Theme in British History in the Long
Twentieth Century', *Twentieth Century British History* 20 (2009), p. 238. Tomlinson's constructivist
approach does not deny that Britain lagged behind its competitors in economic terms. He acknowledges that '[f]rom around 1870, when Britain reached the apogee of its industrial predominance, the
country has experienced relative decline as the size of its economy in relation to the rest of the world
has fallen', Tomlinson, 'Thrice Denied', p. 227.

Thatcher's privatization policies—already reflected the fact that the stock market also encouraged economic behaviour and emotions contrary to Victorian values: speculation, short-termism, gambling, and greed.

The term 'neoliberalism' is used with care in this study. It is reserved for certain journalists, businessmen and Conservative politicians who from the late 1950s lobbied for a more investor-friendly tax code, and who were organized in free-market think tanks like the Institute of Economic Affairs or the Mont Pelerin Society. There is now a vast body of scholarship on these networks and figures, some of which later became influential advisers to or ministers in Margaret Thatcher's cabinet.[51] To be sure, the neoliberal policy mix of privatization and deregulation that was enacted during the 1980s did make Britain a more investor-friendly society. This has led scholars to portray Britain's culture of mass investment as more or less an immediate product and intended outcome of Thatcherite neoliberalism.[52] But we should be wary of ascribing too much explanatory power to neoliberalism, and instead sharpen our focus on the yawning gap between the intentions of neoliberal actors and the outcome of their policies. I will argue in this book that Britain's retail stock market culture has historical roots that are much deeper than Thatcherism. My conception of neoliberalism is therefore a narrow one, and it draws heavily on Quinn Slobodian's recent study of the neoliberal movement. Slobodian has shown that key neoliberal thinkers such as Friedrich August Hayek were more occupied with questions of global governance in the age of decolonization than with plans for lowering taxes or privatizing state assets. In this regard, he describes 'neoliberalism as specific institution-building project rather than as a nebulous "logic" or "rationality"'. This insight has methodological implications for the approach of this book, which disassociates itself from studies on neoliberalism by historians and social scientists that are built on Michel Foucault's concept of 'governmentality'.[53] According to these narratives, 'neoliberal subjectivity' is an all-pervasive force that penetrates quite literally all aspects of public and private life. Such an approach, however, risks distorting our view for ambiguity, contingency, and openness in specific historical settings, because it carries too many assumptions about the direction of social, political, and economic change. If we believe that 'almost every area of economic and social reproduction has been reconfigured under neoliberalism', then 'neoliberal' ideas,

---

[51] See, for instance, B. Jackson, 'The Think-Tank Archipelago: Thatcherism and Neo-Liberalism', in B. Jackson and R. Saunders (eds), *Making Thatcher's Britain* (Cambridge: Cambridge University Press, 2012), pp. 43–61; R. Cockett, *Thinking the Unthinkable: Think Tanks and the Economic Counter Revolution 1931–1983* (London: Fontana, 1995); N. Rollings, 'Cracks in the Post-War Keynesian Settlement? The Role of Organised Business in Britain in the Rise of Neoliberalism before Margaret Thatcher', *Twentieth Century British History* 24 (2013), pp. 637–659.

[52] A. Edwards, '"Financial Consumerism": Citizenship, Consumerism and Capital Ownership in the 1980s', *Contemporary British History* 31 (2017), pp. 210–229; M. Francis, 'A Crusade to Enfranchise the Many: Thatcherism and Property-Owning Democracy', *Twentieth Century British History* 23 (2012), pp. 275–297.

[53] See for instance Edwards, '"Financial Consumerism"', pp. 210–229.

institutions, and discourses are everywhere and nowhere.[54] Neoliberalism explains everything and nothing.

## Rationality and Emotions in Modern Capitalism

Being a modern concept, the history of capitalism is also the history of its competing conceptualizations.[55] Rather than putting down a working definition of capitalism, I wish to draw attention to the ongoing friction between two fundamental ways capitalism has been construed throughout the twentieth century. We can identify two broad strands that had taken shape by the outset of the century as a result of heightened debates over the nature of 'modern capitalism'. The first strand viewed modern capitalism—the interplay of markets, private property, and formally free contractual labour—as a primarily rational endeavour drawing much of its energy from a protestant work ethic built around mundane asceticism, deferred gratification, and prudent calculation. According to this notion, financial speculation was an irrational activity at odds with modern capitalism. This concept was most famously put forward by the German sociologist Max Weber in his 1905 work *The Protestant Ethic and the Spirit of Capitalism*.[56] But the assumption of ongoing rationalization was even shared by capitalism's critics like for instance the Marxist economist Rudolf Hilferding, who observed the 'reduced role of speculation' in the modern business economy:

> Those mass psychoses, which speculation produced at the beginning of the capitalist era, those blessed times in which every speculator felt himself to be God, creating a world out of nothing, all that seems irretrievably lost.[57]

Weber's works had entered Anglo-Saxon academic discourse by the interwar period, and the notion of capitalism relying on bourgeois virtues of thrift and hard work came to hold strong purchase in western political thought. It found its way into British politics in the course of the 'post-war declinist "moment"'[58] in the late 1950s and became a defining element of the New Right, whose explanation for British decline was the alleged demise of these bourgeois or—in Margaret

---

[54] Quote after B. Fine and A. Saad-Filho, 'Thirteen Things You Need to Know about Neoliberalism', *Critical Sociology* 43 (2017), pp. 685–706.

[55] For this argument and an overview of different conceptions of capitalism see J. Kocka, *Capitalism: A Short History*, translated by Jeremiah Riemer (Princeton, NJ: Princeton University Press, 2016), pp. 11–17.

[56] M. Weber, *The Protestant Ethic and the Spirit of Capitalism*, translated by T. Parsons, with a foreword by R. Tawney (London: G. Allen & Unwin, 1930).

[57] Quote in H. James, 'Finance Capitalism', in J. Kocka and M. van der Linden (eds), *Capitalism: The Reemergence of a Historical Concept* (London, New York: Bloomsbury Academic, 2016), p. 158.

[58] Tomlinson, 'Thrice Denied', p. 235.

Thatcher's parlance—'Victorian' values. In Thatcher's case this went along with a life-long suspicion of finance that stemmed from her Methodist upbringing and according to which stock market transactions were merely an economically disguised form of gambling.

Competing with this narrative of rationality was a second understanding of modern capitalism, which saw irrational, emotional, and whimsical aspects at work in its inner fabric, particularly in the financial sphere. Max Weber's counterpart Werner Sombart argued that modern capitalism was just as much driven by rational calculation as by 'hazard [*Spielwut*]', 'instincts', and the 'gamester's passion'.[59] Sombart's ideas were conveyed to a British audience via the liberal thinker and famous theorist of imperialism, John A. Hobson, who acknowledged Sombart's influence on his *Evolution of Modern Capitalism*.[60] Hobson observed the workings of a 'large intricate financial machinery' and concluded that the 'whole system is one of betting: not indeed blind gambling, but speculation in which foresight and chance play parts of varying magnitude'.[61] John Maynard Keynes, another great liberal thinker, was even more convinced that modern finance came almost undistinguishably close to the activities of a casino. Derived from his own experiences speculating in the commodity markets, Keynes came to the conclusion that a certain 'gambling instinct' and what he famously referred to as 'animal spirits', were core elements of financial capitalism.[62] We will come across this tension throughout this book, for instance when the interwar chairman of the Stock Exchange conceded off the record that a certain gambling spirit lay at the heart of his institution. Of course, in public 'The House' would deny any such resemblances and the chairman's post-war successors regularly had to defend it against attacks from Labour frontbenchers who likened the Stock Exchange to a casino, often employing Keynes's famous analogy.[63] But large parts of Britain's investing public were convinced that the stock market was heavily influenced by the 'emotions', 'flair', or 'instinct' of its

---

[59]  Werner Sombart, *The Quintessence of Capitalism: A Study of the History and Psychology of the Modern Business Man*, translated and edited by M. Epstein (London: T. Fisher Unwin, 1915), pp. 45–49.

[60]  The first edition of Hobson's magnum opus was published in 1896 and holds very little reference to finance and speculation. The revised edition of 1926 has an entire chapter on 'The Financier' and pays the following tribute to Sombart in the preface: 'While most of the matter of the earlier historical chapters in the first edition is retained, numerous emendations and additions have been made, and an introductory chapter on the Origin of Modern Capitalism, based largely upon the researches in Professor Sombart's great work, *Der Moderne Kapitalismus*, has been inserted.' J. A. Hobson, *The Evolution of Modern Capitalism: A Study of Machine Production*, new and rev. edn (London: The Walter Scott Publishing Co. Ltd, 1926 [1896]), p. v.

[61]  Hobson, *The Evolution of Modern Capitalism*, p. 243.

[62]  J. M. Keynes, *The General Theory of Employment, Interest and Money* (London: Macmillan, 1961 [1936]), pp. 154–160. On the history of the term see P. Knight, 'Animal Spirits', in P. Crosthwaite, P. Knight and N. Marsh (eds), *Show Me the Money: The Image of Finance, 1700 to the Present* (Manchester: Manchester University Press, 2014), pp. 65–99.

[63]  'When the capital development of a country becomes a byproduct of the activities of a casino, the job is likely to be ill-done.' Keynes, *The General Theory of Employment, Interest and Money*, p. 159.

participants—something that is common knowledge for behavioural economists today.[64] For many small punters this aspect was a key motivation that added to the 'thrill' of playing the stock market. The perception that emotions mattered to finance continued to hold sway in Britain's investing public throughout the decades even as the idea of naturally efficient and rational markets revolutionized politics and economics in the last third of the twentieth century. Particular emphasis will be placed on the tension between rational and irrational elements in financial capitalism that help us gain a better understanding of 1980s popular capitalism. I argue that this has been somewhat impeded by the fact that scholars of Thatcherism have explicitly or implicitly subscribed to a Weberian understanding of capitalism. If we critically reflect on our understanding of capitalism, the history of its expansion in this crucial decade will also appear in new light.

[64] Richard H. Thaler, *Misbehaving: The Making of Behavioural Economics* (London: Penguin, 2016).

# 1

# Bucket Shops and Outside Brokers

## The Interwar Fringe Market for Financial Securities

There were two prime ministers in the twentieth century who left a lasting effect on the way the British people interacted with financial markets: Margaret Thatcher on the stock market and David Lloyd George on the bond market. While Thatcher's controversial give-away flotations turned millions of people into shareholders in the 1980s, Lloyd George made the market for government debt palatable for the nation during the Great War. It was not the first time that a British Government had tapped into ordinary people's savings in order to finance a war. The public had bought government debt during the Napoleonic and Crimean Wars. But the mass participation in this market after 1914 exceeded all prior involvements in terms of scale, propaganda, and repercussions. Throughout the war, mass advertising campaigns appealed to the patriotism of millions of small investors to buy the government's war bonds at their local post office. 'Feed the Guns and Beat the Huns' or 'Turn your Silver into Bullets at the National Post Office' read the posters of the newly founded War Savings Committee that appealed to the subscriber's patriotism. The bonds were issued without a maturity date—known as 'consols'—and with a coupon (the annual interest paid) above the market average. This was considered necessary in order to sufficiently mobilize the nation's finances for the war effort. The advertising agency that advised the wartime government on the marketing campaign for the bonds put it bluntly: 'We must give the investor something for nothing. Why not make patriotism profitable?'[1] While the first issue in 1914 with a 4 per cent coupon was hardly advertised and resulted in a spectacular flop that had to be covered up by the Bank of England, the 1917 issue was subscribed for by more than 2 million investors.[2] Most of the notional amount of 2 billion was sold in small holdings of £100–500 and it is estimated that throughout the war over eight million savers came into touch with war bonds or other savings instruments promoted by the newly-founded

---

[1] Quote after H. Strachan, *Financing the First World War* (Oxford: Oxford University Press, 2004), p. 148.
[2] D. Kynaston, *Till Times Last Sand: A History of the Bank of England 1694–2013* (London: Bloomsbury, 2017), p. 278; 'Bank of England covered up failed first world war bond sale', *The Financial Times*, 8 August 2017.

*Playing the Market: Retail Investment and Speculation in Twentieth-Century Britain.* Kieran Heinemann, Oxford University Press (2021). © Kieran Heinemann. DOI: 10.1093/oso/9780198864257.003.0002

National Savings Movement.[3] The predominance of small holders of these bonds was reaffirmed upon redemption of the 1917 perpetual bond—which had been converted into a 3.5 per cent coupon in 1932. When the Conservative Chancellor George Osborne redeemed the last war bond in 2014, the UK Debt Management Office found that the majority of remaining holders were still retail investors.[4] Against the backdrop of this large-scale foray into the bond market during the Great War, many observers upon Britain's return to a peace-time economy in 1918 expected the investment habit displayed in this exercise in financial patriotism to spill over into the market for industrial shares—for better or worse.

Assessing the outlook for Britain's investing public in 1918, the Liberal politician and tax lawyer, Arthur Comyns Carr,[5] was one of many who expected the number of equity investors to rise and pose new challenges to Britain's existing financial infrastructure:

> We have seen during the war a remarkably widespread diffusion of money, and a wonderful growth in the habit of investment, among classes of the population to whom both are a novelty. [ . . . ] After the war it is expected that a large number of people who never were investors before will be willing to trust their savings to commercial companies, but will not be very well equipped to select those which are worthy of their confidence.[6]

Despite criticism from fiscal hawks, the war bond issues were widely regarded as a necessary effort of war finance and as a successful exercise in financial patriotism. Except for the Labour Party's attacks on the 'rentier class' reaping 'unearned income', which now technically applied to millions of small bond holders, there was little concern about savers having entered the debt market. Government debt offered predictable, if small, returns at a low risk and the average size of the small investor's holding hardly allowed for any risky speculation in a stable and calm market. The prospect, however, of war bonds having prompted an interest in other types of financial securities, not least industrial shares, was met with

---

[3] J. Wormell, *The Management of The National Debt of The United Kingdom* (London: Routledge, 2000), pp. 340–341.

[4] 'UK bonds that financed first world war to be redeemed 100 years later', *The Guardian*, 31 October 2014: 'Of the 11,200 registered holders, 7,700 investors hold less than £1000 nominal, and 92% of holders own less than £10,000 each.'

[5] M. Pottle, 'Carr, Sir Arthur Strettell Comyns (1882–1965)', *Oxford Dictionary of National Biography* (hereafter *ODNB*), 2004.

[6] Quote after R. Michie, 'Gamblers, Fools, Victims, or Wizards?: The British Investor in the Public Mind, 1850–1930', in D. R. Green (ed.), *Men, Women, and Money: Perspectives on Gender, Wealth and Investment 1850–1930* (Oxford: Oxford University Press, 2011), p. 181. Michie notes that '[m]any of these new investors were soon drawn towards joint-stock company shares [...] In addition, investors continued to be drawn into smaller and more speculative concerns offering the prospects of large capital gains.' Michie, 'Gamblers, Fools, Victims, or Wizards?', p. 181.

suspicion in some and great enthusiasm in other sections of British interwar society. The stock market was by and large still the prerogative of wealthy individuals and professional elites who were privileged to reap the rewards, but also able to shoulder the greater risks, of a far more volatile and speculative market that was prone to insider trading and therefore considered unsuitable for investors of modest means. The London Stock Exchange, historically wary of 'amateur' involvement in its market, remained passive, while members of the clergy and the medical profession voiced their fears that increased speculation would erode moral standards, undermine the work ethic, and pose a mental threat to the body politic. On the other hand, however, the interwar years saw the emergence of a loosely connected movement that was more optimistic about the arrival of a new investor class and sought to educate the newcomers into economically enfranchised citizens. This movement was spearheaded by the liberal-minded financial press, which saw a commercial opportunity to expand its readership, but also included the declining Liberal Party and progressive Tories, most notably the Unionist MP, Noel Skelton. Together they argued that if ownership of equities was dispersed more democratically, capitalism would gain a much broader footing in society. This started a national debate over legitimate forms of investment for ordinary people with catchphrases like 'democratisation of investment' or 'property-owning democracy' denoting a normative project of universal share ownership.

Although recent scholarship has called this into question, the financial patriotism small investors displayed in the war-time bond market *did* cause many of them to develop a more active interest in the stock market in the years to come.[7] But in order to capture the nature and extent of this new activity, we must look beyond the official exchanges and turn to the market fringes. For reasons to be discussed further, the exchanges in London and the provinces showed little interest in catering for the new investor class. As a result, unregulated but easily accessible 'outside' brokers and 'bucket shops' filled the gap and serviced the largely uneducated investment newcomers, while at the same time fraudulent share pushers sought to prey on the more gullible among them. These fringe dealers targeted retail investors who did not have access to the regulated exchanges and the majority of transactions they brokered resulted in the physical exchange of stocks, debentures, or government securities. A considerable amount, however, of the new enthusiasm to play the market was channelled into neither the official exchanges nor the outside market. Instead, many punters merely placed bets on the future price movements of financial assets—without ever

---

[7] Rutterford, 'The Evidence for "Democratization" of Share Ownership in Great Britain in the Early Twentieth Century', p. 206. J. Rutterford, D. R. Green, A. Owens, and J. Maltby, 'Who Comprised the Nation of Shareholders? Gender and Investment in Great Britain, c. 1870–1935', *The Economic History Review* 64 (2011), p. 157.

owning the underlying security. They could do so in bucket shops, which acted as bookmakers who made a market not in gambling odds for horse or dog races, but took the opposite view of whatever their customers believed to happen in the securities markets. In the long run, this proved to be a lucrative, yet hugely controversial business model that provoked anger among regulators and financial elites because it blurred the delicate boundaries between organized speculation and frivolous gambling. In this regard, the interwar bucket shop worked in exactly the same way as modern spread betting operators do today. Both then and more recently, retail investors indulging in outright gambling on price movements prompted regulatory intervention, which reveals much about how attitudes towards investment, speculation, and gambling shifted over time.

Commenting on Britain's economic outlook shortly after Armistice Day, the *Financial Times* (*FT*) argued that 'the provision of facilities for the small investor is now more urgent than ever' if the trend of popular capitalism was to be encouraged—and more readers were to buy the *FT*. The mouthpiece of British finance called upon the Stock Exchange to 'devise means to enable its members to be brought into closer touch with the public and so attract a big volume of business which otherwise will be diverted to other, and very frequently undesirable channels'.[8] By 'undesirable channels', the *FT* meant the outside market, which had been allowed to flourish by the exchanges' neglect of new investors in the first place. Because the outside market was unregulated, it was prone to fraudulent share-pushing schemes, which became a national problem by the 1930s and had to be dealt with by the regulator. In 1936 a Board of Trade Committee was commissioned 'to consider the operations commonly known as share-pushing and share-hawking and similar activities and to report what, if any, action is desirable'.[9] Eventually this legal war largely put an end to share frauds by unlicensed dealers and the bucket shop practice of stock price gambling. But tough regulations came at the cost of effectively stifling the retail market for stocks and shares.

## A 'Democratisation of Investment'?

Naturally, the prospect of a crowd of market newcomers in need of investment advice was relished by the financial press which had been growing rapidly since the expansion of share ownership in Victorian times.[10] The decades between 1900 and 1960 marked the emergence of a 'new' or 'popular' financial journalism. In the

---

[8] 'The Prospects of the Stock Exchange', *The Financial Times*, 28 November 1918.
[9] Share-Pushing: Report of the Departmental Committee appointed by the Board of Trade, 1936–7, p. 5.
[10] On the late Victorian trend of wider share ownership see Rutterford et al., 'Who Comprised the Nation of Shareholders?'; J. Maltby and J. Rutterford, '"She Possessed Her Own Fortune": Women

wake of democratization and professionalization, British journalists had moved away from early Victorian elitist ideals and increasingly endeavoured to be 'representative of the people'.[11] Media outlets converged and sought to address the rapidly widening audience in a more accessible and less technical style. This meant that popular newspapers like the *Daily Mail*, the *Daily Herald* and the *Daily Express* entered the field while established journals and papers like *The Economist*, *The Times*, or *The Telegraph* discarded their overly technical approach to financial affairs.[12]

The paper that epitomized this media transformation and became the 'flagship' of the new financial journalism was the *Financial News (FN)*, founded in 1884 by the flamboyant Harry Marks. Marks had gathered his first journalistic experience in the United States and established the *FN* as the leading voice of the 'modern investing public'.[13] He promised its readers a 'Yankee bounce' instead of 'eighteen-hundred-and-fast-asleep conservatism of the old school', but throughout his career 'never quite shook off the suspicion that he was rather shady'.[14] Persistent accusations of fraud surrounded Marks until the end of his life. Perhaps more than any other newspaper the early *FN* highlights the ongoing tension between the professionalization of and fraudulent elements in financial journalism as some newspapers became channels for criminal activities by promoting company fraud[15]—a tension that continued to exist throughout the post-war period as we shall see in Chapter 3. Nevertheless, the growth in financial knowledge and in shareholder numbers was mutually dependent, with the media creating more and more awareness of the stock market and new investors demanding orientation and advice. After 1918, City journalists were further incentivized to promote the ideal of universal share ownership.

In 1919, Marks's successor as editor of the *FN*, Dr Ellis Powell, pinned down the zeitgeist in an essay for the *Financial Review of Reviews*. Powell claimed that as a result of the 'financial patriotism' expressed in the buying of war bonds, Britain

---

Investors From the Late Nineteenth Century to the Early Twentieth Century', *Business History* 48 (2006), pp. 220–253.

[11] M. Hampton, *Visions of the Press in Britain, 1850–1950* (Urbana, IL: University of Illinois Press, 2004), pp. 75–105.

[12] D. Porter, '"Where There's a Tip There's a Tap': The Popular Press and the Investing Public, 1900–60', in P. Catterall and C. Seymour-Ure (eds), *Northcliffe's Legacy: Aspects of the British Popular Press* (London: Macmillan, 2000), pp. 71–96; D. Porter, '"City Slickers" in Perspective: The Daily Mirror, its Readers and Their Money, 1960–2000', *Media History* 9 (2003), pp. 137–152.

[13] D. Porter, '"A Trusted Guide of the Investing Public": Harry Marks and the Financial News 1884–1916', *Business History* 28 (1986), pp. 1–17.

[14] D. Porter, 'Marks, Harry Hananel (1855–1916)', *ODNB*, 2004.

[15] J. Taylor, 'Watchdogs or Apologists?: Financial Journalism and Company Fraud in Early Victorian Britain', *Historical Research* 85 (2012), pp. 632–650; D. Porter, 'City Editors and the Modern Investing Public: Establishing the Integrity of the New Financial Journalism in Late Nineteenth-Century London', *Media History* 4 (1998), pp. 49–60.

would now experience a 'democratisation of investment'.[16] For Powell, the evolution of a 'constantly augmenting financial public'[17] was a natural act of rationalization which was to put an end to the 'continual withdrawal of the life-blood of the body economic into stagnation and unfruitfulness'.[18] A powerful brand of market populism took shape that presented free-market capitalism as a more promising vehicle for equality than the state, and a more viable solution for the problems of the 'small man'—a notion that is pervasive in British politics and business media until this day.[19] It is striking and so far unacknowledged that the idea of a popular capitalism had roots in social Darwinism, which was omnipres-ent in interwar social, political, and economic thought.[20] Powell was convinced, as he had already averred in 1915, that the 'ever-increasing stability and potency of modern finance were attributable to something in the nature of organic develop-ment, operating by means of Natural Selection, and therefore completely in accordance with the main postulate of the Darwinian theory'.[21] Surely not all of Powell's colleagues in City journalism shared his assumption that wider share ownership was an expression of natural selection. But there was certainly a 'Whiggish' sense of determinism in the predominantly Liberal financial press. Hartley Withers, for instance, editor of *The Economist* from 1915 to 1921, was equally impressed by the 'great increase in the investment habit, among classes in which it was formerly uncommon, during and since the war' and was convinced that the 'social importance of this growing democratization of capitalism is difficult to exaggerate'.[22] In a similar vein, *The Economist* declared in 1926 that 'capital ownership in this country is truly a democratic business'.[23] But because 'there were no contemporary estimates of shareholder numbers in the United

---

[16] E. Powell, 'Democratisation of Investment', *The Financial Review of Reviews* 14 (1919), pp. 243–258. A staunch imperialist and social Darwinist, Dr Ellis Thomas Powell, sometimes writing under his nom de plume Robert Ludlow, believed that 'the ever-increasing stability and potency of modern finance were attributable to something in the nature of organic development, operating by means of Natural Selection, and therefore completely on accordance with the main postulate of the Darwinian theory'. Quote from D. Kynaston, *The Financial Times: A Centenary History* (London: Viking, 1988), p. 59.

[17] E. Powell, *Letters to a Small Investor: A Straightforward & Non-Technical Introduction to the Science of Investment* (London: The Financial News, 1916), p. 5.

[18] *Powell*, Democratisation of Investment, p. 250.

[19] D. McKnight, 'The Sunday Times and Andrew Neil: The Cultivation of Market Populism', *Journalism Studies* 10 (2009), pp. 754–768. On the concept of market populism see T. Frank, *One Market under God: Extreme Capitalism, Market Populism, and the End of Economic Democracy* (London: Secker & Warburg, 2001).

[20] On the interwar climate of social engineering and Darwinism see M. Mazower, *Dark Continent: Europe's Twentieth Century* (London: Penguin, 1999), pp. 77–105.

[21] E. Powell, *The Evolution of the Money Market, 1385–1915: An Historical and Analytical Study of the Rise and Development of Finance as a Centralised, Co-ordinated Force* (London: Frank Cass & Co., 1966), pp. vii–viii.

[22] H. Withers, *Hints About Investments* (London: Eveleigh Nash & Grayson, 1926), p. 257. On Withers's influence on financial journalism see D. Porter, 'Withers, Hartley (1867–1950)', *ODNB*, online edn, Oct 2006.

[23] Quoted after Rutterford et al., 'Who comprised the nation of shareholders?', p. 162.

Kingdom', historians need to rely on retrospective estimates, which assume that by the interwar years, the number of people owning shares directly had grown to 1.3 million from 250,000 in 1850.[24]

In addition to journalistic efforts to increase newspaper circulation, the quest for wider share ownership needs to be seen in the context of anti-socialism and the contested debate over earned and unearned income. Increasing the number of investors also held the prospect of mobilizing middle-class voters against the unequal tax treatment of income derived from capital investments as 'unearned', which supporters of free-market capitalism regarded as a fatal disincentive for thrift and deferred gratification. This differentiation had been introduced by the Liberal Party in 1907 and further promoted in form of a surtax by the short-lived first Labour government of Ramsay Macdonald in 1924.[25] Particularly the Labour Chancellor Philip Snowden excelled in denouncing the 'large rich and idle class' of rentiers as 'parasites' of the community.[26] Free marketeers like Ellis Powell were hopeful that a dispersal of equity capital would generate awareness that 'persons who, by thrift, self-denial, and skilful investment, have created and accumulated these financial stores are really the backbone of the community, not thieves exploiting other people's labour'.[27] Another reform-minded journalist who championed the case of wider share ownership by awarding moral authority to the small investor was Hargreaves Parkinson. Praised as a prolific writer on economic affairs, Parkinson had also been with *The Economist* before joining the *Financial News* in 1928 and became editor of the *Financial Times* in 1945, after the two dailies had merged that year.[28] According to Parkinson, a spread of the investment habit would foster the key middle-class virtue of thrift. Under the heading 'The Moral Aspect', he argued:

> Thrift teaches a man dependence on himself rather than on the pity and charity of others. It overcomes the tyranny of chance and misfortune. It confers freedom from anxiety and forms an appropriate background for a serene mind. It enhances self-reliance, and supplies the motive power for the putting forth of one's best in all the affairs of life.[29]

---

[24] Rutterford and Sotiropoulos, 'The Rise of the Small Investor in the US and the UK, 1895 to 1970', p. 495; Michie, *The London and New York Stock Exchanges*, p. 118.

[25] On differentiation and the 1907 budget see M. Daunton, *Trusting Leviathan: The Politics of Taxation in Britain, 1793-1914* (Cambridge: Cambridge University Press, 2001), pp. 98–100. On Macdonald's Labour government and Snowden see M. Daunton, *Just Taxes: The Politics of Taxation in Britain, 1914-1979* (Cambridge: Cambridge University Press, 2002), pp. 66–74, and R. Whiting, *The Labour Party and Taxation: Party Identity and Political Purpose in Twentieth-Century Britain* (Cambridge: Cambridge University Press, 2001), pp. 10–34.

[26] Quote after 'Socialist Attack on Capitalism', *The Financial Times*, 21 March 1923.

[27] Powell, 'Democratisation of Investment', 255.

[28] D. Kynaston, *The City of London: Illusions of Gold 1914-1945* (London, Pimlico, 2000), III, p. 487; p. 505 denotes Parkinson a 'reform-minded financial journalist'.

[29] H. Parkinson, *The Small Investor* (London: Blackie & Son, 1930), p. 112.

In order to assert this moral high ground, however, the small investor's actions had to be rid of the taint of speculation and, to an even greater extent, gambling. More than ever, clear distinctions were needed:

> To put the matter in broad terms, the investor deals in certainties, or, at least, what appear to be such within the limits of this somewhat uncertain world. The speculator takes risks and knows that he takes them, but seeks at the same time to reduce the element of uncertainty to a minimum by ascertaining whatever is ascertainable regarding the matter in hand. He speculates in the light of know-ledge. The gambler—the real villain of the piece—risks all on some casual 'tip' which may have come to his ears without any real understanding of the merits of the case.[30]

The likes of Powell, Parkinson, and Withers were walking a tightrope when defining the lines between investment and speculation as they faced criticism not only from the left, but also concerns over excessive speculation from organized religion. Soon after the end of WWI, a debate over the 'ethics of investment' unfolded in the *Financial Review of Reviews*. One intervention came from H. J. D. Astley, an Anglican vicar from Norfolk and Fellow of the Royal Historical Society, who attempted to erect a moral barrier between 'the proper use of money' on the one hand and the speculator's 'greed and selfishness' on the other.[31] Writing in 1918, he hailed war loans as a 'prudent and patriotic act', leading to 'peace and quiet', but condemned the 'speculation involved in the holding of ordinary shares' as sinful.[32] Unlike the investor, to whom 'worry and anxiety' are unknown, for the speculator 'there lies in wait too often not only loss of goods and loss of self-respect, but the felon's cell or the suicide's grave!'[33] In the mid-1930s, the church intervened again in the debate when it submitted a substantial amount of evidence to the Royal Commission on Betting and Lotteries, which was tasked with investigating the impact of illegal forms of gambling such as off-course betting on horse races. The church also expressed its concern 'regarding the gambling which is associated with financial and com-mercial transactions'. In particular, it wished to ban 'the large number of bucket-shops, or share dealers who are not members of the Stock Exchange' and called upon the government to 'undertake an inquiry regarding the extent and social consequences of the above forms of gambling speculation'.[34] But in this debate the church faced an intricate tension between Mammon and morality. As we shall see,

---

[30] H. Parkinson, *The A B C of Stocks and Shares: A Handbook for the Investor* (London: Longmans, Green and Co., 1925), pp. 30–31.
[31] H. J. D. Astley, 'The Morality of Investment', *The Financial Review of Reviews* 13 (1918), p. 260.
[32] Astley, 'The Morality of Investment', p. 254.
[33] Astley, 'The Morality of Investment', p. 254.
[34] 'Gambling in the City: Concern of the Churches', *The Times*, 30 June 1936.

clergymen recurrently engaged in the stock market—often with devastating consequences—and exposed the church to accusations of double standards.

A similarly dramatic note was struck in an article titled 'The Nemesis of Speculation' by the eugenicist Caleb Saleeby a year later. Saleeby had by the early twentieth century become an internationally acclaimed authority on social problems such as 'venereal disease, insanity, and, in particular, alcohol'.[35] In 1919, he identified speculation as another such 'racial poison' and declared the 'temper of the hour [to be] speculative and inclined to take risks'.[36] 'Lending our money to win the war' may have been entirely legitimate, but now Saleeby sensed a widely held expectation among the British people to 'make money without working for it, by means of speculation and the harassing exploitation of the something-for-nothing instinct'.[37] In the vein of Victorian critics of finance, the trained physician listed addictive behaviour, alcoholism, and suicide among the 'deplorable consequences to mind and body of speculation'. Deeply embedded in the contemporary language of social hygiene, he urged Britain to eradicate this 'injury to the body-politic and to the mind-politic'.[38] Acutely aware that 'speculation is a much-abused word', the likes of Hargreaves Parkinson likewise discarded it for the 'ordinary investor'.[39] It was not the latter's 'business to dabble in speculative share transactions, but to build railways and roads, create industries, and equip them with their necessary resources'.[40]

This integration of shareholding into a twentieth-century model of citizenship found its political expression in the early 1920s. The London-based tax lawyer, Herbert W. Jordan, was commissioned to chair a government committee on employee share and profit-sharing schemes in 1920. He argued that via these means, employees would 'become in a small way capitalists'.[41] Three years later, *The Spectator* published a series of essays entitled 'Constructive Conservatism' by the Scottish Unionist politician Noel Skelton that made a more lasting impact than Jordan's intervention.[42] Skelton envisaged investment—not in the sense of stock dealing or speculation, but of share *ownership*—as a suitable means of bridging the gap between capital and labour. Keen to offer a Conservative alternative to the rise of socialism, he wrote that

---

[35] G. R. Searle, 'Saleeby, Caleb Williams Elijah (1878–1940)', in H. C. G. Matthew and B. Harrison (eds), *The Oxford Dictionary of National Biography* (*ODNB*) (Oxford: Oxford University Press, 2004); for Saleeby's impact on eugenics in Britain see G. Rodwell, 'Dr Caleb Williams Saleeby: The Complete Eugenicist', *History of Education* 26 (1997), pp. 23–40.

[36] C. Saleeby, 'The Nemesis of Speculation', *The Financial Review of Reviews* 14 (1919), p. 26.

[37] Saleeby, 'The Nemesis of Speculation', pp. 29–30.

[38] Saleeby, 'The Nemesis of Speculation', p. 36.

[39] Parkinson, *The A B C of Stocks and Shares*, p. 30.

[40] Parkinson, *The A B C of Stocks and Shares*, p. 33.

[41] H. W. Jordan, 'Profit-Sharing and Co-Partnership', *The Financial Review of Reviews* June (1920), pp. 166–186.

[42] D. Torrance, *Noel Skelton and the Property-Owning Democracy* (London: Biteback, 2010).

To the wage-earner, co-partnery brings a new incentive and a new kind of interest in his work, arising out of his new relation to it; a union of his thrift effort and his work effort; a wider industrial outlook, since, as his savings in the business increase, so does his interest in its general prosperity, for that prosperity affects him directly as a shareholder.

Eventually, Skelton expected, 'workers would become capitalists' and therefore not only politically, but economically enfranchised citizens of a 'property-owning democracy'.[43] Under the term 'co-partnery' he subsumed profit-sharing and employee share schemes, which had already begun to flourish in some industries around the turn of the century.[44] Skelton's ideas were picked up by interwar intellectuals such as Hilaire Belloc and G.K. Chesterton and, as we shall see, the concept of a property-owning democracy went on to leave a significant mark on British politics in the second half of the twentieth century.[45]

While financial journalists, progressive Tories, and Liberals began to promote the benefits of wider share ownership during the interwar period, only a few supporters were found in the City of London, the heart of Britain's financial system. David Kynaston pointed out that the 'Stock Exchange itself hardly encouraged popular capitalism' during the interwar years. Kynaston discusses the following example that illustrates how remote the Stock Exchange's business practice was from the ideal of a 'free and open market place'.[46]

As early as 1923, a year after it began, the BBC asked for permission to broadcast prices—a request granted, with the utmost reluctance, only three years later, a concession rendered almost useless by the stipulation that no prices were to be broadcast prior to 7 p.m., long after the end of trading.[47]

---

[43] N. Skelton, 'Constructive Conservatism IV: Democracy Stabilized', *The Spectator*, 18 May 1923.

[44] On earlier variants of these schemes see E. Bristow, 'Profit-Sharing, Socialism and Labour Unrest', in K. D. Brown (ed.), *Essays in Anti-Labour History: Responses to the Rise of Labour in Britain* (London: Macmillan Press, 1974), pp. 262–289; D. Matthews, 'The British Experience of Profit-Sharing', *Economic History Review* 42 (1989), pp. 439–464.

[45] On the concept's impact on twentieth-century British politics and intellectual landscape see B. Jackson, 'Property-Owning Democracy: A Short History', in M. O'Neill and T. Williamson (eds), *Property-Owning Democracy: Rawls and Beyond* (Hoboken, NJ: Wiley-Blackwell, 2012), pp. 33–52; B. Jackson, 'Revisionism Reconsidered: "Property-Owning Democracy" and Egalitarian Strategy in Post-War Britain', *Twentieth Century British History* 16 (2005), pp. 416–440; M. Francis, 'A Crusade to Enfranchise the Many', pp. 275–297; A. Davies, '"Right to Buy": The Development of a Conservative Housing Policy, 1945–1980', *Contemporary British History* 27 (2013), pp. 421–444.

[46] For a more favourable assessment of the London Stock Exchange in this regard around the turn of the century see Michie, *The London Stock Exchange*, p. 142: 'Accepting that any stock exchange involves a less-than-ideal situation, compared to the free and open market place, then the situation of the London Stock Exchange did not compare unfavourably with any rival or alternatives on the eve of the First World War.'

[47] Kynaston, *The City of London*, III, pp. 294–295.

At the same time, quite a contrary development unfolded on Wall Street, where the New York Stock Exchange embarked on a large-scale marketing agenda and promoted itself as 'the free and open people's market'.[48] While the London Stock Exchange upheld a strict ban on advertising for its members, in the US, financial advertising was a key factor in facilitating a vibrant retail market for stocks and shares.[49] Furthermore, in 1929 and again in 1936, London blocked brokers' initiatives to establish regional branch offices, which would have allowed them to attract regional business as in the US.[50] On the downside, this large-scale participation in the US meant that far more savers and investors got burned in the 1929 stock market crash than in Britain. Particularly small investors had flocked to Wall Street investment trusts who advertised heavily and financed their speculations with enormous amounts of debt. When markets turned on Black Thursday, 24 October 1929, lenders became nervous and in so-called margin calls withdrew the capital the trusts had been using for their unsuccessful bets, leaving the investors to incur heavy losses.[51] These investment trusts were far less popular in Britain, where stock market newcomers nevertheless made their own first painful experiences with a bear market. In total, however, the downswing was less severe and played out more gradually, with the equity market experiencing its first real shock in 1928. In August that year, *The Economist* reported that several Stock Exchange firms were involved in underwriting highly speculative companies with a combined market valuation of £38.5m. By August 1929 they had plummeted to £17.4m.[52]

In Britain, events culminated in September the following year—one month before Wall Street markets collapsed—and until this day are associated with the name Clarence Hatry. Born to Jewish immigrants in 1888, Hatry rose to fame in the 1920s as a flamboyant financier and director of fifteen companies, including Leyland and Debenhams. The City establishment, notoriously suspicious of outsiders, made business with Hatry, but never really accepted him and despised his lavish lifestyle. In 1929 Hatry planned his largest move so far and launched a bid for Britain's largest steelmaker, United Steel, for US$40m. In June that year, however, Hatry's lenders pulled out, not least because they felt anxious about the Labour Party having won for the first time the general elections a month before. Desperate to pull through, Hatry resorted to issuing fake securities in order

---

[48] S. Fraser, *Wall Street: A Cultural History* (London: Faber and Faber, 2006), pp. 310, 347.

[49] See especially J. C. Ott, '"The Free and Open People's Market": Political Ideology and Retail Brokerage at the New York Stock Exchange, 1913–1933', *Journal of American History* 96 (2009), pp.44–71.

[50] C. Swinson, *Regulation of the London Stock Exchange. Share Trading, Fraud and Reform 1914–1945* (Oxford: Routledge, 2018), p. 235.5/749 (pagination refers to the e-book in the online repository of the British Library).

[51] S. Banner, *Speculation: A History of the Fine Line between Gambling and Investing* (Oxford: Oxford University Press, 2017), pp. 178–180.

[52] C. Swinson, *Regulation of the London Stock Exchange*, p. 439.1/749.

to post them as collateral for the loans required to finance the acquisition. By September, the last remaining banks backing Hatry grew suspicious and called in their loans. On 20th September, Hatry turned himself in to the Director of Public Prosecution, Sir Archibald Bodkin, and on the same day, the Stock Exchange suspended trading in Hatry shares inflicting heavy losses on investors small and large.[53] As a result of this scandal, in which renowned stockbroking firms like Foster & Braithwaite were involved, the Stock Exchange established a public compensation fund for investors who lost money as a result of misconduct of any of its members. On the one hand, this meant that the Stock Exchange had begun to accept 'responsibility for protecting the interests of the wider investing public'.[54] But on the other hand, as we shall see, the experience of 1928/1929 further deepened the Stock Exchange's suspicion of outsiders and 'amateurs'. Its willingness to make concessions in regards to investor protection stemmed largely from its nervousness about the shifting political tide and it remained utterly reluctant to cater for the new investor class.

The dominant image in the public propaganda of the interwar Stock Exchange continued to be that of the daring, calculating, professional market operator. While in US discourses, speculation was conceptualized as the ultimate expression of an American 'frontier spirit', British observers employed colonial narratives to fashion speculators as pioneers of imperial capitalism.[55] One example can be found in a standard work on the Stock Exchange, first published in 1934 by Frederick Armstrong who was a senior partner in the renowned stockbroking firm Messrs. Killik & Co.. Armstrong stated that

> All pioneer effort is by its very nature speculative, and efforts to deprecate this natural urge and impulse must, to be consistent, frown on the noblest achieve-ments of man. Columbus, Cook, Livingstone, Pasteur, Alcock, Brown, Marconi, to add to legions of other names famous in history, surely were all speculators.[56]

Francis Hirst, the prominent free trader and editor of *The Economist* from 1907 to 1916, evoked similar images of imperial grandeur when discussing the deeper meaning of investment:

---

[53] C. Swinson, *Share Trading, Fraud and the Crash of 1929. A Biography of Clarence Hatry* (Oxford: Routledge, 2019); A. M. Wright, *The Threadbare Plea: The Hatry Crash of 1929* (Independently published, 2018).

[54] Swinson, *Share Trading, Fraud and the Crash of 1929*, 22.6/749.

[55] On the US self-conception of a 'nation of speculators' see Stäheli, *Spectacular Speculation*, pp. 85–87; also Fraser, *Every Man a Speculator*.

[56] F. E. Armstrong, *The Book of the Stock Exchange: A Comprehensive Guide to the Theory and Practice of Stock and Share Transactions and to the Business of the Members of London and Provincial Stock Exchanges*, 5th edn (London: Pitman, 1934), p. 153.

Our merchants and shippers seek profit in every corner of the globe; our investors large and small have interests in every continent, and the London Stock Exchange List is in itself a sort of key to the distribution of British trade and capital. [ ... ] It will, therefore, be proper within a small compass to take a wide view; for, as Burke says, 'Great empire and little minds go ill together'.[57]

Besides the rhetoric, practical measures were taken to make the exchange difficult to access for outsiders. Not only was admission for membership but also dealing costs were high in London, where the Stock Exchange enforced a unique and strict distinction between stockbrokers (agents) and stockjobbers (dealers or market makers). Brokers charged clients a fixed commission of 2 per cent for processing orders through jobbers who specialized in different markets and aimed to buy low and sell high. Brokers were technically not allowed to deal on their own account—although they did so extensively—and jobbers were forbidden to deal with members of the public.[58] This rule avoided a principal–agent problem, but deterred less affluent investors who could not shoulder paying the broker's commission *and* the jobber's 'turn'—not to mention taxes and stamp duty of 1 per cent on each transaction. As one private investor put it in a reader's letter to the *Financial Times* in 1923:

The game is too much against the punter. He has not a chance to do any good, as he has to placate (1) the broker, (2) the Government, (3) the jobber. All these three take heavy toll before the punter gets anything. I have been a punter for years, but find it a poor game, and I do not wonder that people prefer to back horses. Give the small speculator a ghost of a show and he will come back, but not before.[59]

This *FT* reader was exactly the type of client that Crump, Crosby, and Weber wished to see excluded. They had no time for the 'small speculator who seeks to make earnings out of small differences in prices' and condemned the amateur as a 'superfluous parasite' who was 'not fulfilling any aim of the national economy as a whole'.[60] This conception persisted in British economic thought with the economists Alfred Marshall and John A. Hobson reaffirming the idea of the 'professional financier' who 'manipulate[s] prices, so as to assist his calculations', while 'the amateurs who play with them must lose'.[61]

[57] F. W. Hirst, *The Stock Exchange: A Short Study of Investment and Speculation*, 4th edn (London: Williams and Norgate, 1948), p. 15.
[58] Michie, *The London Stock Exchange*, pp. 495–499.
[59] 'Letters to the Editor: A Punter's Plaint', *The Financial Times*, 29 October 1923.
[60] Weber, 'Stock and Commodity Exchanges', 333.
[61] On Alfred Marshall see M. Dardi and M. Gallegati, 'Alfred Marshall on Speculation', *History of Political Economy* 24 (1992), pp. 571–594. Quotes after Hobson, *The Evolution of Modern Capitalism*, pp. 249–251.

Universal franchise after the war had done little to change attitudes among members of Britain's financial establishment. John Maynard Keynes picked up on this aspect in his *General Theory*. Keynes was of course himself well-acquainted with stock and commodity exchanges, having speculated on heavy margin in derivative markets during the 1920s.[62] Keynes highlighted London's continued aloofness in comparison with Wall Street:

> It is usually agreed that casinos should, in the public interest, be inaccessible and expensive. And perhaps the same is true of Stock Exchanges. That the sins of the London Stock Exchange are less than those of Wall Street may be due, not so much to differences in national character, as to the fact that to the average Englishman Throgmorton Street is, compared with Wall Street to the average American, inaccessible and very expensive. The jobber's 'turn', the high broker-age charges and the heavy transfer tax payable to the Exchequer, which attend dealings on the London Stock Exchange, sufficiently diminish the liquidity of the market (although the practice of fortnightly accounts operates the other way) to rule out a large proportion of the transactions characteristic of Wall Street.[63]

But even though the Stock Exchange could claim that its restrictive attitude avoided a more disastrous outcome of the crash, the concept of professionalism remained elusive and fragile. While Ranald Michie has rejected the characterization of the Stock Exchange as 'the last bastion of the British amateur',[64] David Kynaston has shown how behind a veneer of expertise, members of 'The House' were in fact 'poor at analysing economic fundamentals and distributing financial resources accordingly'.[65] The concept of professionalism was further complicated by the fact that the gentlemanly identity of many Stock Exchange members did indeed entail the self-perception of being amateurs. As Marcus Collins has pointed out, this 'afforded them a disinterestedness, an easygoing generosity, a horror of the small-minded'—character traits that could entail 'an anti-work ethic opposed to the more ruthless and competitive aspects of professionalism'.[66] Up until the post-war decades, leading firms like the blue-blooded stockbrokers Cazenove 'prided [them]selves on being enthusiastic amateurs' in internal correspond-ence.[67] The memoirs of Nicholas Davenport, the left-leaning City editor of *The Spectator*, convey telling insights into the amateurism of the Stock Exchange,

---

[62] On Keynes's career as a speculator see especially M. C. Marcuzzo, E. Sanfilippo and L. Fantacci, 'Speculation in Commodities: Keynes' "Practical Acquaintance" with Futures Markets', *Journal of the History of Economic Thought* 32 (2010), pp. 397–418; also P. Clarke, *Keynes: The Twentieth Century's Most Influential Economist* (London: Bloomsbury, 2009), pp. 49–51.

[63] Keynes, *The General Theory of Employment, Interest and Money*, p. 159.

[64] Michie, *The London Stock Exchange*, p. 99.      [65] Kynaston, *The City of London*, III, p. 298.

[66] M. Collins, 'The Fall of the English Gentleman: The National Character in Decline, c.1918–1970', *Historical Research* 75 (2002), p. 93.

[67] D. Kynaston, *Cazenove & Co: A History* (London: Batsford, 1991), pp. 192–193.

based on experiences with the renowned brokers Rowe and Pitman. Davenport had started working for the firm in the 1920s and described first-hand the nepotism that governed the City and excluded ordinary investors from the privileged networks of information:

> I remembered Hugo Pitman [ ... ] calling me into his room one day to ask me to explain a balance sheet. There was really no reason why Hugo should have bothered to understand a balance sheet. His family's immense clientele was not built up on his understanding of company accounts, but on his integrity and charm. He had rowed for Oxford and was a friend of Augustus John, whose paintings he had collected. He was given the first issue of the Ford Motor Company to handle, because a Ford family connection had been up at Oxford with him and had rowed in his college boat.[68]

Davenport's encounters were far from unusual. George Aylwen of J. & A. Scrimgeour recalled the average life of the interwar stockbroker as follows:

> Most members were merely passers on of information and gossip, there was little or no attempt to sift information, to analyse prospects of equities, or indeed to justify the recommendation of the many and various tips toddled out by the market.[69]

The main reason for this sort of attitude was the City's reliance on insider trading, which had been outlawed in the US in the 1930s, but was not tackled in Britain before the late 1960s. The unique selling position of stockbrokers was whether they could provide wealthy clients with profitable tips—'whom one knew still mattered more than what one knew'.[70] In the 1920s and 1930s, the City was still a bastion of upper-class financiers and therefore woefully unfit, unprepared, and unwilling to accustom itself with the financial consequences of WWI.

We must also challenge the often implied assumption of regular stock market activity as an overly sound, prudent, and calculating affair and bear in mind that the interwar stock market was regularly engulfed in an unusually bullish climate. For a vivid account of interwar speculation we can turn to the journalist and writer Sydney Moseley who published his private diaries in 1960 and wrote in rich details about his—often disastrous—engagement in the stock market. Moseley joined the *Evening Standard* in 1910 and built relationships in the City, which he leveraged to make his mark as an author of critically acclaimed investment guides 'for those

---

[68] N. Davenport, *Memoirs of a City Radical* (London: Weidenfeld and Nicolson, 1974), p. 20.
[69] Kynaston, *The City of London*, III, p. 295.   [70] Kynaston, *The City of London*, III, p. 296.

who desire to have a flutter now and then'.[71] Moseley was not a professional investor by modern standards, but commanding sufficient capital and having access to insider knowledge, he was a professional by nineteenth-century standards, many of which still applied to the interwar City. Moseley's diaries give a very different impression of his stock market dealings than his investment guides. On April 7th 1927, only days before his first book was published, Moseley was in fact '[s]till trying hard to close down on [his] Stock Exchange dealings' and complained that it was 'as hopeless as ever to make money by speculation'.[72] In October that same year, Moseley was found speculating heavily with borrowed money when the market turned against him.

> What I find so heartbreaking is that the money I have made by hard work in writing is simply thrown down the Stock Exchange drain. For some years now I have been trying to reduce my market commitments, but I am no better off for the effort. [ ... ] What's the use of earning a few guineas when one loses hundreds? That, I suppose, is one of the particular evils of speculation: it distorts one's sense of values.[73]

In July 1934—his second investment bestseller, which he advertised as a 'safety-first book' that had 'nothing whatever to do with speculation or speculative investment',[74] had appeared in the meantime—Moseley was 'still in deeply' although he had cleared his 'three biggest stockbroking accounts'. He had six altogether. He promised himself 'that, given the chance, I will get free of the Stock Exchange altogether. At any rate, no more buying! ... Get out! Get out!'[75] No improvement, however, was in sight by March the following year when Moseley was 'tired of "deals", tired of the Stock Exchange, and [hated] to say what else [he was] tired of'. His diary entry of the 26th reveals the enormous leverage of his dealings:

> I must really stop this speculating. [ ... ] My present position is that in one firm I have some £20,000 of stock open for which I am paying a nice interest! [ ... ] I owe my bank about £10,000. And that is not the whole story. So, I repeat, it is very necessary for me to clear out of the Stock Exchange once and for all.[76]

[71] Quote after 'New Investors' Guide', *The Financial Times*, 12 August 1927, a review of S. A. Moseley, *Money-Making in Stocks and Shares: A Popular Guide for Investors and Speculators* (London: Sir Isaac Pitman & Sons, 1927); see also S. A. Moseley, *The Small Investor's Guide*, 2nd edn (London: Sir Isaac Pitman & Sons, 1930).

[72] S. A. Moseley, *The Private Diaries of Sydney Moseley* (London: Max Parrish, 1960), pp. 282–283.

[73] *Private Diaries of Sydney Moseley*, pp. 286–287.

[74] Moseley, *The Small Investor's Guide*, pp. x–xi.    [75] *Private Diaries of Sydney Moseley*, p. 331.

[76] *Private Diaries of Sydney Moseley*, pp. 345–346.

Come September, however, Moseley had found excuses for plunging into shares once again: 'I would put that money I have into the Insurance companies, [ ... ] but look at the silly rates they offer!' Instead, he 'went bang into the gilt-edged market and the so-called high-class investment shares, [buying] 500 Pearl Insurance, followed by another 100 or more'.[77] Moseley's personal writings of that time are not the notes of a rational stock market agent. Instead they reveal a nervous gambler who enjoyed and suffered from the thrills of playing the stock market and who showed many of the symptoms—addiction, suicidal thoughts— his contemporary critics attested to what they saw as the social evil of speculation.

## Catering for 'a Curious Sort of Investing Public': Outside Brokers, Bucket Shops, and Share Pushers

Already by the 1870s, the expansion of the financial press and the establishment of a telegraph network had laid the groundwork for a modern financial infrastructure to serve Britain's growing investing public. As a result, investors whom the Stock Exchange neglected or ignored entirely came into touch with brokers and dealers who were not members of any of the organized exchanges. Outside the institutional market structure, however, they risked falling prey to criminal share pushers who sought to defraud inexperienced members of the investing public. Due to lack of regulations, literally anyone could open a business and call themselves a stockbroker. Thus, both legitimate and fraudulent financial service providers seized upon the retail investor as a business opportunity. The history of this grey market for stocks and shares has often been told through the lens of the 'bucket shop'. Bucket shops were originally betting offices, in which clients could bet on the fluctuations of share and commodity prices without actually dealing in the underlying securities or produce. But unlike in the US, in the British discourse, 'bucket shop' soon became a derogative umbrella term that diluted the difference between respectable outsiders and more dubious intermediaries. These muddled distinctions still characterize historical scholarship which focuses largely on criminal share-pushing activities and less on legitimate outside brokers. David Kynaston's otherwise brilliant account of the *Golden Years* of the City of London, for instance, claims that '[m]ost outside brokers were a lot closer to the bucket-shop' and inhabited 'a pretty squalid, small-beer world [ ... ]—a world from which the main avenue of escape was down rather than up.'[78]

The following survey of the interwar fringe market for financial securities will shed new light on the competing actors and their various commercial as well as fraudulent practices. It draws on an approach developed by Rob Aitken, who has

[77] *Private Diaries of Sydney Moseley*, p. 348.
[78] D. Kynaston, *The City of London*, II pp. 60–62.

argued that 'the fringe finance sector disturbs and complicates our conceptions of finance as a category dominated by rational, technical or respectable sets of relations'.[79] However, I will argue that the financial establishment, and most prominently the London Stock Exchange, sought to delegitimize fringe activity that *was* actually largely respectable. The main sources for this analysis stem from the Board Trade Committee on Share-Pushing, which was appointed in November 1936, and paved the way for new regulations of the stockbroking profession under the Prevention of Fraud (Investments) Act 1939. The act made it compulsory for outside brokers to register with the Board of Trade, since hitherto 'any person with or without special knowledge or experience of stock and share matters may describe himself as a stockbroker'.[80] The committee gathered extensive written and oral evidence from members of the Stock Exchange, solicitors, outside brokers, the police, financial journalists, and defrauded members of the investing public. This material allows us to gain an accurate and nuanced picture of Britain's financial infrastructure for retail investment. Criminal activities in this market certainly posed a serious challenge to the legitimacy of the financial system. However, it will become apparent that the majority of outside brokers provided an entirely legitimate entry point for the growing number of investment newcomers and served as a useful supplement to the wider market.

The Departmental Committee on Share-Pushing soon become known as the Bodkin Committee due to its Chairman, Sir Archibald Bodkin, who had been appointed by Walter Runciman, President of the Board of Trade and National Liberal MP for St Ives. By the time of his appointment, Bodkin was 74 years of age and had risen to legal fame as the Director of Public Prosecutions between 1920 and 1930. During this tenure he prosecuted two of Britain's most notable financial swindlers, Horatio Bottomley in 1922 and Clarence Hatry in 1929, which made him a natural choice for head of the committee. But Sir Archibald had also gained a reputation for his moral conservatism, especially due to his legal war against what he regarded as 'obscene' literature. These endeavours resulted, for instance, in the 1922 ban of James Joyce's *Ulysses*, 'the passages dealing with Molly Bloom's orgasms being enough to convince him of the book's obscenity'.[81] Known to be a strait-laced, at times pedantic character, Bodkin presided over a task force of leading proponents of Britain's legal and financial establishment: his deputy was the Old-Etonian barrister Lionel Cohan; Sir Malcolm Hogg was the Deputy Chairman of the Westminster Bank; Charles Vickers of Slaughter & May and E. T. A. Philips, the Senior Official Receiver topped off the committee's legal

---

[79] R. Aitken, 'Capital at Its Fringes', *New Political Economy* 11 (2006), p. 480.

[80] Share-Pushing: Report of the Departmental Committee appointed by the Board of Trade, 1936–7, London, Printed and Published by His Majesty's Stationery Office, p. 43, The National Archives (henceforth TNA), BT 55/104.

[81] C. Humphreys, 'Bodkin, Sir Archibald Henry (1862–1957)', Online 2006.

expertise; John McEwan represented the Associated Stock Exchanges as their Chairman and the London Stock Exchange commissioned its Deputy Chairman, Robert Pelham Wilkinson.[82] The committee's task was to survey the outside market for financial securities and devise a new regulatory framework that would put an effective end to illegal share-pushing activities. The course of action for this was, in McEwan's words, 'to separate the sheep from the goats among the Outside Stockbrokers'.[83] The compilation of this committee meant that from the outset this legal war was tilted in favour of established financial institutions.

What were the facilities available to ordinary people for investing and specu-lating in financial securities during the interwar period? First of all, local bank managers and solicitors mediated between the public and members of the London Stock Exchange by handling a large chunk of the average private investor's business in return for a share of the broker's commission.[84] This arrangement had grown over the years and brought peripheral business to London, but was resented by the twenty-two Associated Stock Exchanges in Manchester, Birmingham, Glasgow, Belfast, Dublin, and other cities, which together counted around 1,100 members in 1937.[85] Their dealings were largely confined to shares of local companies, but they would also forward clients' orders to London for national and international securities, again sharing the commission.[86] In this business the Associated Exchanges competed not only with named solicitors and banks, but also with the Provincial Brokers Stock Exchange (PBSE), an association of around 275 provincial brokers with an executive committee based in Hull.[87] These provincial brokers 'were regarded as playing a role in mobilizing capital for small companies',[88] but did not have a stock exchange building and carried out their stockbroking business on the side of main professions. Sensing a chance to hamper a competitor, the Associated Exchanges pointed out the ambiguous legal status of the PBSE to the committee and argued that 'their business and the way it is conducted come into the category of Outside

---

[82] 'House of Commons: Share Pushing Inquiry', *The Times*, 27 November 1936.

[83] Council of Associated Stock Exchanges. Memorandum on Share-Pushing, 3 March 1937. Records of the Board of Trade and of successor and related bodies, Departmental Committee on Share Pushing: Evidence and Correspondence. Individual Files of various Witnesses, TNA, BT 55/109.

[84] Michie, The London Stock Exchange, pp. 231–239.

[85] Oral Evidence of Alfred Ainslie Lawrie, Vice-President of the Council of Associated Stock Exchanges, 11 March 1937, TNA, BT 55/109.

[86] W. A. Thomas, *The Provincial Stock Exchanges* (London: Cass, 1973). The Associated Stock Exchanges were and are often referred to as the Provincial Stock Exchanges, but are not to be confused with the Provincial Brokers Stock Exchange.

[87] Oral evidence of Herbert Goodes, Chairman of the Provincial Brokers Stock Exchange, 12 March 1937, TNA, BT 55/109.

[88] R. Michie, 'The Stock Exchange and the British Economy, 1870–1939', in J. J. van Helten and Y. Cassis (eds), *Capitalism in a Mature Economy: Financial Institutions, Capital Exports and British Industry, 1870–1939* (Aldershot: Edward Elgar, 1990), p. 95.

Stockbrokers, and they should be dealt with in the same way'.[89] Also among the list of the 'recognised' markets were several smaller exchanges many of which were obscure and short-lived. But some played an important role in Britain's financial infrastructure. The Mincing Lane Stock Exchange in the City of London, for instance, managed to acquire much of the business in tea and rubber shares. Formed as the Mincing Lane Tea and Rubber Broker's Association in 1909, this exchange was formed 'to provide a market for the vast speculative business in plantation company shares being generated at that time'.[90] Another successful and important institution was the Oldham Stock Exchange near Manchester, which specialized in cotton shares.[91]

The London Stock Exchange, based at the heart of the City of London at Capel Court on Throgmorton Street, was by far the largest market for national and international shares and in 1938 counted 4,132 members, 'of whom 2,491 members were brokers, 1,433 were jobbers and 208 were inactive'.[92] When negotiating business terms with other Exchanges, the General Purpose Committee, London's governing body, always had the upper hand. A non-negotiable condition for cooperation was that brokers did not advertise their services to the general public. The London Stock Exchange had always regarded advertising as 'unprofessional' and moreover unnecessary since its members could rely on personal contacts for their business. When the earliest outside brokers had begun to advertise in an attempt to attract the new late-Victorian investor class, the Stock Exchange imposed an advertising ban on its members in 1885 in order to disassociate itself from outsiders. Brokers of the Stock Exchange were only allowed to circularize about new issues or possible bargains to *existing* clients.[93]

The interwar years saw new calls for a relaxation of advertising, especially from the financial press, but in 1925 the London Stock Exchange demonstrated how serious and relentless it was about this rule. In June that year, the Committee of the Mincing Lane Exchange had decided to expand its business beyond tea and rubber shares and to 'allow the Members [ ... ] to advertise so that members of the public could get into direct communication with brokers'.[94] Naturally City journalists welcomed this move as a new source of revenue and a promising method to popularize share ownership. In 1925, the *Daily Express* published the first

[89] Council of Associated Stock Exchanges. Memorandum on Share-Pushing, 3 March 1937, TNA, BT 55/109.

[90] Michie, *The London Stock Exchange*, p. 85.

[91] Circular on Stockbrokers by R. P. Wilkinson, (Deputy Chairman of the London Stock Exchange), 21 November 1936, TNA, BT 55/104. On the Oldham Stock Exchange see Thomas, *The Provincial Stock Exchanges*, pp. 145–168.

[92] Kynaston, *The City of London*, III, p. 295.

[93] On advertising see A. Jenkins, *The Stock Exchange Story* (London: Heinemann, 1973), pp. 98–99; E. V. Morgan and W. A. Thomas, *The Stock Exchange: Its History and Functions* (London: Elek Books, 1962), pp. 166–167; Michie, *The London Stock Exchange*, pp. 203–205.

[94] Oral Evidence by T. G. Hatherill-Mynott, Member of the Mincing Lane Stock Exchange, 5 March 1937, TNA, BT 55/109.

advertising by the Mincing Lane member firm, Hatherill-Mynott & Co., the same company which would testify to the Bodkin Committee a decade later. The newspaper reckoned that the decision would 'move business from Throgmorton-street to Mincing-lane [sic] and it will increase public interest greatly in stocks and shares'.[95] But the Stock Exchange's uncompromising reaction to this sort of competitive clamour was characteristic. The eminent Cazenove & Akroyds broker Claude Serocold was the first to get wind of the move, even before the ad was published in the *Express*. The Mincing Lane chairman, T. G. Hatherill-Mynott of said company, had approached the Savoy Hotel, offering to list its shares on his exchange. Unfortunately for Hatherill-Mynnot, Serocold happened to be a director of the Savoy and was informed immediately.[96] The same day, he lobbied with the General Purpose Committee and prompted its secretary, Edward Satterthwaite, to address a threatening letter across the Square Mile:

> Sir, The attention of the Committee of The Stock Exchange has been called to statements in the Press that your Association intend in future to allow your Members to advertise for Stock Exchange business and to issue circulars respecting such business to other than their own Principals. They have been further informed that certain Companies not specially connected with Tea and Rubber industries have been invited to apply for a quotation in your Official List. I am directed to enquire whether these statements are correct and if they are to request you to inform your Committee that the persistence in either of the policies mentioned above must inevitably lead to measures on the part of my Committee which they would be very loath to take.[97]

There was a minority of Stock Exchange members who sought to lift the ban on advertising in order to attract business from the growing investing public. But their motions to lift the advertising ban were rejected in 1925, 1927, 1928, 1929, and again in 1934 because 'smaller firms feared that permitting advertising would encourage the development of large firms which would come to dominate business for personal clients'.[98] The General Purpose Committee's only concession was to initiate a corporate advertising campaign in national newspapers and to invite investors to write to the secretary and enquire for a list of brokers. For the curious investor, however, this 'service' was almost entirely useless. As the former

---

[95] 'Stock Exchange Advertiser: History Made in the "Daily Express"', *Daily Express*, 15 June 1925.
[96] J. Slinn, 'Serocold, Claude Pearce (1875–1959)', *ODNB*, 2004.
[97] Cazenove & Akroyds to E. Satterthwaite, Secretary of the Stock Exchange, 12 June 1925; E. Satterthwaite, Secretary of the Stock Exchange to Secretary of the Mincing Lane Tea & Rubber Sharebrokers Association, 15 June 1925, Guildhall Library, Collection Stock Exchange, London, Minutes and Related Papers, General Purpose Committee Minutes, ref code: CLC/B/004/B/01 (henceforth GL), 14,600/116.
[98] Swinson, C., *Regulation of the London Stock Exchange. Share Trading, Fraud and Reform 1914–1945* (Oxford: Routledge, 2018).

City editor of the *Daily Mail*, Herbert Meredith, pointed out: 'If an investor writes to the Secretary of the London Stock Exchange, asking for the name of a stock-broker, he receives a list of over 1,500 names'—and it was highly likely that the chosen broker would not respond to unsolicited requests from small clients unknown to him.

As a result of the Stock Exchange's structural and habitual conservatism, the social and geographical distance between the average small investor and registered stockbrokers was enormous. Therefore, around 800 outside brokers operating in London, other metropolitan areas, and the provinces, sought to fill this gap by employing modern advertising techniques via the press, telegraph, and circulars. They were labelled 'outsiders' because they were not member of any of the 'official' Exchanges. Records show that the average firm of outside brokers in the provinces had a client base between 100 and 1,000, while large firms in metropolitan areas could have up to 7,000 clients. One Mr S. R. Charlesworth, for instance, catered for about 700 active clients from his home office in Grimsby.[99] On the other side, the Stock and Share Dealers Charles W. Gordon & Co. Ltd entertained an office on Old Broad Street, right in the City of London, commanded capital of £30,000 and had 4,600 clients on their books.[100] The social background of these small investors and speculators was highly diverse and included solicitors and accountants, clergymen, widows, and spinsters as well as manual workers and domestic servants.

The relationship between outside firms and members of the Stock Exchange was ambivalent. On the one hand, the outsiders meant serious competition to Throgmorton Street and they 'did not bear the responsibilities or costs of Exchange membership'.[101] On the other hand, a member could profit from the bit of extra business that the outsiders acquired for him because non-member brokers relied on good contact to a jobber inside 'The House' who would process their dealings in return for a share of the commission.[102] In this way members and outsiders complemented each other and in 1893 it was estimated 'that outside brokers paid £53m in commission to 294 members of the Stock Exchange for business transacted on behalf of their clients'.[103] Non-member brokers performed a vital service in that they specialized in niche securities, for which often there was no ready market, thereby fostering 'closer pricing, stability, and liquidity'.[104]

---

[99] Oral Evidence of S. R. Charlesworth, Grimsby, 18 March 1937, TNA, BT 55/110.

[100] Charles W. Gordon to John G. Henderson, Secretary of the Bodkin Committee, 5 February 1937, TNA, BT 55/110. According to the Bank of England Inflation Calculator, £30,000 from 1937 would be worth £1,875,361.45 in 2016. Available at https://www.bankofengland.co.uk/monetary-policy/inflation/inflation-calculator, accessed 16 April 2017.

[101] Robb, *White-Collar Crime in Modern England*, p. 87.

[102] Kynaston, *The City of London*, III, pp. 315–317.

[103] Michie, *The London Stock Exchange*, p. 110.

[104] Michie, *The London Stock Exchange*, p. 82.

One of the biggest and most reputed outside firms was the National Securities Corporation Limited (NSCL). By 1929, the firm employed 140 people in their Cannon Street offices and had capital of approximately £40,000.[105] But the history of this particular outside firm is revealing in another regard. The London as well as the Associated Exchanges refused women to become members. While some Associated Exchanges admitted women as brokers after WWII, the London Stock Exchange did not allow female membership until 1973.[106] This made the outside market an attractive career path for female financial professionals. Arguably the most notable woman stockbroker during the interwar period was the joint managing director of NSCL, Beatrice Gordon Holmes (known as Miss Gordon Holmes). Although born in the City of London in 1884, the daughter of an Irish father and a South African mother was ever so unlikely to become a 'prominent figure' in the Square Mile.[107] After entering working life as typist at the age of 19 and earning £1 a week, she became a clerk with the Canadian City bankers Thorold in 1912. There she was actively involved in the promotion and selling of War Loans, becoming aware of the difficulties of this campaign, since 'the millions of wage-earners of the country had never been appealed to before as potential investors'.[108]

After almost a decade of tutelage and condescension by her employer, she and her colleague, Richard Sefton Turner, decided to launch NSCL in 1921. 'Of course', as Holmes pointed out in her 1944 autobiography, 'we were an "outside House," because the Stock Exchange, like the Church—God and Mammon— refuses to admit women'.[109] As the only woman to be heard by the Bodkin Committee in 1937, Holmes called upon any new regulation for stockbrokers not 'to refuse registration to women merely because they were women' and quoted a recent survey that no woman was member of a British Stock Exchange although London's Vice Chairman Wilkinson pointed out, '[t]here is no rule and nothing in the constitution which prevents it'. The senior stockbroker and Holmes clashed over this, Wilkinson eventually stifling the debate with a remark that revealed he was co-chairing an institution that felt no obligation whatsoever towards the public: 'The London Stock Exchange is a club to elect its members. If the ladies wish to make their own club they can do it quite freely within the provision.'[110]

[105] The Committee on Share-Pushing. Evidence of Mr Richard Sefton Turner, Joint Managing Director of National Securities Corporation Limited, 15 February 1937, TNA, BT 55/109.

[106] A 1962 standard work on the Stock Exchange quotes a poem titled 'Fair Shares' of a 'poetically inclined member' that summed up the stance on women membership: 'We'll share with you gladly / our homes and our hearths / [ . . . ] Our pleasures, and treasures / THOUGH NEVER "THE HOUSE"', Morgan and Thomas, The Stock Exchange, p. 259. On women membership see Michie, The London Stock Exchange, pp. 453–454.

[107] 'Obituary: Miss Gordon Holmes', The Times, 22 November 1951.

[108] B. G. Holmes, In Love With Life: A Pioneer Career Woman's Story (London: Hollis & Carter, 1944), p. 80.

[109] Holmes, In Love With Life, p. 103.

[110] Oral evidence of Richard Sefton Turner and Miss Gordon Holmes of the National Securities Corporation Limited, 26 February 1937, TNA, BT 55/109.

Holmes's autobiography gives an insight into the enormous variety of clients the outsiders catered for, ranging from the careful gilt-edge investor to a clergy-man who deemed Australian government bonds too risky after lengthy and careful consultation—only to part with £20,000 with share pushers running 'some gold-brick swindle' a few months later.[111] Then Holmes recalled 'a client who had been all his life a very big operator with almost "professional" judgment and acumen and reputed success', whom she challenged on his investment philosophy:

> 'Tell me frankly, if you had just put your money in Trustee securities in the first place' (he had inherited a wad), 'wouldn't you have been just as well off by now?'
> 'If I had left it all in three-and-a-half per cents.?' he mused in reply. 'Yes I should have been better off. But'—and he leaned forward emphatically—'I shouldn't have had the fun I've had!'[112]

According to Holmes, investment advice was an unrewarding trade. The average client—seemingly male—demanded 'the highest possible yield on his money, a large increase in capital, absolute safety, and a lot of fun and excitement' and was therefore difficult to please.[113] To Holmes, 'speculation [was] another name for enterprise'[114] and she made no secret of the fact that the outsiders' business was by nature more speculative. Most non-members also acted as principal on a regular basis by taking on shares that members did not frequently deal in. This was mostly the case with small public companies, which were by nature more risky and volatile. One of Holmes's competitors, one Victor Smith of Messrs. George Brodie & Company Ltd elaborated on this practice in his evidence to the Bodkin Committee in order to showcase the outsiders' benefits to both the speculating public and the Stock Exchange:

> Amongst the numerous small Public Companies there are constantly to be found willing buyers and willing sellers for whom the machinery of the Stock Exchange does not cater, and we are frequently approached by potential buyers who require our services to find a seller of such shares, and important business to the satisfaction of both parties often results. [ ... ] Plenty of instances can be cited where the initial activities of an outside Broker have commenced more active dealings in the shares amongst Members, thus generally improving the market-ability of such shares.[115]

---

[111] Holmes, *In Love With Life*, pp. 85–86.    [112] Holmes, *In Love With Life*, p. 85.
[113] Holmes, *In Love With Life*, p. 85.    [114] Holmes, *In Love With Life*, p. 114.
[115] Memorandum of Evidence of Mr G. Victor Smith of Messrs. George Brodie & Company Ltd TNA, BT 55/108.

As mentioned, the outside broker's principal method of marketing shares among investors was to advertise in newspapers and circularize to potential as well as existing clients. Every outside broker summoned by the Board of Trade contended that advertising was the only viable way of reaching out to members of the investing public who did not have contact to a stockbroker. Over the years, outside firms advertised in reputable newspapers like the *Financial Times*, *The Times* or the *Daily Express*. S. R. Charlesworth, the Grimsby stockbroker, boiled down this business approach and explained to the Bodkin Committee: 'There is a curious sort of investing public somewhere in the dark and you have to go out there and search for it.'[116] One member of this curious investing public gave a client's perspective on the matter in a 1925 reader's letter to the *FT*. The investor from Kensington bemoaned that '[m]embers of the Stock Exchange [were] rather snobbishly prohibited from directly advertising in the press'. As a result, he and his fellow punters went 'where we are welcomed—that is, to the outside advertising broker, and even if I take a little more risk my experience has been quite satisfactory so far'.[117]

Since their emergence in the 1880s, outside brokers never enjoyed a good reputation. Throughout the decades, the financial establishment aimed to villainize them by deliberately blurring the lines between honest brokers and fraudulent share pushers. In 1889, an anonymous 'member of the Stock Exchange' wrote in *The Times* that the 'offices of outside brokers are mostly mere bucket shops or gambling hells, and should be put down with a firm hand, in the same interests as low betting clubs are suppressed'.[118] Donald Cobbett, who began his career as a broker on the London Stock Exchange in the 1930s 'vividly recall[ed] that anybody share dealing who was not a member of the London or one of the provincial stock exchanges was contemptuously dismissed as bucketshop'.[119] He insisted, however, that 'one must make a clear distinction between the bucketeers and the respected and honest "outside" stockbrokers. [ . . . ] Many of the latter were both highly reputable and adequately financed'.[120] Financial journalists and solicitors shared this assessment in their oral and written evidence to the Board of Trade Committee, which acknowledged this in its final report:

> We desire to state that we are satisfied that the vast majority of outside brokers are honest [ . . . ]. They transact lawful business and carry it on without

---

[116] Oral Evidence of S. R. Charlesworth, Grimsby, 18 March 1937, TNA, BT 55/110.
[117] 'The Small Investor', *The Financial Times*, 10 December 1925.
[118] 'Letters to the Editor: Servants Speculating On The Stock Exchange', *The Times*, 9 February 1889.
[119] D. Cobbett, *Before the Big Bang: Tales of the Old Stock Exchange* (Horndean, Portsmouth, Hants: Milestone Publications, 1986), p. 101.
[120] Cobbett, *Before the Big Bang*, p. 100.

substantial ground for complaint, and, indeed, are in regard to certain types of stocks and shares of considerable use to the public.[121]

The original practice of the bucket shop was to allow clients to bet on the fluctuations of share and commodity prices without actually dealing in the underlying securities or produce. In a seminal essay, David Itzkowitz has traced the emergence of this practice in the wake of the Royal Commission on the Stock Exchange in 1878, which many observers had taken as a definite acquittal of any gambling accusations hurled at the Stock Exchange.[122] Cunning bookmakers, however, noticed that the majority of transactions on the actual stock and commodity exchanges involved no intention of delivery and therefore had the character of the bet.[123] Hence, they exploited the lack of regulations for stockbroking and, with help of the increasingly affordable stock ticker, popularized betting on stocks and shares as a vicarious type of financial speculation especially among the lower classes.[124] Bucket shops were an Anglo-Saxon phenomenon and the literature on the US is much more elaborate than studies on Britain.[125] On both sides of the Atlantic, as Maurice Cowing has pointed out, they acted 'upon the axiom that "the public is always wrong" [and] assumed they could make a steady profit from the hordes of amateur speculators'.[126] But it is important to stress that only in Britain did the term become a sweeping denigration of any broker or dealer who was not aligned with an official exchange. A letter from the Vice-President of the New York Stock Exchange to the Chairman of the London Stock Exchange illustrates this:

The term 'bucket-shop' may have a *narrower meaning* in this country than in England. It is used here generally to connote an establishment whose proprietors

---

[121] 'A Check on the Share-Pusher: Registration Proposed', *The Times*, 12 August 1937.

[122] 'The testimonial of the Royal Commission to the Stock Exchange is in this way a natural and not an extraordinary result of their labours. It would have been most surprising if the chief business of the Stock Exchange had been found to be gambling and the victimising of the public, and not as it is found to be, a vast amount of buying and selling on behalf of the public, with a facility and convenience such as no other market presents.' 'The Stock Exchange Commission', *The Spectator*, 24 August 1878.

[123] D. C. Itzkowitz, 'Fair Enterprise or Extravagant Speculation: Investment, Speculation, and Gambling in Victorian England', in N. Henry and C. Schmitt (eds), *Victorian Investments: New Perspectives on Finance and Culture* (Bloomington, IN: Indiana University Press, 2009), pp. 98–119. The chapter was a reprint of an article Itzkowitz had first published under the same title in *Victorian Studies* 45 (2002), pp. 121–147.

[124] D. Porter, '"Speciousness is the Bucketeer's Watchword and Outrageous Effrontery his Capital": Financial Bucket Shops in the City of London, c.1880–1939', in J. Benson and L. Ugolini (eds), *Cultures of Selling: Perspectives on Consumption and Society since 1700* (Aldershot, Burlington, VT: Ashgate, 2006), pp. 103–125.

[125] See D. Hochfelder, '"Where the Common People Could Speculate": The Ticker, Bucket Shops, and the Origins of Popular Participation in Financial Markets, 1880-1920', *The Journal of American History* 93 (2006), pp. 335–358; A. Fabian, *Card Sharps, Dream Books, & Bucket Shops: Gambling in 19th-Century America* (Ithaca, NY: Cornell University Press, 1990); de Goede, *Virtue, Fortune, and Faith*, pp. 68–84; Stäheli, *Spectacular Speculation*, pp. 36–70; Ott, *When Wall Street Met Main Street*, pp. 198–211.

[126] Cowing, *Populists, Plungers, and Progressives*, p. 28.

purport to execute orders for customers on the stock exchange, but who in fact simply take the side of the market opposite to their customers without executing orders upon the exchange at all.[127]

The most common practice of doing this was for bucket shops to provide so-called marginal or deferred delivery accounts: against a small deposit, clients could speculate over an extended account period of several months—as distinguished from the fortnightly settlements on the Stock Exchange. This meant, of course, that the 'broker' hardly ever had to actually purchase the securities dealt in as positions were usually opened and closed within this excessively long period.[128] This practice was heavily frowned upon among the financial establishment because it blurred the carefully drawn line between organized speculation and gambling. Deferred delivery was also associated with share pushers who would manipulate the quotations to their advantage. For this reason, the majority of outside brokers summoned by the committee stressed that they did not offer deferred delivery accounts in order to avoid any impression or accusation of fraud. They argued that this type of business would be 'throwing the door wide open for all sorts of abuses',[129] but had to acknowledge that most firms who ran these accounts were operating in accordance with the law: 'You cannot say legally they are wrong, they are not, they are acting legally right, but morally their actions are questionable. [ ... ] I avoid any immorality I possibly can in my transactions.'[130] It is important to note that not every firm dealing in deferred delivery accounts was of a criminal nature, since the literature often conflates share gambling with criminal share-pushing. Newman, for instance, claims that with all of these bookmakers the 'end product was the same, large numbers of investors parting with their money which they would never see again'.[131] But the editor of the *Investors' Chronicle*, the leading financial weekly that had been spearheading a media campaign against criminal share-hawking activities, stressed in his hearing that '[t]here are "firms" doing business on these lines [deferred delivery system] who are as honest as any reliable bookmaker'.[132] Any gambling establishment that emulated 'professional' stock market activity posed a threat to the financial sector's reputation. But these bookmakers as well as the share pushers among

---

[127] Extract from a letter, dated December 11th 1936, from Mr Dean K. Worcester, Executive Vice-President of the New York Stock Exchange to Mr R. B. Pearson, Chairman of the Stock Exchange, London. BT 55/109 (my italics).

[128] Porter, 'Speciousness is the Bucketeer's Watchword and Outrageous Effrontery his Capital'.

[129] Oral Evidence, Charles William Gordon, a Director of Charles W. Gordon and Company Limited, 5 February 1937, TNA, BT 55/110.

[130] Oral Evidence of S. R. Charlesworth, Grimsby, 18 March 1937, TNA, BT 55/110.

[131] K. Newman, *Financial Marketing and Communications* (Eastbourne: Holt, Rinehart and Winston, 1984), p. 63.

[132] Memorandum of Evidence of Mr G. J. Holmes, 21 March 1937, TNA, BT 55/108. On efforts by financial journalists against share-pushers see Porter, 'Speciousness is the Bucketeer's Watchword and Outrageous Effrontery his Capital', 105.

them were a problem of the Stock Exchange's own making, a result of its plutocratic outlook. Bucket shops—as well as outside brokers—attracted clients because they were much cheaper, easily accessible, and allowed clients to avoid the 'tiresome formalities of dealing with a member of the Stock Exchange'.[133]

Arguably the most successful outside house that ran enormous profits with deferred delivery accounts were A. W. Cornforth & Co. of Old Broad Street. The name Cornforth stood for more than half a decade of outside stockbroking in the City of London, as a synonym for financial ruin and suicide. After serving in the Air Force during the war, Athelstane Wilson Cornforth launched the company in 1919,[134] thereby following in the dubious steps of his father Athelstane Arthur, who had also been an outside broker between 1886 and 1910. After graduating from Cambridge, Cornforth senior had become a clergyman, but soon left the Church of England to start A. Cornforth & Co., Stock and Share Brokers, which seemed like an unnatural career move at that time, considering that religious apprehensions towards stock market finance were still strong. His business grew very successful, but in 1910, he committed suicide in New York, where he had travelled to using a false name to evade £1,696 of debt.[135] In 1926, Athelstane's second-born son and A. W.'s brother, Charles, 'was found dead in a gas filled room in a [London] boarding house on the day he was due to appear at the Mansion House charged with a serious criminal offense'.[136]

At that time, A. W.'s company had grown into a highly profitable enterprise and was capitalized at £250,000. On a weekly basis, the firm listed advertisements in the *Financial Times* and the *Daily Telegraph*. When explaining his business model to the Bodkin Committee in 1937, Cornforth revealed that it was built on the assumption that there was 'a kind of natural tendency for people to speculate in something' and that 'over a long period of time [ . . . ] most speculators, whether they are speculating on the Stock Exchange or outside, lose money and [although] most speculators recognise that, they all hope they will be the exceptions'. By simply taking the opposite view to any given bet on price movements, Cornforth generated profits in the long run. Bear markets allowed him to exploit the bullish mood of his clients even more drastically: 'in a big slump we would stand to make quite a considerable profit'.[137] Bodkin noted that Cornforth had a 'reputation of

---

[133] Porter, 'Speciousness is the Bucketeer's Watchword and Outrageous Effrontery his Capital', p. 116.

[134] Records created or inherited by the Air Ministry, the Royal Air Force, and related bodies, Officers' Service Records, Cornforth, Athelstane Wilson, TNA, AIR 76/106/8.

[135] 'Strange Career of Athelstane Cornforth, Wrecked by Illness and Domestic Trouble', *New York Times*, 22 July 1910. Cornforth had £1,696 of debt. 'Creditors' Meetings', *The Times*, 5 August 1910. An obituary said that in 1909 'while his run of prosperity was still unbroken, he was seized with a kind of melancholia', after which his business rapidly declined. 'Business Romance: From Holy Orders to "Outside" Stockbroking', *Daily Mail*, 22 July 1910.

[136] *Daily Mail*, 3 November 1926; 'Accused Man's Suicide', *Daily Telegraph*, 4 November 1926. The reports did not give any details about the 'serious criminal offense'.

[137] Oral Evidence of A. W. Cornforth of Messrs. Cornforth Ltd, 7 April 1937, TNA, BT 55/111.

always paying'[138] and never pleading the Gaming Act, according to which neither party in a wager had been able to legally enforce the contract since 1845. It was a common practice among less honest bucket shop operators to make use of this legal loophole if bets had moved against a shop, thereby evading payment. One such firm that had come under the scrutiny of the committee were F. Reid Price & Co. Ltd. Its operator, Arthur Savile, defaulted in 1940 for £70,000 and in 1945 was fined £350 for 'carrying on business of dealing in securities without a [Board of Trade] licence'.[139]

This brings us to the last type of fringe market operator: the outright share pusher, manipulator, and fraudster. As George Robb has pointed out, since the Victorian period, Britain 'had few illusions regarding the world of finance' and financial fraud is as old as the stock market itself.[140] But this phenomenon of confidence men seeking to manipulate the ticker tape in stock betting, to promote bogus companies, or to offload worthless shares on the investing public came to bother British authorities around the turn of the century.[141] Financial fraudsters generally thrived in bull markets and exploited their victims' temporary penchant for unbridled speculation in view of prices on a seemingly endless rise. As Charles Kindleberger, the eminent historian of financial crises, has noted, the 'propensities to swindle and be swindled run parallel to the propensity to speculate during a boom'. Comparing a 1936 bull market to the 1929 frenzy, *The Times* commented that the 'only important feature common to both "booms" is that promoters of fraudulent "bucket shops" and the equally undesirable fabricators of fraudulent optimism, have as usual been quick to take advantage of the growth of the speculative spirit'.[142] Public outcries and calls for legislation grew louder over time, with the Lord Chief Justice, Russell of Killowen, in 1898 denouncing an 'unscrupulous minority [that] was systematically undermining the commercial probity of the financial sector'.[143] In the early twentieth century, several writers and journalists began to openly attack outside brokers and bucket shops. So far unacknowledged by scholars is that this campaign was deeply embedded in the 'widespread anti-Semitic prejudice in the City'[144] and at times escalated into unabashed racial slurs of Jews in British finance.

---

[138] Oral Evidence of A. W. Cornforth of Messrs. Cornforth Ltd, 7 April 1937, TNA, BT 55/111.

[139] See for instance the correspondence between F. Reid Price & Co. Ltd and the Bodkin Committee from 26 February, 2 March, 9 March, 1 April 1937, TNA 55/111. 'Gambling In Share Margins: Unlicensed Dealers Fined', *The Times*, 12 March 1945.

[140] Robb, *White-Collar Crime in Modern England*, p. 3.

[141] G. R. Searle, *Corruption in British Politics: 1895–1930* (Oxford: Oxford University Press, 1987), pp. 33–40.

[142] C. Kindleberger, *Manias, Panics, and Crashes: A History of Financial Crises*, 5th edn (Hoboken, NJ: John Wiley & Sons, 2005), p. 73. 'City Notes: The Growth of Speculation', *The Times*, 2 November 1936.

[143] Porter, 'Speciousness is the Bucketeer's Watchword and Outrageous Effrontery his Capital', p. 108.

[144] Kynaston, *The City of London*, III, p. 337.

The banker and prolific financial author, Henry Warren, for instance, published two books in 1906 and 1908 that stereotypically identified the bucket shop swindler as of Jewish origin. In the first book, Warren described an encounter with a German-Jewish outside broker in the West End, who had approached him for some journalistic work. But Warren accused the broker of being a fraudster: 'I felt that I would rather sit under a Kaffir than under that little Jew broker, or dig in a trench alongside a nigger before I would work for so low class a Jew.' Warren also vilified another bucket shop keeper by the name of George Algernon Taylor as follows: 'Pale of face, with a decidedly Hebrew nose, and somewhat large, Eastern eyes, which seemed full of craft, the man looks a Jew. His narrow, retreating forehead, and his heavy, fleshy chin, do not suggest either intellect or strength.'[145] The example of Warren furthermore illustrates that historical scholarship has not distinguished carefully enough between the contemporary usage of 'bucket shops' and 'outsiders'. Warren, like so many others, deliberately conflated the two categories. Yet Dilwyn Porter, for instance, takes Warren's accounts of outsiders and bucket shops at face value, glaringly unaware of his anti-Semitic outbursts and also of the fact that his source was convicted for libel and extortion of an outside broker.[146]

All this is not to suggest that criminal share pushers were not a serious problem in the City of London. In 1911, the Home Office, the Board of Trade, and the Director of Public Prosecution discussed legislative action against 'bucket shops'.[147] The Home Secretary, a young Winston Churchill, had learnt from his brother Jack, who worked in the City, about a 'case of a housefull [sic] of domestic servants losing all of their savings through one of these tricks'.[148] The Solicitor to the Corporation of the City of London also suggested that Churchill should raise the issue of 'bucket shops' in the House of Commons to 'warn the public against being made the dupes of these outside Brokers [sic]'.[149] Yet, no measures were taken. As Porter has observed, this laissez-faire stance only changed after the 1929 crash and the ensuing slump had changed the political climate: 'With economic liberalism under pressure, especially from the political left, it was prudent for

---

[145] H. Warren, The Modern Bucket Shop: A description of the wiles of the 'outside' stockbroker or dealer, of the manner in which he runs his gambling den, of the London gutter Press which assists him, and of the shearing of the lambs (London: Everett, 1906), p. 142. H. Warren, Dr Taylor of London Wall: Prince of Bucket-Shop Swindlers, An Account of the Greatest Bucket-Shop Fraud the World has Ever Known (London: Robert Sutton, 1908), p. 4.

[146] Porter, 'Speciousness is the Bucketeer's Watchword and Outrageous Effrontery his Capital', pp. 108–117. For Henry Warren's trial and sentence to '12 months' imprisonment with hard labour' see 'The Police Courts', The Times, 12 June 1906; 'Central Criminal Court', The Times, 28 July 1906.

[147] J. S. Webster (Board of Trade) to S. Harris (Under Secretary of State, Home Office), 22 February 1911, The Churchill Archives Centre, Cambridge, (henceforth: CHAR), 12/9/54.

[148] J. S. Churchill to W. Churchill, 1 March 1911, CHAR 12/9/85–87.

[149] Sir Homewood Crawford, Solicitor to the City of London to Sir Charles Mathews, Director of Public Prosecutions, 25 February 1911, CHAR 12/9/80–82. Note that Crawford, in line with common parlance, conflates bucket shops with outside brokers and dealers.

those who believed in capitalist free enterprise to put their houses in order.'[150] Until then, the Stock Exchange saw no need to proceed against criminal bucke-teers and adhered to its 'prevailing orthodoxy of "caveat emptor"'.[151] Even in 1925, when share-hawking activities were ripe in the City, the Chairman of the London 'House' played down the problem, writing to his counterpart in New York that 'the danger here [in Britain] from Bucket Shops and Share Pushers is not so intense'.[152]

The techniques of criminal bucket shops that operated in the City of London were various and at times highly sophisticated. Gordon Cummings, a financial journalist on the *Daily Herald*, described them in rich detail in his written evidence to the Bodkin Committee. Cummings, who later rose to fame as a stock market guru during the post-war period as an author of best-selling invest-ment guides,[153] was the head of the *Herald's* Investment Advice Bureau. In this capacity, he had come 'in very close touch with the working man [ ... ] through the letters that we get in every day'. He witnessed a 'very wide practice of investment by working people', which was 'definitely increasing', but since 'they know nothing about investments', they were more prone to falling prey to share pushers.[154] Driven by this experience, Cummings began to act as decoy to many outside houses in order to separate between commercial strategies of legitimate firms and bogus schemes of bucket shops. One common method of the latter was rigged 'option dealing' in which buyers were lured into buying the right but not the obligation to buy or sell securities, but were fleeced whenever they sought to execute their right to 'call' or 'put'. In 1925 the *Financial Times* reported an instance of a bucket shop operator who was trialled for running this kind of scheme and sentenced to 'fifteen months hard labour for the fraud charges'.[155] Then there were the already mentioned 'deferred delivery accounts', mere wagers on share prices, of which Cummings, however, acknowledged that '[t]his method [ ... ] is used by perfectly reputable outside Broking Houses, against which complaints of unfair dealing have never been registered'. Furthermore, bucketeers sought to impose on credulous clients 'unmarketable securities', often from dubious 'gold mining companies'. 'When unfortunate holders tried to sell, how-ever, they found it impossible to deal at the prices given in these circulars'. Finally, share pushers also engaged in 'straightforward sales' of listed securities on which they had taken a bear position, aiming to deliver after prices had fallen and

[150] Porter, 'Speciousness is the Bucketeer's Watchword and Outrageous Effrontery his Capital', pp. 120–121.
[151] Michie, *The London Stock Exchange*, p. 264, caveat emptor being Latin for 'let the buyer beware'.
[152] A. C. Campbell to E. H. H. Simmons, President of the NYSE, 22 June 1925, GL, MS 14600/116.
[153] See Chapter 2.
[154] Oral Evidence of R. Gordon Cummings, 28 January 1937, TNA, BT 55/108.
[155] 'Options Frauds: City Bucket Shop Principal Sentenced', *Financial Times*, 7 February 1925.

coming up with excuses or simply disappearing if the market had moved against them.[156]

Like outside brokers, share pushers made avid use of modern advertising techniques. They printed advertisements in more or less respectable newspapers, depending on the reputation or criminal record of the operator. Perhaps the most common method of reaching out to potential victims was to circularize aggressively or to send out telegrams, 'sometimes accompanied by a reply paid form, urging immediate purchase of shares recommended in the circular'. Cummings had also come across victims who had received telephone calls or even personal home visits from share pushers, who were always 'well dressed, opulent looking, and very persuasive in their manner'.[157] Like many others who testified to the Departmental Committee, Cummings suggested that share brokers and dealers should only be allowed to conduct business if they were registered with the London, one of the Provincial Stock Exchanges, or a government department. Cummings, however, was one of the few summoned who suggested that new legislation should entail a comprehensive ban on advertising for any broker so that investors could identify delinquents by their advertising activities. In line with the General Purpose Committee, he was of the opinion that a 'professional man does not advertise'.[158]

Who was the average 'client' of a bucket shop or most common victim of a share pusher? Other sources support Cummings's view that fraudsters deliberately targeted people of modest income and with little financial knowledge. The London-based bank clerk and book author, F. J. Lewcock, also stated that

It is these small people who are tempted to part up with hard-earned £10 and similar sums to 'obtain control'—the favourite bucket shop phrase—over a large number of shares and so-called 'margin' schemes. [ ... ] In the course of the last five years or so I have come into contact with innumerable cases where working people have been let in in this way, having spent considerable time in a social work which has involved addressing working men's clubs and similar organizations on various aspects of finance and financial matters.[159]

The Bodkin Committee found that 'clergymen, widows, and spinsters are perhaps more frequently victimized than other members of the public'.[160] The involvement of these groups in bucket shop frauds was indeed a recurring theme. Already in 1911 'Widow's [sic] and Clergymen [ ... ] appear to be easily duped; the latter class [ ... ] being only too anxious to endeavour to increase their very small incomes by

---

[156] Written evidence by R. Gordon Cummings, 21 January 1937, TNA, BT 55/108.
[157] Written evidence by R. Gordon Cummings, 21 January 1937, TNA, BT 55/108.
[158] Oral Evidence of R. Gordon Cummings, 28 January 1937, TNA, BT 55/108.
[159] 'Letters to the Editor: Stock Exchange Rules', *The Times*, 22 August 1930.
[160] 'A Check on the Share-Pusher: Registration Proposed', *The Times*, 12 August 1937.

indulging in this kind of speculation, although always ready to condemn it in the pulpit!'[161] In 1936, the Labour MP for North Tottenham, Robert Morrison, called Parliament's attention to a case of a defaulted bucket shop, whose 'list of creditors included 220 women and 120 clergymen'.[162] That same year a conference of legal scholars estimated that 'somewhere between £5,000,000 and £6,000,000 went into the pockets of share pushers every year'.[163]

The conclusion many financial observers and advisers drew from this was to warn investment newcomers against any dealings with outside brokers, deeming it too difficult for the uninitiated investor to tell apart an honest broker from a trickster. Sydney Moseley, for instance, was particularly sceptical of non-members: 'I admit that there are one or two unofficial stock and share dealers who are honest. But how are you to know? In any case, I cannot see that you have anything to gain from dealing even with an honest outside broker.'[164] While the authorities assumed 800 outside brokers to be operating across the country in 1937, the police only 'identified a total of 177 [illegal] shops as having operated within the City of London *between 1910 and 1936*' according to Porter.[165] Most share pushers misled their victims into thinking they were dealing with a serious broker. Once deceived, most of them felt too embarrassed to testify against perpetrators in court, which hampered effective prosecution.[166] But vice versa, many investors confused legitimate outside brokers and dealers for swindlers. This can be illustrated by a letter to the Bodkin Committee from a retired Army officer from Surrey, who had previously 'suffered from the operations of Share Pushers'. He had written because he was 'still in receipt of Share Pushers' circulars' which he offered as evidence to the committee.[167] Among his list of alleged criminals, however, were the outside firms Cornforth Ltd, George Brodie & Co., and Charles W. Gordon & Co., all of which the committee later found to be perfectly honest enterprises. Naturally, this confusion was a problem for both the investors and the outsiders. There was a fundamental difference between those non-members who provided a useful service to the wider system and refused to gamble on share prices, those who acted as honest bookmakers, and those who were sheer criminals. The problem was that many members of the investing public could not tell the differences to their disadvantage, which made effective regulation such a pressing matter.

---

[161] Sir Homewood Crawford, Solicitor to the City of London to Sir Charles Mathews, Director of Public Prosecutions, 25 February 1911, CHAR 12/9/80–82.

[162] *HC Deb* 314, c.2114, 15 July 1936.

[163] 'Solicitors at Nottingham: "Share-Pushing" Evil', *The Times*, 23 September 1936.

[164] Moseley, *The Small Investor's Guide*, p. 129.

[165] Porter, 'Speciousness is the Bucketeer's Watchword and Outrageous Effrontery his Capital', p. 104.

[166] Porter, 'Speciousness is the Bucketeer's Watchword and Outrageous Effrontery his Capital', p. 118.

[167] Lieut-Colonel W. J. P. Hume, CMG to The Secretary, Committee of Share Pushing, 21 December 1936, TNA, 55/104.

A more detailed picture of the periphery of interwar financial markets urges us to rethink the verdict of Rutterford et al. that contemporary talk about a 'democratisation of investment' was merely a mirage. Based on an analysis of share registers of large public companies, the authors conclude that the 'democratization of investment ownership does not appear to have increased over the later nineteenth and early twentieth centuries, despite the arguments put forward by several commentators at the time'.[168] To be sure, democratization in terms of a more equal distribution of listed equity capital was indeed far from becoming a socioeconomic reality. But an approach that merely samples shareholder registries of large public companies overlooks that much of the deliberately constrained market activity spilt over into other, no less relevant areas. If we take into account the Stock Exchanges' aloofness, it becomes apparent that smaller investors could not easily invest in listed securities. Without access to a Stock Exchange broker, many investors and speculators of modest means did business with an outsider, dealing instead in smaller companies or in unlisted securities of which no registers existed. Others merely gambled on share prices in bucket shops or were fleeced by share pushers. Treating their experiences as void or irrelevant would amount to a crude and positivistic understanding of what constitutes a market. Turning a spotlight on the fringes of financial markets does not enable us to determine more accurately Britain's shareholder population and ownership patterns. But this perspective does bring forward strong evidence that the stock market came to occupy Britain's public imagination on an unprecedented scale during the interwar period.

Summing up the entanglements and complexities of the interwar grey market for stocks and shares, it becomes apparent that fringe operators posed three major challenges to Britain's financial system. First, legitimate and well-organized outside brokers and dealers who advertised their services to a wider audience posed serious competition to members of the organized Stock Exchanges in London as well as other metropolitan areas. Second, outside houses and bookmakers exposed the striking similarity between organized stock exchange activity and gambling, when they allowed punters to wager bets on the movements of share and commodity prices without dealing in the market. This unmasking put the Stock Exchange's reputation at stake, given that stockbrokers, investors and speculators spent much of the nineteenth century facing off accusations that their business was in any way akin to gambling. Third, the activities of a minority of criminal share pushers among the outsiders had over time grown into a problem of significant proportion and undermined confidence in the probity of Britain's financial sector. What legislative action did the Bodkin Committee recommend

---

[168] Rutterford, 'The Evidence for "Democratization" of Share Ownership in Great Britain in the Early Twentieth Century', p. 205.

for coping with these challenges and what were the consequences of these suggestions for Britain's financial infrastructure?

## The Prevention of Fraud (Investments) Act 1939

The Bodkin Committee's recommendations laid the legal groundwork for the Prevention of Fraud (Investments) Act 1939, which legal scholars regard as 'the first major piece of legislation in the United Kingdom concerned specifically with the protection of the interest of the individual investor'.[169] However, this assessment does not stand up to a source-based look behind the scenes of the making of this act. Bodkin's team of senior financiers and solicitors devised a new regulatory framework for stockbroking and share dealing that was very much geared in favour of institutionalized finance. This can be demonstrated by the committee's hearing of Robert Barclay Pearson, the Chairman of the London Stock Exchange whose recommendations were implemented almost in full. To be sure, Pearson readily acknowledged that the 'the great majority' of the 800 or so outside brokers were 'carrying on their business on an honourable and upright way' and that they 'come in rather useful' when it came to marketing 'shares which are not dealt in on the Stock Exchange'. Yet he still urged the committee to 'rule them out' regardless, claiming 'that the advantage is [not] worth the disadvantage' as the facilities of the outside broker were 'too often used by unscrupulous persons as a means of touting and hawking'.[170] Under Pearson, the Stock Exchange had come to discover fraudulent share pushers as a useful villain, the scale of whose threat had to be exaggerated in order to eliminate outside competition.

Pearson's proposition of 'ruling them out' was to place a duty on outside brokers to register with the Board of Trade and furthermore to have them banned from engaging in any form of advertising. Pearson was unimpressed by the committee's observation that advertising techniques seemed to allow a broker to do 'the initial work of popularising or getting known the shares which he offers'.[171] The senior stockbroker stood by his line that 'advertising serves no useful purpose to the Stockbroking profession and is a source of danger to the public'.[172] Was Pearson's radical stance on the matter shaped by a critical perception of the American experience, where critics held advertising responsible for enticing millions of savers into fuelling a speculative bubble that resulted in the 1929

---

[169] J. Fisher and J. Bewsey, *The Law of Investor Protection* (London: Sweet & Maxwell, 2003), pp. 13–14.

[170] Oral Evidence of R. B. Pearson, Chairman of the London Stock Exchange, 11 March 1937, TNA, BT 55/109.

[171] Oral Evidence of R. B. Pearson, Chairman of the London Stock Exchange, 11 March 1937, TNA, BT 55/109.

[172] Memorandum of Evidence by Mr R. B. Pearson, Chairman of the Stock Exchange London, 1 February 1937, TNA, BT 55/109.

stock market crash? The available evidence suggests otherwise. First, the London Stock Exchange was already relentless on advertising before the Great Slump as the 1925 quarrel with the Mincing Lane Exchange demonstrates. Then, the debate between Pearson and the Bodkin Committee over advertising and a potential widening of the investing public, reveals that the Stock Exchange was suspicious of a mass market in stocks and shares for other reasons. Bodkin challenged Pearson by describing how he had recently sold some shares through his broker, who was a member of the London Stock Exchange, but wondered whether 'a stranger [would] have as good a chance' to be catered for in this fashion. Pearson's reply reveals the enormous class prejudices that stood in the way of this becoming a reality:

> That is the point—the stranger. If you will allow me to suggest a broker of the London Stock Exchange gets a letter from an unknown small person in the country, whether he may be a gardener or a domestic servant, or someone without any great attachments or any position, and the broker is quite willing to do that business, but the broker must, surely, find out first of all if that person is, shall we say, verified by reference. The person is unknown to the broker. [...] It is quite obviously dangerous for a broker in London to deal with some quite unknown person in the country without any further reference. That, I suggest, is one difficulty.[173]

Pearson's hearing furthermore reveals the remarkable way in which the question of deferred delivery accounts or other practices that amounted to share gambling was negotiated. The committee was very sceptical of this practice and the public outcry that it caused. It had received letters from the public that called upon Bodkin and his team to establish once and for all a solid distinction between speculation and gambling. One investor from East Devon, for instance, assuming that the committee's 'wide terms of reference may include ethical, moral and commercial aspects', made the following remark in a letter:

> I suggest that your Committee should make a carefully considered statement on the ethics and advisibility [sic] of speculation in share values, that may be characterised as Gambling, as distinct from investment. As your Committee is independent of Lobby majorities and election results, the result of evidence and deliberations may bring out a clear line of demarkation [sic] and be definitely stated.[174]

---

[173] Oral Evidence of R. B. Pearson, Chairman of the London Stock Exchange, 11 March 1937, TNA, BT 55/109.

[174] Walter A. Welshman to J. G. Henderson, Secretary to the Committee on Share Pushing, 15 January 1937, TNA, BT 55/104.

The Stock Exchange's official line on the matter was that '[w]e hold no brief for gambling, being of the opinion that this is a vicious propensity quite apart from speculation, with which by some it is always associated'.[175] Off the record, however, Chairman Pearson spoke more ambiguously on the matter and revealed a glaring discrepancy between his own views and the public communication of his institution. On the one hand he called 'decidedly' for a ban on deferred delivery dealing as it led members of the public to confuse Stock Exchange dealings with betting. On the other hand he conceded that it would be impossible to conclusively distinguish between gambling and speculation:

> I do not think I would venture a definition as differentiating gambling from speculation; I agree it would be very difficult; they are very much allied, due to some spirit of adventure which will be found in most of us if we were only to confess it, I think.

Banning deferred delivery accounts was to convey to the public a clear distinction between desirable speculation and outright gambling[176]—even though privately, Stock Exchange representatives of the highest level held this differentiation to be void. The Prevention of Fraud Act eventually did impose on stockbrokers an obligation to register for a licence with the Board of Trade, condition of which was that they did not advertise. Honest companies like the NSCL or Gordon & Co. helped form the Association of Stock and Share Dealers, an organization of outside brokers that aimed to 'avoid certain handicaps which might arise under the Government's promised share-pushing Bill'.[177] The new legislation did eventually ban any form of betting on share or commodity prices, which outlawed the practices of companies like Cornforth Ltd who had to go into 'voluntary liquidation'.[178] On the one hand, the Bodkin Committee's legal efforts did put an end to share-pushing activities although due to the outbreak of the war, the Prevention of Fraud Act was not enforced until 1944.[179] Ranald Michie has pointed out that the Act granted the Stock Exchange 'a virtual monopoly over security trading within

---

[175] Armstrong, *The Book of the Stock Exchange*, p. 154.

[176] For this line of argument in view of Victorian struggles over this distinction see Itzkowitz, 'Fair Enterprise or Extravagant Speculation: Investment, Speculation, and Gambling in Victorian England', 98: 'By allowing the new speculation alone to carry the moral opprobrium that had once applied to all speculation, late Victorian society ensured that speculation in general would remain legitimate.'

[177] 'Association Of Stock And Share Dealers', *The Times*, 16 August 1938.

[178] 'Cornforth to be Liquidated', *Financial Times*, 30 December 1939. However, the late 1950s liberalization of gambling markets under the government of Harold Macmillan legalized gambling on stock market prices through the back door. See the discussion in Chapter 2.

[179] 'Bucket-Shop Law', *The Financial Times*, 2 February 1944; 'Bucket Shop Adieu', *The Financial Times*, 8 August 1944.

Britain'.[180] In line with its then chairman, one could add that the law effectively also gave the Stock Exchange a monopoly on share gambling.

On the other hand, the law entailed regulations that effectively killed off the retail market that the outsiders were facilitating. With the new regulations the Skeltonian ambition and liberal optimism came to a halt, which had defined views on wider share ownership in the early 1920s. In this way, Britain took a trajectory very different from developments in the United States, where the public had bought war bonds in a similarly enthusiastic manner, but were afterwards ensnarled by Wall Street as part of the New York Stock Exchange's agenda of promoting itself as the 'free and open people's market'.[181] It is worthwhile, however, to compare the British interwar experience with Germany, another country that had used modern propaganda techniques to prompt millions of citizens to buy war bonds (*Kriegsanleihen*).[182] But the German Reich lost the war, and the newly formed democracy of the Weimar Republic struggled to pay back the Draconian reparations laid down in the Versailles Treaty. The government resorted to printing money, leaving millions of savers and first-time investors to see 'their holdings eroded, and eventually wiped out, by galloping inflation'.[183] Together with the ensuing hyperinflation of the mid-1920s, the war bond disaster was a financial trauma for the German investing public, which until then had not been unfamiliar with retail investment in the stock market, but now developed a serious aversion towards any form of financial risk taking.[184] Therefore, the contributing factor of Britain's overall positive experience with war bonds towards a culture of mass investment becomes even more to the fore when compared with Germany's negative experience.

Finally, the Bodkin Committee and the ensuing legislation reflect Paul Johnson's insight that Britain's financial infrastructure is a 'complex web of competing economic, legal, political and moral claims'.[185] His study on the 'Victorian origins of corporate capitalism' argues that the institutions, customs, and practices of modern capitalism were largely *made* during the nineteenth century. Well into the twentieth century, however, a substantial component of Britain's financial landscape was still in the making. Its securities market was challenged by a large intake of new investors, which resulted in a resurgence of financial fraud and a new struggle over the distinction between speculation and

---

[180] R. Michie, *The City of London: Continuity and Change since 1850* (London: Macmillan, 1991), pp. 137–138.

[181] See the chapter 'Mobilizing the Financial Nation' in Ott, *When Wall Street Met Main Street*, pp. 75–100.

[182] K. Roesler, *Die Finanzpolitik des Deutschen Reiches im Ersten Weltkrieg* (Berlin: Duncker & Humblot, 1967).

[183] 'Why are German so obsessed with saving money?', *Financial Times*, 22 March 2018.

[184] On retail activity in the German stock market between c.1860 and 1914 see Buchner, *Spielregeln der Börse*, pp. 198–233.

[185] Johnson, *Making the Market*, p. 3.

gambling. Britain's way of dealing with these challenges was somewhat counter-intuitive to a country whose elites took pride in having invented free-market capitalism. After a surge in political democratization, its financial and legal decision makers did not seek to enfranchise as many people as possible in its economy, but deliberately took a conservative stance on popular capitalism. This stance did not change after WWII. But as we will see in Chapter 2, that did not keep the stock market from surging in popularity in some parts of British post-war society.

# 2

# The Stock Market Game in Post-war Britain

In one of her first speeches in Parliament in April 1960, a young Conservative backbencher denounced the 'speculator in stocks and shares' who was making easy profits in the current stock market boom. Her attack tapped into conservative as well as left-wing resentment of the stock market in post-war Britain, and she sounded almost like the opposition Labour Party whose MPs frequently attacked the Stock Exchange as a glorified casino or an upper-class betting shop. The MP's name was Margaret Thatcher. Of Methodist upbringing, Thatcher drew upon the age-old Protestant criticism of speculative finance being a commercially disguised form of gambling that violated Christian morality and traditional notions of property ownership. To be sure, profiting from financial investments was perfectly legitimate for Thatcher, who liked to invoke the Parable of the Talents in which the 'the successful servant turned his five talents into ten'.[1] Speculation, however, was deplorable because the speculator was 'making a business of buying and selling shares, not to hold them for their income producing properties, but to live on the profit which he makes from the transactions'. In hindsight, Thatcher's scathing critique of speculators seems remarkable against the backdrop of her eleven years as prime minister, when she presided over a decade of exuberant speculation. In 1960, however, her jibe was made in the context of widespread and ongoing concern in Westminster and the City of London that small savers could get sucked into a speculative frenzy of the scale of the great stock market crash of 1929. The chairman of the Stock Exchange warned that '[n]othing could be better than a large number of small investors—but nothing worse than a large number of small speculators'.[2] Labour politicians were even more alarmist and deplored the 'encouragement which is given to the ordinary man in the street to take part in the gamble for quick wealth through speculation', which would see Britain become 'a nation of chancers' and result in 'the emergence of the "gamblers' State" as a successor to the Welfare State'.[3] But how was it possible that Britain's financial and political establishment feared a repeat of 1929 if, since the end of WWII, its political economy had taken a more social democratic direction and both parties had done much to tame the rampant excesses of financial capitalism?

---

[1] M. Thatcher, 'Speech to American Chamber of Commerce', 20 October 1976.
[2] 'Helping the Small Investor', *The Sunday Times*, 28 February 1960, p. 7.
[3] Maurice Edelman, Labour MP for Coventry North, *HC Deb* 625, c. 832, 24 June 1960; Cyril Bence, Labour MP for Dunbartonshire East, *HC Deb* 634 c. 148, 6 February 1961.

*Playing the Market: Retail Investment and Speculation in Twentieth-Century Britain.* Kieran Heinemann, Oxford University Press (2021). © Kieran Heinemann. DOI: 10.1093/oso/9780198864257.003.0003

The political and economic consequences of WWII had had a profound impact on the City of London and Britain's investing public. The City's decline as the financial node of an empire had become irreversible and the London Stock Exchange had lost its role as the world's leading market for financial securities to its counterpart in New York measured by trading volume and market capitalizations of listed companies.[4] The Stock Exchange had come under immense political scrutiny after the Labour Party won a sound majority in the General Election of July 1945, and the following six years had seen the establishment of a more regulated and productionist economic settlement, including a wide-ranging nationalization programme.[5] Clement Attlee's Labour governments brought key sectors such as coal, the railways, and the Bank of England under public ownership, which limited the scope for popular investment. In the following thirteen years of Conservative rule (1951–64), the Tory leadership for electoral reasons did very little to dismantle the post-war settlement and in 1962 even introduced a short-term capital gains tax, with Tory backbenchers arguing that 'it must seem unjust to the vast majority of taxpayers that a short-term speculator can make a large, quick profit without paying one penny in tax'.[6] Throughout these years, the Stock Exchange and the City more generally were exposed to polemic attacks from Labour and at times even Conservative backbenchers like Thatcher. Harold Wilson, for instance, shadow chancellor at the time of Thatcher's speech, repeatedly employed John Maynard Keynes's famous warning that 'when the capital development of a country becomes a byproduct of the activities of a casino, the job is likely to be ill-done'.[7] In an ongoing national debate over the role of British finance, in which Wilson was to play a prominent role up until the late 1970s, the labour movement accused the City of depriving domestic industry of capital at the expense of pursuing higher yielding investments overseas. The financial sector, in turn, held state intervention and political commitment to full employment responsible for the country's growing lack of international competitiveness.[8] But in 1960, at least, the City had lost the argument and after the 'golden years' at the

---

[4] Hannah, 'London as the Global Market for Corporate Securities before 1914', p. 127.

[5] J. Tomlinson, 'Labour Party and the City 1945–1970', in R. Michie and P. Williamson (eds), *The British Government and the City of London in the Twentieth Century* (Cambridge: Cambridge University Press, 2004), pp. 174–192.

[6] J. Tomlinson, '"Liberty with Order": Conservative Economic Policy, 1951–1964', in M. Francis and I. Zweiniger-Bargielowska (eds), *The Conservatives and British Society, 1880–1990* (Cardiff: University of Wales Press, 1996), pp. 274–288; E. Green, 'The Conservative Party, the State and the Electorate, 1945–64', in J. Lawrence and M. Taylor (eds), *Party, State and Society: Electoral Behaviour in Modern Britain* (Aldershot: Scolar Press, 1997), pp. 176–200; quote after Ian MacArthur, Conservative MP for Perth and East Perthshire, *HC Deb* 634 c. 148, 6 February 1961.

[7] Keynes, *The General Theory of Employment, Interest and Money*, p. 159. *HC Deb* 608, cc. 34–36, 29 June 1959. See also the Cambridge economist and Labour MP for Sheffield Park, Fred Mulley, citing this passage in the Commons, *HC Deb* 545, c. 455–456, 27 October 1955.

[8] Whiting, *The Labour Party and Taxation*, pp. 123–124; A. Davies, *The City of London and Social Democracy: The Political Economy of Finance in Britain, 1959–1979* (Oxford: Oxford University Press, 2017).

turn of the century, had to content itself with taking a backseat in the post-war economic settlement of state interventionism, planning, and high taxation.

As much as this new regime was to some extent 'financially repressive' for savers and investors,[9] full employment and high wages coupled with redistributive measures resulted in an unprecedented rise in living standards. Therefore, the post-war welfare state enabled lower as well as higher income groups potentially to invest considerable amounts of their disposable income in the stock market, and markets recovered as the period of austerity drew to a close in the early 1950s. Between June 1952 and July 1955 and again from February 1958 to January 1960, the Stock Exchange experienced prolonged bull markets. During these periods, the *Financial Times* Index which tracked Britain's 30 largest public companies grew by a staggering 111.7 per cent and 122.1 per cent respectively. The year 1959 was a particularly bullish one, prompting Labour's Shadow Chancellor, Harold Wilson, to question whether Britain was 'to counter the Soviet industrial developments with an economic system the higher manifestations of which are the take-over bid and a Stock Exchange behaving like a casino run mad?'[10] That year, the volume of new issues rose to £435m from £255m in 1958, and, as we shall see, small speculators played a pivotal role in this 'primary' market where companies raised capital in initial public offerings. Long before Margaret Thatcher coined the term in the 1980s, financial commentators who were less concerned about a new wave of retail investors and speculators would herald the coming of 'popular capitalism'[11] in Britain and the dawning of an 'age of the small investor'.[12]

The 1950s and 1960s brought dramatic changes to Britain's investing public. In these decades, the institutionalization of the stock market gained momentum, meaning that large investors like pension funds and insurance companies shifted their holdings from fixed income into equity on an unprecedented scale.[13] This 'Cult of Equity' went hand in hand with a continued expansion of stock market coverage in the press and wider media—a development that was much to the dismay of Labour backbenchers like Cyril Bence who deplored that 'the financial columns of the newspapers are getting bigger and bigger with reports of Stock

---

[9] In this vein Hannah, *London as the Global Market for Corporate Securities before 1914*; Rutterford and Sotiropoulos, 'The Rise of the Small Investor in the US and the UK, 1895 to 1970'. Financial repression refers to measures governments implement to reduce foreign debt—which in the case of the UK after WWII amounted to £21 billion to the US alone—at the cost of domestic savers.

[10] Quote after *HC Deb*, 612, c. 264, 28 October 1959. On the bull markets see Littlewood, *The Stock Market*, pp. 120–137.

[11] 'Widening Share Ownership: Meeting at Westminster', *The Times*, 21 November 1958; 'Giving Small Savers A Stake In Industry', *The Times*, 29 April 1959; 'Changing Face of Thrift', *The Guardian*, 24 September 1961.

[12] A. H. Thrower, *How to Invest for Profit in Stocks and Shares: A Guide for the Small Investor* (Preston: Thomas, 1961), p. 7.

[13] Y. Avrahampour, '"Cult of Equity": Actuaries and the Transformation of Pension Fund Investing, 1948–1960', *Business History Review* (2015), pp. 281–304.

Exchange gambling'.[14] From the mid-1950s, statistical data on ownership patterns and shareholder numbers were gathered and came to be seen as relevant economic indicators while attempts were made to survey the attitudes of Britain's shareholder population. These surveys found that the stock market was entering into more and more British households during the post-war period and gradually climbed down the social ladder. Investors small and large made and lost fortunes in two unprecedented boom markets while the burgeoning climate of affluence and permissiveness further loosened traditional reservations against stocks and shares. This expansion occurred against considerable resistance from the City of London and revealed frictions between different types of investors who held competing notions of legitimate investment activity. As a reaction to increased speculation—especially in new issues—traditional shareholders who were after long-term income began to fashion themselves as 'genuine investors'. This concept took share ownership literally and—in line with Thatcher's critique of speculation—claimed moral superiority over frequent buying and selling of shares. 'Genuine investors' fashioned their actions as an exercise in self-styled middle-class virtues of thrift and financial patriotism.

Again, it was not only economic factors but social and cultural developments that drew people into the market. When the Conservative governments liberalized gambling laws in the 1950s in recognition of a wider relaxation of social attitudes towards gambling, this had a profound impact on the investing public. Facing much criticism from the churches and their own grass roots, the Tory leadership went as far as to conflate elements of public finance with betting in the 1956 introduction of Premium Bonds and decriminalized most gambling formats in the 1960 Betting and Gaming Act. Because there were overlaps between gambling and the investing public, we can see how the dismantling of restrictions in the former led on to more relaxed attitudes in the latter. In the course of this, the church's own position on stock market investment took a spectacular turn. It is often overlooked that in the 1950s the Church of England—previously a vocal critic of finance—became a major player in the 'Cult of Equity' by also selling considerable amounts of its holdings in government and corporate debt and piling into equities instead. As an unacknowledged side effect, the church undermined its own religious criticism of the stock market that had previously held strong purchase in conservative milieus. If we shift our focus away from elite discourses on share ownership and the inner workings of the engine rooms of high finance and instead look towards the everyday knowledge and practices of the stock market, we can reveal rich—and at times—surprising stories about British post-war capitalism. In this way, debates over popular investment and speculation serve as a window into negotiations over the profit motive, the changing character of Christian morality

---

[14] *HC Deb* 634 c. 148.

and reveal the influence of economic individualism as a social force that ran counter to the corporatist character of post-war economic policy.

## Surveying the Small Investor: Shareholder Population, Patterns of Ownership and Investment Behaviour

In the summer of 1960, HM Treasury was annoyed by the London Stock Exchange. The stock market was booming and Whitehall civil servants were busy preparing a speech for the economic secretary, which he was due to give during a Parliamentary debate on the 'Wider Ownership of Industrial Shares'.[15] But Treasury staff were struggling to find accurate data on the extent of share ownership in Britain. For such information, they had to rely on 'articles in the financial Press [sic]' which were 'far from complete' and the Stock Exchange was simply unable to 'provide any facts about the breadth of shareholdings in companies'. The Treasury had furthermore learned 'from the Bank [of England] that the Stock Exchange have come down firmly against any scheme to encourage small investors in equities'.[16] Why was an institution whose chairman affirmed in public that its 'main aim is to maintain a fair and free market and to make its facilities known as widely as possible to anyone who may want to use them',[17] so opposed to the idea of wider share ownership? Why did the Stock Exchange not have at hand—and did not feel responsible for providing—reliable information on Britain's shareholder population like in other countries? The first shareholder surveys were carried out by hobby statisticians and financial journalists in the late 1940s. The 1950s saw economists and social scientists developing an interest in the subject. But it was not until the mid-1960s that Britain's leading market for financial securities, the London Stock Exchange, bowed to political and public pressure and commissioned the first comprehensive survey on Britain's shareholder population. The Stock Exchange's reluctance in this field stemmed from the conservative attitude its patrician-minded members adhered to at a time when British society came to challenge paternalism in many aspects of public and private life.

Partly, this reluctance rooted in the City of London's 'instinct for secrecy'[18] and its anti-intellectualism. In-depth financial analysis and number crunching caused

---

[15] *HC Deb* 625, cc. 823–920, 24 June 1960. The economic secretary was the Conservative Anthony Barber, later Chancellor of the Exchequer under Edward Heath. For the context of the debate in which Barber represented the government's line against the motion of his backbencher colleague, Gresham Cooke of the Wider Share Ownership Council, see Chapter 4.

[16] J. F. Barrow to J. I. Mck. Rhodes, 10 June 1960, TNA, T 326/285, Investment of Small Savings in Industry, 1962–64. Wider Ownership of Shares.

[17] The chairman in question was Lord Ritchie of Dundee (1959–65). Quote after. Jenkins, *The Stock Exchange Story*, p. 184.

[18] Littlewood, *The Stock Market*, p. 133.

suspicion in a community of bankers and stockbrokers who relied primarily on personal contacts and a 'sense of smell' or 'deeply entrenched habits and instinct [ ... ] a sea of experience [and] a good pinch of flair or hunch'.[19] A 1963 publication by the PR department that the Stock Exchange grudgingly called into life, illustrates what 'The House' regarded as its members' job requirements. Becoming a jobber or broker, the leaflet explained, 'is helped by an instinct or flair for this rather special type of business'.[20] The post-war City in general, and the Stock Exchange in particular, took pride in maintaining a conservative, paternalist, and restrictive mentality that had guided Britain's financial elites through the Victorian and the interwar period. Outside the City, of course, this code of conduct was derided at best and the way in which stockbrokers were seen as out of touch with society is perhaps best captured by the 1976 Monty Python sketch about the 'The Dull Life of a City Stockbroker'. Throughout the decades, most London brokers were suspicious of the small investor and relied on their client base of wealthy individuals and financial institutions 'with contact being of a personal nature, reinforced through family, educational, or other ties'.[21] Subscribing to the view that the Council 'must guard its members from the public, not the reverse',[22] hardly anyone in the Stock Exchange saw the need of, or felt responsible for gathering information on investors.

To be sure the Stock Exchange did open up ever so slightly under the chairmanship of Sir John Braithwaite (1949–59). With an 'austere cast of mind' that eschewed 'speculation and dangerous gambling', the senior stockbroker took into account the new political climate and was keen to shed the image of the Stock Exchange as a private members' club, or worse, an upper-class betting shop.[23] He was known to take public attacks of this kind very seriously, in fact personally, and one example where he did bow to political pressure was his strict stance against the reintroduction of dealing in options, derivative contracts that granted the buyer the right, but not the obligation to buy or sell an underlying financial security. Options had been banned with the outbreak of WWII in an effort to curb speculation and Braithwaite, acutely aware that options trading had a strong gambling element, upheld the ban until 1958 in order not to give the government arguments in favour of taking the Stock Exchange under public control.[24] Under his chairmanship, the Stock Exchange finally opened a Visitors' Gallery in 1953— something the Royal Commission of 1877 had already urged 'The House' to do—

---

[19] On anti-intellectualism in the City see D. Kynaston, *The City of London: A Club No More 1945–2000* (London: Pimlico, 2001), IV, pp. 199–209. Quote on central bankers requiring a 'sense of smell', Kynaston, *The City of London, IV*, p. 208, flair etc. pp. 170–172.

[20] Public Relations Department of the London Stock Exchange, *A Career on the London Stock Exchange* (London: London Stock Exchange, 1963).

[21] Michie, *The London Stock Exchange*, p. 203.     [22] Kynaston, *The City of London*, IV, p. 31.

[23] J. Slinn, 'Braithwaite, Sir John Bevan (1884–1973)', *ODNB*, 2004.

[24] Michie, *The London Stock Exchange,* pp. 368–401.

and furthermore formed said PR department in 1957.[25] But although Braithwaite pledged 'to attract a whole new class of investors', these were more acts of political opportunism than serious attempts to promote brokerage services to smaller clients. The City's conservative stance towards popular capitalism becomes clear when we compare the London Stock Exchange with its counterpart in New York, particularly the different approaches towards advertising. There, in 1952, the New York Stock Exchange (NYSE) commissioned a leading advertising company to conduct a comprehensive survey about the number, age, gender, and regional dispersion of US shareholders. The European pioneer in this regard was Sweden, where the Stockholm Stock Exchange initiated a similar survey on shareholdings and ownership, which found that between 50 per cent and 70 per cent of the shareholder population were women.[26] On Wall Street, these regular surveys were part of a public relations campaign that aimed to generate new business for a market that still had not fully recovered from the 1929 crash. It seemed self-evident to the NYSE, which had been fashioning itself as 'the people's market' since the interwar years, to provide stockbrokers with valuable information on their client base for advertising—which was allowed in the US.[27] In Britain, however, the interwar resistance against retail stockbroking continued and the majority of members of the Stock Exchange Council refused to lift the ban on stockbrokers' advertising, arguing that this 'could all too easily attract the wrong type of client, the outright small speculator'.[28]

As a result of the financial establishment's lack of interest in the small investor, the first efforts in surveying the shareholder population were undertaken by private stock market experts and financial journalists with naturally amateurish methods. It was the experience of nationalization and economic planning during the first Labour administration that first led liberal financial observers to probe into the extent of popular share ownership in Britain.[29] The first systematic attempt to estimate the number of shareholders was undertaken by Alec Ellinger who became a popular persona in the investment world who is worth shedding some further light on.[30] In a series of articles for the *Financial Times* (*FT*) in 1949, Ellinger evaluated the share registers of 40 British companies and by 'comparing duplication of holdings between shareholders' estimated that about

---

[25] For Braithwaite's chairmanship see W. J. Reader, *A House in the City: A Study of the City and of the Stock Exchange Based on the Records of Foster & Braithwaite, 1825–1975* (London: Batsford, 1979), pp. 173–177.

[26] *The Financial Times*, 23 January 1951.

[27] Ott, *When Wall Street Met Main Street*, pp. 191–213.

[28] 'The Stock Exchange Grapples With a Social Revolution', *The Times*, 24 October 1960.

[29] Rutterford and Sotiropoulos, 'The Rise of the Small Investor in the US and the UK, 1895 to 1970', p. 487.

[30] Rutterford and Sotiropoulos, 'The Rise of the Small Investor in the US and the UK, 1895 to 1970', p. 36.

1.25 million Britons owned industrial shares and that 40 per cent of these investors were women.[31]

After ten years in a London broker's office, Ellinger started his own investment firm in Cambridge, where he hired university graduates to manage the portfolios of wealthy individuals and published his investment ideas in the *Monthly Investment Letter*, one of the growing numbers of newsletters at that time carrying investment advice. In his famed anthropology of the City of London, novelist Paul Ferris spent a day with Ellinger and they met again for the 1964 BBC documentary *Men and Money*.[32] Ellinger promoted an active investment philosophy that revised holdings 'not only from month to month but from week to week and day to day'.[33] But what marked him somewhat of a City outsider was not his speculative investment strategy but the analysis it was based on. Ellinger was a pioneer of what today is referred to as 'technical analysis', which at that time was becoming known ironically as 'chartism'. Ellinger, who became known as the 'doyen of British chartists', was somewhat of a City outsider, not necessarily because his firm was located in Cambridge, but because he promoted a semi-scientific investment strategy.[34] Chartists aim to use past performances of certain securities to predict future price movements—a concept that bordered on charlatanry for many City people. For instance, the *Daily Telegraph's* assistant City editor and later unit trust director, Percie Naish, could only turn up his nose at this 'curious technique of investment'. He scoffed 'that most chart readers have had to invent their own special brand of gibberish with which to describe their technique gives extra force to my feeling that often they are entrapped by their own enthusiasm'.[35] One impact critics believed chartism to have was to distort markets by producing self-fulfilling prophecies. 'If a large number of people believe that a share's price is about to move up and that the time is right to buy', one author lamented, 'their very act of purchasing the share will inevitably exert an upward pressure on its price, so validating their earlier predictions'.[36] More ironically, Ferris commented on this detached and more speculative investment philosophy that a 'day with Ellinger provided an academic, uncoloured view [of the stock market], like football seen through pools coupons'.[37] In spite of the criticism, Ellinger became a prominent figure in Britain's investment community, and with

---

[31] Quote after Rutterford and Sotiropoulos, 'The Rise of the Small Investor in the US and the UK, 1895 to 1970', p. 36; see furthermore A. Ellinger, 'The Owners of Industry', *The Financial Times*, 28 February 1949; A. Ellinger, 'How many Investors are There?', *The Financial Times*, 2 March 1949.

[32] P. Ferris, *The City* (London: Penguin, 1960), pp. 52–57. Ferris described Ellinger as 'the better type of English academic: dry, precise, perpetually amused and unlikely to put his faith in one solution'.

[33] A. G. Ellinger, *The Art of Investment*, 1st edn (London: Bowes and Bowes, 1955), p. 37.

[34] Quote after J. Rowlatt and D. Davenport, *Guide to Saving and Investment*, rev. edn (Newton Abbot: David & Charles, 1971), p. 121.

[35] P. J. Naish, *The Complete Guide to Personal Investment* (London: C. Tinling, 1962), p. 131.

[36] T. M. Ryan, *Theory of Portfolio Selection* (Basingstoke: Macmillan, 1978), p. 123.

[37] Ferris, *The City*, p. 57.

his standing as an author of several investment guides he added to the popularization of investment in the post-war period.[38]

The early 1950s saw further modest interest in Britain's shareholder population. In 1951, Hargreaves Parkinson, the interwar champion of the small investor and since 1945 the editor of the newly-merged *FT*, came to more or less identical results as Ellinger.[39] He also counted 1.25 million shareholders, but while Ellinger's interest in the matter was more academic, Parkinson's intervention was of a political nature. He argued 'that ownership could not be more democratic if the companies concerned were indeed nationalized'[40] and made public ownership responsible for the lack of share ownership growth since the interwar years, when Britain was thought to have had about 1.1 million private equity investors.

Between 1958 and 1960—when the *FT* 30 index was climbing to ever new heights—*The Times* published a series of articles, in which the stock market expert Gordon Cummings produced estimates of the shareholder population. These are the articles the Treasury civil servants were referring to when writing their reports and complaining about the lack of official data from the Stock Exchange. From a background similar to Alec Ellinger's, Cummings had experience in financial journalism, the private sector as well as book-writing. After a spell at the *Daily Herald's* City desk in the 1930s—during which time he testified against bucket shops to the Board of Trade Committee—Cummings settled as a chartered accountant in Mayfair. He remained an acclaimed financial writer, became PR adviser of the merchant bank Lazard Brothers, and went on to gain a reputation as Britain's 'stock market sage'.[41] Between 1953 and 1956 he was a regular contributor to the BBC's personal finance programme *Money Matters*, where he educated listeners about their income tax allowances, house purchase, life insurance, and the facilities available to the small investor on the Stock Exchange. In 1963, he published for the first time his *Complete Guide to Investment*, which in the following three years alone sold 'more than 120,000 copies'. In a review essay of investment books for beginners, a genre that 'had seen a steady flow over the past year or so', *The Economist* singled out Cummings's book as 'ideal for the absolute beginner' due to its 'wide range and simple language'.[42] Renamed *The Investor's Guide to the Stock Market*, what was arguably Britain's most successful investment

---

[38] Ellinger, *The Art of Investment*. This book reached its third edition in 1971. See also Ellinger, *The Investor's Progress: From Money Box to Stocks and Shares* (London: Bowes and Bowes, 1958); 'Congenial Talk About Money: Investment Clubs in Conference', *The Times*, 26 September 1960.

[39] H. Parkinson, *Ownership of Industry* (London: Eyre & Spottiswoode, 1951). By the time of the publication of his book, however, The *FT* editor had already died prematurely.

[40] Rutterford and Sotiropoulos, 'The Rise of the Small Investor in the US and the UK, 1895 to 1970', p. 520.

[41] 'Gordon's Golden Rules', *The Financial Times*, 20 February 1982.

[42] 'Investment Guide', *The Times*, 31 March 1966. 'Blackboard or Platform? Books for Beginners', *The Economist*, 25 March 1967. The book reached its 7th edn in 1975.

book continued to be published until 1988.[43] In opposition to Ellinger's chartist approach, however, Cummings promoted a concept that is known today as 'value investing' and most commonly associated with the US billionaire investor Warren Buffet. This investment strategy is guided by company fundamentals and for Cummings was furthermore rooted in the belief that speculation 'is not for the small investor with only a few hundred pounds of hard-won savings behind him'.[44] Familiar with the opportunities and pitfalls for investment newcomers since the interwar period, Cummings now grappled with the question of how many shareholders there were in the UK.[45] He analysed the share registers of Britain's ten largest companies and found that small holdings of '£500 or below are predominant' among corporations such as Unilever, Imperial Tobacco or the Midland Bank and estimated the number of shareholders to be about three million.[46]

By then, another trend had begun to dramatically change Britain's financial landscape. Even before the number of direct shareholders had been established with any certainty, it was becoming apparent that pension funds and life insurance companies had shifted their clients' savings from fixed-income securities such as Gilts and corporate bonds into corporate shares as a hedge against inflation thereby turning these savers into indirect shareholders (Figure 2.1).[47] The face of this transformation was George Ross Goobey, manager of the Imperial Tobacco pension fund who earned spectacular returns by following an equity-only investment policy for his fund. Known as the 'Cult of Equity', this trend entailed the private investor's relative decline in terms of corporate ownership. Between 1957 and 1963, individual investors' share of overall listed equity declined from 61.8 per cent to 54 per cent although the real value of their holdings increased significantly due to the prolonged bull market.[48] Another consequence of the Cult of Equity was that stockbroking firms had further incentives to attract large orders from institutional clients on a fixed-commission basis of 2 per cent, thus making it even

[43] G. Cummings, *Investor's Guide to the Stock Market*, 5th edn, repr. with amendments (London: Financial Times Business Information, 1988).

[44] G. Cummings, *The Complete Guide to Investment*, 1st edn (Harmondsworth: Penguin, 1963), p. 139.

[45] Cummings, *The Complete Guide to Investment*, p. 139. 'How Many Small Shareholders?', *The Times*, 13 November 1958; 'Widening Ordinary Share Ownership I', *The Times*, 8 January 1959; 'Widening Ordinary Share Ownership II', *The Times*, 9 January 1959.

[46] Cummings, *The Complete Guide to Investment*, p. 139. 'WHO Owns The Capital Of Unilever Ltd.?', *The Times*, 2 June 1959; 'WHO Owns The Midland Bank's Share Capital?', *The Times*, 4 August 1959; 'WHO Owns Imperial Tobacco And B.A.T.?', *The Times*, 29 September 1960.

[47] Kynaston, *The City of London*, IV, pp. 160–165; A. Davies, *The City of London and Social Democracy*, pp. 37–74; Littlewood, *The Stock Market*, pp. 100–108.

[48] J. Revell and J. Moyle, *The Owners of Quoted Ordinary Shares: A Survey for 1963* (London: Chapman and Hall for the Department of Applied Economics, University of Cambridge, 1966), vol. 7, p. 6. See J. Moyle, *The Pattern of Ordinary Share Ownership 1957-1970* (Cambridge: Cambridge University Press, 1971), p. 8. For this trend in context see R. Michie, 'Financial capitalism', in L. Neal and J. G. Williamson (eds), *The Spread of Capitalism: From 1848 to the Present*, The Cambridge History of Capitalism (Cambridge: Cambridge University Press, 2014), pp. 230–263.

| Column1 | Column2 | Column3 | Column4 | Column5 | Column6 | Column7 | Column8 | Column9 | Column10 | Column11 | Column12 | Column13 |
|---|---|---|---|---|---|---|---|---|---|---|---|---|
| Percent of total equity owned | | | | | | | | | | | | |
| | | 1963 | 1969 | 1975 | 1981 | 1989 | 1990 | 1991 | 1992 | 1993 | 1994 | 1997 |
| Rest of the world | | 7 | 6.6 | 5.6 | 3.6 | 12.8 | 11.8 | 12.8 | 13.1 | 16.3 | 16.3 | 24 |
| Insurance companies | | 10 | 12.2 | 15.9 | 20.5 | 18.6 | 20.4 | 20.8 | 19.5 | 20 | 21.9 | 23.5 |
| Pension funds | | 6.4 | 9 | 16.8 | 26.7 | 30.6 | 31.7 | 31.3 | 32.4 | 31.3 | 27.8 | 22.1 |
| Individuals | | 54 | 47.4 | 37.5 | 28.2 | 20.6 | 20.3 | 19.9 | 20.4 | 17.7 | 20.3 | 16.5 |
| Unit trusts | | 1.3 | 2.9 | 4.1 | 3.6 | 5.9 | 6.1 | 5.7 | 6.2 | 6.6 | 6.8 | 6.7 |
| Investment trusts | | | | | | 1.6 | 1.6 | 1.5 | 2.1 | 2.5 | 2 | 1.9 |
| Other financial institutions | | 11.3 | 10.1 | 10.5 | 6.8 | 1.1 | 0.7 | 0.8 | 0.4 | 0.6 | 1.3 | 2 |
| Charities | | 2.1 | 2.1 | 2.3 | 2.2 | 2.3 | 1.9 | 2.4 | 1.8 | 1.6 | 1.3 | 1.9 |
| Private non-financial corporations | | 5.1 | 5.4 | 3 | 5.1 | 3.8 | 2.8 | 3.3 | 1.8 | 1.5 | 1.1 | 1.2 |
| Public sector | | 1.5 | 2.6 | 3.6 | 3 | 2 | 2 | 1.3 | 1.8 | 1.3 | 0.8 | 0.1 |
| Banks | | 1.3 | 1.7 | 0.7 | 0.3 | 0.7 | 0.7 | 0.2 | 0.5 | 0.6 | 0.4 | 0.1 |
| Total | | 100 | 100 | 100 | 100 | 100 | 100 | 100 | 100 | 100 | 100 | 100 |

**Figure 2.1** Beneficial equity ownership

*Note:* The data for 1963 and 1969 are taken from the Cambridge Department for Applied Economics as listed in note 48.
*Source:* Office for National Statistics (London: The Stationery Office, 1997).

more difficult for investors of modest means looking to process smaller orders to find good investment advice.

An important undercurrent of the Cult of Equity was the rise of the unit trust industry. Unit trusts were first launched during the interwar period as mediated investment vehicles that pooled their clients' small amounts of capital and charged a management fee for investing them in a diversified portfolio of equities, fixed income, and other financial securities depending on investor's risk appetite. This allowed smaller investors, who normally could not afford this, the benefits of portfolio diversification. Hence, unit trusts were advertised as a vehicle enabling the 'small man' to enjoy the benefits of equity investment.[49] The long-serving Bank of England director, George Booth, is credited with launching the first unit trust in 1931 and people like Iain Fairbairn or the left-leaning financier William Piercy did much to pioneer this form of investment in subsequent years.[50] Counter to the democratizing narrative of this investment vehicle, Fairbairn later acknowledged that there was a paternalistic element behind the idea, explaining that unit trusts came into being because 'most responsible and well-informed people in the City were on principle against equity investment for any but those experienced enough to look after themselves'.[51] But for a long time the Stock Exchange refused to list the securities because several directors had been caught out manipulating the price of the units and for much of the 1950s unit trusts continued to struggle getting off the ground because of this suspicion.[52]

By the late 1950s, however, Sir John Braithwaite, the Stock Exchange chairman who had vowed to attract a new class of investors, recognized unit trusts as a suitable tool of including the ever-growing number of small investors while at the same time barring them from making their own, potentially harmful, investment decisions. In 1957, the Stock Exchange decided to lift the ban on unit trust advertising. Beginning in the early 1960s, the industry virtually exploded. While fifty-one unit trusts managed £200m worth of clients' money in 1959, there were 208 companies investing £1,400m by 1969, marking a fivefold increase in real terms.[53] This growth was fuelled by enormous sums unit trust managers invested in advertising campaigns in the quality and popular press, thereby contributing to the growth of financial journalism across all outlets.[54] From a purely financial perspective, unit trusts were indeed the safest and least troublesome form of equity investment for the small investor who sought protection from inflation and gradual long-term growth. At the same time, however, many advocates of wider

---

[49] Michie, *The London Stock Exchange*, pp. 282–3, 317–318; A. Gleeson, *People and Their Money: 50 Years of Private Investment* (Norwich: Fletcher & Son, 1981).

[50] On Booth and his role in developing the first unit trust see D. Crow, *A Man of Push and Go: The Life of George Macaulay Booth* (London: R. Hart-Davis, 1965), pp. 175–180.

[51] 'Unit Trusts—Past and Future I', *The Investors' Chronicle*, 13 August 1955.

[52] See for instance the dubious practices of the unit trust pioneer, Denys Lowson; R. Davenport-Hines, 'Lowson, Sir Denys Colquhoun Flowerdew, first baronet (1906–1975)', *ODNB*, 2004.

[53] Newman, *Financial Marketing and Communications*, p. 152.       [54] See Chapter 3.

share ownership disliked that a unit trust disconnected an investor from direct ownership of a company and bemoaned the decreased level of excitement when investing this way. In the words of one contemporary, '[i]nvesting through the medium of a management company takes the thrill out of backing one's own judgment against that of the market'.[55] As we shall see later, the advancement of unit trusts industry and other vehicles of managed investment meant that *direct* trading in stocks and shares was increasingly practised as a sort of hobby and source of entertainment.

By the late 1950s a new interest in the shareholder population emerged. While economists and statisticians probed into the number of investors and ownership patterns, social scientists now entered the field and sought to explore the social background of these investors. Jon Lawrence has noted that in 'Britain, it was only after World War Two that social science shifted its focus from the marginalized and disadvantaged—the "social problem" groups—to "ordinary" or "average" Britons'.[56] As part of this shift, social scientists now discovered the small investor as an object of enquiry and sought to explore 'ordinary' people's attitudes towards the stock market. What was the socioeconomic position of the average investor? What motivated him or her to buy shares while others shied away from the stock market? What investment vehicles did investors use and what influenced their decisions? These attitudinal surveys have often been neglected by historians, which is a reminder that scholarship has tended to reduce the actual investors to statistics, numbers, and anonymous recipients of political catchphrases.

In 1959, the Acton Society Trust, a non-profit organization that promoted research in the social sciences, published a pioneering study in this field that received wide attention in the daily and financial press. The papers of the trust have not survived but correspondence with several politicians, academics, and businessmen give some insight into the organization. For instance, William Piercy, the centre-left pioneer of the unit trust movement gave his financial support to the trust's work and provided input for *Wider Shareholding*.[57] *The Times* commented on *Wider Shareholding* that the '[d]iscussion about the small investor can at last proceed on the basis of fact', indicating that the investor was no longer just a macroeconomic variable, but a social figure.[58] The first half of the survey was based on 2,761 questionnaires that small clients of London stock-brokers had returned, naturally resulting in a regional selection that the research

[55] R. Taylor, *Investment* (London: Collins, 1963), p. 55.
[56] J. Lawrence, 'Social-Science Encounters and the Negotiation of Difference in Early 1960s England', *History Workshop Journal* 77 (2014), p. 215.
[57] R. Stewart to W. Piercy, 25 June 1959; W. Piercy to R. Stewart, 26 October 1959, 2 November 1959, London School of Economics Library, collection of William Piercy (1886–1966); 1st Baron Piercy, PIERCY 15/1.
[58] 'What IS Needed To Expand Share Ownership', *The Times*, 14 December 1959. See also the welcoming review in *The Investors' Chronicle*, 'Small Investor in Profile', 18 December 1959.

team was well aware of. A total of 42 per cent of returned questionnaires were from the East and South East of England including London, while 20.7 per cent came from the North and 15.7 per cent from the Midlands with the rest divided over the South West, Scotland, Wales, and Ireland.[59] The 'small investor' had been defined beforehand as someone who had 'invested to date a total of £1,000 or less' and had a 'maximum weekly income of £50'.[60] The survey found that share ownership had climbed down the social ladder, the average small investor being 'probably a member of the lower middle class, or possibly the upper working class'.[61] Overall, the authors remained cautious and stressed that due to lack of material available for comparison 'no claims regarding the representativeness of our sample are made'.[62] Yet the research team identified important trends in retail investment, which more comprehensive surveys would later confirm. The average small investor, for instance, would almost certainly have a bank account, very likely some money in National or Post Office Savings accounts, and life insurance. Keen to find out what motivated investment newcomers to enter the stock market, the researchers learned that private study, friends, and family as well as the financial press were the most likely reasons. The survey also found strong evidence that higher occupational grades were far more likely to consult a stockbroker before making investment decisions. The *FT* singled out as a 'particularly signifi-cant' finding of the survey that small investors were becoming not only 'more numerous', but also 'on average, becoming smaller' in comparison to their inter-war counterparts, thereby supporting Gordon Cummings's earlier observation that small holdings were becoming ever more common among share registers of public companies.[63]

The Acton Society Trust also aimed to sound the potential for further expan-sion and to identify obstacles for wider share ownership. For this purpose, the second half of the survey examined working-class attitudes towards stocks and shares. The researchers carried out 210 interviews with workers in five different factories of companies operating employee share schemes. These first-hand state-ments of working-class investors were mostly brushed aside in contemporary newspaper reports and are absent from the historical literature, but they made the survey a treasure house of qualitative material. They challenge us to build on Paul Johnson's insight that a 'knowledge of individual responses to material or financial problems can inform a discussion of topics that are social and collective' and serve as a reminder 'that behaviour which is apparently determined by selfish economic motives can significantly affect and be affected by social and

---

[59] Acton Society Trust, *Wider Shareholding* (London: The Society, 1959), p. 21.
[60] Acton Society Trust, *Wider Shareholding*, p. 20.
[61] Acton Society Trust, *Wider Shareholding*, p. 51
[62] Acton Society Trust, *Wider Shareholding*, p. 21.
[63] *The Financial Times*, 'The Small Investor', 14 December 1959.

non-economic forces'.[64] In this case, the interviews reveal highly diverse attitudes towards investment and speculation among the respondents. On the one hand, employee shares could be perceived as a medium of creating strong links between a business and its workforce. A 50-year-old foreman, for example, explained that he bought his shares 'from a patriotic standpoint to support my own firm'. Likewise a semi-skilled worker aged 22, 'did not invest for the money or to make my job more secure but to feel that I had a stake in the company'. Another respondent found that share ownership 'helps keep interest in the firm and a man sees that if he lets the firm down he lets himself down'.[65]

Some workers, on the other hand, held a fundamentally different notion of stock market investment. In some factories the researchers noticed 'the formation of gambling groups' and one supervisor confirmed that 'the *Financial Times* was commonly seen on the bench, which it had not been "in his younger days"'.[66] A foreman, aged 41, reported that '[t]here is a work-group who are doing speculating. They are not out for dividends. They started in the last six or nine months, possibly due to the selling of shares here'. One of his colleagues, a skilled worker aged 48, indeed described how 'years ago' he used to do 'a little Football Pools', but now he found 'the Stock market more enlightening and exciting'. Other workers admitted that 'watching the fluctuations is after all a bit of fun' or described the stock market as a casino with slightly better odds but no less addictive than the pools: 'a man in my shop who used to back horses told me that he had found a better method-industrial shares-and now he has got me and several others doing it too'.[67] The experiences of these workers turn a spotlight on an aspect of investment that the City establishment was keen to deny in public discourse: the striking resemblance between stock market activity and gambling. Share investment could provide entertainment and excitement, not because playing the stock market necessarily *was* gambling, but because it promised similar thrills of risk and reward to betting on horses, football, or dog races. As we will see, this appealed not only to those working-class investors who viewed the stock market as merely another betting format, but to many middle-class investors as well.

The survey material, furthermore, suggests we need to call into question Richard Whiting's assessment that wider share ownership 'failed' in the post-war period because 'shares, in fact, reinforced a lesson about short-term insecurity and instability, and this was what most workers were trying to guard against'.[68]

[64] P. Johnson, *Saving and Spending: The Working-Class Economy in Britain, 1870–1939* (Oxford: Clarendon Press, 1985), p. 5.
[65] Acton Society Trust, *Wider Shareholding*, pp. 63–65.
[66] Acton Society Trust, *Wider Shareholding*, p. 64.
[67] Acton Society Trust, *Wider Shareholding*, pp. 50, 63–64.
[68] R. Whiting, 'The City and Democratic Capitalism', in R. Michie and P. Williamson (eds), *The British Government and the City of London in the Twentieth Century* (Cambridge: Cambridge University Press, 2004), p. 114.

The experiences of the workers who *did* get in touch with the stock market were clearly too diverse to warrant such generalizations. Besides, the research team found that more workers stayed away from shares due to a *lack of interest* than because of *insufficient capital*. In fact, some interviewees contended that if investment was better explained and advertised, more workers would be drawn into the stock market. A 'working-class man in his thirties', for instance, opined that 'share buying should be advertised and made as easy for the working classes to understand as are, say, football pools or what is running in the 2.30'.[69] The social barriers to investment were another issue. Addressing the aloofness of the City, a chargehand, aged 40 suggested: 'Brokers should be more accessible. The first time [visiting a stockbrokers' office] my knees were knocking. You have to move in a different circle to brave it, but I have always been a gambler and like a flutter, so carried on.'[70] Only a minority of the interviewed workers—ten out of 210—objected to investment on moral or political grounds: 'It's not for the working man to buy shares, to gamble. For some rich people it's a living isn't it?' Other respondents explained that they did 'not buy ordinary shares because that is unfair profit-making. I don't like to think that people are living on other people—buying and selling without producing'.[71] These findings, albeit drawn from firms with company share schemes, suggest that class-based objections against investment may not have been as deep-rooted among working-class communities as Labour critics of the Stock Exchange asserted them to be.

Reviewing *Wider Shareholding*, *The Economist* lauded it as a 'pilot survey', but stated that 'if the small investor is to become the infantryman of a property owning democracy it will have to be supplemented by a wider survey of what makes people save and invest'.[72] The newly-founded Wider Share Ownership Council (WSOC), a lobby group of mainly Conservative backbenchers and City men, heeded this call and commissioned a survey on *Savings and Attitudes to Share Owning*.[73] In the meantime, a Gallup poll on *The Private Investor* was published in the *News Chronicle*.[74] Both surveys stood out by making bold—and as it turned out wrong—claims about the number of shareholders in Britain

---

[69] Acton Society Trust, *Wider Shareholding*, p. 12.

[70] Acton Society Trust, *Wider Shareholding*, p. 78.

[71] Acton Society Trust, *Wider Shareholding*, p. 69. Workers interviewed in later surveys believed that investment income would mean to 'derive benefits from others' exertions' or categorically stated that 'people of our class don't invest'. G. Naylor, *Sharing the Profits: An Inquiry into the Habits, Attitudes and Problems of Employees' Shareholding Schemes*, with an intro. by Nancy Seear and George Copeman. Foreword by Lord Shawcross and Maurice Macmillan (London: Garnstone Press, 1968), pp. 44, 47.

[72] *The Economist*, 'The Small Investor: Who is He?', 3 January 1960.

[73] Research Services Limited, *Savings and Attitudes to Share Owning* (London: Wider Share Ownership Committee, 1962); on the WSOC see A. Edwards, '"Manufacturing Capitalists": The Wider Share Ownership Council and the Problem of "Popular Capitalism", 1958–92', *Twentieth Century British History* 27 (2016), pp. 100–123 and Chapter 4.

[74] 'Do you know how to set about buying some shares?', *News Chronicle*, 4 May 1960.

having climbed to three-and-a-half or four million respectively. Although the WSOC survey was presented prominently at the group's annual conference, it failed to make any impact. Having received a copy from the WSOC during its annual Budget presentation, Treasury officials did 'not think that this is a very good survey' and concluded with relief that it did 'not fortunately give the Wider Share Ownership Committee any stick with which to beat the Treasury'.[75]

In 1966, the London Stock Exchange finally published its first survey with reliable estimates of 1.8 million owners of industrial shares in Britain (3.3 per cent of the population), and 800,000 holders of UK government bonds.[76] Three years later, a team of researchers from Imperial College, London carried out another comprehensive survey counting 2.3 million (4.1 per cent) and in addition presenting an in-depth analysis of private shareholders' investment behaviour.[77] To some extent, these numbers confounded earlier expectations of Britain developing into a share-owning democracy. Britain lagged behind US growth, where shareholder numbers sky-rocketed from 6.5 million in 1952 (4.2 per cent of population) to about 20 million in 1965 (14.6 per cent).[78] Yet, by the late 1960s the UK shareholder population had still almost doubled since the war and was steadily growing. Previewing the 1966 results in *The Stock Exchange Journal*, Gordon Cummings introduced Britain's average private investor as '[a]bove average age; with a professional, managerial, or higher administrative job; educated until at least 16; tending to live more in the South than in the North; with money in other forms of investment, and possibly living in a mortgaged home'.[79] While middle income groups, 53 per cent of the population, were numerically the largest shareowner group with 48 per cent, higher income groups accounted for 40 per cent of all shareholders while constituting only 13 per cent of the overall population.[80]

According to the survey, 57 per cent of shareholders were men and they were over-represented in industrial shares while women held the majority of

[75] J. I. McK. Rhodes to T. H. Caulcott, 13 March 1962; R. W. Phelps to J. I. McK. Rhodes, 15 March 1962, TNA, T 326/285, Investment of Small Savings in Industry. Wider Ownership of Shares. Indeed the sample of the survey only included 568 men and 178 women.

[76] London Stock Exchange, *How Does Britain Save?: A summary of the results of a survey conducted for the London Stock Exchange by the British Market Research Bureau Limited* (London, 1966). These numbers did not include holders of unit trusts (700,000), investment trusts (200,000), or 'Government and Local Authority Securities' (800,000).

[77] R. A. Vernon, M. Middleton, and D. G. Harper, *Who Owns the Blue Chips?: A Study of Shareholding in a Leading Company* (Epping: Gower Press, 1973). The research team comprised an economist, a statistician, and a psychologist.

[78] J. M. Traflet, *A Nation of Small Shareholders: Marketing Wall Street after World War II* (Baltimore, MD: Johns Hopkins University Press, 2013), p. 153.

[79] G. Cummings, 'Who are the Shareholders?', *The Stock Exchange Journal* 11 (1966), pp. 4–5.

[80] London Stock Exchange, *How Does Britain Save?*, pp. 16–17. Socioeconomic groups were defined as 'AB: higher managerial, administrative or professional, and intermediate managerial administrative or professional; C1: Supervisory or clerical, junior managerial, administrative or professional; C2: skilled manual; DE: Semi and unskilled manual, and State pensioners', p. 7.

government bonds.[81] Women were found to be less active traders, more risk averse, and not as up to speed about market developments as their male counterparts. In this context, it is important to point out the highly gendered nature of the relationship between market masses and individual market actors.[82] On the one hand, market crowds and institutions—take, for instance, the Old Lady of Threadneedle Street—have always been feminized and described with stereotypes of feminine behaviour: markets were claimed to be emotional, moody, or hysterical. On the other side, we can detect with Marieke de Goede a 'distinctively masculine conception of agency'[83] in financial markets. The *individual* investor or speculator was almost exclusively fashioned as a male operator, whose 'emotions need to be kept in check' in order for him to stay on top of the market.[84]

While women investors may have been less risk-taking, plenty of evidence suggests that they were certainly more successful investors, which is highlighted forcefully by the phenomenon of investment clubs. In the late 1950s and early 1960s, privately organized investment clubs of hobby investors mushroomed across the country. In May 1959, the newly founded National Association of Investment Clubs (NAIC) presided over seventy registered clubs, together disposing of capital of about £50,000.[85] By September the following year, there were 400 investment clubs and the funds invested through them estimated at £600,000.[86] Pooling their members' money and investing it collectively, investment clubs essentially worked with a logic similar to unit trusts. The difference of this non-corporate equivalent was that members could socially interact, devise common strategies, and engage more actively with the business world by deciding over the club's portfolio democratically. Again, the direct involvement, whether individually or collectively, was furthermore celebrated as a more exciting experience than the institutional investment vehicles that were continuing to grow: 'Investing through the medium of a management company takes the thrill out of backing one's own judgment against that of the market and, although it minimises likely losses, investing in this indirect way also minimises the gains that can be expected from a successful investment policy.'[87]

By 1964, the NAIC was publishing a monthly newsletter, the *Stockholder*, which kept members informed of investment opportunities and social events, as well as

---

[81] London Stock Exchange, *How Does Britain Save?*, pp. 14–15.

[82] U. Stäheli, *Spectacular Speculation*, pp. 137–139.

[83] M. de Goede, 'Mastering "Lady Credit"', *International Feminist Journal of Politics* 2 (2000), pp. 58–81.

[84] B. H. Barrada, *How to Succeed as an Investor* (London: Newnes, 1966), p. 18.

[85] 'Growing Number of Investment Clubs', *The Times*, 5 May 1959.

[86] 'Clubs For Small Capitalists', *The Times*, 5 September 1960; 'Investment Club X-Ray', *The Investors Chronicle*, 4 November 1960; R. Kellett, *Ordinary Shares for Ordinary Savers*, Hobart papers (London: The Institute of Economic Affairs, 1962), vol. 16, p. 25.

[87] Taylor, *Investment*, p. 55. See also C. Gifford and J. A. Stevens, *Making Money on the Stock Exchange: A Beginner's Guide to Investment Policy*, 2nd edn (London: Macgibbon & Kee, 1960), p. 180: 'I must admit they [unit trusts] don't sound very exciting. Why does anybody buy them?'

serving as a discussion forum for all kinds of questions surrounding the stock market.[88] Curiously, the National Association's annual meeting brought regular embarrassment to all-male clubs as they were repeatedly 'soundly beaten by the women in a test of investing skill'.[89] For the 'interesting fact that on average all-female clubs outperform their all-male opposites'[90] two reasons were given: women's 'chariness of anything that might be considered speculation' and their choice of investments in 'companies they are familiar with from shopping'. A far more convincing explanation than the patronizing guesswork of the predominantly male 1960s investment world is the more recent empirical evidence gathered by behavioural economists that men tend to overtrade and trading frequently results in below-market performance.[91]

In regard to the Stock Exchange's place in society, its official survey did not reflect well on the institution as it highlighted the social distance between stockbrokers and 'ordinary' members of the investing public. Only 32 per cent of respondents—again predominantly the upper income groups—dealt directly through a stockbroker. The majority, 53 per cent, bought stocks and shares through their bank manager.[92] Here it is worth exploring the broker–client relationship in a brief excursion and pointing out the problem of workable source material in this regard. Not many archives of stockbroking firms survived the series of takeovers by merchant banks in the 1980s and 1990s. Those collections that have survived are largely comprised of ledgers and account books, and rarely contain personal material or correspondence with clients. Against this backdrop, it is of great value that the private papers of Terence Rattigan, the famous dramatist of the post-war period,[93] contain letters from his stockbroker over a period of eight years. They throw a rare light on the privileges that a close relationship with a stockbroker could bring to a 'celebrity investor' like Rattigan—and illustrate *ex negativo* the informal resources as well as information networks more modest investors were excluded from.

In November 1959—at the height of the second post-war bull market—Terence Rattigan became a client of the stockbroking firm Fielding, Newson-Smith & Co. and, under the guidance of senior partner J. D. C. Noble, built up an equity portfolio worth £8,781.[94] In April 1960 Rattigan must already have given Noble

---

[88] In 1970, the newsletter was renamed *The Shareholder and New Investor*.

[89] 'Congenial Talk about Money: Investment Clubs in Conference', *The Times*, 26 September 1960.

[90] 'Female clubs in the lead', *The Times*, 5 September 1967.

[91] 'In the Money: Investment Clubs', *The Times*, 9 July 1962. B. M. Barber and T. Odean, 'Boys will be Boys: Gender, Overconfidence, and Common Stock Investment', *The Quarterly Journal of Economics* 116 (2001), pp. 261–292; B. M. Barber and T. Odean, 'Trading Is Hazardous to Your Wealth: The Common Stock Investment Performance of Individual Investors', *The Journal of Finance* 55 (2000), pp. 773–806.

[92] London Stock Exchange, *How Does Britain Save?*, pp. 28–29.

[93] M. Arditti, 'Rattigan, Sir Terence Mervyn (1911–1977)', *ODNB*, online edn, January 2008.

[94] Rattigan Papers. Vol. ccl (ff. 192), Western Manuscripts, Add MS 74537, The British Library (henceforth: Rattigan Papers, BL), J. D. C. Noble to Terrence Rattigan, Summary of portfolio, 26

permission to act on short-term fluctuations on his behalf, because the stock-broker sold short 792 Great Universal Stores shares at 47/3 shilling and repurchased them at 46/3 the same day, of course 'free of stamp and subject to commission only'. Brokers would only deal on account for clients with sufficient capital, and positions opened and closed within a fortnightly period were exempt from stamp duty. This was much to the anger of many long-term small investors, one of which complained in the *Financial Times*:

> At present, an 'investor' buying and selling stocks or shares in the same Account period, possibly without any of his own money changing hands (which is more in the nature of a gamble than an investment) is excused liability to the £2 per cent. Stamp Duty, whereas the longer-term investor, holding over a period of years and genuinely paying for his investments, has the £2 per cent. stamp duty imposed on his purchase.[95]

While the time bargain carried out on Rattigan's behalf already smacks of insider dealing, Noble's next deal leaves no doubt about this. He bought a significant amount of shares of an American manufacturing firm for his client after having had lunch with the company's chairman, who had told Noble that he 'anticipates earnings [to be] \$3 against 2.37\$ [sic!] last year'.[96] Soon broker and client were on first-name basis after Rattigan had invited Noble to the London premiere of his 1960 play, *Ross*. Later the writer gave Noble carte blanche over his portfolio, further highlighting that the classic broker–client relationship was one of personal proximity and mutual trust.[97]

After Labour's election victory in October 1964, Noble increasingly began to shift his client's capital from British to foreign companies and the ensuing correspondence gives valuable insight into the contemporary debate over Britain's declining competitiveness. The stockbroker had a negative outlook on British business and advised his client to 'have further funds abroad especially in view of the Socialist Government here'.[98] As a result, Rattigan sold his Unilever shares and went into BASF, a German competitor in the chemical industry. A few months later, Noble pushed this strategy further, advising that '[w]ith the advent

November 1959. Fielding, Newson-Smith & Co were in fact one of the more progressive, medium-sized companies that unsuccessfully lobbied for broking firms to be allowed to advertise. Michie, *The London Stock Exchange*, p. 433.

[95] Noble to Rattigan, 22 April 1960. 'Letters to the Editor: Stamp Duty', *The Financial Times*, 4 May 1957.

[96] Noble to Rattigan, 10 May 1960. David Kynaston emphasizes the importance of City lunches for sharing insider knowledge, Kynaston, *The City of London*, IV, pp. 198–9, 231–2, 470.

[97] Noble to Rattigan, 7 June 1961; Rattigan's private secretary to Colegrave & Co., 17 December 1963: 'Mr. Rattigan will accept Mr. Noble's advice and you can go ahead and reinvest the money without further consultation with Mr. Rattigan.' Noble had moved on to Colegrave & Co. in the meantime, but kept Rattigan as a client underlining further the personal nature of this connection.

[98] Noble to Rattigan, 9 March 1965.

of the Corporation Tax in the Finance Bill [ ... ] I would prefer that you had further funds abroad'.[99] Noble's portfolio management epitomizes the view of the entire City of London. Bankers, stockbrokers, and fund managers regarded British industry as uncompetitive and increasingly sought higher returns abroad on their clients' capital. On the other hand, the Labour Party, trade unions, and New Left intellectuals accused the City of being ignorant of manufacturing's needs and of systematically depriving British industry of much-needed capital. Noble lost a prime client in 1967, when Rattigan moved to Bermuda—he had come to dislike 1960s London—and liquidated his £12,422 share portfolio as well as £32,067 of 3.5 per cent War Loan.[100] What this relationship helps to illustrate beyond the personal character of financial relations and the growing tensions between the City and industry, are the myriad advantages more affluent investors had over investors of more modest means. Stockbrokers were far more likely to share insider knowledge with wealthy clients and might also deal on the account for them, thereby evading transaction costs that conventional dealers had to pay.

Coming back to the Imperial College survey, it is difficult to compare its results with the one commissioned by the Stock Exchange as the former was carried out based on the share register of *one* anonymized 'blue chip' company. In regards to social background, gender, regional distribution, education, and age of investors both surveys came to similar conclusions. The 1968 survey, however, is more important in view of the claims it makes about the behaviour, attitudes, and motivations of the average shareholder. Were Britain's shareholders better characterized as investors or speculators? The London Stock Exchange survey found that only 6 per cent of respondents bought stocks and shares 'for short-term speculative purposes' without further elaborating on its definition of short-term speculation. The majority, 43 per cent, stated to aim for 'capital appreciation' and 40 per cent were 'concerned to receive a steady income' when investing in equities, which was in line with the WSOC survey whose respondents had also listed capital gain before dividends as their prime motive for buying equity.[101] Over a third of respondents in the Gallup poll stated they 'bought shares to take a gamble'.[102]

According to the Imperial College survey, however, Britain's shareholders were far more apathetic and risk-averse. The researchers came to the mixed conclusion that 'many private shareholders are apathetic about their holdings' while nevertheless, 'a substantial proportion do take an active interest in investment matters'.[103] Most respondents listed 'steady income' (54 per cent) and 'hedge against

[99] Noble to Rattigan, 4 August 1965.
[100] Coutts & Co. to Rattigan, 5 and 7 September 1967, 11 November 1967. Coutts were Rattigan's bankers.
[101] London Stock Exchange, *How Does Britain Save?*, p. 28; Research Services Limited, *Savings and Attitudes to Share Owning*, p. 3.
[102] Whiting, 'The City and Democratic Capitalism', p. 105.
[103] Vernon et al., *Who Owns the Blue Chips?*, p. 124.

inflation' (34 per cent) as the 'main attractions' of shares.[104] It found that only 11 per cent of blue chip holders listed 'capital gain profits' as a motivation for equity investment and averred that 'most respondents revoke the idea of shares as a hobby or a gamble'.[105] Findings were frequently backed up with personal statements retrieved from interviews with shareholders such as: 'Only a fool gambles with capital and you don't do this sort of thing as a hobby. I regard investment as a very serious business.' The survey did conjure up a minority of people who did regard investment as a hobby as one respondent recounted: 'I was sick in bed after a coronary for about three months. A stockbroker friend suggested that I pass away the time with a little flutter on the stock market.'[106] Overall, however, the private investor was depicted as risk-averse, prudent, and interested in long-term income.

However, several factors complicate the firm distinction these surveys suggest between sound investment, risky speculation, and reckless gambling. First of all, the Imperial College survey had a selection bias. Shareholders of blue-chip companies—who comprised the sample exclusively—are more risk-averse than investors in growth shares of small and medium-sized companies, which are by nature more volatile and speculative. Then, more generally, we must deconstruct the linguistic peculiarities in Britain's economic language and take into account that many of its terms had a persistently negative connotation. Take for instance the term 'profit', the linchpin of capitalist vocabulary. Bernard Hollowood, the editor of the satirical magazine *Punch*, pointed out that 'even dyed-in-the-wool capitalists shrink from using it blatantly' and instead 'replace it with such euphemisms as margin, gain, balance, earnings, recompense and remuneration'.[107] This applied more specifically to financial terms like 'speculation', which was still surrounded by a whiff of indecency leading even professionals to avoid it. The 1960 City novel, *Bargains at Special Prices,* satirized 'the City convention that "speculation" was as unmentionable a word as "cancer" in an old folk's home'—instead, the group of shady stockbrokers, who were the main protagonists of the novel, 'talked of "avoiding stagnation", "watching trends", "making your money work for you", and so on'.[108] Restrained language of this kind also underlay the 1966 Stock Exchange survey, which claimed that only 6 per cent of British shareholders were speculators, while those 43 per cent who sought 'capital appreciation' were not classified as such. This interpretation strikes as odd

---

[104] Vernon et al., *Who Owns the Blue Chips?*, p. 93.

[105] Vernon et al., *Who Owns the Blue Chips?*, p. 93. However, 27 per cent of respondents listed 'capital gain profits' as a 'secondary transaction'.

[106] Vernon et al., *Who Owns the Blue Chips?*, pp. 93, 85.

[107] B. Hollowood, *Funny Money* (London: Macdonald and Jane's, 1975), p. 62.

[108] A. Clark, *Bargains at Special Prices* (London: New Authors, 1960), p. 20. The author, Alan Clark, gained a reputation as an amateur historian and became the Conservative MP for Plymouth Sutton in 1974, later serving as Minister of State for Trade in Margaret Thatcher's second government. See J. Ure, 'Clark, Alan Kenneth (1928–1999)', *ODNB*, online edn, Oct 2006.

when read against conventional City definitions, according to which 'the specu-lator buys for capital appreciation'.[109] But the Stock Exchange's wariness was probably down to Labour having won the 1964 general election. Naturally it did not want to provide Harold Wilson's government with any evidence that could be used in support of Labour's claim that the Stock Exchange was fostering specu-lation. In a similar fashion, the various guide books by and for small investors would not openly encourage their readers to speculate, but to apply 'intelligent anticipation'[110] or to 'launch out on the high seas of equity investment, trusting in skill and good seamanship to bring us to prosperous shores'.[111]

Against the backdrop of this language regime, survey respondents were also likely to have been reluctant to concede to be 'speculating'. But investors who sought capital gain were basically anticipating to buy low and sell high—and therefore could rightfully be regarded as speculators. At closer scrutiny, it becomes apparent that the 'separation of investment from speculation is not easy'.[112] Several guides for the private investor 'admit[ted] that just as there may be an investment element in most speculations, there is a speculative element in most investments'.[113] Francis Hirst, the erstwhile *Economist* editor and early pioneer of popular capitalism, believed that 'even in an old and conservative country like England the average investor is a speculator in the sense that he not only wishes his investment to yield him interest but also hopes to sell out at a profit'.[114] The two practices were frequently referred to as the 'twin sisters of Stock Exchange activity. By nature closely related, they provide subject-matter for constant debate by moralists, theorists, and economists.'[115] The discursive struggles that unfolded in post-war Britain over the boundaries of these concepts were not just of economic, but social and cultural significance. They are indicative of changing notions of economic prudence, financial morality, and the profit motive more generally. If we want to gain a more accurate picture of the stock market's place in British post-war society, we need to complement the findings of contemporary surveys with an analysis of more open-ended material in a wider historical context.

[109] Quote after H. Withers, *Stocks and Shares*, 4th edn (London: J. Murray, 1948), p. x.
[110] J. P. Warren, *Pounds, Shillings and Sense: A Guide for the New Investor* (Sensible Investments Publications, 1959), p. 43.
[111] Barrada, *How to Succeed as an Investor*, p. 11. In line with these imperial metaphors the author declared: 'The spirit of investment is the spirit of discovery and adventure.'
[112] C. Wallace, *The Investor's Pocket Book* (London: Evans Bros, 1955), pp. 9–10.
[113] Gifford and Stevens, *Making Money on the Stock Exchange*, p. 215.
[114] Hirst, *The Stock Exchange*, p. 164
[115] Armstrong, *The Book of the Stock Exchange*, pp. 151–152. See this allegory also in W. W. Duncan, *Duncan on Investment and Speculation in Stocks and Shares*, 2nd edn (London: E. Wilson, 1894), p. 5: 'Investment and speculation are twin sisters, and so nearly alike that it is almost impossible to discriminate between them. [...] All investments of money are more or less speculations as surely as that all speculations are investments of money.'

## Playing the Stock Market in 'Affluent' Britain

In his detailed study of black markets in wartime and Austerity Britain, Mark Roodhouse has restated the importance of the 'moral dimension of exchange' for historical inquiries into market activity and convincingly dismissed 'the idea that economic activity is in some subtle and fundamental way distinct from social life'.[116] This observation is just as valid for the stock market. Popular forms of investment and speculation were not just affected by changes in Britain's political economy, but by the social and cultural transformations of the post-war period that historians subsume under the term 'affluence'. Arguably the most prominent strand of research under this moniker have been studies on the manifold 'consequences associated with the growth of postwar consumerism' for British society.[117] Historians of post-war 'affluence' have in common that they locate the origins of social change not only on the level of party politics and economic structure, but on 'the inner, small-scale workings of society itself as people went about their daily lives'.[118] This approach continues to go along with a marked focus on consumer practices like spending, shopping, or travelling, often in relation to burgeoning youth cultures.[119]

As a result of this emphasis on the 'consumer citizen',[120] less attention has been paid to the ways in which ordinary people actively appropriated other market practices such as investing, dealing, trading, collecting, or speculating throughout this period.[121] If we assume that the 1950s and 1960s saw 'the erosion of customary restraints on assertive individualism across British society',[122] then foregrounding this neglected, more commercial set of market practices enhances our understanding of this social transformation. More specifically a close examination of ordinary people's involvement in the stock market beyond textual sources lends new support to the assumption that the 1950s and 1960s were a

---

[116] M. Roodhouse, *Black Market Britain, 1939–1955* (Oxford: Oxford University Press, 2013), p. 262.

[117] L. Black and H. Pemberton, 'Introduction: The Uses and (Abuses) of Affluence', in L. Black and H. Pemberton (eds), *An Affluent Society?: Britain's Post-War 'Golden Age' Revisited* (Aldershot: Ashgate, 2004), pp. 1–13.

[118] M. Savage and S. Majima, 'Contesting Affluence: An Introduction', *Contemporary British History* 22 (2008), p. 446.

[119] See for instance K. Bradley, 'Rational Recreation in the Age of Affluence: The Cafe and Working-Class Youth in London, c.1939–1965', in E. D. Rappaport, S. T. Dawson, and M. J. Crowley (eds), *Consuming Behaviours: Identity, Politics and Pleasure in Twentieth-Century Britain* (London: Bloomsbury Academic, 2015), pp. 71–86.

[120] M. Daunton and M. Hilton (eds), *The Politics of Consumption: Material Culture and Citizenship in Europe and America* (Oxford: Berg, 2001).

[121] For a welcome shift of perspective that traces the 'popularisation of antique collecting' and ordinary people rehearsing market practices in the interwar period see H. Egginton, 'In Quest of the Antique: *The Bazaar, Exchange and Mart* and the Democratization of Collecting, c.1926–1942', *Twentieth Century British History* (2016), pp. 159–185.

[122] J. Lawrence, 'Class, "Affluence" and the Study of Everyday Life in Britain, c.1930–1964', *Cultural and Social History* 10 (2013), p. 289.

formative period for the kind of economic individualism that 'fed the shift to neo-liberalism and free market ideology in the 1980s'.[123]

Having sketched the economic scale of share ownership and the social background of Britain's shareholder population, we can now conceive of private investment as a social sphere in which contested debates over the profit motive were argued out. Examining the ways in which legitimate and illegitimate ways of moneymaking were negotiated over time reveals the extent to which economic individualism gained a foothold in post-war Britain. One such debate unfolded over the practice of 'stagging' in the late 1950s and early 1960s. Most people are familiar with the bull and the bear epitomizing the endless ups and downs of the stock market, but the stag is a less commonly known animal in the zoology of finance. The stag is a short-term speculator who targets new issues by trying to subscribe to as many shares as possible, but then merely aims to re-sell allotted stock swiftly in order to gain a quick profit. For this reason, stags complicate reliable surveys on shareholder data as they are not investors in a narrower sense—much less share*holders* from a legal point of view—and yet the stag is certainly a stock market participant. The term was first coined during the 1840s wave of speculation in railway companies for small speculators who bought shares only to sell them on straight away in the hope of a quick profit. Given Victorian aversion against financial speculation, stags always carried a whiff of indecency around them with contemporaries describing them as 'penniless adventurers who could only secure letters of allotment or shares by using fictitious names and false addresses'.[124] Together with the bull and the bear, the stag underscores the importance of 'animal spirits' to stock market behaviour and offers valuable insights into the emotional economy of investment.[125] Observers contended that overall, 'investment, with its element of uncertainty, stimulates the excitability arising from expectation of gain or fear of loss'.[126] Stagging promised an even larger 'thrill', but could also be 'a very hazardous occupation'.[127] Success required the skills of 'an amateur psychologist' because stags do not analyse the intrinsic value of a share, but essentially anticipate the market behaviour of others.[128] This aspect of 'stagging', by the way, illuminates why financial sociologists conceive of speculation as a highly self-referential 'second-order economic observation'.[129] During a new issue boom in the late 1950s and early 1960s, stagging became a

---

[123] Black and Pemberton, 'Introduction', p. 8.

[124] Robb, *White-Collar Crime in Modern England*, pp. 39–40:

[125] 'There has arisen a third brand of Stock Exchange speculator-animal to range himself alongside the bull and the bear—the stag.' B. Whitehouse, *Investing Your Money* (London: Foyle, 1961), p. 70.

[126] Barrada, *How to Succeed as an Investor*, p. 18.

[127] 'Two Rules for Stagging', *The Daily Telegraph*, 7 March 1960.

[128] Naish, *The Complete Guide to Personal Investment*, p. 227.

[129] Stäheli, *Spectacular Speculation*, p. 56.

'popular pastime' and a national 'town and country sport'.[130] But while this new hobby brought pleasure and excitement to some punters, it caused enormous outrage among those members of the financial community who thought of themselves as 'genuine investors' and considered stagging a violation of financial morality.

When journalists set out to profile the average stag during the new issue scramble, they were surprised by the diversity of people engaging in this type of speculation. In 1961, a *Times* story found stags 'grey-suited in country vicarages, tweedy in public school common rooms, bath-chaired at Bournemouth'.[131] The following year *The Guardian* noted that the practice of stagging had 'spread excessively' and 'oddly enough [was] practised more by people of moderate means such as bank clerks, parsons, and suburban housewives, than by speculators in the surtax class'.[132] Apparently there was an 'increasing tendency for investors to stag new issues without the resources to back their application',[133] a trend that most financial observers condemned as dangerous. But proponents of stagging within the speculator's means not only praised it as a 'cheap method of gambling'[134] but pointed out the stag's 'important, if occasionally invidious, part in the mechanism of company launchings'.[135] As with any type of speculation, there were advocates who saw wider economic benefits in stagging; in this case the speculator's pursuance of a short-term profit was held to be conducive to an active and liquid new issue market. One particularly emphatic laud on the stag came from Nigel Lawson, then City editor of the *Sunday Telegraph* and later Chancellor of the Exchequer under Margaret Thatcher, who argued that 'there can be no doubt that on balance the new issue stag [...] is an animal to be cherished. Without him a good many issues might get off to a very sticky start indeed.'[136]

But long-term investors began to take issue with this practice when they increasingly lost out to armies of stags in new issues. Several of them complained in the press that 'the genuine investor is left out in the cold, and what should be a normal business procedure becomes a mad scramble for quick gamblers' profits'.[137] They described scenes of issuing houses being 'besieged by groups of stags with armfuls and case-fulls [sic] of application forms in the process of

---

[130] 'Is L.C.C. paying too much?: An expensive gamble', *The Guardian*, 6 February 1958; 'Stags Lurk in Surprising Places: A Town and Country Sport', *The Times*, 19 May 1961. On the post-war new issue market see D. Chambers, 'Gentlemanly Capitalism Revisited: A Case Study of the Underpricing of Initial Public Offerings on the London Stock Exchange, 1946–1986', *Economic History Review* 62 (2009), pp. 31–56.

[131] 'Stags Lurk in Surprising Places', *The Times*, 19 May 1961.

[132] 'Taxing capital gains', *The Guardian*, 4 April 1962.

[133] 'I.C.F.C. Move to Discourage Stagging', *The Financial Times*, 2 May 1961.

[134] Taylor, *Investment*, p. 116.

[135] J. Rowlatt and D. Davenport, *The Handbook of Saving and Investment* (London: Arthur Barker Ltd, 1965), p. 130.

[136] N. Lawson, 'Talking of Money Stagomania', *The Sunday Telegraph*, 14 May 1961.

[137] 'Letters to the Editor: New Issues and Stags', *The Financial Times*, 24 August 1963.

shuffling their forms into piles, some of these piles being built up on the pavement outside and then handed into the receiving clerks'.[138] Rallying behind the term 'genuine investors' critics decried stagging as 'one of the things which bring[s] the Stock Market into disrepute'[139] and 'which all responsible parties should cooperate to stamp out'.[140] It is worthwhile to quote at length one 'true investor', who criticized stagging extensively in a reader's letter to the *FT* as late as 1973. By that time, the stag's activity had long been curbed to some extent by the introduction of a short-term capital gains tax in 1962, but the reader's intervention highlights the continued appeal of this pastime as well as the resentment it caused. His letter is revelatory as it allows us to flesh out an essentially conservative critique of financial speculation that highlights a tension between private property rights and the responsibility of ownership—two elements that according to advocates of wider share ownership constituted a capitalist society:

> A share certificate is not a mere commodity but a certificate of membership. A company is a living entity affecting the welfare and livelihood of a lot of people. Capital is its lifeblood, and the investor has a proper and honourable part to play in providing that capital. [ ... ] It is no bad thing for members to cultivate a sense of identity with the company and try a little loyalty, rather than behave like soccer fans who cheer wildly in the good times and revile and desert their club when it is down. [ ... ] Playing the exchange is a far more deplorable form of gambling than roulette: and stags, of course, are merely Wembley ticket touts with posher accents. Maximum gain is made the only consideration, a view which not everyone is ready to share. Naturally we all buy hoping that the company will prosper and we may sometimes have to sell, but as true investors we dislike speculators.[141]

It is important to point out the fine line that is being drawn here between legitimate expectation of a fair return for providing industry with an amount of capital, however small, and, on the other hand, a condemnable intangible trade in financial securities for maximum profit. This critique had deep roots in Britain's economic mentality and was in fact much older than the socialist critique of speculation as a parasite of physical labour. James Taylor has portrayed this

---

[138] 'Letters to the Editor: Stagging Menace', *The Financial Times*, 21 May 1966.

[139] 'Letters to the Editor', *The Investors' Chronicle*, 28 April 1961: 'What the small investor complains of is not the balloting but the stags. It is a great scandal that the genuine investor should be held to ransom by these spivs.'

[140] 'Capital Issues: Letters to the Editor', *The Times*, 12 April 1958.

[141] 'Letters to the Editor: Investment Philosophy', *The Financial Times*, 11 January 1973. The then incumbent Heath government sought to compel institutional investors to similar obligations. See Davies, *The City of London and Social Democracy*, p. 41.

'pervasive culture of antipathy to speculation in nineteenth century Britain'[142] that stemmed largely from a romanticized notion of ownership and evangelical morality. According to the latter, financial speculation was a 'godless activity which undermined habits of hard work and thrift' because it resembled gambling in its reliance on chance.[143] Gambling, on the other hand, from an evangelical point of view, 'subverted the meritocratic principles of the Puritan work ethic, in which capital was earned by hard work, talent and deferred gratification'.[144] We can see remnants of this Victorian aversion resurface in the post-war critique of stagging and of speculation more generally, for instance in Margaret Thatcher's aforementioned critique of 'the speculator in shares [ ... ] the person who is making a business of buying and selling shares, not to hold them for their income producing properties, but to live on the profit which he makes from the transactions'.[145] What we can conclude from the post-war debate over stagging, is that, on the one hand, the profit motive was to some extent still tamed by a financial morality that stemmed primarily from a traditional understanding of shares as a form of ownership and a Protestant antipathy towards excessive speculation. According to this notion, speculation perverted the principle of ownership and was merely a disguised form of gambling. On the other hand, however, 'stagging' and other forms of popular speculation carried on in spite of this public morality and, after all, no post-war government undertook deliberate action to curb the stagging of new issues.

## The Church of England Becomes a Player

Simon Green has suggested that 'Britain had ceased to be a Christian country by 1960'.[146] Did religious apprehensions about moneymaking and speculation wane in line with religious belief? It would seem far-fetched to assume a causal link between Britain becoming a more secular society and the growth of shareholder numbers during the post-war period. However, there is a religious side to the history of Britain's changing financial landscape in this period which has not yet been explored. During the 1950s and 1960s, the Church of England became a pioneer of the 'Cult of Equity' and the country's second largest holder of financial securities. Seminal works on the post-war City and the Stock Exchange only touch

---

[142] J. Taylor, *Creating Capitalism*, p. 89. For religious antipathy towards speculation in 19th-century Britain see also B. Hilton, *The Age of Atonement: The Influence of Evangelicalism on Social and Economic Thought, 1785–1865* (Oxford: Clarendon Press, 1991), pp. 115–136; G. R. Searle, *Morality and the Market in Victorian Britain*, pp. 82–86; Johnson, *Making the Market*, pp. 213–214.
[143] Taylor, *Creating Capitalism*, p. 56.     [144] M. Clapson, *A Bit of a Flutter*, p. 20.
[145] *HC Deb* 638, c. 1227, 19 April 1961.
[146] S. Green, *The Passing of Protestant England: Secularisation and Social Change, c.1920–1960* (Cambridge, New York: Cambridge University Press, 2011), p. 32.

briefly upon what contemporaries described as a 'remarkable transformation',[147] while Andrew Chandler has chronicled the Church of England's 'Age of Speculation' in his exhaustive history of the institution during the second half of the twentieth century.[148] But so far the historiography has neglected the extent to which the church's involvement in the stock market helped to dismantle older restraints and weaken traditional Christian suspicion of investment and speculation in the stock market.

After the war, the church intervened once again in the national debate over gambling when yet another Royal Commission on Betting, Lotteries and Gaming was set up from 1949 to 1951. The church repeated its condemnation of horse and dog racing, of football pools, gaming machines—and of the 'gambling transactions of the Stock Exchange'.[149] But the church was also in a dire financial position as many of its assets had lost value due to war damage and inflation. As a remedy, it merged its two previous funding bodies, Queen Anne's Bounty and the Ecclesiastical Commissioners, into the Church Commissioners. This allowed the commissioners to reinvest church funds—the majority of which were in bonds and real estate—and by 1953 the church had become Britain's second largest holder of financial securities after the insurer Prudential.[150] There were two key architects in this restructuring process, the First Commissioner, Sir Malcolm Trustram Eve, and his Financial Secretary, Sir Mortimer Warren, who had 'advised the commissioners that they must take the revolutionary change of investing for growth, including investing in equity shares'.[151] According to Chandler, Eve was 'something of a genius'.[152] A trained lawyer and chairman of many government commissions, he commanded the respect of the archbishop, and the *Daily Mail* approvingly dubbed him the 'Church's No. 1 share buyer' or the 'Man Who Gambled the Church's Money'.[153] His biographer points out that 'Trustram Eve's appointment had been actively sought by the archbishop of Canterbury, Geoffrey Fisher, not least for his ability to bring his experience of modern business to bear on the church's financial affairs'.[154] Warren was a chartered accountant who 'understood the intricacies of the finances and

[147] 'How the Church Doubled its Income in 13 Years', *The Times*, 5 June 1961.
[148] A. Chandler, *The Church of England in the Twentieth Century: The Church Commissioners and the Politics of Reform, 1948–1998* (Woodbridge: Boydell Press, 2009), pp. 34–63.
[149] 'Churches' Views on Gambling', *The Times*, 14 December 1949.
[150] 'Church Income and Property', *The Times*, 12 October 1954; 'Church's S. E. Portfolio', *The Financial Times*, 24 October 1959; 'The Cult of Equity', *The Observer*, 5 April 1959.
[151] 'Obituary: Sir Mortimer Warren', *The Times*, 21 February 1972.
[152] Chandler, *The Church of England in the Twentieth Century*, p. 36.
[153] 'Share Boom Doubles Church Income in 13 Years', *Daily Mail*, 5 June 1961; 'The Man Who Gambled the Church's Money', *Daily Mail*, 20 October 1961.
[154] R. Woolven, 'Eve, (Arthur) Malcolm Trustram, first Baron Silsoe (1894–1976)', *ODNB*.

investments better than any other' and, besides managing the church's wealth, authored a critically acclaimed investment guide.[155]

Writing in the *Stock Exchange Journal* in 1961, Warren explained how the commissioners had come to own £128.1m worth of industrial ordinary shares. In order to protect the church's funds from inflation, ordinary shares now amounted to 33.4 per cent of its entire assets; in addition to 11.9 per cent in gilts and a further 10.8 per cent in corporate bonds, preference shares, and investment trusts, meaning that more than half of the church's income was invested in financial securities. In this context it needs to be noted that the market value of ordinary shares had increased by 70 per cent compared to book value (75.2 per cent to 128.1 per cent). The market value of bonds, on the other hand, had dropped by 10.8 per cent due to inflation (26.8 per cent to 23.9 per cent).[156] By that time, the commissioners were holding annual press conferences where Eve and Warren gave assurances that they were managing the church's portfolio conservatively, favouring long-term growth over capital appreciation and even pursuing an ethical investment policy that forbade holdings in breweries, tobacco companies, cinemas, or the arms industry.[157] There is furthermore evidence that Warren spurned brokers' offers for short-term speculations due to 'political expediency'.[158] But the public eye was not always ready to take such a nuanced perspective and viewed with scepticism that the church had ventured 'onto the ocean of speculation'.[159]

The church's involvement in the stock market became the object of a heated debate for the first time in June 1956. That month the archbishop publicly criticized Chancellor Harold Macmillan's introduction of Premium Bonds which sought to encourage savings through a regular prize draw. At the same time it was rumoured that the commissioners had made an enormous profit in the takeover of the Trinidad Oil Company, of which the church was a major shareholder.[160] Premium Bonds introduced elements of chance into National Savings

---

[155] Chandler, *The Church of England in the Twentieth Century*, pp. 46–47. M. Warren, *Investment for the Ordinary Man* (London: Macgibbon & Kee, 1958); see review in *Sunday Times*, 22 May 1960. The *Sunday Telegraph* called Warren a 'financial wizard', 'Steward of Millions', *The Sunday Telegraph*, 22 March 1964.

[156] M. Warren, 'Number One, Millbank, and the Market', *The Stock Exchange Journal* 6 (1961).

[157] 'No Beer Money', *The Financial Times*, 6 April 1961. Lord Ritchie, the Chairman of the Stock Exchange, alluded to this policy in a joke he shared during a speech at the centenary dinner of the *Investors' Chronicle* in 1960: 'We had a client who was a very rich man [ ... ]. He was a leading light in the Nonconformist Church and a very strict teetotaller. One day we bought him a series of investments which included a parcel of Debenture Stock in the then Niger Company, and after he had held the stock for about six months he found out to his horror that one of the activities of the company was selling beer to the natives. (Laughter). Well this shook him very much, and he got on to us on the telephone, hot foot, and said would you please sell the investment at once—but not below 95. (Laughter).' 'Lord Ritchie's Congratulations', *The Investors' Chronicle*, 17 June 1960.

[158] Chandler, *The Church of England in the Twentieth Century*, p. 49.

[159] Chandler, *The Church of England in the Twentieth Century*, p. 45.

[160] Kynaston, *The City of London*, IV, pp. 108, 114.

and therefore the church, Christian Conservative MPs, and Labour alike—in accordance with traditional Protestant morality—condemned them as gambling.[161] Against the backdrop of its investments, however, the church's criticism appeared hypocritical and in the ensuing debate, Macmillan deliberately blurred the line between gambling and investment in an act of political expediency. In parliament, the Conservative backbencher Charles Mott-Radclyffe assisted his chancellor by arguing that 'that the moral issue ought not to be voiced too loudly by clergy of the Church of England. [ . . . ] Where their investments have been switched from gilt-edged to ordinary shares, that, too, is a gamble.'[162] Both the Conservative MP for Louth, Cyril Osborne, who was a stockbroker by profession, and the Labour MP for Nelson and Colne, Samuel Silverman, criticized Premium Bonds for promising a 'something for nothing' mentality.[163] But Macmillan shrugged off such accusations, stating sardonically that 'I really do not see any great difference between the prize which they [the Church Commissioners] have drawn unexpectedly [from Trinidad Oil] and the prize of a man who might draw a Premium Savings Bond prize'.[164] Later as Prime Minister, Macmillan was more candid wih his chancellor and noted that 'buying equities to the ecclesiastical mind has all the fascination of gambling without its moral guilt'.[165] A *Telegraph* reader from Queen's Park London would have agreed with Macmillan's assessment but did not share the chancellor's penchant for permissiveness. He took issue with the fact that

> No pronouncement has been made by any leaders of the Church on the gradual switch of a large proportion of the funds of the Church Commissioners from gilt-edged securities to industrial equities. Many of the laity believe there is just as much an increase in the gambling element arising from this switch as there is in the switch from Orthodox government saving schemes to premium bonds.[166]

In October 1956, it was confirmed that the church had indeed made a capital gain of £160,000 as a result of the takeover of the Trinidad Oil Company. Eve felt this 'was a most embarrassing thing for us' and spoke of an 'unwanted profit' at the commissioners' first press conference.[167] Somewhat ironically, it was Nicholas Davenport, the *Spectator's* left-leaning City editor, who struck a blow for the

---

[161] B. Harrison, *Seeking a Role: The United Kingdom 1951–1970* (Oxford: Oxford University Press, 2009), pp. 480–481. For the Labour Party's deep-rooted aversion of gambling see G. McClymont, 'Socialism, Puritanism, Hedonism: The Parliamentary Labour Party's Attitude to Gambling, 1923–31', *Twentieth Century British History* 19 (2008), pp. 288–313.

[162] *HC Deb* 554, cc. 1097–1098, 18 June 1956.    [163] *HC Deb* 554, cc. 1093 and 1104.

[164] *HC Deb* 554, c. 1182.

[165] Quote after M. Jarvis, *Conservative Governments, Morality and Social Change in Affluent Britain, 1957–64* (Manchester: Manchester University Press, 1990), pp. 69–70.

[166] 'Letters to the Editor: Church Gambles', *The Daily Telegraph*, 5 June 1956.

[167] 'Church Switched £30m of Investments Last Year', *The Daily Telegraph*, 19 October 1956; 'Church made £160,000 on Oil Deal', *Daily Mirror*, 19 October 1956.

church's investment strategy. He argued that 'the Stock Exchange need the Church Commissioners, who possess accumulated savings, just as much as the Church Commissioners need a Stock Exchange where they can put their savings to work and provide income for their beneficiaries'. Davenport highlighted the ambiguity between stock market investment and Christian ethics, musing that the 'parable of the talents might well be written on the wall of the House of Mammon as well as being framed in the office of the Church Commissioners'.[168] Subsequently, investors regularly employed the parable of the talents to legitimize investment and speculation as in line with Christian moral standards: 'As the parable of the forty talents so forcefully reminds us, money hidden away is sterile. It earns nothing for its owner; it does no useful work.'[169] Naturally, even more outright support came from the City. One senior stockbroker pointed out candidly that 'surely the Commissioners should be aware by this time that when some eight years ago they switched a large proportion of their gilt-edged holdings into equities they inevitably entered the field of speculation'. But, having 'still to encounter one who has taken a capital profit with any feeling of shame', he urged the Church Commissioners not to shun the pursuit of wealth, but to embrace it.[170]

But local parishes did not necessarily share this notion. Throughout these years, Warren had to reply to letters from clergy and laity voicing concern over the church's investments. Chandler paraphrases one clergyman who 'wrote that he had been leading a course on the Church's teaching on gambling, and had found himself asked to talk about the Church Commissioners' "gambling on the Stock Exchange"'.[171] Another struggled to bring in line the archbishop's critique of Premium Bonds with the church's stock market investments, wondering 'whether you [Warren] could give me a little help over this question as I know little or nothing about financial speculation'.[172] One Richmond clergyman was less acquiescent about the commissioners' 'investments and dealings on the Stock Exchange', arguing that '[i]f the essence of gambling is to receive money for which no equivalent service is given, it concerns equally speculation on the Stock Exchange'.[173] In the 'Church oligarchy', however, there was little 'soul-searching' or disagreement over the new financial strategy—the end justified the

---

[168] N. Davenport, 'The Church and the Stock Exchange', *The Spectator*, 2 November 1956.

[169] Cummings, *The Complete Guide to Investment*, p. 10. See also: 'The Stock Market is really one of the few places where the reader, if so disposed, can take literally and put into practice the exhortation in the parable of the talents. Go out and do something with your spare capital; do not dig a hole to put it in.' J. Medomsley, *Opportunities for the Small Investor* (Durham: MEL Publications, 1978), p. 7.

[170] 'Church Profits: Letters to the Editor', *The Daily Telegraph*, 12 November 1956. The author, Marno Slorach, was a senior partner in the stockbroking firm Atchley and Heron.

[171] Chandler, *The Church of England in the Twentieth Century*, p. 54. Unfortunately, according to the website of the Church of England Record Centre, these letters 'have been destroyed in line with standard appraisal procedure'.

[172] Chandler, *The Church of England in the Twentieth Century*, p. 54.

[173] 'Letters to the Editor: Gambling Ethics', *The Daily Telegraph*, 15 June 1962.

means: Eve and Warren sustainably consolidated the church's financial position, allowing it, for instance, to double the average clergy stipend.[174] But the first-hand statements from vicars and worshippers reveal that the commissioners' stock market activity meant predicaments for everyday parish life and must have diluted previously held beliefs in financial morality. All this had effects on the wider investing public. One of its members, Sybil Burrows from Hampshire, encapsulated the consequences of the church's policy for the 'small punter' in the *Daily Mail*: 'It was most gratifying to read of Sir Malcolm Trustram Eve's brilliant gambling on the Stock Exchange on behalf of the Church. Now perhaps we small punters can carry on with our own little each-way bets without fear of criticism from the Church.'[175] The various ramifications of the church's involvement in the stock market urge us to reassess the Cult of Equity. David Kynaston has argued that '[t]he trend would mean, among other things, that the City seemed an irrelevance in the day-to-day lives of most people'.[176] Certainly, the actions of private investors, small and large, became less and less relevant in a market dominated by institutions. But the commissioners' 'widely publicised and widely copied'[177] engagement in the stock market caught the public's imagination and thereby played its part in popularizing share ownership and City affairs more generally.

Britain's gambling public overlapped with its investing public, and related debates were often entangled. This became apparent again during the preparation and implementation of the 1960 Betting and Gaming Act, when the Conservative government clashed again with the church over this sweeping liberalization of gambling laws. Macmillan and his ministers pushed through the legislation against criticism from the Archbishop of Canterbury and the free churches, all of whom branded gambling as a 'social evil' that 'wasted manpower and drained the economy'.[178] Mark Jarvis has pointed out that one of the unintended consequences of Conservative modernization efforts was the rise of 'a powerful commercial gambling market'.[179] But very little attention has been paid to the Act's consequences for Britain's financial landscape. The new legislation effectively legalized the bucket shop—only 21 years after these establishments had been clamped down on in an enormous legal effort. Claire Loussouarn has recently shown how the 1960s gambling reforms technically legalized the practice of betting on the price movements of financial securities without legally owning them, thus laying the foundation for Britain's spread betting industry. As a result,

---

[174] Chandler, *The Church of England in the Twentieth Century*, p. 41.
[175] 'Gambling: Letters to the Editor', *Daily Mail*, 23 October 1961.
[176] Kynaston, *The City of London*, IV, p. 101.     [177] Michie, *The London Stock Exchange*, p. 417.
[178] Jarvis, *Conservative Governments, Morality and Social Change in Affluent Britain, 1957–64*, pp. 66–70.
[179] Jarvis, *Conservative Governments, Morality and Social Change in Affluent Britain, 1957–64*, p. 73.

she argued, 'the Victorian divide between speculation and gambling eroded'.[180] Indeed, an overlooked, but immediate result of the Betting and Gaming Act was the establishment of so-called 'stock market pools'. One of the first, the Mancunian firm Bulls and Bears Ltd, was formed in 1960 and none other than Matt Busby, the legendary manager of Manchester United, was a founding director. Punters could have a 'modest flutter on the Stock Exchange' by picking the most successful shares over a fortnightly period.[181] As with bucket shops during the interwar period, the Stock Exchange fretted about this betting format as it blurred the carefully drawn line between gambling and organized speculation. Lord Ritchie, the Chairman, disapproved that his institution 'should be linked to a sheer gamble'.[182]

But the Victorian distinction between speculation and gambling did not collapse as conclusively during the 1960s as Loussouarn suggests. Shared notions of investment, speculation, and gambling changed more subtly not least because linguistic reservations against profit and speculation persisted in British common parlance. A widely publicized 1962 court case forcefully reminded the British investing public that 'stock market gambling' in everyday use remained a term to denigrate reckless, fraudulent, and indeed criminal financial conduct. That year, Ronald Houlden, a 42 year-old correspondence clerk from Kent, stood trial at the Old Bailey in London and was accused of obtaining more than £4,000 of credit by false pretences from several London stockbrokers. Houlden earned £1,000 a year, meaning that he owed four times his annual salary to various City firms. The defendant, who pleaded not guilty, stated that '[f]or the past two years [i.e. during the enormous bull market] I have been interested in the movement of shares and studying the financial columns of the newspapers'.[183] To the prosecution, however, it was evident that he had been 'speculating and indeed gambling on the Stock Exchange'.[184] Eventually, Houlden was sentenced to a conditional discharge of 12 months for his 'fierce and futile flutter on the Stock Exchange'.[185] The clerk explained: 'I decided to buy some shares in the hope the prices would rise and that I would gain the financial benefit my friends appeared to be having.'[186] Certainly,

[180] C. Loussouarn, 'Spread Betting and the City of London', in R. Cassidy, A. Pisac, and C. Loussouarn (eds), *Qualitative Research in Gambling: Exploring the Production and Consumption of Risk* (New York, London: Routledge, 2013), p. 240.

[181] 'Busby Forms Shares Betting Pool', *Daily Mail*, 15 March 1960; 'New Pool On Stocks And Shares: Mr. Matt Busby a Director', *The Times*, 5 May 1960.

[182] 'Bulls & Bears Pools: Lord Ritchie's Disapproval', *The Financial Times*, 10 June 1960; 'Stocks & Shares Pool Attacked', *The Daily Telegraph*, 10 June 1960.

[183] Quote after 'Clerk Gambled on Stock Exchange', *The Times*, 7 March 1962. See also 'Clerk Gambled on Stock Exchange: Prosecution', *The Financial Times*, 7 March 1962; 'Clerk Used False Names, Say Police', *The Daily Telegraph*, 9 March 1962.

[184] '£4,000 Lost in Boom, Court Told', *The Times*, 3 April 1962; 'Shares man "lost during boom"', *Daily Mail*, 3 April 1962.

[185] '"Fierce and Futile Flutter"', *The Times*, 4 April 1962; 'Fierce flutter was futile', *Daily Express*, 4 April 1962; *Daily Mirror*, 4 April 1962.

[186] 'Clerk Accused of Share Deal Fraud', *The Daily Telegraph*, 3 April 1962.

Houlden represents the very fringes of the stock market. But his statement nevertheless urges us to conceive of 'affluence' not just as a socioeconomic condition that widened the number of investors. 'Affluence' also encompassed a climate of non-economic factors such as social envy, group pressure, or desire for status recognition that also influenced financial decisions and could lead to disastrous consequences.

But the case of Ronald Houlden is revelatory in another regard. In his *History of Financial Speculation,* Edward Chancellor has noted one pattern of speculative manias being that 'the leading speculators [...] are pilloried, stripped of their wealth, and imprisoned. [...] They become scapegoats for the sins of the community and are sacrificed so that normality can return.'[187] To be sure, Ronald Houlden was only a small-time villain and the post-war stock market rally did not result in a financial crash. Nevertheless we can see something similar play out as the 'gambling clerk' was a welcome scapegoat at the end of an extraordinary bull market. The prosecution deliberately pointed out that Houlden made his losses 'at a time of boom when it was almost impossible to lose money on share transactions',[188] thereby highlighting the extraordinariness of the late 1950s bull market. Scapegoating Houlden was thus part of restoring financial normality and a way of appealing to the investing public's virtue and prudence.

Nevertheless, in the wake of rising disposable incomes, the liberalization of gambling and the decline of traditional restraints of investment and speculation, resemblances between the stock market and the world of gambling *did* increasingly shine through in financial discourses. On the one hand, this affinity continued to be a source of moral outrage; either in the form of a left-wing critique of the Stock Exchange as a casino or expressed as a conservative critique of excessive speculation. On the other hand, this was the reason why the stock market fascinated, enthralled and attracted so many people. As mentioned earlier in this chapter, one did not have to gamble recklessly in stocks and shares to enjoy the thrills of equity investment. While high finance was determined to demarcate itself from any gambling accusations, most investors were well aware of the similarities and drew analogies to the turf when explaining the market to a wider audience. Fledgling investors were told that 'there are no "certainties" on the Stock Exchange any more than at a race meeting, even if the odds are very much more in your favour'.[189] But then again, as the same investment guide insisted, the 'uncertainty is one of the fascinations of investment'.[190] More and more it became justifiable and acceptable not only to reap the pecuniary benefits of share investment, but to indulge in 'the fun of watching your own shares

---

[187] E. Chancellor, *Devil Take the Hindmost: A History of Financial Speculation* (London: Plume, 1999), p. 28.
[188] '£4,000 Lost in Boom, Court Told', *The Times,* 3 April 1962.
[189] Whitehouse, *Investing Your Money,* p. 64.       [190] Whitehouse, *Investing Your Money,* p. 41.

perform'.[191] Popular investment guides were perfectly clear about investment having the double function of being economically prudent and entertaining at the same time: 'Investment, in short, has become mass business, or mass entertainment, if you prefer.'[192] Numerous authors advertised the stock market as 'a pleasant as well as a profitable pastime' or 'one of the most fascinating hobbies in the world' that provided an 'exciting daily interest', thereby giving rise to a notion that ran counter to traditional understandings of share*holding* as a form of ownership.[193] One investor from Cheshire elaborated on this aspect in a letter to the *Financial Times*. Replying to a previous correspondent, who had insisted that 'if one must invest, speculate or gamble, Premium Bonds are by far the best', he argued:

> Although a good return on one's investment is an essential, it is not the only criterion; surely the amount of pleasure one gets from the medium of investment is important and explains why people have such diverse investments as stock and shares, stamp and coin collecting, property, antiques, jewellery, paintings, etc.[194]

A large part of the fun was drawn from 'the pleasure of knowing that you have played the game successfully',[195] which for many investors was as important as the prospect of financial gains. If 'intelligent anticipation' was a euphemism for speculation, it was precisely this aspect that could 'make investment such an absorbingly interesting subject, because nothing is more satisfying than to obtain reward from the successful application of one's own common sense'.[196] To some investors, dealing directly in stocks and shares was not primarily a means of providing for old-age or protecting their savings from inflation, but an end in itself.

We can see this gaming approach to the stock market gaining popularity in Britain by the late 1960s. For instance, in 1968 the US investment classic, *The Money Game*, written by the *New York* magazine journalist George Goodman under the pseudonym Adam Smith, also became a critically acclaimed bestseller in Britain, with the *Sunday Times* labelling it the 'the funniest money book of all times'.[197] Goodman was an ardent admirer of John Maynard Keynes—not of the

---

[191]  P. Sergeant, *Money Matters* (London: Bancroft, 1967), p. 121.

[192]  Rowlatt and Davenport, *The Handbook of Saving and Investment*, p. 7.

[193]  ' Investors' Chronicle, *Beginners, Please*, 2nd edn (London: Eyre & Spottiswoode, 1960), p. ix; E. Westropp, *Invest £100: A Guide to Investment*, 4th edn (London: Oldbourne, 1964), p. 9. Barrada, *How to Succeed as an Investor*, p. 17.

[194]  'Letters to the Editor: The Best Bet', *The Financial Times*, 4 May 1968.

[195]  A. H. Thrower, *How to Invest for Profit in Stocks and Shares: A Guide for the Small Investor* (Preston: Thomas, 1961), p. 7.

[196]  Warren, *Pounds, Shillings and Sense*, p. 43.

[197]  Originally published in 1968 by Random House, New York it was distributed in the UK by Michael Joseph Ltd that same year and reached its fourth impression by April 1969. *The Sunday Times* 31 October 1968.

economist, but 'Keynes the writer and speculator'.[198] The book polemicized against the perceived Anglo-Saxon dogma 'that money is A Very Serious Business' and built on Keynes's aphorism that 'the game of professional investment is intolerably boring and over-exacting to anyone who is entirely exempt from the gambling instinct; whilst he who has it must pay to this propensity the appropriate toll'.[199] Note that Keynes spoke deliberately of 'professional' investment, not the investing public as a whole, assuming that 'many Englishmen' still invested 'for income'.[200] But this seems to have changed by the late 1960s. *The Economist*'s review of *The Money Game* reasoned that one side effect of the rise of institutionalized investment was that those who continued to invest directly, increasingly did so for the excitement involved in making your own investment decisions. One of the book's 'serious lessons', according to the magazine, was that 'most private investors are not interested primarily in making money (or they would have their money managed for them) but in getting some other satisfaction out of playing the market'.[201] By that time, the stock market game had already found new, colourful representatives in Britain in a new generation of young and aspiring financiers like Tiny Rowland, James Goldsmith, or Jim Slater who had upended the City's traditional financial order by the late 1960s and early 1970s. Out of this group, Slater was arguably the most illustrious proponent and his dubious career as a financial journalist and corporate raider will be discussed in more detail in Chapter 3. After a three-year spell with the *Sunday Telegraph* as a flamboyant share-tipper, Slater had gained the attention of the investing public and from 1964, took on British companies with his asset-stripping vehicle,[202] Slater & Walker, which he founded with his friend Peter Walker, the Conservative MP for Worcester. In a 1969 interview with the *Daily Mail*, he explained the essence of his investment philosophy:

> Any game you play is a reflection on you, on the way you won or lost. In this game, if you're not making money, then you're not playing the game well. It's the game not the chips. [...] You are pitching your judgment against the market, and it's very pleasant to be right. [...] I eat well, I drink well. I have slightly better suits. [...] I have slightly better holidays. [...] What doesn't change is the game. I find it completely enjoyable. I don't think I could give it up. [...] Having made three million I shall regard myself as having played the game badly if I don't

---

[198] A. Smith, *The Money Game* (London: Michael Joseph, 1968), p. 8.

[199] A. Smith, *The Money Game*, p. 9.

[200] A. Smith, *The Money Game*, p. 159. Keynes contrasted the image of the prudent average English investor with that of the more risk-taking American speculator who would 'not readily purchase an investment except in the hope of capital appreciation',

[201] 'The New World of Adam Smith', *The Economist*, 10 August 1968.

[202] Asset stripping refers to the financial practice of buying an undervalued company with the intention of reselling its assets separately in pursuit of short-term profits.

make six million. [ ... ] I regard it all as an intellectual challenge. You are really playing against yourself, as you do in golf or chess.[203]

We should not underestimate the fascinating appeal of this 'game'. There is a growing consensus among scholars of finance that 'modern capitalism required not only Protestant techniques of self-discipline but also the Dionysian spirit of the gambling table'.[204] Throughout the nineteenth century, institutions like the Stock Exchange demarcated their business from gambling and reinforced this distinction in the interwar period by clamping down on bucket shops and outside brokers. Post-war affluence, however, began to dismantle this Victorian veneer of economic rationalism and capitalist sobriety. As a result of the sweeping social and cultural changes of the post-war decades, an economic individualism took shape in British society that increasingly tolerated the gambling element of the stock market. For a comprehensive understanding of retail investment in post-war Britain, we must take into account that throughout the period, playing the stock market became a popular and socially acceptable hobby of predominantly middle-class households. In turn, the experiences of ordinary people with the stock market as a source of excitement and fascination helped to legitimize the profit motive. However, this trend was by no means all-pervasive, and the reappraisal of the free market had yet to find its expression in Britain's political economy. But analysis of this chapter suggests that by the dawn of the 1960s, attitudes towards profiteering, moneymaking, and speculation had already loosened among many households, families, and individuals—prior to the rise of the New Right, the arrival of monetarism, and the election of Margaret Thatcher which we will turn to in later chapters.

---

[203] V. Mulchrone, 'When making millions is just a game!', *Daily Mail*, 1 January 1969.
[204] Stäheli, *Spectacular Speculation*, p. 27; Chancellor, *Devil Take the Hindmost*, p. 44.

# 3

# The Financial Press and the Investing Public

On Wednesday, 18 December 1957, the stockbrokers Patrick Somerset Gibbs of Sir R. W. Carden & Co. and Albert Samuel Ashby of B. Hansford & Co. were sworn and examined by the Bank Rate Tribunal. This tribunal had been appointed on 18 September of the same year by the Home Secretary, Rab Butler, to inquire 'whether there is any justification for allegations that information about the raising of Bank Rate was improperly disclosed to any person, and whether if there was any such disclosure any use was made of such information for the purpose of private gain'.[1] Gibbs and Ashby were two of many market players who on 1 September 1957 had made substantial profits in the gilt-edged market by selling large amounts of government debt hours before the Bank of England announced a steep interest rate hike from 5 per cent to 7 per cent—when interest rates go up, bond yields rise accordingly and prices fall as a result of the inverted relationship between yield and price of fixed-income securities. Observers took this behaviour as a clear sign that the information had been leaked in advance, allowing insiders to trade accordingly. In their attempt to gather evidence for financial misconduct, the tribunal repeatedly came across the role of the financial press. When the Attorney-General, Edward Milner-Holland, inquired where the stockbrokers had got their information from, they listed the various daily and weekly newspapers which members of their profession consulted. Ashby, who, like many of his colleagues, resided in the 'stockbroker belt' of Surrey, explained to the tribunal how his daily train journey to London included reading the *Financial Times*, the *Times*, the *Mail* and the *Express* and if anybody else has a *Telegraph*, or something like that, I borrow theirs to read the City article'. The tribunal wanted to get a clear picture of this morning habit of City men:

'So instead of doing the crossword puzzle, you study the markets on the train?'
Ashby: 'Yes.'
'And have your daily gamble?'
'Yes.'

The attorney-general was surprised to hear that 'brokers, as it were, take their line from the newspapers, and not the newspapers from the brokers'. He pointed out

---

[1] *HC Deb* 477, *c.* 1149, 14 November 1957, Bank Rate Increase (Tribunal of Inquiry).

*Playing the Market: Retail Investment and Speculation in Twentieth-Century Britain*. Kieran Heinemann,
Oxford University Press (2021). © Kieran Heinemann. DOI: 10.1093/oso/9780198864257.003.0004

that surely as professionals they must be 'closer to the atmosphere of the market than the newspapers'. In reply, Gibbs ventured a more refined explanation of the complex interplay between the financial press and the market, arguing that 'the prices are made by the great body of the investing public, and they take their immediate line more from the newspaper than from brokers'. The tribunal kept stressing that 'the newspapers play a very important part' in guiding financial speculation, and asked the senior stockbroker whether 'the public are more apt to rely on the newspapers than on their brokers'. Challenged in this manner, Gibbs said he 'would not be so disloyal to my own profession as that', but conceded that any member of the investing public may have had 'a chance to see his morning paper before the market opens, but they have not had a chance to speak to their broker by then'.[2] What can this conversation between the tribunal and two stockbrokers tell historians about the relationship between the financial press, the stock market, and its participants?

Eventually, no stockbroker, jobber, or financier was charged with financial misconduct after the Bank Rate Tribunal.[3] But this anecdote illustrates a rare incidence of City elites being pressed to speak openly about the crucial role of the financial press for the markets. Two essential aspects transpire from the conversations between the investigators and the two senior stockbrokers that structure the analytical framework of this chapter. First, smaller investors ranked among the lower end of what Paul Johnson called the 'multiple layers of information and knowledge' that has characterized UK financial markets since the early Victorian period, and 'only some of which were accessible to the public at large'.[4] Although the interwar years had brought new laws of investor protection, small investors of the post-war period continued to be disadvantaged in the stock market due to the prevailing practice of insider dealing—in Gibbs's words, the millions of small holders of government bonds did not have the 'chance to speak to their broker' in time.[5] Well-connected stockbrokers—as the examination of the relationship between the writer Terence Rattigan and his broker has illustrated in Chapter 2—were by the nature of their business far more inclined to share delicate information with more affluent clients. Hence the small investor was sidelined from the tightly-knit information network that permeated the City of London. Second, newspapers were of crucial importance to the investor, whether small or large. What Britain's small investors knew about prices, listed companies, or takeovers, they knew largely from the financial press. But even bigger players had to acknowledge the power of certain newspapers and influential columnists, and their potential to move the market with a scathing headline or a favourable

---

[2] Bank Rate Tribunal, Transcripts of Proceedings, Day 10, 18 December 1957, Mr Albert Samuel Ashby; Mr Patrick Somerset Gibbs, The National Archives, TS 58/3.
[3] D. Kynaston, *The City of London*, IV, pp. 94–101.     [4] P. Johnson, *Making the Market*, p. 195.
[5] For post-war accounts of insider trading see Kynaston, *The City of London*, IV, pp. 172–173; R. Michie, *The London Stock Exchange*, pp. 376–377.

leader—otherwise they would not have read the City pages as eagerly as Ashby described. Therefore, we need to take into account that newspapers do not merely mirror, reflect, or disseminate information about an 'ontological, available, object-ively accessible reality', in this case of the market.[6] Instead, by judging company performances, evaluating market behaviour, and advising the investing public, financial journalism can *create* its own reality with consequences for the market and its participants.

We have discussed the enormous expansion of the financial press from the late Victorian into the interwar period, resulting in the emergence of what Dilwyn Porter has called a new or popular financial journalism.[7] In the post-war decades both the broadsheet and tabloid branches of this trade expanded even further. Again this trend was accompanied by a large intake of new investors once Britain entered an age of mass affluence and left austerity behind, as detailed in Chapter 2. Traditionally, as Wayne Parsons has argued, the financial press had confidently seen 'its role in defining a capitalist language and culture: free markets, individu-alism, profit and speculation'.[8] The post-war generation did so in spite of post-war politics having come to embrace planning, nationalization, and demand manage-ment as new economic orthodoxies. City journalists forcefully challenged political leaders of all parties who attacked the City of London and corporate Britain or expressed doubts over the profit motive.

Britain's financial press catered for multiple audiences within the investing public and in order to account for this complexity, I will scrutinize three different formats and practices of financial journalism that addressed different types of readerships. I will first focus on the educational agenda of Harold Wincott, editor of the *Investors' Chronicle* and influential columnist for the *Financial Times*. Wincott was a leading figure of the New Right and a vocal advocate of wider share ownership and popular capitalism. He tirelessly explained the inner work-ings of the stock exchange to a wider audience, always highlighting the relevance of finance within a broader economic, political, and social context. The second section examines the common journalistic practice of share-tipping. While jour-nalists like Wincott sought—through careful education—to turn their readers into self-reliant decision makers, tipsters aimed to attract readers by giving them immediate investment advice. I will contrast the 1960s share-tipping column of the notorious financial guru, Jim Slater, with Wincott's more didactical approach. This serves to highlight the emergence of a more speculative approach to invest-ment, which I argue is an early indicator of financialization in Britain. With the social historian Jürgen Kocka, we can think of financialization as '[t]he tendency

---

[6] N. Luhmann, *The Reality of the Mass Media* (Stanford, CA: Stanford University Press, 2000), p. 7.
[7] Porter, 'City Editors and the Modern Investing Public, pp. 49–60; Porter, '"Where There's a Tip There's a Tap, pp. 71–96.
[8] W. Parsons, *The Power of the Financial Press: Journalism and Economic Opinion in Britain and America* (New Brunswick, NJ: Rutgers University Press, 1989), p. 41.

to detach economic action from social contexts, the concentration on goals of profit and growth coupled with a simultaneous indifference to other goals' and a growing predominance of 'the autotelic character of capitalism'.[9] The extent to which broader 'masses' were encouraged to participate in the financialization of public culture—or warned of its dangers—is thematized in a concluding section that deals explicitly with the popularization of financial knowledge in the tabloid press.

## Harold Wincott Educates the Investing Public

Post-war contemporaries already dubbed the stark increase in press coverage of financial affairs as the 'most explosive expansion in British journalism since the end of the war'.[10] This enormous growth affected all segments of journalism: up-, mid- and downmarket papers. An important driver behind this expansion was a new flow of advertising revenue, which resulted from financial institutions expanding rapidly in the wake of rising wages and living standards in the mid-1950s. Stockbrokers continued to be banned from advertising by the Stock Exchange Council. But savings banks, building societies, pension funds, life insurances, and unit trusts eagerly competed for prime advertising space in their battle over the disposable incomes of increasingly affluent savers and investors. Though institutional shareholdings were soon to outweigh private investment in financial securities, a steadily increasing amount of Britain's small savers ventured some of their capital directly into industrial shares. Newspaper space dedicated to personal finance matters was a growth sector at this time with more and more households looking for sound advice on mortgages, life insurance, their pensions, and the latest stock market developments.[11] The new interest in City and stock market affairs was a development somewhat contrary to the interventionist character of the post-war economic settlement. Hence, in many ways, financial journalism was a free-market bastion against the mixed economy and many financial journalists and City editors were openly hostile towards the welfare

[9] J. Kocka, *Capitalism*, p. 114. In this context, Kocka also stresses 'the epitome of business transactions that have little to do with production and exchange of goods but that are made above all with money and (in the milieu of) money changers, brokers, banks, stock exchanges', p. 115. Kocka's assessment is built mainly on the empirical findings of G. R. Krippner, *Capitalizing on Crisis: The Political Origins of the Rise of Finance* (Cambridge, MA: Harvard University Press, 2011), who defines financialization more broadly as 'the growing importance of financial activities as a source of profits in the economy' of Western market societies, p. 27.

[10] P. Bareau, 'Financial Journalism', in R. C. Bennett-England (ed.), *Inside Journalism* (London: Owen, 1967), p. 153.

[11] A. Davis, *Public Relations Democracy: Public Relations, Politics and Mass Media in Britain* (Manchester: Manchester University Press, 2002), pp. 60–83; J. Tunstall, *Newspaper Power: The New National Press in Britain* (Oxford: Clarendon Press; Oxford University Press, 1996), pp. 354–362; Newman, *Financial Marketing and Communications*, pp. 174–199.

state and nationalization. Consequently, economic and financial journalists like Samuel Brittan, Peter Jay, William Rees-Mogg, and Patrick Hutber, who rose to fame in the 1970s, have been credited with playing a crucial role in the New Right's economic counter revolution.[12]

But arguably the most vocal and influential voice in this journalistic resistance during the post-war decades was Harold Wincott. Often overlooked by scholars, perhaps because of his early death in 1969 at the age of 62, contemporaries regarded him as the 'doyen of financial journalists'.[13] Having started his career as a statistician for a stockbroking firm, Wincott soon switched to journalism, but for the rest of his career maintained from his first job a penchant for stats, charts, and yield curves. In 1930 he became a subeditor with the *Financial News*, and the paper's championship of popular capitalism was to leave a lasting impact on the young journalist.[14] Eight years later, he was made editor of the *Investors' Chronicle*, Britain's most important investment journal, 'from which platform he emerged as probably the leading financial journalist of the day'.[15] During his time at the *Financial News*, Wincott became a close associate of Oscar Hobson and Paul Bareau, two other high-profile proponents of 'the new breed of columnists who could broaden coverage beyond straightforward market reporting to more general economic analysis'.[16] After the war, in 1955, the three helped set up the Institute of Economic Affairs (IEA), the libertarian think tank and melting pot for disillusioned capitalists, gathering around the Austrian economist, Friedrich August Hayek.[17] Their journalistic contribution to defending free-market capitalism against the perceived socialist threat included authoring popular books that sought to explain to a wider audience the City's key role for British industry and its central place in a capitalist society.[18]

Harold Wincott's political stance defies simple definition. He was right of centre, but harboured deeply anti-paternalistic instincts and was at times progressive. As an editor he set an example with his meritocratic work ethic and was one of the first in his profession to promote female journalists. His obituary in *The Times*, for instance, noted that 'Margot Naylor, the first woman financial journalist and now on the *Daily Mail*, started under him. In those days he [Wincott] had

[12] Jackson, 'The Think-Tank Archipelago', pp. 52–55.
[13] R. Harris, 'Foreword: Harold Wincott—Doyen of Financial Journalism', in G. E. Wood (ed.), *Explorations in Economic Liberalism: The Wincott Lectures* (Basingstoke: Macmillan, 1996), at p. xi.
[14] Porter, '"A Trusted Guide of the Investing Public"', pp. 1–17.
[15] D. Kynaston, *The Financial Times*, p. 126.
[16] J. Tomes, 'Bareau, Paul Louis Jean (1901–2000)', *ODNB*. On Hobson's editorship at the *FN* see Kynaston, *The Financial Times*, pp. 115–120. Both Hobson and Bareau later moved on to the *News Chronicle*.
[17] Parsons, *The Power of the Financial Press*, pp. 93–94.
[18] H. Wincott, *The Stock Exchange* (London: S. Low, Marston, 1947); H. Wincott, *The Business of Capitalism: A Selection of Unconventional Essays on Economic Problems of the 1960s* (London: The Institute of Economic Affairs, 1968); O. Hobson, *How the City Works*, 4th edn (London: Dickens Press, 1954); P. Bareau, *The Future of the Sterling System* (London: The Institute of Economic Affairs, 1958).

to resist the sort of pressure exerted by some City chairmen who sent him invitations for "you or one of your young gentlemen"'.[19] Wincott's staunch belief in economic individualism, which he regarded as 'a fundamental part of the British character',[20] qualified him as one of the most prolific apologists of the post-war Stock Exchange. He regarded a private marketplace for trading financial securities as vital to the national interest, and left no doubt about his belief that it was 'impossible to run a free market without speculation'.[21] Accordingly, he supported the reintroduction of option dealing in 1958 against resistance from the Bank of England.[22] However, at the same time he relentlessly criticized what he regarded as deficiencies in the London Stock Exchange, especially in comparison to its sister institution on Wall Street. For example, during the 1959 bull market, he called for the establishment of a British equivalent to the US Security and Exchange Commission, the supervisory body established as a response to the Wall Street crash of 1929. Such an agency was to curb 'undesirable speculation', which—in his 'old-fashioned, sound-money'[23] attitude—he defined as 'speculation which involved you in greater sums than you could meet *from your own resources* if the speculation comes unstuck'.[24] In a catchy analogy for the Stock Exchange he once noted that 'any efficient sewage system has a nasty smell about it!', and argued that an independent watchdog was required to moderate the stench.[25] As late as 1966 he wrote critically 'that the London Stock Exchange hasn't erected very reliable signposts over an extended period'.[26] He was also suspicious of the self-styled amateurism of the City establishment and pushed for the professionalization of stock market affairs, which gained significant traction in the following decades. In this regard, he helped found the Society of Investment Analysts in 1955, when 'investment analysis was in its infancy in this country and few stockbrokers and merchant bankers had research departments'.[27]

Wincott was an admirer of American capitalism and he saw himself in the tradition of US financial reformers of the Progressive Era, many of whom had been journalists as well and who 'sought to eliminate fraud and unethical dealers, educate the investing public, and rally the broker fraternity to pride in their

[19] 'Harold Wincott', *The Times*, 7 March 1969.

[20] Wincott, *The Stock Exchange Journal*, p. 164.

[21] Wincott, *The Stock Exchange Journal*, p. 164. Wincott grappled a lot with the question of legitimate and unsound speculation, see H. Wincott, 'What is a Speculation?', *The Financial Times*, 20 July 1954; H. Wincott, 'The Speculator', *The Financial Times*, 21 June 1960.

[22] H. Wincott, 'Back to Options', *The Investors' Chronicle*, 30 May 1958.

[23] Kynaston, *The City of London*, IV, p. 45.

[24] H. Wincott, 'S.E.C. (G.B.)?', *The Financial Times*, 17 November 1959. For earlier calls, see for instance, H. Wincott, 'Failures in the Stock Exchange', *The Investors' Chronicle*, 24 November 1956.

[25] H. Wincott, 'The Economic Scene', *The Investors' Chronicle*, 4 March 1960. Sewage analogies were quite commonly applied when explaining and vindicating the Stock Exchange. In the 1870s, Charles Branch, a senior stockbroker had stated that 'the Stock Exchange is a channel, not a filter [and] it argues no fault in the construction of an aqueduct that the water it conveys is often dirty'. Quote after Kynaston, *The City of London*, IV, p. 31.

[26] Kynaston, *The City of London*, IV, p. 173.      [27] 'Harold Wincott', *The Times*, 7 March 1969.

calling'.[28] But perhaps even more important for understanding Wincott and his lasting legacy is the sincere admiration he had for West Germany and the ordoliberalism underpinning its post-war economic miracle, the *Wirtschaftswunder*. Towards the late 1950s he compared Britain unfavourably with the Federal Republic's economic performance in several articles. He especially flagged up the country's apparent thriftiness, which was in perfect line with his own idolatry of thrift as a cardinal economic virtue. Sceptical about the economic consequences of post-war affluence at home, he praised West Germany for having 'one of the lowest consumption ratios and the highest investment ratio in recent years of a group of six European countries and the US and Canada'.[29] By popularizing this 'mounting evidence of the dynamism of the Western European economies' in an increasingly alarmist fashion, Wincott played an active part in bringing about the 'initial postwar declinist "moment" [that] came at the end of the 1950s and early 1960s'.[30]

The resulting obsession with Britain's relative economic decline became a central theme in the New Right's political agenda and so did Wincott's idolization of the West German economy. In the 1970s, leading Thatcherites like Keith Joseph and Geoffrey Howe argued that if Britain was to reverse its economic decline, it would have to draw lessons from the Federal Republic's 'social market economy'.[31] For Wincott and the New Right, contrasting Britain's alleged backwardness with West German economic superiority was a deliberate attempt to mobilize popular sentiment against the post-war social democratic settlement. In this political battle, it mattered less that Germany's middle classes were in many ways—by Thatcherite standards—much less capitalistic than their British counterparts, at least when it came to investing their disposable incomes in the stock market. In spite of the German Christian Democratic government's experiments with privatization and peoples' shares in the 1950s and 1960s, which we will scrutinize further in Chapter 4, retail investment in the stock market was not very common in Western Germany until after its reunification with the East in 1990. This was mirrored in the fact that the Federal Republic's press landscape did not develop a popular brand of financial journalism before the 1990s. Until then, private

---

[28] Cowing, *Populists, Plungers, and Progressives*, p. 38.
[29] H. Wincott, 'How Germany does it', *The Financial Times*, 29 April 1958. See also H. Wincott, 'Germany: Prosperous and Imperturbable', *The Financial Times*, 19 July 1960.
[30] Tomlinson, 'Thrice Denied', p. 235.
[31] See for instance *Why Britain Needs a Social Market Economy: With a foreword by Sir Keith Joseph* (London: Centre for Policy Studies, 1975), which was one of the first CPS pamphlets. See also Richard Vinen's point that 'Conservative enthusiasm for European integration during the 1970s and early 1980s had gone, in part, with a belief that British capitalism had lessons to learn from France and West Germany'. R. Vinen, *Thatcher's Britain: The Politics and Social Upheaval of the 1980s* (London: Simon & Schuster, 2009), p. 189.

investors had to resort to the high-brow *Frankfurter Allgemeine Zeitung*, the pro-business newspaper most closely resembling the *FT*.[32]

In 1963, Wincott was knighted for—as a London stockbroker phrased it in his congratulatory letter—'the extra curricular duties that you have undertaken to disseminate financial knowledge to the uninitiated as well as the initiated'.[33] Likewise, members of the business community praised Wincott's efforts 'over the years to raise the standard of financial integrity in the country and to educate and enlighten investors of all categories'.[34] The list of people who congratulated Wincott on his knighthood is illustrative of his standing among his peers and reveals him as an authoritative figure in the City and Westminster establishment. Patrick Sergeant, the long-time City editor of the *Daily Mail*, labelled him a 'great credit to our craft' and expressed his delight 'that the best of us has been chosen for dignifying in this way'.[35] Among others who heaped praise on Wincott were the Chancellor of the Exchequer, the Chairman of the London Stock Exchange, and several other financiers and Conservative politicians such as the unit trust manager Edward du Cann. Leslie O'Brien, later governor of the Bank of England, outed himself as a Harold Wincott 'fan'.[36]

Arguably the first and foremost reason why Harold Wincott became 'the City's conscience'[37] was his weekly column for the *Financial Times*. It was launched in 1950—the programmatic title of the first article was 'Rediscovering Capitalism'— and continued until his death in 1969.[38] From this platform Wincott intervened in virtually every major financial, monetary, and political debate of the post-war era, heavily criticizing the interventionist direction of both Labour and Conservative economic policy. In the resulting clashes, Wincott's polemic was his strength, but at times he overstepped the mark. There was public outcry, for instance, in 1951 when he called Hugh Gaitskell 'Herr Finanzminister' and again in 1964 when he attacked the tax policy of Nicholas Kaldor, the Cambridge economist and Labour's special economic adviser, saying there had been 'Nothing like it since Mein Kampf'.[39] But normally Wincott blended anti-socialist bite with a genuine effort

[32] M. Kutzner, *Marktwirtschaft schreiben: Das Wirtschaftsressort der Frankfurter Allgemeinen Zeitung 1949 bis 1992* (Tübingen: Mohr Siebeck, 2019), p. 293.

[33] Victor Brooks of Kitcat & Aitken to H. Wincott, 10 June 1963, Harold Wincott Foundation, Archive at the University of Buckingham (hereafter HEW), Item 25: Letters of Congratulations on C.B.E.

[34] Francis Andrew of Unilever to H. Wincott, 10 June 1963, HEW, Item 25.

[35] P. Sergeant to H. Wincott, 10 June 1963, HEW, Item 25.

[36] R. Maudling to H. Wincott, 11 June 1963; Lord Ritchie of Dundee to H. Wincott, 10 June 1963; E. du Cann to H. Wincott, 10 June 1963; L. O'Brien to H. Wincott, 10 June 1963, HEW, Item 25.

[37] Kynaston, *The City of London*, IV, p. 297.

[38] H. Wincott, 'Rediscovering Capitalism', *The Financial Times*, 11 July 1950.

[39] H. Wincott, 'Herr Finanzminister', *The Financial Times*, 7 August 1951; H. Wincott, 'Nothing Like it Since "Mein Kampf"', *The Financial Times*, 15 December 1964. Both articles elicited an enormous amount of responses from readers with most letters supporting Wincott. However, the *Financial Times* rang Kaldor to apologize for Wincott's lapse after Chancellor Jim Callaghan had written a letter of protest. Kynaston, *The Financial Times*, pp. 323–324.

to highlight the intersections between industry and the City, as an article on the tax plans of Harold Wilson's Labour government exemplifies.

> But I would like to see a much better job done to counteract the insidious propaganda of the spotty ones [a metaphor Wincott used for Labour's far left]. I would like it to be made plain to every holder of a with-profit life policy, to every contributor to a company pension scheme, to every vicar and curate whose increased stipends spring from the Church Commissioners' decision in 1948 to buy equities, to every widow the Public Trustee looks after, to every unit-trust investor and investment club member, what the result would have been over the last 20 years if these Socialist ideas had been implemented.[40]

As a rule, Wincott never told his readers which shares to buy, since he did not see it as a financial journalist's purpose to show readers how to make money. Instead, he strove after the Victorian ideal of the 'press as an educational agent', which entailed 'a wide elite optimism in England's institutions',[41] and wanted his readers to make their own political and financial decisions. His articles were educational in ambition and even more so in tone as they often took the form of imaginary conversations between the author and his fictional son.[42] This earned Wincott the reputation of having developed a new, vernacular, and less technical language for the stock market and financial affairs. Alan Jenkins's 1974 *Stock Exchange Story* lauds Wincott for having 'first showed how to educate people in finance and business and investment by means of satire'.[43] At least one of his personal friends was clearly inspired by this pedagogical approach when he told Wincott that he bought 'small holdings in different companies' for his 'three children (now aged 16½, 14½, 12½) to develop their already existing interest in shares'.[44] But not everyone was a fan of Wincott's style. Nicholas Davenport, for example, City editor of *The Spectator*, 'could not stand his conversational articles which began "Hello Son"—"Hello Dad"'. Yet even Davenport credited Wincott for having 'won journalistic fame as the simple, honest guy who stood up against the nonsense of socialism in the City'.[45]

Wincott's personal papers, though piecemeal, allow for a good impression of his professional life, particularly of how he wrote his articles. Needless to say, Wincott was himself an avid investor and speculator who discussed his broad portfolio with his stockbroker once a week and kept meticulous notes on shares.[46]

[40] H. Wincott, 'How to Counteract the Spotty Ones', *The Financial Times*, 31 August 1965.
[41] M. Hampton, *Visions of the Press in Britain, 1850–1950*, p. 69.
[42] See H. Wincott, 'Investmanship', *The Financial Times*, 21 October 1952, for example. Here the father explains to his son the risks and benefits of investment at times of inflation and budget deficits.
[43] Jenkins, *The Stock Exchange Story*, p. 4.
[44] Frank W. [na] to H. Wincott, 8 September 1967, Item 24: Correspondence of Harold Wincott.
[45] Davenport, *Memoirs of a City Radical*, p. 112.
[46] HEW, Item 20: Harold Wincott's Address Book.

But more importantly, his private correspondences reveal that Wincott, who never left a letter unanswered, indeed drew much inspiration from his readers. For instance, they frequently provided him with 'ammunition' for his ongoing personal feud with Nicholas Kaldor.[47] Other issues concerned the supposed inefficiency of the nationalized industries or a 'Campaign Against Capital Gains Tax', initiated by a reader from Luton who feared 'the further subjugation of the middle-class [sic] in aid of communism'.[48] The thrust of these correspondences is revelatory in various ways. It shows that taxation of investment income was regarded as an attack on self-ascribed middle-class values of thrift and deferred gratification. This unrest needs to be seen in the context of the late 1950s 'middle-class revolt', the growing discontent of traditional Tory voters with the party leadership's dirigisme during the 1950s and 1960s.[49] But the relationship between Wincott and his readers also puts into perspective more elitist readings of the financial press that overstate its function of merely interpreting 'the views and values of a more limited and narrower élite', an analysis which downplays a newspaper's 'ability to change the attitudes and opinions of its readers'.[50] Instead, these findings provide empirical evidence for David Kynaston's claim that Wincott's *FT* column 'acquired a devoted following—especially among small investors, whose steadfast champion he was'.[51] In a relationship of mutual inspiration, Wincott mattered to his readers and they mattered to him.

Early on, Wincott discovered wider share ownership as his pet issue. The idea of making Britain a share-owning democracy appealed to him as an educational agenda for liberal capitalism. As early as 1951, he argued the case for wider share ownership as an alternative to nationalization—and curiously lauded the example of Sweden. In spite of the Scandinavian country being the epitome of post-war social democracy, the Stockholm Stock Exchange was running regular public lectures and courses about the workings of the financial system, which turned out to be immensely popular, particularly among female investors. For Wincott, only a broader spread of ownership in industry could 'secure the type of real property-owning democracy which is surely the only answer to the otherwise inexorable drift towards the totalitarian state'.[52] It is not surprising that this radical stance echoed the core message of Friedrich Hayek's *Road to Serfdom* given Wincott's role in setting up the IEA.[53] We do not know whether the

---

[47] Sir Thomas Hutton to H. Wincott, 18 March 1964; Brigadier, A. D. Bridge to H. Wincott, 15 January 1965, Item 24.

[48] J. D. Tigert to H. Wincott, 5 September 1963; E. K. Sandeman to H. Wincott, 'Campaign Against Capital Gains Tax', 14 January 1965, HEW, Item 24.

[49] Green, 'The Conservative Party, the State and the Electorate, 1945–64', pp. 183–186.

[50] Parsons, *The Power of the Financial Press*, p. 3, 7. For a similar line of argument see Davis, *Public Relations Democracy*, pp. 60–61.

[51] Kynaston, *The Financial Times*, p. 226.

[52] H. Wincott, 'Learning to be an Investor', *The Financial Times*, 23 January 1951.

[53] F. A. Hayek, *The Road of Serfdom* (Chicago, IL: The University of Chicago Press, 1944). For Hayek's reception see Jackson, 'The Think-Tank Archipelago'.

Austrian economist, who had famously argued in 1944 that any middle way between capitalism and socialism would end in totalitarianism, had a close relationship with Wincott. In the vein of the IEA, Wincott called for comprehensive tax cuts on investment income, but nevertheless remained sceptical of the government's capacity to bring about popular capitalism. For example, he considered the wider share ownership proposals laid out in the 1959 pamphlet *Everyman a Capitalist* by Conservative MP Toby Low as to 'too paternalistic', because they resembled Labour's 'revisionist' considerations for a state-sponsored unit trust.[54] Instead, in the wake of rising shareholder numbers following the late 1950s bull market, he saw the most promising approach in 'educating this unknown body of new and potential investors about the merits, and possible snags, of share ownership'.[55]

As part of this endeavour, Wincott reshaped the *Investors' Chronicle* (IC) before stepping down as editor in 1959 (he continued to advise the journal until his death). In 1955, due to the 'remarkable revival of interest in Stock Exchange investment by personal investors in the last two or three years' he published for the first time *Beginners' please,* the *Chronicle's* popular investment guide, which reached its fifth edition in 1975. Mirroring Wincott's hard-money principles and adulation of thrift, each edition was dedicated 'to the small investors of Britain, the men and women who have proved they can be trusted to save'.[56] In these books, as well as in the eponymous new column in the print edition of the *IC*, Wincott sought to correct what he felt was the prevailing image of the Stock Exchange: 'a place where wealthy capitalists with top-hats and cigars speculate and gamble, making large fortunes without performing any useful service to the community.'[57] Wincott knew, however, that in order for this to happen, 'the House' had to retreat from its paternalistic attitudes. He acknowledged that 'certain members' wished to 'persuade the lower income groups to save *direct through the Stock Exchange*'. But he was equally aware of those stockbrokers who 'have long ago decided that the small investor is an uneconomic proposition, is more trouble than he's worth'.[58] It was the latter group which he held responsible for 'the failure of the House to move with the times, to get away from the concept that it is still a private club'. Like many of his colleagues, Wincott desperately urged the Stock Exchange to abolish restrictive practices and 're-establish contact with the individual investor'.[59] He proposed to end fixed commissions, which made the handling of

[54] H. Wincott, 'Investment for All?', *The Investors' Chronicle*, 1 May 1959. The Low plan is discussed in more detail in Chapter 4. On Labour ideas for a state unit trust see Jackson, 'Revisionism Reconsidered, pp. 416–440.

[55] H. Wincott, 'Shares for All: The Movement Towards Wider Share Ownership', *The Investors' Chronicle*, 26 February 1960.

[56] Quote after Investors' Chronicle, *Beginners, Please*, p. vii.

[57] Investors' Chronicle, *Beginners, Please*, p. xi.

[58] H. Wincott, 'Can the House Attract Small Savings?', *The Financial Times*, 1 August 1950.

[59] H. Wincott, 'The Stock Exchange of 1978', *The Investors' Chronicle*, 31 January 1958.

smaller deals unprofitable, and to lift the council's ban on advertising for broker members. Last but not least, Wincott insisted on the opening of a long-promised visitors' gallery in the Stock Exchange.[60]

During his lifetime, many of Harold Wincott's efforts were in vain. Britain did not have a financial supervisory body until 1985, when the Securities and Investments Board was established. Furthermore, the Stock Exchange did not allow its members to advertise until 1973, and upheld its fixed commissions of 2 per cent until they were abolished by the Big Bang deregulations of 1986.[61] The London Stock Exchange's persistent conservatism massively hampered the establishment of a US-style retail market for stocks and shares that arguably would have further boosted not only popular investment, but also speculation.[62] Wincott's campaigning against restrictive practices in the City needs to be seen in the wider context of post-war declinism. Like his companions at the IEA and leading Thatcherites after him, he shunned structural explanations of Britain's waning political and economic clout, favouring technical and cultural interpretations instead. Wincott had long viewed Britain to be suffering from the alleged fact that 'share investment in this country has come to be regarded as a spivish business'.[63] For him, the reasons for national decline were 'many and deep-rooted' and the City was part of the problem:

Too much protection, too many restrictive practices all round, insufficient incentives, overfull employment, governments which are too timorous to do what they know must be done, mediocre standards in reporting on the results of investment, and above all, I suspect, our besetting sin of thinking profits and dividends to be immoral.[64]

For Wincott, the solution lay in creating the right tax incentives for thrift and financial risk-taking, in exposing the City of London to international competition and in preaching the moral benefits of capitalism. While many of his assessments and recommendations were specific to the historical moment, the public awareness he created for these themes is arguably his most lasting legacy for the decades following his untimely death in 1969.

---

[60] H. Wincott, 'Silence in the Gallery', *The Financial Times*, 3 March 1953. David Kynaston notes that the Visitors' Gallery was opened 'almost three-quarters of a century after it had been recommended by the Royal Commission [in 1878]', Kynaston, *The City of London*, IV, p. 38. On advertising and commissions see H. Wincott, 'Protecting the Investor', *The Investors' Chronicle*, 12 December 1958; 'The New Small Investor', *The Investors' Chronicle*, 13 March 1959.

[61] On the liberalization of advertising see Michie, *The London Stock Exchange*, pp. 482–484; on fixed commissions Michie, *The London Stock Exchange*, pp. 213–218, 483–484.

[62] Ott, '"The Free and Open People's Market"', pp. 44–71.

[63] H. Wincott, 'The Investment League', *The Financial Times*, 3 July 1956.

[64] H. Wincott, 'Investment: Home and Overseas', *The Financial Times*, 22 February 1966.

Several later Thatcherites like Alan Walters, Chief Economic Adviser from 1981 to 1983, as well as leading financial journalists like Samuel Brittan and Peter Jay, who played a crucial part in making economic liberalism the mainstream of British politics again, cited Wincott as an important source of influence.[65] At the *FT*, to this day Martin Wolf upholds the tradition of the respected financial columnist: male, careful in approach and crunching economic data in order to provide a comprehensive view on market developments rather than tipping money-making shares to his readers. In the year of Wincott's death, the IEA created a foundation in his name with the financial support of friends, benefactors, and readers.[66] Until today, the Wincott Foundation presents an annual award 'for outstanding achievement in economic and financial journalism'[67]—Brittan was the first awardee in 1970; Jay followed in 1973. The foundation also hosts an annual Wincott Lecture, the first of which in 1970 had already made a significant impact: Chicago-based economist Milton Friedman gave a paper on the 'Counter-Revolution in Monetary Policy' and acquainted Britain's political and financial establishment with the theory of monetarism. In his seminal study of the intellectual network behind the *Economic Counter Revolution* of neoliberalism, Richard Cockett states that 'the 1970 Wincott Lecture was very important in the dissemination of monetarism to a wider audience, as were Friedman's frequent subsequent [sic] IEA publications'. He also points out that the audience 'included, amongst others, James Callaghan, the former Labour Chancellor and the politician who, as Prime Minister, would put the control of the money supply at the top of the political agenda in 1976'.[68] Harold Wincott did not live to see the resurgence of economic liberalism that unfolded over the course of the 1970s and which many on the now emergent New Right pursued as an agenda of moral rejuvenation.[69] But his posthumous influence throughout the following decades should not be underestimated.

## 'Capitalist': Jim Slater's 'New Approach to Investment'

Not all readers followed the financial press because they sought to have stock market activity explained to them in a wider political and economic context as provided by the likes of Harold Wincott, Oscar Hobson, or Paul Bareau. Other

---

[65] Parsons, *The Power of the Financial Press*, p. 183.

[66] 'Wincott Foundation', *The Times*, 22 April 1969.

[67] Quote from the website of the Wincott Foundation, available at http://www.wincott.co.uk/about. html. Accessed 19 August 2016.

[68] 'Friedman view of monetary theory', *The Times*, 17 September 1970. Cockett, *Thinking the Unthinkable*, p. 154.

[69] F. Sutcliffe-Braithwaite, 'Neo-Liberalism and Morality in the Making of Thatcherite Social Policy', *The Historical Journal* 55 (2012), pp. 497–520; M. Grimley, 'Thatcherism, Morality and Religion', in B. Jackson and R. Saunders (eds) *Making Thatcher's Britain* (Cambridge: Cambridge University Press, 2012), pp. 78–94.

newspapers—the *Daily Telegraph*, the *Daily Express* and the *Daily Mail* in particular—ran regular tipping columns whose authors gave specific investment advice on what they regarded as money-making shares. Patrick Sergeant, the City editor of the *Mail* and his rival, Frederic Ellis of the *Express*, for instance, developed a reputation as sound advisors of the investing public over the decades.[70] Due to their day-to-day contact with market operators and company bosses, financial journalists had privileged access to sensitive information; a position which they could exploit for their own pecuniary benefit. In the words of Paul Bareau:

> His criticism or commendation can move markets. He is, therefore, always in a position in which he could profit by speculative operations based on the views he expounds.[71]

Tips came in various forms, but mostly they were based on one of the City's most valuable, yet unreliable currencies: gossip and rumours. The memoirs of *Observer* columnist William Keegan, who worked on the *Mail's* City desk in the 1960s, provide a vivid account of the genesis of Sergeant's hotly anticipated 'Share of the Year' tip: 'He went around his staff, asked for our views and then declared, "Well, you are all wrong. I have just been playing squash with the chairman of [a well-known machine tool company] and they are my choice."'[72] Sergeant lived by the motto that 'an ounce of information is worth a ton of theory'.[73] Yet he urged his readers to treat any tip with utmost care: 'Do remember that where there's a tip there's a tap, and the greedy small investor usually pays for the tap'.[74] It was an open secret that, in Sergeant's words, the 'City has always lived by inside information, and still does, however hard the insiders protest to the contrary'.[75] Hence, when it came to acting on insider information, it was widely agreed that the odds were stacked heavily against the small investor as a popular book on the Stock Exchange explained in 1966:

> You must remember that if you, an outsider, start speculating, as opposed to investing, the odds are fairly heavily against you. To begin with, by the time the tip reaches you, it is probably already too late; then, as you are not on the spot you cannot take advantage of a momentary rise to 'get out.'[76]

---

[70] S. Fay, 'Share tippers and financial writing', *The Spectator*, 30 March 1990.

[71] Bareau, *Financial Journalism*, p. 160.

[72] W. Keegan, *Nine Crises: Fifty Years of Covering the British Economy from Devaluation to Brexit* (London: Biteback Publishing, 2018), p. 18.

[73] Keegan, *Nine Crises*, p. 14.

[74] Quote after Porter, 'Where There's a Tip There's a Tap', p. 92.

[75] P. Sergeant, 'Tip for Tap in the City', in A. Ewart and V. Leonard (eds), *100 Years of Fleet Street: As Seen through the Eyes of the Press Club* (London: Press Club, 1982), p. 66.

[76] H. D. Berman, *The Stock Exchange: An Introduction for Investors*, 5th edn (London: Pitman Publishing, 1966), p. 132.

And although investors were advised to 'be on guard against being tempted by the "straight from the horse's mouth" tip'[77] and told that financial columnists were 'neither more nor less reliable than racehorse tipsters',[78] share-tipping remained a common journalistic practice. Between 1963 and 1965, however, the scene was dominated by one particularly flamboyant share-tipper, who wrote a monthly column for the newly-founded *Sunday Telegraph* under the pseudonym 'Capitalist'. The paper's City editor who hired Capitalist at that time was Nigel Lawson, later Chancellor of the Exchequer under Margaret Thatcher. By then, only a few people on the newspaper's staff knew that 'Capitalist' was a young chartered accountant by the name of Jim Slater, who would later rise to fame as a pioneer of investment banking and a notorious asset stripper of post-war British industry.

Jim Slater played a key role in the transformations that swept Britain's industrial and financial landscape during the 1960s and 1970s. David Kynaston, though critical of his methods, acknowledges that 'he already had something special about him' before his City career.[79] Slater was born in 1929, raised in Wembley by modest parents, and later qualified as a chartered accountant. By the early 1960s he had already secured a top position at British Leyland, the car manufacturing conglomerate. In 1964, however,—while still writing 'Capitalist'—he left industry behind and founded Slater Walker Securities (SWS) together with his business partner, the self-made millionaire Peter Walker.[80] At that time, Walker was the Conservative MP for Worcester and had previously worked in the unit trust industry together with fellow MP, Edward du Cann.[81] Slater and Walker's arcane asset stripping vehicle soon began to shake up Britain's financial and industrial establishment in a series of takeover battles. By the early 1970s SWS was valued at £200m and Slater's former employer Nigel Lawson reckoned that 'most people feared having their companies taken over by it more than they feared nationalization'.[82]

In public perception, Jim Slater became the most prominent face of a generation of 'corporate raiders' that personified the transition from the old 'gentlemanly' to the new meritocratic City of London.[83] Other representatives included Tiny Rowland of the mining company Lonrho—whom Edward Heath as Prime Minister deemed to embody 'the unpleasant and unacceptable face of

[77] Warren, *Pounds, Shillings and Sense*, p. 10.
[78] R. Heller, *The Naked Investor: Cautions for Dealing with the Stock Market* (London: Weidenfeld and Nicolson, 1976), p. 19.
[79] Kynaston, *The City of London*, IV, p. 350.
[80] Kynaston, *The City of London*, IV, pp. 350–353.
[81] M. Garnett, 'Walker, Peter Edward, Baron Walker of Worcester (1932–2010)', *ODNB*, first published January 2014.
[82] Lawson gave this assessment in an internal policy document in 1973. See Vinen, *Thatcher's Britain*, p. 118.
[83] For this terminology and a detailed account of the changes it denotes see the chapter 'Old City, New City' in Kynaston, *The City of London*, IV, pp. 117–234.

capitalism'[84]—and billionaire merchant banker, James Goldsmith. Public opinion on these financiers was tremendously polarized. Large parts of the financial press celebrated them as the rescuers of Britain's industrial base, suggesting their entrepreneurial ruthlessness would end the alleged persistence of anti-industrial mentalities in the City and largely family-owned corporations.[85] Critics, on the other hand, condemned Slater's pursuit of moneymaking as an apparent end in itself, and his failure to acknowledge broader industrial or even social considerations.[86] Slater, Rowland, and Goldsmith had close ties to each other. They frequently convened at the Clermont Club in Mayfair, a luxurious gambling club and hotspot for right-wing entrepreneurs founded in 1960 by the extravagant bookmaker John Aspinall, shortly after the Macmillan governments had liberalized gambling laws.[87] Aspinall took pride in hosting what he referred to as 'risk-takers' and was convinced that financial expansion went hand in hand with a certain gambling spirit. In a 1971 interview he characterized his clientele and its activities as follows:

> Some people actually seek risk and they put themselves at risk voluntarily and I think that is a spirit that is to be admired; I think it's the spirit that built the prosperity that everybody in this country is enjoying today; [it] was created by adventurers, by merchant adventurers, by pirates if you like.[88]

To be sure, Slater denied that he was ever an active member of the 'Clermont Set' and claimed to prefer chess or bridge over roulette and card tables.[89] But as we shall see later, Slater was not always too particular about the truth. Either way, his affinity to gaming is crucial for understanding his approach to investment, which

---

[84] *HC Deb* 856, c. 1243, 15 May 1973. 'Mr Heath calls Lonrho affair "the unpleasant and unacceptable face of capitalism"', *The Times*, 15 May 1973.

[85] The argument of anti-industrialism among British elites still holds sway in the financial press. It was recently employed by the *Financial Times* to explain Westminster politicians' apparent indifference towards the consequences of Britain's departure from the European Union for domestic business. See 'The fatal divide for business in Brexit Britain', *The Financial Times*, 13 July 2017.

[86] For a contemporary account in awe of Slater see G. McKnight, *The Fortunemakers* (London: Michael Joseph, 1972); see on the other hand R. Spiegelberg, *The City: Power without Accountability* (London: Blond & Briggs, 1973), p. 172, arguing that Slater's values were 'established essentially by the City, for the City, in the City'.

[87] On gambling laws see Jarvis, *Conservative Governments, Morality and Social Change in Affluent Britain, 1957–64*, pp. 65–85; on Aspinall see R. Davenport-Hines, 'Aspinall, John Victor (1926–2000)', *ODNB*; 'Mayfair's wheel of fortune', *The Guardian*, 16 July 1999.

[88] BBC 2, *The Mayfair Set: Entrepreneur Spelt 'SPIV'*, documentary, 1999. Available at https://www.youtube.com/watch?v=yuN6onlQLNA, (hereafter Mayfair Set) Aspinall interview at 15:02. Accessed 13 December 2020.

[89] Slater recalled in 2006: 'People say I was a member of the "Clermont Set" but it's not true. I was never a frequent visitor. In fact I think I only visited the club about five times. I wasn't heavily into gambling and didn't play at the tables. I enjoyed a game of bridge because more skill is needed.' 'An era was born in Berkeley Square', *Daily Telegraph*, 26 August 2006.

involved frequent dealing, invariably placing shareholder return over long-term business strategy—an approach which Slater simply referred to as 'the game'.[90]

Early in 1963, Jim Slater approached Nigel Lawson and suggested he should write a monthly tipster column for the newly-launched *Sunday Telegraph*. Slater had recently 'discovered the joy—and profit—in share dealing, a hobby he developed while incapacitated with the debilitating effects of a virus'.[91] Lawson was impressed by Slater's proven ability to outperform the market by rooting out undervalued shares in smaller companies. However, this was exactly the reason why the *Sunday Telegraph* was hesitant about engaging Slater as an external contributor. Lawson was well aware that any tipster's leeway for moving the market was enhanced when it came to smaller companies that had fewer shareholders and were therefore more volatile. Were Slater to take advantage of this, he could well place the paper's reputation at stake. Therefore, the new arrival 'agreed orally with Nigel Lawson that I would not, for example, invest a few days before the articles or sell a few days afterwards' as Slater's biographer has him stating for the record.[92]

And so on 3 March 1963 'Capitalist' made his debut, promising a 'highly successful new approach to investment'.[93] Before examining this approach, Slater's chosen pseudonym deserves brief scrutiny. Clearly, it encapsulated the columnist's resentment of the post-war economic settlement. More specifically, it was a jibe against the interventionist revival in Conservative economic policy led by Chancellor Selwyn Lloyd in the early 1960s, which included, for instance, the introduction of a short-term Capital Gains Tax in 1962.[94] But what type of capitalism did 'Capitalist' stand for? Like Harold Wincott, who urged Britons to 'rediscover capitalism', Slater regarded the social democratic order of nationalized industries and interventionist policies as fundamentally wrong. Furthermore, Wincott, and Slater were in tune in so far as they harboured strong free-market instincts and were convinced that Britain's reticence towards the profit motive spelt economic disaster. However, upon closer inspection, they differed substantially in what they regarded as legitimate means of achieving their common purpose. This is demonstrated, for instance, by how Slater earned his first £20,000 playing the markets with

---

[90] V. Mulchrone, 'When making millions is just a game!', *Daily Mail*, 1 January 1969.

[91] 'Jim Slater obituary', *The Guardian*, 22 November 2015. For Slater's early career as a hobby speculator see also Heller, *The Naked Investor*, pp. 164–165.

[92] C. Raw, *Slater Walker: An Investigation of a Financial Phenomenon* (London: Deutsch, 1977), p. 95.

[93] Capitalist, 'A New Approach to Investment', *The Sunday Telegraph*, 3 March 1963.

[94] On this background see J. Tomlinson, 'Managing the Economy, Managing the People: Britain c.1931–70', *Economic History Review* 58 (2005), pp. 555–585; J. Ramsden, *The Winds of Change: Macmillan to Heath, 1957–1975* (London, New York: Longman, 1996), pp. 158–164.

enormous leverage, the details of which he explained in a 1973 interview with *Accountancy Age*:

> I saved about £2,000, and I didn't start investing till I was 32. [ ... ] I borrowed £8,000, so I had £10,000 to invest; and then the £10,000 became £20,000, I repaid the £8,000 which left me with £12,000.[95]

These early dealings earned Slater the status of a 'guru' in the investment community where 'the strength of his share-dealing acumen' became object of many legends.[96] Wincott was also convinced that new incentives for financial risk-taking were needed to reverse Britain's alleged decline and regarded speculation as essential for a functioning market. But trading with borrowed money was exactly the type of speculation which he labelled as 'undesirable' and wished to ban with the aid of a supervisory body. Both columnists fashioned themselves as champions of the small investor. Yet they addressed Britain's investing public very differently. Wincott wished to see speculation delegated to a professionalized body of market operators and envisaged the 'genuine' investor, the small shareholder as an economic citizen who was enfranchised in British industry via his or her investments. The veteran journalist also included the potential investor in his audience whom he wished to convince of the benefits of a 'property-owning democracy'. Slater's 'New Approach to Investment', on the other hand, sought to turn shareholders into share dealers, investors into speculators, and was only concerned with making profits.

At outset, 'Capitalist' laid down nine principles regarding the dividend yield, earnings ratio, and liquidity of companies that were to govern his investment decisions. Besides these rather technical aspects, a ground rule was that 'the company should not be family controlled'. Arguing against the nascent efficient market or random walk hypothesis,[97] Slater stated that 'the market is not perfect: if it were there would be no point in buying one share rather than another'. Shares worthy of consideration for Capitalist's portfolio were to be found 'among the smaller and lesser known companies'. This and the fact that capital was not to be spread over a larger number of shares, led the tipster to concede that there was 'an extra element of risk in my system'. There is a striking resemblance between Capitalist's approach to investment and Slater's practice of asset stripping which he commenced a few years later. The columnist declared that 'capital gain and not income is the real object of the exercise'.[98] This meant that investors were advised

[95]   Raw, *Slater Walker*, p. 75.
[96]   M. Walters, *How to Make a Killing in the Share Jungle*, 3rd edn (London: Sidgwick & Jackson, 1987), p. 2.
[97]   F. Jovanovic, 'The Construction of the Canonical History of Financial Economics', *History of Political Economy* 40 (2008), pp. 213–242.
[98]   Capitalist, 'A New Approach to Investment', *The Sunday Telegraph*, 3 March 1963.

not to buy shares with the intent of generating a long-term income, which contemporaries referred to as 'genuine investment'. Least of all should they identify with the company or its workforce or become emotionally attached to it. Instead, Capitalist and his followers were solely interested in the profits that could be made from buying and selling shares at the right moment. In this column, as in his later dealings, Slater detached financial securities from their underlying businesses and thereby severed the link between finance and industry that Wincott made such an effort getting across. Hence, we can regard the 'Capitalist' column as a harbinger of financialization in Britain.

'Capitalist' was off to a flying start. Within three months the column boasted 'an overall capital appreciation of roughly 30 p.c.'.[99] By its first birthday, the portfolio had appreciated by 48 per cent.[100] Its success made 'Capitalist' tremendously popular. Charles Raw, the chronicler of Slater Walker Securities and himself a former financial journalist, gives an estimate of the column's impact. During his spell as City editor of *The Guardian*, Raw perused the share registers of the companies Slater tipped, and singled out Clear Hooter, a small manufacturing company from Birmingham with about 250 employees. An employee of Clear Hooter remembered Slater tipping the company at a time when it had 'only had about 900 shareholders and the publicity resulted in an increase to around 2,000'.[101] This enormous influence over companies and stock prices earned Capitalist a 'challenger' shortly after the column's first-year anniversary. The reader claimed he could outperform Capitalist with a different selection of stocks—he lost eventually.[102] But the challenger rightfully lamented that Capitalist's tips had the character of a self-fulfilling prophecy, which made it impossible for small investors to get anywhere near the column's success:

It should be pointed out that to some extent your performance is self-generated. In cases where you select shares in narrow markets the price on Monday morning is very often above the price you quote. [...] Another point is that when you do follow your admirable policy of cutting losses, your recommendation to sell a share may cause a downward movement so that once again readers do not benefit at the price you quote. Therefore, readers who have followed your good advice to date have been unable to achieve anything like the performance you publish.[103]

This circumstance of Slater's column is revelatory in two regards. It highlights from a small investor's perspective that the function of the financial press reached

[99] Capitalist, '30 p.c. Profit in under Three Months', *The Sunday Telegraph*, 26 May 1963.
[100] Capitalist, 'Cannon for my Birthday', *The Sunday Telegraph*, 1 March 1964.
[101] Raw, *Slater Walker*, p. 80.
[102] Capitalist, 'Not so much a bear, more a wiser bull', *The Sunday Telegraph*, 10 January 1965.
[103] 'Capitalist—a Challenge', *The Sunday Telegraph*, 22 March 1964.

beyond merely representing or mirroring market information. Share-tipping is one instance in which the financial press creates its own reality, thereby *making* the market—rarely to the benefit of small investors. As it turned out, Slater did break his agreement with Lawson and used 'Capitalist' for his personal gain. Tracking down Slater's name on share registers, Charles Raw was able to prove that he had indeed—in spite of all assertions—'on a number of occasions either bought shortly before tipping, or sold shortly afterwards'.[104]

However, the case of 'Capitalist', whose last column was printed in February 1965, transcends the story of an ordinary share tipster, even that of a fraudulent one.[105] Jim Slater was a forerunner of a new type of financial capitalism. First as share tipster and later as asset stripper, he anticipated many of the changes that reshaped international finance during the 1970s and 1980s: the growing self-reference of financial activity; its disengagement from broader social context; and the emergence of a fast-paced, quixotic trading culture.[106] His first public appearance as 'Capitalist' makes him a progenitor of financialization in Britain and urges us to take seriously the media history of this complex phenomenon. Britain's small investors were the main audience in this narrative and Slater started off by introducing them to his self-referential game of anticipating price movements and spotting market anomalies. For Britain Slater epitomizes the rise of the financial trader more than anybody else. In a 1971 television interview, he was presented as a 'new breed of person in British industry' that does not 'deal with any one thing other than money'. Slater agreed: 'That is in a sense our product. We are concerned with making money. That is what we are trying to do. I regard my prime job, if I can put it that way, as a responsibility to my shareholders to provide for them an increasing return per annum on their capital employed. And this to my mind is what it's all about.'[107] Strictly speaking, however, he was not a trader but a manipulator. He may have promoted a highly speculative approach to investment. But neither was he a speculator in the proper meaning of the term, because he did not take on the risks that genuine speculators carry. Instead he frequently offloaded risk to buyers he had generated himself.[108]

What do Wincott and Slater reveal about the post-war history of British capitalism? Although fellow advocates of free markets, they represent contrasting trajectories of financial capitalism that we need to take into account if we want to get a better understanding of its history. Slater is often depicted as '*the* epitome of new business and new City', but Wincott's case complicates this narrative since he was equally at war with the paternalist and patrician elements of the Old

---

[104] Raw, *Slater Walker*, p. 95.

[105] 'Capitalist and his successor', *The Sunday Telegraph*, 7 February 1965.

[106] For recent accounts that regard this trading culture as a key component of financialization see Foroohar, *Makers and Takers*; J. Kay, *Other People's Money: Masters of the Universe or Servants of the People?* (London: Profile Books, 2015).

[107] Mayfair Set, Slater interview at 23:46.       [108] Raw, *Slater Walker*, p. 98.

City.[109] Unlike Slater, however, Wincott worked towards a regulatory framework that envisaged the Stock Exchange as a private institution, yet fettered by a public watchdog and mandated to build a share-owning democracy by serving the interest of investors small and large. Slater, by contrast, had no stake in this moderated form of democratic capitalism. Contrasting the two protagonists and their notions of capitalism allows us to highlight the temporary availability of more tamed and regulated avenues towards financialization. Wincott exemplifies that not only critics, but also proponents of capitalism made the case for a stronger institutional framework, capable of enforcing a clear set of rules in a bid to spread the benefits of a free-market economy more equally. Paying close attention to these variants allows us to highlight the contingent elements of capitalism's history. Wincott is still widely regarded as an ancestor of British neoliberalism. But there is a significant divergence between his vision of a nation of shareholders and the type of predatory capitalism that Slater promoted first as 'Capitalist' and later pursued as a corporate raider. We shall discuss in chapter 6 the paradox that although the Thatcher governments had intended to realize Wincott's vision of a share-owning democracy, the 1980s came to be more closely associated with Slater's buccaneering, rapacious variant of capitalism.

## Midmarket and Popular Financial Journalism: Frederick Ellis and Patrick Sergeant

Harold Wincott was arguably the most prominent post-war voice in Britain in favour of a popular, free-market capitalism as an economically, socially, and morally desirable order. But it is difficult to ascertain the extent to which his message reverberated beyond his readership, which comprised London-based members of the financial and political establishment and the experienced invest- ors that followed the *FT* and the *Investors' Chronicle*.[110] This type of initiated, urban, and market-attuned milieu is likely to have overlapped with the armchair speculators that followed Slater's 'Capitalist'. But who then catered for the less- moneyed members of the investing public and explained the benefits and pitfalls of stock market investment to lower middle- and working-class audiences? Although the new financial journalism of the late Victorian and interwar period had helped fuel the expansion of share ownership, the 'development of a distinct- ive midmarket pattern of financial journalism only really took place in the 1950s'.[111] In this emerging market, the *Daily Express* and the *Daily Mail* were the two most active newspapers. They competed fiercely over largely provincial

---

[109] Quote after Kynaston, *The City of London*, IV, p. 411.
[110] Kynaston, *The Financial Times*, pp. 299–300.
[111] Tunstall, *Newspaper Power*, p. 358; Porter, 'Where There's a Tip There's a Tap'.

established middle- and lower middle-class readers and the associated advertising revenue, with the *Express* also being more successful at reaching out to working-class readers.[112] The ways in which the two papers addressed these income groups can perhaps be best understood with Thomas Frank's concept of 'market populism', the notion that 'markets were a friend of the little guy; markets brought down the pompous and the snooty; markets gave us what we wanted; markets looked out for our interests'.[113] Accordingly, the core message of Britain's popular financial press was that a free-market economy served ordinary peoples' interests better than the interventionist and welfare-based politics of post-war governments. A similar type of market populism was even peddled by the *Daily Mirror*, the left-leaning tabloid. Its City editor, Derek Dale, likewise sought 'to translate the jargon of the City into language that all will understand' and declared at the height of the post-war bull market that 'there has been a revolution in the savings habits of Britain. No longer is The City the exclusive domain of Big Money'.[114] For the sake of argument, however, the following analysis will focus on the financial journalism of the *Daily Mail* and the *Daily Express*. I will readdress the *Daily Mirror's* role in popularizing share ownership in Chapter 6, when discussing Margaret Thatcher's 'popular capitalism' of the 1980s.

While market populism was the common thread of tabloid City journalism, these papers also revealed crucial differences. For instance, the *Mail* and the *Express* took different stances when negotiating the morality of financial practices and the inclusion as well as the exclusion of lower income classes in and from the stock market. Contrasting the two papers, and their respective City editors, reveals diverse and to some extent opposing approaches to investment. This was partly due to differences in style and personality of these two editors. To be sure, following Adrian Bingham, historians should not treat the popular press as a 'convenient and unproblematic window into society' that 'accurately and unfailingly reflected the "reality" of social attitudes'.[115] We need to bear in mind that personal finance pages of the tabloid press merely convey representations of the stock market, investors, and economic mentalities. As we have seen in Chapter 2, members of the investing public could share a common socioeconomic

---

[112] For the *Mail–Express* rivalry see T. Jeffery and K. McClelland, 'A World Fit to Live in: The *Daily Mail* and the Middle Classes 1918–1939', in J. Curran, A. Smith, and P. Wingate (eds), Impacts and Influences: Essays on Media Power in the Twentieth Century (London, New York: Methuen, 1987), pp. 27–52; on working-class readers see A. Bingham and M. Conboy, *Tabloid Century: The Popular Press in Britain, 1896 to the Present* (Oxford: Peter Lang AG, 2015), p. 178.

[113] Frank, *One Market under God*, p. xiv.

[114] Quotes after Porter, '"City Slickers" in Perspective', pp. 138, 141.

[115] A. Bingham, *Gender, Modernity, and the Popular Press in Inter-War Britain* (Oxford: Oxford University Press, 2004), p. 11. Ranald Michie has called for an equally careful approach to media sources when assessing the public perception of investors: 'These [sources] allow conclusions to be drawn about how investors and their actions were being judged [...]. This testimony should not be taken as an accurate representation of the behaviour of investors,' Michie, 'Gamblers, Fools, Victims, or Wizards?', p. 170.

background, yet still harbour opposing and very complex attitudes towards investment. Revealingly, while newspapers competed over readers of more or less the same income bracket, they also reflected the fine divisions between traditional and more permissive attitudes towards stock market investment. Accordingly, the diversity of the cultural norms and moral assumptions under-pinning the media discourse surrounding retail investing is indicative of an investing public that was more complex than scholars have acknowledged so far.

In 1948, Frederick Ellis became the new City editor of the *Daily Express*, which shortly before the war had superseded the *Daily Mail* as the best-selling mid-market daily.[116] With paper rationing still effective and finance on the political back foot, Ellis would only write two or three City articles per week, their main theme being the consequences of Labour's nationalization programme for Britain's economic landscape (an 'assault on free enterprise').[117] In the 1950s, however, the paper's financial page grew proportionately with the incomes and living standards of its readers. By 1955, Ellis presided over a separate, daily City page, which appeared towards the back of the paper, usually right next to the summary of the races in the sports section. Throughout the 1950s and 1960s, Ellis 'pioneered popular financial journalism', as his adversary at the *Daily Mail*, Patrick Sergeant, would later acknowledge.[118] The *Express* City office received thousands of readers' letters per year and in exchange provided financial advice on housing, insurance, car purchase as well as the stock market. Over the years, Ellis established a reputation as a reliable share tipper who received information 'straight from the horse's mouth' as his 'racing colleagues would say'.[119] But sound advice went along with serious misjudgements, for instance when Ellis strongly advised his readers against buying shares in Northern Songs, the Beatles' highly profitable record company, noting that 'Show Biz is a mercurial one and today's stars are often tomorrow's memories'.[120]

In the same year Ellis started at the *Express*, Patrick Sergeant decided to quit the firm of stockbrokers he had joined a year earlier, in order to embark on what he deemed a more promising career in financial journalism. Like Harold Wincott before him, Sergeant seemed convinced that writing about the City held better prospects than actually working in the markets. He joined the *News Chronicle* in 1948, where the eminent Oscar Hobson took him under his wing. But Sergeant moved on to the *Daily Mail* in 1953 and became its City editor in 1960 with the

[116] Jeffery and McClelland, 'A World Fit to Live in', pp. 27–28; on post-war circulation trends see A. Bingham, *Family Newspapers?: Sex, Private Life, and the British Popular Press 1918–1978* (Oxford: Oxford University Press, 2009), pp. 15–20; also the graphs in Tunstall, *Newspaper Power*, pp. 42, 49, 55.

[117] F. Ellis, 'Socialists plan more take-overs', *Daily Express*, 3 May 1948.

[118] 'Frederick Ellis: Obituary', *Daily Mail*, 9 April 1979. The *FT* also credited Ellis with having done 'much to popularise the reporting of City and company affairs', 'Frederick Ellis', *The Financial Times*, 9 April 1979.

[119] F. Ellis, 'The "tapes" go up next Tuesday', *Daily Express*, 21 February 1959.

[120] F. Ellis, 'Nay, nay, nay', *Daily Express*, 9 February 1965.

clear object of challenging the *Express's* pole position in midmarket investment advice. The soaring advertising income from the now booming unit trust industry—especially that of the Unicorn Trust run by Sergeant's close friend, Edward du Cann—allowed the editor to expand coverage and establish *Money Mail*, the weekly personal finance supplement.[121] In his new position, Sergeant developed an approach very different from that of his earlier mentor Hobson. First, he quenched the post-war investing public's rekindled thirst for share tips, a trend that Hobson viewed 'with alarm, regarding it as one of the "less creditable" development of postwar journalism'.[122] Second, Sergeant dedicated his work to the credo of Lord Northcliffe, the founder of the *Daily Mail*, who had revolution-ized Britain's press landscape with the notion 'that newspapers should captivate readers, amusing and entertaining rather than merely informing them'.[123] Accordingly Sergeant, who throughout his career enjoyed a reputation as a '*bon vivant*',[124] held that his role as City editor was, in turn, 'to entertain, to inform and to advise'[125] his readers.

Ellis and Sergeant shared the strong anti-socialist sentiment that was all-pervasive in the post-war City and financial journalism.[126] Both fashioned them-selves as champions of the small investor and conjured up the social goal of a share-owning democracy in which members of all social backgrounds were to have a stake in British industry. But unlike the City editors of the established newspapers, the popular financial journalists focused more on conveying practical investment knowledge to 'those of limited experience and relatively modest means'[127] rather than explaining the workings of City institutions in a wider economic, industrial, and political context. This included clear warnings that shares were not for everyone. Sergeant's ground rule was to 'put a year's pay in the bank before you buy an Ordinary share'.[128] He warned workers of employee share schemes—since they would lose job and capital if their company went bust—and advised investing in unit trusts instead, thereby keeping his advertisers happy. Nevertheless both *Express* and *Mail* criticized that many of those who did have the financial capacity to invest in shares directly were not encouraged to do so—neither by the government nor by the Stock Exchange. Both wished, for

---

[121]  Personal information by Sir Patrick Sergeant, 31 May 2016.
[122]  Porter, 'Where There's a Tip There's a Tap', p. 82.
[123]  Hampton, *Visions of the Press in Britain, 1850–1950*, p. 40; on Northcliffe's target group see also C. Seymour-Ure, 'Northcliffe's Legacy', in P. Catterall and C. Seymour-Ure (eds), *Northcliffe's Legacy: Aspects of the British Popular Press* (London: Macmillan, 2000), pp. 9–25.
[124]  Nigel Lawson refers to Patrick Sergeant as 'the financial journalist, successful businessman and *bon vivant*'. N. Lawson, *Memoirs of a Tory Radical* (New York: Biteback Publishing, 2011), p. 293.
[125]  Sergeant, 'Tip for Tap in the City'.
[126]  For anti-socialism in the post-war City see Kynaston, *The City of London*, IV, pp. 8–46, 208–209.
[127]  Porter, 'Where There's a Tip There's a Tap', p. 74.
[128]  P. Sergeant, 'Is the Stock Exchange behind the times?', *Daily Mail*, 17 November 1958.

instance, to see the government abolish the stamp duty and stockbrokers to be allowed by the Stock Exchange Council to advertise.[129]

However, Sergeant and Ellis revealed substantial differences when challenging the City establishment and these approaches are revelatory of their general attitudes to investment. On the one hand, Sergeant would criticize companies, but entertain excellent personal relationships with their bosses and the wider City elite. For instance, he reported annually from Ascot, tipping shares based on information he obtained over lunch with the captains of industry.[130] Ellis, on the other hand, was known for his 'style of attacking company bosses' and regularly had an axe to grind with members of the financial elite.[131] The most prominent figure in the editor's firing line was Sir John Braithwaite, the strait-laced Chairman of the Stock Exchange (1949–59), whom he listed among 'the men who have the brakes hard on against the expansion of investment by the little fellow'.[132] Sir John had pledged in 1956 to attract 'a new whole class of investors',[133] but Ellis keenly disavowed this as a meaningless phrase by reproducing the experience of one of his readers in dealing with the Chairman's stock-broking firm, Foster & Braithwaite:

One of our readers, a gentleman from Worthing, wrote to Foster and Braithwaite asking if they would sell some I. and R. Morley shares he holds. And what did Foster and Braithwaite reply to this small investor? Why that 'We regret, however, that before we accept a new client, we require an introduction from clients already known to us.' [ . . . ] The letter was dictated by 'J. D. C. B.'—son of Sir John Braithwaite. Well, I will tell Sir John that this is no way to attract the 'cloth cap' investor that he is so keen on in his speeches.[134]

The episode reveals Ellis as the financial journalist at war with anything in the City that smacked of class-snobbery. In this instance his anger was fuelled further by the chairman's son remarking that the firm's name was mentioned in the *Express* 'without our knowledge or approval'.[135] The Stock Exchange Council in fact reprimanded newspapers for unapproved mentions of members until a 'minor

---

[129] P. Sergeant, 'Budget should help share-buyers', *Daily Mail*, 23 February 1960; P. Sergeant, 'Ten years of do-nothing', *Daily Mail*, 20 March 1962; F. Ellis, 'Drop stamp duty, Mr. Lloyd! And then on with capital gains tax', *Daily Express*, 27 March 1962.

[130] P. Sergeant, 'A good place to find those inside stories', *Daily Mail*, 20 June 1968.

[131] Tunstall, *Newspaper Power*, p. 359.

[132] F. Ellis, 'Cut cost of "cloth-cap" share deals', *Daily Express*, 9 March 1959; the other man was the Chancellor, Derick Heathcoat-Amory. For Braithwaite's mindset of 'hard work & self-denial' and his 'austere cast of mind' that included 'eschewing speculation' and 'dangerous gambling' see J. Slinn, 'Braithwaite, Sir John Bevan (1884–1973)', *ODNB*, 2004.

[133] 'Wider Holdings Of Stocks', *The Times*, 16 March 1956; Reader, *A House in the City*, p. 173.

[134] F. Ellis, 'Sir John brushes off "cloth cap" investor', *Daily Express*, 17 July 1956.

[135] F. Ellis, 'Sir John brushes off "cloth cap" investor', *Daily Express*, 17 July 1956.

relaxation in the rules in 1965'.[136] But the episode further illustrates how little the Stock Exchange had opened up to the wider investing public since the interwar period, in spite of the chairman's progressive statements in the press. Having fretted about the 'stranger' during the interwar years, the bête noire of the post-war Stock Exchange was now the cloth cap investor. The 1964 BBC documentary *Men and Money* includes a revelatory interview with a senior stockbroker recounting doing business with this new class of investors. In one instance, the broker had ordered £200 worth of shares for the client and was astonished by what happened next.

> He literally turned up the next afternoon although payment wasn't due for about 15 days and he turned up with a cloth cap literally—we hear a lot about the cloth cap investor—he literally had a cloth cap on and out he doled his £200 for us [ . . . ] We get some quite funny ones coming into the office—and they know nothing, absolutely nothing and this is a problem as far as we are concerned because the chaps must be protected against themselves, this is frightfully important. [ . . . ] They must first of all have some sort of security like a little money in perhaps the Post Office savings bank, some cash which they can draw on if they're out of work, if anything goes wrong.[137]

This paternalism was an anathema to Ellis. In his audacious, confrontational manner he railed against 'share gamblers' and 'Stock Exchange spivs' with 'shiny toppers' who 'get fat' on takeover deals.[138] But it is important to point out that for Ellis, it was not financial capitalism as a system that was harmful to the interests of the 'ordinary chap', but rather a small, conservative elite at the top of its institutions—not to mention interventionist governments—that constrained the market from benefiting the 'little fellow'. Sensitive to the class-based inequality in the stock market, Ellis claimed to advocate the interests of the 'cloth-cap' or 'genuine' investors who launched moralized attacks on speculative exuberances like the stagging of new issues during the post-war bull markets.[139] Sergeant, on the other hand, avoided moral judgements and nonchalantly envisaged his readership as the 'world's best savers and biggest gamblers'.[140] Accordingly he tailored his advice not only to the needs of the ordinary private investor, whose shareholdings were to provide for his or her old age, but also to

[136] Michie, *The London Stock Exchange*, p. 433.
[137] BBC Online Archive, *Men and Money: The Golden Eggheads*, documentary, 1964. Available at http://www.bbc.co.uk/archive/menandmoney/6803.shtml, interview with unnamed stockbroker at 43:20. Accessed 14 December 2020.
[138] F. Ellis, 'Store investors get quit option', *Daily Express*, 30 July 1951.
[139] F. Ellis, 'Rothschilds put on cloth caps: New unit trust launched with £20 minimum', *Daily Express*, 30 January 1959.
[140] P. Sergeant, 'Is the Stock Exchange behind the times?', *Daily Mail*, 17 November 1958.

the small speculator and 'punter'—those who 'want the fun of watching your own shares perform'.[141]

These images and selective replication of readers' experiences are indicative of the two papers' subtle differences regarding their conceptions of and attitudes towards stock market investment. The opposing conceptions become even clearer if we discuss them by means of a specific example. When the Conservative Chancellor, Selwyn Lloyd, considered the introduction of a short-term capital gains tax in 1961, the idea provoked an enormous outcry in the City and the financial press.[142] The tax aimed at capital gains realized within a period of six months and was eventually introduced in 1962 'as a way of dealing with resentment against speculators in the take-over and property booms'.[143] While Sergeant uttered his disbelief that 'a Conservative Government could possibly approve an impost so penal, so unfair, and so likely effectively to prevent the City becoming the financial centre of Europe', Ellis revealingly took a different line. He repeatedly assuaged concerns against the tax, arguing that '[t]o the ordinary investor who is seeking to protect his capital against the ravages of inflation or to save for his old age a capital gains tax is something that holds no dangers'.[144] He mocked Braithwaite's successor at the Stock Exchange, Lord Ritchie of Dundee, for frantically distributing 4,000 leaflets against the 'coming tax on share gamblers' in the City and concluded: 'This column always supports investors. But the capital gains tax is not to be aimed at investors. Its target will be gamblers.'[145]

At the core of Ellis's and Sergeant's opposition on the matter of capital gains lay fundamentally different notions of the meaning of share ownership. At the *Express*, Ellis promoted a conservative concept that bears witness to the traditional reservations towards financial speculation as well as to the moral anxieties surrounding the stock market's affinity to gambling that still held sway in the post-war decades. According to this notion, industrial shares were not to be regarded an object of trading, but held as a certificate that represented co-ownership in a business. Time was an important factor when determining legitimate and illegitimate ways of financial profit making. Ellis regarded 'genuine investment in British industry' as a long-term commitment to the nation's economy and accordingly flagged up the income-producing qualities of shares for retirement planning or their benefit of providing a hedge against inflation. Short-term speculation, on the other hand, was decried as indecent 'share gambling' and therefore constituted the opposite end of the moral yardstick that the *Express* applied to financial practices. Of course, neither could Ellis justifiably determine

[141] P. Sergeant, *Money Matters* (London: Bancroft, 1967), p. 121.

[142] Kynaston, *The City of London*, IV, pp. 289–292. See also the discussion in Chapter 4.

[143] Daunton, *Just Taxes*, pp. 260–261.

[144] F. Ellis, 'Who's afraid of a capital gains tax?', *Daily Express*, 17 April 1961.

[145] F. Ellis, 'Lord Ritchie has leaflet raid: Warns Governments of Gains Tax', *Daily Express*, 15 December 1961.

what was to be regarded as short- and long-term, but he agreed with the government's benchmark by pointing out that 'the genuine investor does not fear the Capital Gains Tax for he does not often sell under six months'.[146] Evidently, the categories of short-term and long-term as well as speculation and investment are largely arbitrary. But Ellis's conservative definition comes to the fore more clearly when held against that of Jim Slater, who argued in the early 1970s 'that any share he held for as long as three, four or six months was a long-term investment to him'.[147] In fact, Slater stretched conventional notions of 'long-term' even further when stating that 'any share not bought and sold within a two-week Stock Exchange account could be said to be long-term investment'.[148]

Nothing demonstrates more clearly the extent to which the *Daily Mail* departed from the *Express's* conservative notion than Patrick Sergeant's admiration for Jim Slater and his investment philosophy. We do not know what Frederick Ellis thought of Slater; he left the *Express* City office in 1968, enjoyed another three years as the paper's New York correspondent and died in 1979. But Sergeant began to actively promote Slater in 1968, when he strongly advised his readers to invest in Slater Walker's newly set up Invan unit trust, which naturally was 'more speculative than most' since their managers believed in 'changing their holdings often'.[149] In 1971 and 1973, the *Mail* City editor picked Slater and Walker as his 'share of the year' in his annual pre-Christmas tipping column.[150] Even when he later advised against one of Slater Walker's takeovers—that of Samuel Hill, the prospect of which had ruinous consequences for Slater—Sergeant stated that he admired 'them as brilliant traders' and made clear that he held 'foolish the present fashion that damns people who make money but praises those who make things'.[151] Whereas Ellis advocated the concept of share ownership or shareholding in its literal sense, Sergeant essentially promoted share *dealing*: He made this conviction very clear in an article he wrote after having discussed the state of UK shares over lunch with Jim Slater: 'Shares are for buying and selling, not putting away in the old oak chest. There is no such thing as a permanent investment.'[152] More importantly for the context of the early 1970s, Sergeant recited Slater's assessment that 'our shares are between too high and much too high', which is why the financier's 'advice to small investors [was] to weed out shares'. Sergeant's piece, 'one of those rare articles that truly made the financial weather',[153] triggered an enormous wave of selling among small investors, heralding the 1973–74 bear

---

[146] F. Ellis, 'Brokers hit by gains tax plan to quit', *Daily Express*, 12 November 1962.

[147] Raw, *Slater Walker*, p. 94.      [148] Raw, *Slater Walker*, p. 94.

[149] P. Sergeant, 'Go-Go with Shore', *Daily Mail*, 5 April 1968.

[150] P. Sergeant, 'Oh, sunny Jim!', *Daily Mail*, 21 December 1970; P. Sergeant, 'Now face the future with Pearl—and Jim Slater!', *Daily Mail*, 19 December 1972.

[151] P. Sergeant, 'Jim Slater must stop this disastrous bid', *Daily Mail*, 18 June 1973.

[152] P. Sergeant, 'Jim Slater says shares are still too high', *Daily Mail*, 25 January 1973.

[153] Kynaston, *The City of London*, IV, p. 470.

market and once again testifying to Slater's—and Sergeant's—potential to move the market.

Historians seeking to explain why economic liberalism became fashionable again in Britain during the 1970s should take into account that for more than two decades, millions of midmarket newspaper readers had been increasingly exposed to the asserted benefits of free-market capitalism and were actively encouraged to appropriate a popular financial knowledge. In a recent assessment of the entangled relationship between party politics, the financial press, and City institutions, Amy Edwards has contended that the 'newspapers and financial journalists of the popular press, no matter their political allegiances, had an important function regarding the progress of popular capitalism. They helped make the language of the Conservative Party more visible, more profuse and perhaps, even, more believable.'[154] She stresses the primacy of political elites in making neoliberalism, by furthermore arguing that 'Thatcher developed a concept of citizenship which was intrinsically linked to the consumption of capital. And it was this narrative of consumption, present in popular capitalism, which was appropriated by the financial press and financial institutions selling their wares'.[155] The prominent and ambiguous role popular financial journalism played in 1980s popular capitalism will be addressed in Chapter 5. But the findings of this chapter already urge us to reconsider such arguments that play down the agency of financial journalism and underestimate its wider trajectory—one that transcends political attempts to widen share ownership. When it comes to popular capitalism, Britain's financial press was not an echo chamber of Westminster politics—it set the tone of the agenda. Before Conservative politician Noel Skelton promoted the dispersal of industrial shares in his 1920s concept of a property-owning democracy, financial journalists were heralding the 'democratisation of investment'. In the same way, financial journalists during the 1980s did not appropriate the language of Thatcherism, much less the language of consumption. Instead, the Thatcherite rhetoric of thrift, profits, and risk-taking drew from the language financial journalists had been speaking for decades—a language that was brought into the Conservative Party by former journalists like Nigel Lawson.

However we should be wary of an all-too homogenous interpretation of the popular financial press. This chapter has suggested a more nuanced reading by paying close attention to the diverse, at times opposing, notions of stock market investment expressed in the *Daily Mail* and the *Daily Express*. Ironically, the *Express*, viewed as having come to terms more easily with post-war affluence than the *Daily Mail*,[156] upheld traditional stigmas surrounding unfettered speculation in its City coverage. Yet the two prominent tabloids—as well as the *Daily*

---

[154] Edwards, '"Financial Consumerism"', p. 218.
[155] Edwards, '"Financial Consumerism"', pp. 224–225.
[156] Bingham and Conboy, *Tabloid Century*, p. 184.

*Mirror*—shared a market populism that couched stock market investment in powerful terms and metaphors of freedom, democracy, and empowerment. Owing to its simplicity and straightforwardness, this narrative is likely to have had a more compelling appeal to largely middle-class and increasingly affluent working-class audiences than its more technocratic counter-arguments of demand management, planning, and Keynesian fine-tuning.[157] Peter Mandler has urged us to 'evaluate not only the meanings of a text but also its relations to other texts, its significance in wider discursive fields, its "throw", its dissemination and influence'.[158] Many intellectual histories of neoliberalism have emphasized the power of political discourse and the role of academics of the 'neoliberal thought collective' in shaping ideas about the free market.[159] But the columns of Harold Wincott, Jim Slater, Patrick Sergeant, and Frederick Ellis arguably did more to shift British public opinion towards individualism and free-market capitalism than Hayek's *Road to Serfdom*.

[157] For this line of argument see A. Burgin, 'Age of Certainty: Galbraith, Friedman, and the Public Life of Economic Ideas', *History of Political Economy* 45 (2014), pp. 191–219; S. Brandes, '"Free to Choose": Die Popularisierung des Neoliberalismus in Milton Friedmans Fernsehserie (1980/90)', *Zeithistorische Forschungen* 12 (2015), pp. 526–533. Comparing Friedman's TV show *Free to Choose* with Galbraith's *Age of Uncertainty*, which sought to popularize their neoliberal and Keynesian ideas respectively, Burgin and Brandes argue that Friedman was much more successful because of his 'populist persona' and 'the force of the market metaphor', while 'Galbraith never found a way to distill his views in simple and broadly applicable terms', Burgin, *Age of Certainty*, p. 216.

[158] P. Mandler, 'The Problem with Cultural History', *Cultural and Social History* 1 (2004), p. 96.

[159] For this line of argument see D. Stedman Jones, *Masters of the Universe: A History of Neoliberalism* (Princeton, NJ: Princeton University Press, 2012); D. Plehwe, 'Introduction', in P. Mirowski and D. Plehwe (eds), *The Road from Mont Pèlerin: The Making of the Neoliberal Thought Collective* (Cambridge, MA: Harvard University Press, 2009), pp. 1–44.

# 4

# The Politics of Wider Share Ownership

The question of whether ordinary people should own stocks and shares has a longer political trajectory that transcends the history of the Thatcher period. When the idea of creating a property-owning democracy of small shareholders took shape in the interwar period, there was still a consensus among Britain's political and financial elites that ordinary people should stay away from the stock market. By the end of the century, however, politicians welcomed the fact that there were more private shareholders in Britain than trade union members, and investment banks like Kleinwort and Benson had reaped handsome profits from fees for floating nationalized industries on the stock exchange during seventeen years of Conservative reign.[1] Tracing the various ideas for creating a 'popular capitalism' throughout the century refines our understanding of the changing relationship between state and individual in British politics. Revealingly, the idea of wider share ownership had come to appeal to backbenchers from all major parties by the post-war period, but no government took legislative action because schemes were difficult to reconcile with the mixed economy. Housing had become a pressing policy matter after the war and Labour was pursuing an agenda of democratic socialism, prompting advocates of free-market capitalism to make the private provision of affordable homes the cornerstone of a property-owning democracy.[2] In this context, share ownership and housing became two key tenets of anti-socialist ideas that viewed private property as a generator of moral values such as responsibility and thrift, which were considered to be the foundation of a capitalist society.[3]

Recent scholarship has widened our scope on the history of the Conservative neoliberal revival of the 1980s by taking into account a more diverse range of actors other than politicians like Thatcher and her closest allies or intellectuals like the economists Friedrich Hayek and Milton Friedman.[4] In this vein, this chapter

---

[1] D. Parker, *The Official History of Privatisation: The Formative Years 1970–1987* (London: Routledge, 2009), vol. I; D. Parker, *The Official History of Privatisation: Popular Capitalism, 1987–1997* (London: Routledge, 2012), vol. II.

[2] Davies, '"Right to Buy", pp. 421–444.

[3] E. H. H. Green, *Thatcher* (London, New York: Hodder Arnold, 2006), pp. 83–101; Jackson, 'Property-Owning Democracy'; Francis, 'A Crusade to Enfranchise the Many'; see also R. Stevens, 'The Evolution of Privatisation as an Electoral Policy, c. 1970–90', *Contemporary British History* 18 (2004), pp. 47–75.

[4] Edwards, '"Manufacturing Capitalists"'; Rollings, 'Cracks in the Post-War Keynesian Settlement?'.

*Playing the Market: Retail Investment and Speculation in Twentieth-Century Britain.* Kieran Heinemann, Oxford University Press (2021). © Kieran Heinemann. DOI: 10.1093/oso/9780198864257.003.0005

focuses not only on Westminster MPs, but journalists and businessmen of the increasingly influential New Right who advocated a return to economic individualism that was motivated by a perceived decline of allegedly middle-class, bourgeois, or 'Victorian' values. This 'declinism' shaped Thatcherite plans in opposition for a new tax code that would 'allow more direct personal engagement with capitalist enterprise'.[5] Small investors and speculators were expected to provide the risk capital and entrepreneurial spirit deemed necessary for an economic recovery. Eventually, the economic hardship of the 1970s brought a noticeable shift in attitudes towards mass participation in the stock market. Eager to foster a 'nation of shareholders', the Thatcher governments from 1979 implemented many of these reforms such as the 1984 abolition of the tax discrimination against investment income as 'unearned' income.

Throughout the decades, however, policymakers and advocates of wider share ownership realized that stock market investment lent itself not only to an exercise in bourgeois values of thrift and deferred gratification, but could also foster speculation and gambling. The line between prudent saving, beneficial investment, and speculative risk-taking always proved difficult to draw and crossing it demanded careful communication. By paying close attention to these boundaries we can make sense of the inherent tension between moralizing and the more adventurous aspects of investment, which later also characterized the popular capitalism of the Thatcher years.

## The Wider Share Ownership Movement

Britain's post-war era began with a political earthquake. Labour won a large majority in the general election held in July 1945 and the party launched a full-scale programme of nationalization. In the following six years of government, Labour won the argument that key industries and services such as coal, steel, and the railways should be managed in the public interest by civil servants no longer saddled with the need to keep shareholders in line. Labour's corporatist regime and expansion of welfare provision required higher taxes on corporate profits and dividends.[6] As we have seen in Chapter 2, Labour assumed a widespread resentment against high finance and the profit motive across British society—not always accurately—and sought to tap into this mood with public attacks on high finance.

---

[5] M. Daunton, 'Creating a Dynamic Society: The Tax Reforms of the Thatcher Government', in M. Buggeln, M. Daunton, and A. Nützenadel (eds), *The Political Economy of Public Finance: Taxation, State Spending and Debt since the 1970s* (Cambridge: Cambridge University Press, 2017), p. 37; on Conservative plans for tax reform in opposition see A. Williamson, *Conservative Economic Policymaking and the Birth of Thatcherism, 1964–1979*, Palgrave Studies in the History of Finance (Basingstoke: Palgrave Macmillan, 2015), pp. 85–88.

[6] Daunton, *Just Taxes*, pp. 194–228; Whiting, *The Labour Party and Taxation*, pp. 61–90.

During the 1959 election campaign, the party claimed that eight years of Conservative reign had given 'the "expense account" man an easy run, and [let] the spiv and the speculator off scot free'.[7] In the run-up to Labour's return to power, party leader Harold Wilson denounced 'share-pushers take-over bidders, land and property speculators' in the City of London.[8]

The Conservatives Party's conclusion from six years of opposition (1945–51) was to acknowledge the apparent public acceptance of Labour's post-war economic settlement. In the following years, the party's libertarian strand had to carry the blame for the 1945 election disaster. Staunch libertarians like the party chairman and former stockbroker, Ralph Assheton, stood down and a young generation of progressively-minded Tories like Anthony Eden, Rab Butler, and Harold Macmillan gained the upper hand within the party.[9] Having made their first political steps in the 1920s, these 'One-nation Conservatives' concurred with Labour's agenda in so far as they gave priority to full employment and good industrial relations over monetary stability, the traditional creed of Britain's political economy. To be sure, Conservatives continued to be a party of private enterprise, but remained cautious to avoid any impressions of a return to the unfettered capitalism of the interwar period. In the run-up to the 1951 election, Harold Macmillan—by then already very influential on Conservative policy— noted an episode in his diary that illustrates Tory reluctance in this field, especially in view of the City.

> But he [Churchill] raised one most important question of policy. He felt concerned about the stock exchange boom and the general feeling which might be created, and exploited, by the Socialists that the Conservative party was that of business and profits and dividends. Something must be done (from the political point of view) to counter this.[10]

Eden and Macmillan, the next two Prime Ministers, had been personal friends of the Scottish Unionist MP, Noel Skelton, who had been an influential 'middle way' thinker in the 1920s. Philip Williamson has noted that '[Skelton's] ideas appealed strongly to a loose group of younger, idealistic Conservatives in the 1924 parliament [ ... ] who supported the progressive elements in Baldwin's Conservative government against what they regarded as the party's reactionary business

[7] Labour Party, *Your Personal Guide to the Future Labour Offers You* (London, 1959).

[8] Harold Wilson and the Labour Party, *The New Britain: Labour's Plan*, Selected Speeches 1964 (Harmondsworth, 1964), p. 13.

[9] Green, 'The Conservative Party, the State and the Electorate, 1945–64', pp. 179–180.

[10] H. Macmillan, *Macmillan Diaries: The Cabinet Years 1950–1957*, Edited and with an Introduction by Peter Catterall (London: Macmillan, 2003), p. 101.

members.'[11] Chapter 1 has shown how Skelton made his mark as an astute political observer when he published a series of essays entitled 'Constructive Conservatism' in the Spectator in 1923.[12] A gifted writer, he used this platform to unfold his vision of making Britain a 'property-owning democracy', the core of which concept was the spread of industrial shares. At a time when financial observers proclaimed the 'democratization of investment' in Britain, Skelton advocated co-partnership, the participation of workers and employees in industry via share ownership, as a suitable means of bridging the gap between capital and labour. Skelton reminds us that the Conservative Party was occupied with wider share ownership long before Thatcher and we shall see that the party maintained an ambiguous relationship with the issue throughout the twentieth century.[13]

However, we should be wary of drawing an all-too direct line of continuity from Skelton to Thatcher. For one reason, it was not the Conservative, but the Liberal Party which first took up Skelton's ideas and made co-partnership a key social policy in its 1928 manifesto *Britain's Industrial Future*. The Liberal manifesto wished to see an expansion of employee share schemes, 'because it helps to bring about a wider diffusion of ownership' and would mean 'a real advance towards that goal of Liberalism in which everybody will be a capitalist'.[14] This strand continued to shape Liberal policies throughout the post-war period, when the party complained 'that the ownership of industry, like the ownership of property in general, was in the hands of a tiny minority'.[15] Under Jo Grimond's charismatic leadership (1956–67), the Liberals remained a prominent political voice in favour of a society of small shareholders, championing wider share ownership and industrial co-partnership as a road towards a more participatory and less paternalist political economy.[16] But, as we shall see later, Britain's third party had to wait until 1978 for an opportunity to see parts of its long-championed ideal turned into legislation.

---

[11] P. Williamson, 'Skelton, (Archibald) Noel (1880–1935)', *ODNB*. For Skelton's influence on Eden, Macmillan, and Alec Douglas-Home, Macmillan's successor, see also Francis, 'A Crusade to Enfranchise the Many', 277.

[12] N. Skelton, 'Constructive Conservatism IV: Democracy Stabilized', *The Spectator*, 18 May 1923.

[13] 'Whilst it is true that widening share ownership became a mainstay of Conservative policy-making in the 1980s, it is important not to overemphasise the novelty of the Party's concern with share ownership. The broadening of share holding [sic] had formed a central part of the "property-owning democracy" in its original articulation by Unionist MP Noel Skelton in 1923, who saw co-partnership and profit-sharing as a way to distribute property more widely and improve industrial relations.' Edwards, '"Financial Consumerism"', pp. 213–214.

[14] Liberal Party of Great Britain, *Britain's Industrial Future: Being the report of the Liberal Industrial Inquiry* (London: E. Benn Ltd, 1928), pp. 198–204, 249–261.

[15] G. Foote, *The Republican Transformation of Modern British Politics* (New York: Palgrave Macmillan, 2006), p. 100.

[16] G. Sell, *Liberal Revival: Jo Grimond and the Politics of British Liberalism 1956–1967*, University of London, PhD thesis (1996), pp. 52, 194–195.

Foote, *The Republican Transformation of Modern British Politics*, pp. 89–101; S. White, '"Revolutionary Liberalism"? The Philosophy and Politics of Ownership in the Post-War Liberal Party', *British Politics* 4 (2009), pp. 164–187.

The Conservative Party did not incorporate Skeltonian ideas of wider share ownership until its 1947 *Industrial Charter*, which is widely held as an attempt to come to terms with the post-war economic order of nationalization, planning, and social welfare.[17] Written chiefly by the new head of the Conservative Research Department, Rab Butler, the manifesto lauded 'schemes of profit-sharing or employee-shareholding', but stressed that '[s]uch schemes do not by themselves necessarily create good industrial relations; they follow from them'.[18] This position of welcoming a capital-owning democracy on the one hand, but not actively encouraging it on the other, was to encapsulate the Conservative Party's awkward relationship with wider share ownership during its time in office, 1951–64. After returning to power in 1951, first Winston Churchill and then his successor Eden, expressed support for employee share schemes. In opposition Deputy Leader Anthony Eden had already revived Skelton's call for a property-owning democracy and sought to rally the party behind this term as a conservative yet participatory and inclusive alternative to socialism.[19] His biographer notes among Eden's domestic achievements as Prime Minister (1955–57) the 'improvement of industrial relations, through share ownership, employee participation, and profit sharing'.[20] But any legislation was deemed 'extremely complex and technical' and the room for tax cuts 'very limited indeed' with the result that both Churchill and Eden stuck to the passive line spelt out in the *Industrial Charter*.[21]

Towards the end of the 1950s, the party leadership's adherence to economic 'dirigisme' caused a 'middle-class revolt', with the Conservative grass roots becoming concerned that a disengagement from free-market principles would alienate the party's electoral base.[22] In this vein, Tory backbenchers began to advocate wider share ownership both as a bulwark against socialism and a counter project to nationalization. In November 1958 the Conservative MP for Halifax, Maurice Macmillan—the Prime Minister's eldest son—brought into life the Wider Share Ownership Council (WSOC), a group consisting of 'joint stock and merchant bankers, stockbrokers, unit trust and investment trust directors, well-known industrialists, trade union officials, back-bench members of Parliament and others, of every shade, of political opinion interested in spreading the ownership

---

[17] E. Green, *Ideologies of Conservatism: Conservative Political Ideas in the Twentieth Century* (Oxford: Oxford University Press, 2002), pp. 170–171.

[18] *The Industrial Charter: A Statement of Conservative Industrial Policy* (London: Conservative and Unionist Central Office, 1947), pp. 33–34.

[19] Stevens, 'The Evolution of Privatisation as an Electoral Policy, c. 1970–90', 67.

[20] D. R. Thorpe, 'Eden, (Robert) Anthony, first earl of Avon (1897–1977)', *ODNB*, 2004; see also D. R. Thorpe, *Eden: The Life and Times of Anthony Eden, First Earl of Avon, 1897–1977* (London: Chatto & Windus, 2003), p. 340.

[21] R. A. Butler to W. Churchill, Profit-Sharing and Co-Partnership, 18 November 1954; H. Brooke to A. Eden, 7 June 1955, The National Archives (hereafter TNA), PREM 11/2669. See also P. Dorey, *British Conservatism and Trade Unionism, 1945–1964* (Aldershot: Ashgate, 2009), pp. 68–70.

[22] Quote after Green, *Thatcher*, p. 58; in more detail Green, 'The Conservative Party, the State and the Electorate, 1945–64'. See also the discussion in Chapter 3.

of industrial shares'.[23] This illustrious list included Stock Exchange members such as Anthony Hornby, of leading brokers Cazenove & Co, or the legendary jobber Esmond Durlacher.[24] Even Siegmund Warburg, the pioneering merchant banker, was a member of the WSOC. However, these memberships should not be mistaken as an indicator for a broad alliance in the City in favour of wider share ownership. As discussed earlier, influential firms like Cazenove had long inhibited any motions from fellow Stock Exchange members who sought to abolish the advertising ban for brokers and make commissions more flexible in order to reach out to potential retail investors.

The political membership of the council is more noteworthy. Although the council was dominated by Conservatives such as Macmillan and the later party chairman and Unit trust manager, Edward du Cann, the council could boast a cross-party membership throughout the 1960s and 1970s. The Liberal MP for Bolton, Arthur Holt, and Labour's 'expert on financial matters', Harold Lever, both served as vice chairmen at points.[25] Lever was known for his 'commercial acumen', but unpopular within the party's left wing because of 'his reputation for great wealth and his right-wing views on policy'.[26] He would later, in the spirit of the WSOC, publicly oppose Callaghan's 1965 budget for its inclusion of a comprehensive capital gains tax. Besides Lever, many Labour 'revisionists' like Douglas Jay and Hugh Gaitskell, who were sceptical of full-scale nationalization and 'concerned about the consequences of such an approach for flexibility and dynamism', considered wider equity ownership to have an egalitarian potential.[27] Together with the social–liberal economist James Meade, they pondered the idea of a state-run unit trust—a plan that never materialized.[28]

The WSOC lobbied for tax cuts on dividends and capital gains deriving from investment income, and called for the abolition of the 2 per cent stamp duty on share transactions.[29] The lobby group vigorously challenged the 'Fabian consensus' underpinning Britain's tax system, the unequal treatment of 'earned' and 'unearned' income, with a bias towards the former as being morally superior.[30] This differentiation had been introduced in 1907 by the Liberal Chancellor David Lloyd-George, 'on the grounds that [income from investments] was "unearned"

---

[23] M. Macmillan, 'Wider Shareholding', *The Times*, 18 December 1959; founding of WSOC: 'Encouraging Wider Shareownership: Meeting in the City Next Week', *The Times*, 13 November 1958; 'Widening Share Ownership: Meeting at Westminster', *The Times*, 21 November 1958.

[24] On Durlacher's status within the 'House' see Kynaston, *The City of London*, IV, pp. 184–185.

[25] Quote after Davies, *The City of London and Social Democracy*, p. 117; on Lever and Holt in the WSOC see R. Whiting, 'The City and Democratic Capitalism', p. 101.

[26] E. Dell, 'Lever, (Norman) Harold, Baron Lever of Manchester (1914–1995)', *ODNB*.

[27] Quote after Daunton, *Just Taxes*, p. 364.

[28] B. Jackson, 'Revisionism Reconsidered'; R. Whiting, 'The City and Democratic Capitalism', p. 104.

[29] Wider Share Ownership Council, *Growth in a Responsible Society* (London, 1961); Wider Share Ownership Council, *The Shareholder's Rights and Responsibilities* (London, 1963).

[30] C. Munro, 'The Fiscal Politics of Savings and Share Ownership in Britain, 1970–1980', *The Historical Journal* 55 (2012), pp. 757–778.

by active exertion, imposing a parasitical drain of rents and interest payments on enterprising members of society'.[31] Notions of entrepreneurialism and how the tax system could reward risk-taking remained highly contested over time, the unequal tax treatment of 'unearned' income, for instance, coming under frequent attack by the financial press, Tory backbenchers, and libertarian think tanks.[32]

When the stock market underwent its second post-war bull market in the late 1950s, the WSOC sought to capitalize on this momentum. Fuelled by full employment, economic growth, and rising wages, the boom in stocks and shares resulted in a large intake of small investors and a growth in employee share schemes as laid out in Chapter 2. These trends caused anxiety and criticism on the left. Senior Labour politicians launched public attacks on the Stock Exchange. The trade unionist Labour Research Department published a *Poor Man's Guide to the Stock Exchange*, warning that working-class share ownership threatened 'to undermine trade union solidarity by making the workers feel that they have a stake in the success of capitalism'.[33] In light of the late 1950s share fever, the Chancellor of the Exchequer, Peter Thorneycroft, pointed out to his Prime Minister, Harold Macmillan, that '[w]e must now decide whether to take a positive line on this, or whether we should deliberately leave these various schemes to evolve on their own'. Macmillan agreed to set up a working group at the Treasury in order 'to study the whole question urgently'.[34]

This 'Committee on Wider Ownership of Shares in Industry' began its work in January 1959. Parallel to the Treasury committee, the Conservative Political Centre (CPC) set up a taskforce on wider share ownership chaired by Sir Toby Low, the MP for Blackpool North. Low had been appointed minister of state at the Board of Trade under Churchill, but 'in January 1957 left office at his own request to seek better-paid work in the City'.[35] He remained an MP and was a founding member of the WSOC. Low was supposed to become the group's chairman instead of Maurice Macmillan, but stepped back as he was appointed the Conservative Party's deputy chairman shortly afterwards. Nevertheless he oversaw the policy work of the CPC taskforce, which in April 1959 resulted in the publication of a pamphlet carrying the telling title *Everyman a Capitalist*.[36] The Low group called for wide-ranging tax incentives for equity investment in order to

---

[31] Daunton, *Just Taxes*, p. 23.

[32] Munro, 'The Fiscal Politics of Savings and Share Ownership in Britain, 1970–1980', 758: 'The notion that income accruing to one person might have been earned in part by another had been adopted by the Fabians to promote state control, but gained traction during the first half of the twentieth century, especially in relation to income arising from investments. Wide acceptance of this moral judgement underpinned the differential income tax rules that prevailed until the 1980s.'

[33] F. Simmery, *The Poor Man's Guide to the Stock Exchange* (London: Labour Research Department, 1959), p. 55.

[34] P. Thorneycroft to H. Macmillan, 21 November 1958, TNA, PREM 11/2669.

[35] J. Ure, 'Low, Austin Richard William [Toby], first Baron Aldington (1914–2000)', *ODNB*.

[36] 'Call for Incentive to Buy Shares: Sir Toby Low's Aim of "Everyman a Capitalist"', *The Times*, 14 April 1959; see also Green, *Thatcher*, p. 88.

'promote a wider understanding of the working of the free enterprise system' and to 'tap a new source of saving for industry'.[37] But the document is revelatory in another regard, since it highlights the Conservative Party's careful approach when challenging the post-war economic settlement. Considerate of the stock market's bullish outlook and the heated political situation, the authors wished Britain to become a 'share-owning democracy', but felt the need to stress that they were 'concerned here with investment and not with speculation'.[38]

The late 1950s prominence of wider share ownership among free-market liberals as a way of boosting Britain's investment rate coincided with the growing awareness that Britain lagged behind its European competitors in this regard.[39] We have already seen how declinist commentators like Harold Wincott advocated popular capitalism as a means of tackling Britain's proclivity for over-consumption and its relatively low economic growth. In 1961, the Tory financial expert and WSOC member, William Clark, picked up on this in another early proposal for wider share ownership published by the Junior Carlton Club. Like Wincott, he compared Britain's investment rate of 19 per cent unfavourably against Germany's 29.1 per cent, yielding 1.6 per cent and 4.3 per cent of economic growth respectively.[40] Clark argued that 'capital investment is a key factor in economic growth' and 'that we are spending too much of our income on expendable goods and not enough on investment in modernising Britain'.[41] His companion Maurice Macmillan struck a similar chord, when advertising a recent WSOC pamphlet in a Parliamentary debate the same year:

Broadly, those views [of the pamphlet] are based on the belief that there is a need for more voluntary savings both to combat inflation and to aid growth through investment, and that there is an unused capacity to save and invest which has not yet been tapped. I believe that on the whole people spend what they do not save rather than save what they do not spend. Therefore, to increase saving and to encourage investment, new incentives are needed: on the lines of making legal company thrift plans, tax relief for income from small savings invested directly in industry on the same lines as now obtains for income from National Savings, and

---

[37] Green, *Thatcher*, p. 9.

[38] T. Low, *Everyman a Capitalist: Some Proposals for the Small Saver in Industry* (London: Conservative Political Centre, 1959), p. 12.

[39] 'The initial post-war declinist "moment" came at the end of the 1950s and early 1960s. A combination of general angst caused by the Suez debacle and the decline of Empire, political positioning by the opposition Labour Party and mounting evidence of the dynamism of the Western European economies, combined to create a "What's Wrong with Britain" furore that led to a culture of declinism that has persisted, albeit with considerable waxing and waning, ever since.' Tomlinson, 'Thrice Denied'.

[40] *Owning Capital: Proposals of a study group formed by the Political Council of the Junior Carlton Club* (London: Conservative Political Centre, 1963), p. 17.

[41] *Owning Capital*, pp. 5–6.

the same concessions for all retained savings as for assurance and deferred annuities.[42]

The wider share ownership movement sought to reverse the moral charge of 'speculation' by contrasting sound investment with frivolous consumption— something the Labour left was also uneasy with.[43] Distinctions familiar from matters of saving and spending were translated into the world of investment. In this regard, Martin Daunton has pointed out that the 'cultural distinction between visceral, immediate gratification and prudential deferred gratification in consumption and saving is reflected in the debate over speculation as unregulated emotion and greed, and investment as rational, calculating, and careful'.[44] Advocates even suggested channelling funds 'wasted' on gambling—another Labour anxiety—into industry via the stock market.[45] *Everyman a Capitalist*, for instance, suggested that 'investment in industry may actually attract money from the pools'.[46] In 1956, John Braithwaite, the Chairman of the London Stock Exchange had already stated that '[i]f only some of the hundreds of millions that are poured down the drain each year in betting on horses, dogs, and football could be attracted into investment in British industry, what a fine start could be made.'[47] But the argument also revealed a certain concession that gambling and stock market activity were essentially not too different from each other, as William Clark's more elaborate remarks on the matter illustrate:

> There is basically no reason to suppose that someone who can understand the complications of the Pools or of racing 'form' cannot distinguish between a good company and a bad one. [ ... ] We are aware of the argument that small savings should not be put to too much risk. But nor should the investment be too dull. It would be a great advantage if some of the huge sums now devoted to betting could be diverted to investment in industry.[48]

---

[42] *HC Deb* 634, c. 90, 6 February 1961.
[43] L. Black, *The Political Culture of the Left in Affluent Britain, 1951–1964: Old Labour, New Britain?* (Basingstoke: Palgrave Macmillan, 2003).
[44] M. Daunton, 'Afterword', in N. Henry and C. Schmitt (eds), *Victorian Investments: New Perspectives on Finance and Culture* (Bloomington, IN: Indiana University Press, 2009), p. 216.
[45] On Labour's ambiguous relationship with gambling see McClymont, 'Socialism, Puritanism, Hedonism'. On further considerations to divert gambling funds into the stock market see Whiting, 'The City and Democratic Capitalism', p. 101: 'What convinced Labour people that wider share ownership was practicable were the sums regularly spent on the main forms of working-class gambling. Joel Barnett, a friend of Lever's, recommended "the transfer of funds from bingo halls and betting shops to better forms of investment in unit trusts, which would provide both a gain to the holders and a gain for the country"'.
[46] Low, *Everyman a Capitalist*, p. 9.
[47] 'Wider Holdings Of Stocks', *The Times*, 16 March 1956.
[48] *Owning Capital*, pp. 14–15. For Labour considerations in this regard see Whiting, 'The City and Democratic Capitalism', p. 101.

These suggestions did not seem to strike a chord with the party leadership or the higher civil service. Rab Butler commented that the Low Report was 'rather negative and unhelpful'.[49] The Treasury working group on wider share ownership provided a very restrained outlook on the matter, possibly because it was chaired by William Armstrong, at that time already an aspiring Treasury Secretary. Armstrong was one of the most influential civil servants of the post-war era and adhered to 'the dominant Keynesian policy framework of the period'.[50] He went on to become Permanent Secretary to the Treasury in 1962 and Head of Home Civil Service in 1968 and would later incur the wrath of Tory libertarians for orchestrating Edward Heath's interventionist policy 'U-turn' in 1971–72.[51] Echoing the position already laid down in the *Industrial Charter*, Armstrong concluded early on that although 'a widening of the ownership of industrial shares was desirable on general social grounds, this ought to be regarded as a gradual and long-term development. Rapid change was neither to be expected nor desirable.'[52] Two months later, the Prime Minister's office received the Treasury committee's final report. This cautious paper came to define the line of future governments on wider share ownership and was very much in tune with the government's 'conciliatory, middle-way approach' towards housing. Already as Housing Minister, Macmillan publicly committed himself to creating a property-owning democracy and he was able to preside over a considerable increase in privately owned homes. However, he shied away from the more radical proposals pitched by the party grassroots such as a 'Right to Buy' policy for council houses, which was later promoted on a grand scale by Margaret Thatcher.[53] Similar to the Tory leadership's reluctance when it came to housing, the apprehensions spelt out in the Treasury report on wider share ownership testify to the economic paternalism prevalent in post-war Whitehall politics and reveal the nervousness of high-ranking Conservatives to unpick elements of the corporatist post-war settlement.[54]

The report included a detailed assessment of the facilities for equity investment available to the small saver. They ranged from trading through a broker of the Stock Exchange—'expensive and inaccessible'—over the mediated form of unit trusts to the increasingly popular format of investment clubs, which were 'popular in America [and] spreading gradually in the United Kingdom', and eventually

[49] Butler scribbled this assessment on a minute from Chancellor Heathcoat Amory to the Prime Minister, 24 March 1959, TNA, FO 1109/321.

[50] K. Theakston, 'Armstrong, William, Baron Armstrong of Sanderstead (1915–1980)', *ODNB*.

[51] R. Lowe, *The Official History of the British Civil Service: Reforming the Civil Service, Volume I: The Fulton Years, 1966–81* (London, New York: Routledge, 2011), pp. 163, 444, nn 114–115.

[52] Committee on the Wider Ownership of Shares in Industry, 1st meeting, 19 January 1959, TNA, T 277/802.

[53] Davies, '"Right to Buy"', p. 430. Davies notes that prior to Thatcher, 'Conservative councils enacted profitable local sales schemes during the late 1960s'.

[54] J. Lawrence, 'Paternalism, Class and the British Path to Modernity', in S. Gunn and J. Vernon (eds), *The Peculiarities of Liberal Modernity in Imperial Britain* (Berkeley, CA: University of California Press, 2011), pp. 147–164.

employee share schemes. The problem with the latter was that 'all eggs are in one basket', meaning that workers would not only lose their job, but also their capital should their companies go out of business. In spite of viewing a wider spread of private capital ownership as socially desirable, the government had to consider economic as well as moral arguments against pursuing any such policies. First and foremost, the Treasury report saw equity investment as too risky for the average saver whose priority was deemed to be 'liquidity with no risk of capital loss'. The report furthermore mirrored policymakers' distrust of market mechanisms. An increase in retail share investing was deemed to inevitably come at the expense of National Savings. Such a shift away from conventional savings in government bonds to equities—something that was already happening in the market—was considered to 'reduce the area over which the Government can influence the total volume of credit and therefore the general level of economic activity'. Statements like this mirror the strong belief in the state's entrepreneurial qualities prevalent in Whitehall at that time and which Thatcher and her allies later declared war on. The government was advised only to remove such obstacles in the way of ordinary investors which were 'not involving serious revenue loss'. Giving way, for example, to the WSOC's calls for tax concessions on investments was out of the question for a government relying on a constant flow of revenue for demand management.[55]

In addition, ministers urged Macmillan to consider religious opposition against the spread of share ownership. Early on, the Lord President of the Council, Lord Hailsham, a devout Christian, wrote to the Prime Minister:

> We must be extremely careful that any policy we propose does not incur the wrath of the Churches, some of whose zealots regard any form of purchase of shares as a form of gambling. This is of course rubbish, but operating on the Stock Exchange can be a form of gambling and I see no particular reason why we should encourage it unless we have this danger fully in mind.[56]

On this, Macmillan merely noted: 'We must await the report. But I do not share your apprehensions.' We have seen in Chapter 2 in connection with the church's increased involvement in the stock market how Macmillan as Chancellor had already laughed off religious protest when he introduced Premium Bonds in his 1956 budget. He followed the same line when he presided over the sweeping liberalizations of gambling markets as Prime Minister in the late 1950s, gleefully pointing out the church's double moral standards in this regard.[57] On wider share ownership, he took a similar stance: the state should not object on moral or

[55] Report of the Committee on the Wider Ownership of Shares in Industry, 24 March 1959, TNA, PREM 11/2669.
[56] Lord Hailsham to H. Macmillan, 24 Nov 1958, TNA, PREM 11/2669.
[57] Jarvis, *Conservative Governments, Morality and Social Change in Affluent Britain, 1957-64*, pp. 65–85.

religious grounds, if people wanted to take a flutter, be it in dogs and horses or stocks and shares. They should not, however, take higher economic risks if the government could be made responsible for financial losses. Last but not least, encouraging the electorate to invest in stocks and shares was a delicate matter of timing. The report pointed out that a bull market was the worst possible moment for encouraging people to buy shares:

> The risk of capital loss is, of course, aggravated, if the wage-earner makes his investment at a time when share prices are high. In the nature of things equities tend to gain in popularity after a rise in prices rather than before it and this makes it particularly important that investors should have access to sound advice and should have some understanding of the risks that are involved.

Two apprehensions were at play here. On the one hand, if voters felt politically encouraged to buy potentially overpriced shares and then burnt their fingers, this would backfire electorally. Tory policymakers were well aware that 'an ill-timed marketing campaign could result in financial losses by the investing public and consequent electoral ignominy'.[58] On the other hand, the financial crash of 1929 was still a bogeyman in British post-war politics. Financial observers had pointed out the danger of a repeat of 1929 should the mid-1950s' bull market develop into another 'share-buying craze'.[59] Harold Wincott, whose articles were circulated in 10 Downing Street, picked up on this widely spread anxiety in a review of John Kenneth Galbraith's seminal account, *The Great Crash, 1929*.[60] Wincott did not think that 'there's the slightest chance of a repetition of 1929 in our lifetime', but his optimism, somewhat contradictory, was based on the awareness that 'the fear is still prevalent in men's minds that such a slump can recur'. It is likely that this resonated with politicians like Macmillan, who had experienced at first hand the devastating social consequences of the Great Slump in his Stockton constituency during the 1930s. As share prices rose further in January 1960, the new Chancellor Derick Heathcoat-Amory circulated among Treasury staff a letter from J. R. Cuthbertson, Head of the Economic Intelligence Department at the merchant bank of Lazard Brothers. The senior banker was concerned about the 'current Stock Exchange boom' and warned the Chancellor against applying the proposals laid out in Toby Low's pamphlet, *Everyman a Capitalist*:

> It seems to me that it would be inviting disaster to initiate such a scheme at a time when stock market prices are heading straight for lunatic levels. One would be risking putting a lot of small people with very limited financial means into the

---

[58] Munro, 'The Fiscal Politics of Savings and Share Ownership in Britain, 1970–1980', p. 769.
[59] Acton Society Trust, *Wider Shareholding*, p. 90.
[60] Candidus [i.e. H. Wincott], 'Can 1929 Come Again?', *The Investors' Chronicle*, 5 November 1955.

concluding phase of a South Seas' [sic] bubble. [ ... ] One would not wish to see the small investor, particularly the working man, given such a fear of equity investment that several decades will pass before he can once again be induced to consider it. The 1929 crash on Wall Street had just that effect.[61]

We have already seen in Chapter 2 how several months later, in June 1960, the Treasury learned from the Bank of England, 'that the Stock Exchange have come down firmly against any scheme to encourage small investors in equities'.[62] However, we should not mistake the resulting inactivity as evidence in support of the popular argument 'which claims that the City and its representatives have been able to determine and dictate the economic policies of the British State to the benefit of international financial and commercial interests at the expense of domestic industry'.[63] On the contrary, the Stock Exchange had very little impact on government policy during the post-war period, as the debate surrounding the introduction of a short-term capital gains tax by the Conservative Chancellor Selwyn Lloyd will show. According to Ranald Michie, '[i]n areas that really mattered to the Stock Exchange, such as taxation, there is little evidence to suggest that it made any difference whether Labour or the Conservatives were in power.'[64] What we can conclude from this episode is that financial elites shared with Whitehall officials concerns regarding a large intake of new investors. The more specific context of this back-channel communication between the Treasury and the Stock Exchange was the preparation of a House of Commons debate on 'Wider Ownership of Industrial Shares'. The Economic Secretary, Anthony Barber—who would later ignite the 'Barber boom' with his expansionist budget during Heath's U-turn—had poured cold water over a motion proposed by Gresham Cooke, the Conservative MP for Twickenham and WSOC member. Barber's intervention illustrates vividly how the Treasury sought to keep a lid on wider share ownership proposals. Cooke's original motion read:

> That this House, believing that economic stability, political freedom, and social justice require a wider spread in the personal ownership of the industrial wealth of the country, calls upon Her Majesty's Government to *take action*: both to remove obstacles which may prevent the small saver investing in industrial shares, and to encourage the small investor to invest in equities by measures

---

[61] J. R. Cuthbertson to D. Heathcoat-Amory, 5 January 1960, TNA, T 233/1851.

[62] J. F. Barrow to J. I. Mck. Rhodes, 10 June 1960, TNA, T 326/88.

[63] Quote after Davies, *The City of London and Social Democracy*, p. 31; on a critical assessment of this argument see R. Michie, 'The City of London and the British Government: The Changing Relationship', in R. Michie and P. Williamson (eds), *The British Government and the City of London in the Twentieth Century* (Cambridge: Cambridge University Press, 2004), pp. 31–55.

[64] Michie, *The London Stock Exchange*, p. 425. Michie contends that 'there is a total absence of evidence to indicate that the Stock Exchange was able to exert much influence on the government' in the 1950s and 1960s; Michie, *The London Stock Exchange*, p. 425.

similar to those already taken to further encourage investment in National Savings; and, as a first step, to consider reducing the Stamp Duty on all share transfers, and amending the Income Tax Act 1952 so as to permit Company Thrift Plans for investment, part in National Savings part in industrial shares, to be set up.

After Barber's amendments, the motion merely '[ ... ] call[ed] upon Her Majesty's Government to consider whether any action can be taken to remove obstacles which may deter the small saver from investing in industry and to encourage him to make such investments'.[65]

In spite of this setback, the WSOC established a 'tradition of access' to the Treasury over the course of the decade.[66] Before each budget, the Chancellor or the Economic Secretary would meet a council delegation at the Treasury and listen to policy proposals. Members made specific proposals that '[d]iscrimination against securities as forms of property subject to capital gains tax should be ended' and called for a 'less unfavourable treatment of the fruit of investment'.[67] The latter point referred to 'the present unequal treatment of so-called "unearned" as compared with "earned" income',[68] which middle-class taxpayers had long regarded as 'a tax on thrift and self-reliance'.[69] In addition to that, the WSOC wished to extend personal allowances on capital income, cut or abolish stamp duty, and exempt unit trusts from corporation tax. As a way of spreading the investment habit among working-class communities, the council even 'suggested that it would be a good idea to inspire the working man to have a gamble on shares, instead of on the pools'.[70]

But minor achievements like the halving of stamp duty in 1963, raised to 2 per cent by Labour in 1947, were outweighed by bitter pills the council had to swallow. In his 1962 budget, Selwyn Lloyd introduced a short-term capital gains tax in a bid to 'counter criticism of the Conservatives as the party of speculators and shady financiers'.[71] The tax was both a concession to union opinion and 'a way of dealing with resentment against speculators in the take-over and property booms',[72] which had gripped the City in the wake of the Aluminium War 1959. The London Stock Exchange was outraged when it heard about Lloyd's intentions and its Chairman, Lord Ritchie of Dundee, used the WSOC's annual conference

---

[65] Gresham Cooke to P. M. Hewlett, 26 April 1960, TNA, T 326/88. *HC Deb* 625, c. 823, 24 June 1960; J. F. Barrow to E. W. Maude, 2 May 1960, TNA, T 326/88.

[66] R. J. Painter to W. Armstrong, 28 February 1969, TNA, T 326/917.

[67] Memorandum of the Wider Share Ownership Council to the Chancellor of the Exchequer, 31 January 1967, TNA, T 326/917.

[68] Memorandum of the Wider Share Ownership Council to the Chancellor of the Exchequer 1971, 5 November 1970, TNA, T 306/42.

[69] Daunton, *Just Taxes*, p. 116.

[70] WSOC Deputation to Chancellor of the Exchequer, minutes of meeting, 29 January 1964, TNA, T 326/285.

[71] Daunton, *Just Taxes*, p. 260.   [72] Daunton, *Just Taxes*, p. 261.

for launching a scathing critique of the Conservative government. The senior stockbroker argued that 'the City ha[d] not reached its pre-eminence by taxation and restriction' and lamented that 'the subject of investment, the subject of freedom of markets, the subject of the importance of the stock market to the country, to industry, and to us all is constantly bedevilled by the Government'.[73] Harold Wilson's Labour government (1964–70) took further action against capital gains by introducing a long-term tax in 1965, designed by the Cambridge economist Nicholas Kaldor.[74] Even when the WSOC had a 'friend at court'[75]—from 1967 to 1969, Deputy Chairman Harold Lever was Financial Secretary to the Treasury—its efforts were in vain. In 1969, the Chief Secretary, John Diamond, felt obliged to point out to the council's deputation that 'a lesson could perhaps be drawn from the fact that the council found themselves compelled to repeat their representations year after year'. The Treasury's view on the WSOC's ideas is perhaps best encapsulated by a scribbled remark by an unidentifiable civil servant regarding a proposal on Incentive Share Schemes by the Council's Honorary Secretary, George Copeman: 'If any employer offered me this thing as an incentive I'd go and work elsewhere.'[76]

In June 1970, the Conservatives returned to power after party leader Edward Heath seemed to have re-embraced economic liberalism, with the manifesto promising to foster a 'capital-owning democracy'.[77] This, of course, spelt hope for the wider share ownership movement, especially when Iain Macleod was announced to be Heath's new chancellor. Macleod was a staunch free-market liberal and had gained a reputation as a self-proclaimed critic of the 'nanny state'.[78] When the shadow cabinet met for its seminal conference at Selsdon Park Hotel in January 1970—the birth of the party's new free-market manifesto—Macleod put the abolition of the investment income surcharge at the top of the agenda.[79] As part of reintroducing free market policies, he showed interest in a WSOC proposal for an equity-linked Save As You Earn (SAYE) scheme, which the Treasury described as 'the best starter there is for fulfilling the Conservative Party Manifesto pledge'.[80] But only a month after his appointment,

---

[73] For the Aluminium War and its political implications see Kynaston, *The City of London*, IV, pp. 108–15.;'City "At The End of Tether"', *Financial Times*, 21 March 1961; '"House" Chairman Tilts at Capital Gains Tax', *Daily Telegraph*, 21 March 1961.

[74] Whiting, *The Labour Party and Taxation*, pp. 159–168.

[75] M. Macmillan to H. Lever, 14 February 1969, TNA, T 326/917.

[76] Minutes of meeting with WSOC deputation at Treasury, 13 March 1967, TNA, T 326/917.

[77] *A Better Tomorrow: The Conservative Programme for the Next 5 Years*, (London: Conservative Central Office, 1970).

[78] After refusing to serve under Macmillan's successor, Alec Douglas-Home, Macleod was the editor of *The Spectator* for two years. Here he wrote a weekly column under the pseudonym 'Quoodle', firing 'salvos in the direction of what I call the Nanny State.' *The Spectator*, 3 December 1965.

[79] Quote after Munro, 'The Fiscal Politics of Savings and Share Ownership in Britain, 1970–1980', p. 760.

[80] C. D. Butler to Inland Revenue, Equity-linked version of SAYE, 18 September 1970, TNA, T 326/1275.

Macleod died of a heart attack and was succeeded by Anthony Barber. It will remain unknown whether Macleod would have thwarted the Tory leadership's renunciation of its free-market agenda during the winter of 1971–72. But in view of drastically increasing unemployment levels, Heath's government introduced wide-ranging interventionist policies and Barber's expansionist budget.[81] At any rate, in the course of this 'U-turn', the equity-linked SAYE scheme was dismissed because the Treasury suddenly had 'very strong objections on principle to the proposed tax concessions'. The text did point out 'that officials should given [sic] further study to the kind of scheme which might be introduced if a change in economics warranted this, including the question of a time-scale'.[82] But in conclusion, the Conservative leadership was not ready to move away from the restrictive stance it had spelt out in the 1950s, and shelved yet another plan for widening equity ownership.

## Thinking the Unthinkable: Conservative Opposition Plans for 'Grass-Roots Capitalism'

After two narrow election defeats to his nemesis Harold Wilson in February and October 1974, Heath was replaced in February 1975 as Leader of the Opposition by Margaret Thatcher, who had been the Secretary of State for Education and Science under Heath. Thatcher, a proponent of the right wing and party grass roots, was not seen as a long-term solution. Yet her election revealed the waning belief in post-war economic wisdoms of planning, nationalization, high taxes, and public expenditure. As the second half of the 1970s witnessed a global comeback of economic liberalism and a growing belief in the social benefits of the profit motive, Thatcher radically refashioned her party's policies along these lines.[83] Under her leadership the Conservatives took up many of the radical free-market alternatives offered by those who had been 'thinking the unthinkable' in the past decades—mainly outside the party.[84] Think tanks like the Centre for Policy Studies (CPS) or the neoliberal Institute of Economic Affairs (IEA) gained key influence on Tory policy. While the CPS had been founded by Thatcher and two of her closest allies, Keith Joseph and Alfred Sherman, in 1974, the IEA had been

---

[81]  B. Harrison, *Finding a Role?: The United Kingdom 1970–1990* (Oxford: Clarendon Press, 2011), pp. 316, 435. For the New Right's reaction to the U-turn see Green, *Thatcher*, pp. 34–37.

[82]  C. W. Fogarty, Memorandum on Wider Share Ownership Council proposals for an equity-linked contractual savings scheme, 10 May 1972, TNA, T 326/1605.

[83]  For Thatcher's general realignment of the Conservative Party see the detailed study by D. Geppert, *Thatchers konservative Revolution: Der Richtungswandel der britischen Tories 1975–1979* (München: R. Oldenbourg Verlag, 2002). More specific on Conservative tax policy and wider share ownership is Munro, 'The Fiscal Politics of Savings and Share Ownership in Britain, 1970–1980'; for social policy see Sutcliffe-Braithwaite, 'Neo-Liberalism and Morality in the Making of Thatcherite Social Policy'.

[84]  Cockett, *Thinking the Unthinkable*; B. Jackson, 'The Think-Tank Archipelago'.

championing the case of wider share ownership since the early 1960s.[85] These think tanks and their 'academic' influence were important for the rise of what later became labelled 'Thatcherism'. But recent scholarship has urged historians of that period to 'throw light on individuals other than the academic economists commonly seen as lying at the heart of neoliberal ideas'.[86] In this vein, we shall see how throughout the 1970s the case for wider share ownership was taken up and advocated by a diverse group of politicians, businessmen, and journalists.

It is important to base the analysis on this broader movement for wider share ownership—in which the WSOC was one player—and not to conflate issues of popular share ownership with the 1980s. This loosely connected movement did not only lay the intellectual foundation for Margaret Thatcher's privatization programme of the 1980s. Thinking in radical alternatives, it also put forward the spread of individual capital ownership as a major tool against what the Selsdon Manifesto had decried as 'the paternalism of the Welfare state'.[87] Early pioneers of this movement outside the WSOC were the *Sunday Times* journalist, Richard Kellett; head of the Conservative Political Centre and influential Tory right-winger, Russell Lewis; as well as his political idol, Enoch Powell, then the libertarian New Right's leading figure. Their visions of dispersed, individual, and direct capital ownership inspired Thatcherite conceptions of a capital-owning democracy.

Amy Edwards has recently suggested that 1980s popular capitalism brought about the emergence of a new economic regime, which she describes as financial consumerism: 'the convergence of the practices, mentalities and subjectivities of consumption with the mechanisms, service providers and investors of financial products'.[88] To be sure, in the 1980s, due to the process of disintermediation, large financial conglomerates did come in more direct contact with individual savers and investors, thereby applying more aggressive marketing techniques than ever before in Britain. But the moniker of 'financial consumerism' risks muddling the fundamental distinction between the employment of capital for the sake of its accumulation, as is the case in saving, investing, or speculating, and the act of consuming goods, resources, or experiences for instant gratification. Furthermore, the concept of financial consumerism obscures the specific historical backdrop of this key Thatcherite project, which was in many ways directed *against* consumerism.

---

[85] J. E. Powell, *Saving in a Free Society* (London: The Institute of Economic Affairs, 1960); Kellett, *Ordinary Shares for Ordinary Savers*.

[86] Rollings, 'Cracks in the Post-War Keynesian Settlement?', p. 656.

[87] The Selsdon Manifesto, 19 September 1973, Margaret Thatcher Foundation Website. Available at www.margaretthatcher.org/document/110860, accessed 17 December 2020. MTF 110860 (hereafter MTF).

[88] Edwards, 'Financial Consumerism', 222.

In order to explain the wider trajectory of Conservative plans for wider share ownership in the 1970s and 1980s we must take into account the New Right's obsession with Britain's alleged national and industrial decline. Scholars widely agree that this provided an important motivational background for Thatcher, who is widely considered one of the 'most important declinist politicians of the twentieth century'.[89] Thatcherites denied structural explanations that Britain's economic and political clout was waning as a consequence of two world wars, resulting in US dominance and decolonization. Instead, the New Right largely subscribed to a pseudo-cultural interpretation of decline. A key tenet in this reading was the assumption that Britain's elites had long adhered to traditional aristocratic ideals of rural nostalgia and anti-industrialism, as a result of which Britain's captains of industry, politicians, academics, and financiers lacked the industrial 'spirit' of their bourgeois European counterparts, leading to the country's long-term economic demise.[90] Taking this questionable interpretation of history further, Thatcherites claimed that the post-war expansion of the welfare state, inflation, and consumerism had further eroded bourgeois or, in Thatcher's parlance, 'Victorian' values of thrift, hard work, self-help, and enterprise.[91] Large sections of the right-wing press and libertarian think tanks shared this assessment and deliberately peddled fears over the corrosion of purportedly middle-class values of long-term financial prudence, thrift, and independence. This zeitgeist was famously pinned down by Patrick Hutber in his 1976 book *Decline and Fall of the Middle Class*. Hutber was Nigel Lawson's successor as the *Sunday Telegraph's* City editor, closely associated with the IEA and 'especially close' to Margaret Thatcher.[92] He singled out 'thrift' or the 'readiness to postpone satisfaction', which he saw 'deeply imbued with the Puritan ethic', as the most characteristic middle-class virtue that had come under threat from taxation and inflation.[93] After Thatcher's election victory in 1979, the New Right's declinism was given an academic veneer by Martin Wiener's 1981 book *English Culture and the Decline of the Industrial Spirit*. The American historian's account impressed Thatcher's

[89]  Tomlinson, 'Thrice denied', 235. The other one was Joseph Chamberlain.

[90]  Daunton, ' "Gentlemanly Capitalism" and British Industry 1820–1914'; M. Daunton, 'Financial Elites and British Society, 1880–1950', in Y. Cassis (ed.), *Finance and Financiers in European History 1880–1960* (Cambridge: Cambridge University Press, 1991), pp. 121–146.

[91]  Green, *Thatcher*, pp. 55–57.

[92]  Quote after his obituary 'Champion of the middle classes', *Sunday Telegraph*, 6 January 1980; on Hutber's connection with the IEA see Jackson, 'The Think-Tank Archipelago', pp. 48, 55, 57. Ironically Hutber was the only City editor who was explicitly sceptical of wider share ownership and adhered to the City's paternalist view on the matter. He was of the opinion that 'direct equity investment carries risk and requires time and skill to make it remotely successful. Very few men in the street have the time or the skill.' P. Hutber, 'Why Barber can't give much away . . . The case for Narrower Share Ownership', *Sunday Telegraph*, 7 March 1971.

[93]  P. Hutber, *The Decline and Fall of the Middle Class, and How It Can Fight Back* (London: Associated Business Programmes, 1976), p. 13. On Hutber's book see also Sutcliffe-Braithwaite, 'Neo-Liberalism and Morality in the Making of Thatcherite Social Policy', 514–515.

chief ideologue Keith Joseph so much that he allegedly 'distributed copies of Mr Wiener's book to every member of the cabinet'.[94]

This notion also shaped thinking and policy design on wider share ownership and popular capitalism as a means to reverse decline and alleged middle-class corruption. Rendering Britain's economic dismay as a cultural and moral crisis allowed Thatcherites to present the rejuvenation of 'industrial', 'Victorian', or 'bourgeois' values and related changes in the tax system as a promising way of reversing decline. Hence, we can conceive of the quest for wider share ownership as a social as well as economic project that pursued 'the re-establishment of an economic and legal framework, and a cultural ethos which rewarded proper bourgeois behaviour'.[95] As will become clear, this does not mean to view the politics of privatization and deregulation of the Thatcher years as a successful restoration of Victorian values in Britain.

In a 1962 essay for the IEA, the *Sunday Times* City correspondent Richard Kellett delivered a comprehensive analysis of the economic and social function of individual share owners. An economics graduate from Oxford, Richard Kellett was member of the Conservative Bow Group, the intellectual melting pot for young Tories, where he gained a reputation as an expert on taxes. To borrow Hayekian terminology, Kellett was only a small 'second-hand dealer of ideas' and never a kingpin in politics, journalism, or the world of think tanks, but he occupied the intersections of these three realms, publishing widely on financial and economic affairs.[96] His notion of private share ownership encapsulated the IEA's radical marriage of Hayekian individualism and economic liberalism that came to influence the Conservative Party's neoliberal overhaul under Thatcher. Kellett's declinist assumption was that Britain had long suffered from a still widely held belief that investment was 'anti-social and objectionable'. As a cause of this perception he identified a 'fifty-year record of radical attacks' on the shareholder, ranging 'from Lloyd George in 1906 [sic] with his discrimination against "unearned" income, to Cripps with his stamp duty in 1946, to Mr Selwyn Lloyd with his long-expected expedient of a capital gains tax'.[97] But surveying the market

---

[94] Quote after 'Empty shelves', *The Economist*, 27 April 2010. While this assessment is hard to verify, Wiener's book definitely 'captured the attention of Margaret Thatcher's cabinet', G. Ortolano, *The Two Cultures Controversy: Science, Literature and Cultural Politics in Postwar Britain* (Cambridge: Cambridge University Press, 2009), p. 13. For a critical discussion of Wiener's book see Mandler, 'The Problem with Cultural History'; also J. Raven, 'British History and the Enterprise Culture', *Past and Present* 123 (1989), pp. 178–204.

[95] Sutcliffe-Braithwaite, 'Neo-Liberalism and Morality in the Making of Thatcherite Social Policy', p. 516.

[96] See R. Kellett, *Taxes for Today* (London: Conservative Political Centre on behalf of the Bow Group, 1958); R. Kellett, *City Page* (London: Newman Neame Take Home Books, 1962); R. Kellett, *Money on Your Mind: A Simple Guide to Successful Share-Buying*, Corgi Books (Transworld, 1964); R. Kellett, *The Merchant Banking Arena: With Case Studies* (London: St. Martin's Press, 1967).

[97] Kellett, *Ordinary Shares for Ordinary Savers*, p. 9. Lloyd George introduced differentiation in his 1907 budget.

position of Britain's small investors in the early 1960s, Kellett also identified restrictive practices in the City of London as part of the problem. He accused the London Stock Exchange's conservative outlook of hampering the development of a share-owning democracy along the lines of the United States, where shareholder numbers had skyrocketed since the mid-1950s. Like many financial journalists, Kellett criticized the London Stock Exchange for its refusal to lift the ban on advertising for stockbrokers, and bemoaned that '[t]here is nothing comparable here to the American or Continental networks of brokers' offices spread widely across the country'.[98] But Kellett's main object of criticism was the unequal treatment of 'earned' and 'unearned' income, which he slammed as an incentive to indulge in consumption instead of postponing gratification by providing capital for industry. This was completely in line with the IEA's wider agenda of promoting thrift as a cardinal economic virtue:

> Behind all borrowings and lendings—at home or abroad—lies the basic, simple fact: someone is going without immediate consumption, someone is saving to finance someone else, somewhere else, to build up more productive equipment.[99]

Last but not least, Kellett pointed out that 'tax reliefs for savings through pension funds or life insurance policies' had caused a rapid institutionalization of British stock markets—a trend worrying many advocates of wider share ownership.[100] For this reason, he deplored not only the growth of pension funds and insurance companies, but also that of unit trusts. As discussed in Chapter 2, unit trusts were experiencing enormous growth at that time and were advertised as a vehicle to enable the 'small man' to enjoy the benefits of equity ownership. But Kellett and other IEA libertarians like Enoch Powell criticized unit trusts as an oblique and anonymous affair, depriving the unit holder of economic enfranchisement and co-ownership. In another IEA pamphlet, Powell bemoaned that with a unit trust

> The investor is not brought into touch as a shareholder with the fortunes or management of firms; and he has no concern with or knowledge of the problems and prospects of the businesses or industries whose securities underlie the units

---

[98] Kellett, *Ordinary Shares for Ordinary Savers*, pp. 20–21.

[99] Kellett, *Ordinary Shares for Ordinary Savers*, p. 9. The IEA's creed that productivity relied immensely on deferred gratification was spelt out in G. Hutton, 'All Capitalists Now', in R. Harris (ed.), *Radical Reaction: Essays in Competition and Affluence* (London: The Institute of Economic Affairs, 1961), p. 35.

[100] Kellett, *Ordinary Shares for Ordinary Savers*, p. 30. See also a WSOC's internal strategy paper on this issue: London School of Economics Library, London, Wider Share Ownership Council Collection (hereafter, LSE, WSOC), Box 9, 'How to halt the trend towards institutional dominance of the stock market' (undated, c.1979).

and he has no responsibility or voice (beyond the selection of his trust) in the direction of the purchase of securities.[101]

In the same vein, Kellett claimed that these 'anonymous trusts [ ... ] cannot by their nature appeal to people who want to invest directly in real companies and products'.[102] In order to reverse the growth of institutional investment, Kellett and Powell suggested extending the 'small army of people who put savings not into bonds or building societies but into industrial shares'.[103] In accordance with the WSOC's agenda, the IEA papers called on politicians to cut taxes and urged the City and the Stock Exchange to open up to the investing public. Going even further than Tory backbenchers with their emphasis on employee share owner-ship schemes, Kellett fashioned the small investor as an indispensable risk-bearer in a free economy governed by dispersed market power. Providing evidence from industrial leaders, he demonstrated that institutional investors were traditionally risk-averse and tended to invest conservatively in large 'blue chip' corporations, hence depriving smaller, but more dynamic start-up com-panies of crucial venture capital. In contrast to this, the private investor func-tioned as a type of capitalist 'truffle pig' that invested in companies 'at an early stage', hence injecting 'valuable risk capital' and a 'spirit of adventure' into the market.[104] In this sense, small investors were—without labelling them as such—rendered small speculators since shares of small and medium enterprises (SMEs) are commonly prone to violent fluctuations, thereby giving the investment a more than average risk. It is revelatory to note the similarities between Kellett's notion of the small investor and the classical definition of a speculator put forward by the eminent financial journalist Charles Duguid (1864–1923) in his popular guide to the stock exchange:

> The speculator, less conservative, risks money the loss of which he is perfectly well able to afford, *in the furtherance of experiments in commerce and industry*, be it the trial of a patent or the opening up of a mine. He expects a big return should the experiment prove successful, but is prepared to face the loss should it turn out otherwise. He hopes to enrich himself, and without his aid commerce and industry would make none of those rapid strides which are for the welfare of the world, for speculation is the handmaid of enterprise.[105]

---

[101] Powell, *Saving in a Free Society*, p. 106. For this line of argument see also Daunton, 'Creating a Dynamic Society', p. 45.
[102] Kellett, Ordinary Shares for Ordinary Savers, pp. 24–28.
[103] Kellett, *Ordinary Shares for Ordinary Savers*, p. 9.
[104] Kellett, *Ordinary Shares for Ordinary Savers*, p. 45.
[105] C. Duguid, *The Stock Exchange*, 5th edn (London: Methuen and Co, 1926), p. 131; my emphasis.

Kellett was concerned with bridging the gap both between capital and labour as well as 'between the City and small savers'.[106] He was fairly optimistic about this, invoking the sociologist and proponent of the embourgeoisement hypothesis Ferdynand Zweig, who had famously contended that '[p]eople who once thought of themselves as exclusively working-class are taking on middle-class habits, are starting to save, and are being more ambitious with their savings'.[107] By invoking Zweig, 'Thatcherites' most favoured sociologist in the 1970s', Kellett anticipated wider share ownership as a tool for embourgeoisement, a concept leading Thatcherites like Keith Joseph later referred to as 'the object of our lifetime'.[108]

Another second-hand dealer of ideas and pioneer of wider share ownership— and, as we shall see, of privatization—with close links to the IEA as well as the Conservative Party was Russell Lewis. After an early career in stockbroking and standing unsuccessfully as a Conservative candidate for Parliament in 1959, the Cambridge-educated economist became a leading figure of the Bow Group.[109] There he worked closely with Cambridge contemporaries John Biffen and Geoffrey Howe, all of whom became followers of Enoch Powell.[110] After serving as director of the CPC (1966–75) and president of the Selsdon Group (1973–75), he switched to journalism, became a leader writer at the *Daily Mail* and also Margaret Thatcher's first biographer.[111] During Thatcher's first term, he maintained close ties to Alan Walters, her Chief Economic Advisor, whom he met for occasional lunches.[112]

Lewis was a free-market enthusiast, inspired by a deep belief in the 'economic value of the market' and in 'its efficiency in the right overall conditions in guiding the everyday business of our lives'.[113] In 1954, he made his mark by urging a party rhetorically committed to building a 'property-owning democracy' to create the 'fiscal concessions' for small investors. Seventeen years after outside and provincial brokers failed to make the case to the Board of Trade Committee on Share-Pushing, Lewis called upon his fellow Tories to compel the Stock Exchange to launch a large-scale advertising campaign—again in vain.[114] A rampant critic of

---

[106] Kellett, *Ordinary Shares for Ordinary Savers*, p. 25.

[107] Kellett, *Ordinary Shares for Ordinary Savers*, p. 14.

[108] Like Zweig, Joseph and Thatcher conceived of the middle classes as a 'value system' that was characterized by having a 'further time-horizon [than the poor] and willingness to defer gratification.' Sutcliffe-Braithwaite, 'Neo-Liberalism and Morality in the Making of Thatcherite Social Policy', pp. 514, 515. On Thatcherite receptions of Ferdynand Zweig see furthermore J. Lawrence and F. Sutcliffe-Braithwaite, 'Margaret Thatcher and the Decline of Class Politics', in B. Jackson and R. Saunders (eds), *Making Thatcher's Britain* (Cambridge: Cambridge University Press), pp. 139–143 .

[109] Cockett, *Thinking the Unthinkable*, pp. 162–163.

[110] Geppert, *Thatchers konservative Revolution*, p. 248.

[111] R. Lewis, *Margaret Thatcher: A Personal and Political Biography* (London, Boston: Routledge and K. Paul, 1975).

[112] Alan Walters diary, 21 July 1981, MTF 137536; 24 February 1982, MTF 144222.

[113] R. Lewis, *Industry and the Property Owning Democracy* (London: Bow Group, 1954), p. 15.

[114] Lewis, *Industry and the Property Owning Democracy*, pp. 20–21, 30.

the mixed economy, Lewis called for a 'radical Toryism to attach itself to the task of simplifying government' and to restructure the nationalized industries along 'commercial principles'.[115] Together with the Tory MP for Guildford, David Howell, whom he had known from at least 1968 through several IEA seminars,[116] Lewis linked the policy of denationalization with the long-term goal of wider share ownership. Howell, in 1969, identified telecommunications as the 'number one growth industry in the coming decade' and marked the telephone system as a target of denationalization—fifteen years before the privatization of British Telecom under Thatcher. This would 'give the industry back to the people' thereby realizing such 'ambitious social goals like wider share ownership'.[117] Echoing the New Right's admiration for Western Germany's economy, both Howell and Lewis invoked the example of the denationalization of Volkswagen in 1960 as a role model for a 'social market economy [*Soziale Marktwirtschaft*] and modern popular capitalism'.[118]

Pondering for the first time in a 1968 *Telegraph* article on 'How to Denationalise', Lewis struck an even more emphatic tone, envisaging that 'shares for the people' could create a 'vested interest' against nationalization.[119] Having in mind 'the same principle as Henry VIII did when denationalising the monasteries', Lewis suggested to essentially dole out to voters free shares in privatized industries—a proposition also floated by Milton Friedman, but dismissed in the 1980s by Chancellor Geoffrey Howe during the early stages of privatization.[120] The resulting 'popular capitalism' would not only 'have the merit of educating large numbers of citizens in the workings of the capitalist system'. It would furthermore add 'a little spice to economic life [and] should appeal to the British sporting instinct'.[121] Conceding that the idea of free shares might jar with the 'puritanical streak in the national character', Lewis was nevertheless optimistic that a 'mass market would arise devoted to transactions in ordinary shares for ordinary people'.[122] This idea of an 'exciting', 'sporting', popular capitalism resonated with the vision of a market society governed by adventurist small speculators envisaged earlier by Lewis's fellow Bow Grouper, Richard

[115] R. Lewis, *A Bonfire of Restrictions* (London: Conservative Political Centre, 1965), pp. 3, 13.

[116] Cockett, *Thinking the Unthinkable*, pp. 193–195.

[117] D. Howell, 'Who wants private lines?', *The Spectator*, 6 February 1969.

[118] Quote after D. Howell, 'Which way now for democrats?', *The Daily Telegraph*, 9 March 1977. Lewis devoted a sub-chapter to 'The German example' of Volkswagen in R. Lewis, 'How to Denationalise', in R. Boyson (ed.), *Goodbye to Nationalisation* (London: Churchill Press, 1971), pp. 85–87. See also a 1976 speech Lewis gave at the Selsdon Group Seminar: 'In fact denationalization is perfectly practicable, and there are many examples of it being carried out. [...] The most encouraging example however is that of Volkswagen which was sold in 1960 to a million and a half shareholders. That is the example for Conservatives.' Cockett, *Thinking the Unthinkable*, pp. 215–216.

[119] R. Lewis, 'How to Denationalise: First Steps', *The Daily Telegraph*, 4 October 1968.

[120] Lewis, 'How to Denationalise', pp. 80–93. See Chapter 5 for Howe's dismissal of free give-away flotations.

[121] Lewis, 'How to Denationalise', p. 84.     [122] Lewis, 'How to Denationalise', p. 85.

Kellett. These remarks further demonstrate that throughout the post-war decades, protagonists of the wider share ownership movement negotiated themes of investment and gambling alongside each other and were furthermore aware of the potential 'exuberance of emotions' inherent in stock market activity.[123] This uneasy coexistence of moralistic and swashbuckling elements in the quest for wider share ownership was to come to the fore again during the public's participation in the privatization issues of the Thatcher years. As we shall see in Chapter 6 the flotations of state assets in the 1980s lent themselves more to a popular gambling spirit than to an exercise in Victorian values, prompting the 'wet' minister Richard Needham to comment that the 'British have always been followers of horse-racing who like to put a few shillings on a winner— privatisation was putting a few bob on a sure winner'.[124]

However, in spite of the overlapping rhetoric, it would be simplistic to draw a direct line of continuity between the ideas the likes of Howell, Lewis, and Kellett had entertained since the 1960s and the policies the Thatcher governments eventually implemented in the 1980s to bring about popular capitalism. Tracing backwards Thatcher's politics and rhetoric in government inevitably conjures up evidence in support of seemingly linear arguments. If we pay attention to the various circumstantial factors and to the evolutionary character of wider share ownership as well as privatization plans, the contingent element in the development of Thatcherite policy comes to the fore. First of all, Howell and Lewis were aware of the utopian character of their ideas. Indeed they were sceptical whether the stock market could actually absorb the flotation of large state assets—concerns still prevalent among privatizing ministers and City seniors in the 1980s.[125] Then there was confusion over terminology. In 1970 Howell introduced the term 'privatization' into the British debate, although not in the context of selling state assets. Pointing out, however, that the term was 'hideously clumsy' and that 'something better must be invented', Howell used it when discussing his proposals of implementing modern management techniques into government.[126] This means that although the two libertarian right-wingers had spelt out what became the predominant method of privatization during the Thatcher years, denationalization and wider share ownership were still widely treated as separate issues, deemed having to be achieved by different means.

This is illustrated further if we look at the structure of the various policy groups Thatcher set up during opposition. The taskforce on the Nationalised Industries,

---

[123] Quote after Naish, *The Complete Guide to Personal Investment*, p. 123.

[124] Quote after E. J. Evans, *Thatcher and Thatcherism*, 3rd edn (London, New York: Routledge, 2013), p. 35.

[125] Kynaston, *The City of London*, IV, pp. 659–660.

[126] D. Howell, *A New Style of Government: A Conservative View of the Tasks of Administrative, Financial and Parliamentary Reform Facing an Incoming Government* (London: Conservative Political Centre, 1970), p. 8. The ambiguity in early uses of the term 'privatization' is stressed by Stevens, 'The Evolution of Privatisation as an Electoral Policy, c. 1970–90', 49–50.

for example, was chaired by Nicholas Ridley, one of Thatcher's earliest political allies. In 1976, the group compiled a detailed assessment of 'possible treatment[s]' for nationalized industries that listed Telecommunications and Gas—the two most successful privatizations of the Thatcher period—to have 'no potential for denationalisation by selling shares'.[127] Even the notorious 1977 'Ridley Report' remained undecided whether denationalized industries should 'issue their own equity shares, convertible shares, or loan stock to the public'.[128] On the other hand, Howell—by now Thatcher's speech writer and right-hand man on taxation—chaired the policy group on wider share ownership which he set up with Keith Joseph's approval in October 1975.[129] 'Wider Share Ownership' was a sub-group of the 'Taxation' unit, also led by Howell, which ranked third after 'Economic Reconstruction' and 'Public Sector' in the Shadow Cabinet.[130] This testifies to both the influence of Howell on the policymaking process and to wider share ownership having priority over denationalization.

Between 1975 and 1978—when he passed the chairmanship of the group on to MP Peter Hordern—Howell and his group devised plans for a new regime of capital taxation designed to foster 'popular', 'grass-roots', and 'mass capitalism'.[131] Anticipating the language of Margaret Thatcher's 'capital-owning democracy' of the 1980s, Howell and his colleagues suggested abolishing capital gains tax, stamp duty, and the investment income surcharge to create incentives for direct equity investment and employee share schemes.[132] These measures were to encourage the private investor to provide capital for SMEs, which were regarded as 'critical to the nation's economic success', and the spearhead of an economic recovery.[133] At this stage, wider share ownership was less about employee share schemes and more about incentivizing the private investor to invest in small businesses.[134] Thatcherites argued that the 'real rate of return on capital is pathetically low'[135] and envisaged comprehensive tax cuts as a means of providing start-ups with necessary venture capital and of changing popular attitudes towards risk-taking.

---

[127] Policy Recommendations of the Smaller Business' Group and the Nationalised Industries Group, Table I, 13 July 1976, MTF 110163.

[128] Report of Nationalised Industries Policy Group, 30 June 1977, MTF 110795.

[129] M. Thatcher to D. Howell, 2 August 1975, David Howell papers, Churchill Archives Centre, Cambridge, HWLL, 2/4/1/10 (hereafter HWLL), M. Thatcher to D. Howell, 5 May 1979; D. Howell to K. Joseph, 2 October 1975.

[130] Conservative Research Department, List of Policy Groups, 12 December 1975, HWLL, 2/4/1/1.

[131] Progress Report on Policy Groups, Taxation, 13 December 1975, HWLL 2/4/1/1; D. Howell, speech draft 'wider share ownership' (undated, c.1976), HWLL 2/4/1/17; Wider Ownership Group. Proposals for Employee Profit-Sharing, 25 May 1976, the papers of Baroness Thatcher LG, OM, FRS, Churchill Archives Centre, Cambridge, THCR 2/6/1/36 (hereafter THCR).

[132] Minutes of the Second Meeting of the Wider Share Ownership Group, 24 November 1975, LSE, WSOC, Box 9. The group's first meeting on 21 October was not minuted.

[133] Shadow Cabinet, Smaller Business Policy Document, 22 July 1977, MTF 110198.

[134] Williamson, *Conservative Economic Policymaking and the Birth of Thatcherism, 1964–1979*, pp. 84–85; Daunton, 'Creating a Dynamic Society', p. 41.

[135] D. Howell, Speech to Brecon and Radnor Branch of Conservative Small Businesses Bureau, 1 September 1977, HWLL 2/4/1/8.

Again, what amounted to mass speculation—ordinary savers putting up capital at an over-average ratio of profit and loss—had to be couched in less problematic terms. Hence, people were to be encouraged to participate in a 'fertile climate [ ... ] where initiative will be rewarded and where proper incentives for risk-taking, skill and hard work will exist'.[136]

In the development of the group's policies, Howell relied heavily on private sector input, mirroring Thatcher's ambition of 'transferring the business ethic into the heart of government administration'.[137] One important figure in this regard was the libertarian tax-lobbyist Barry Bracewell-Milnes, Economic Advisor to the Institute of Directors and libertarian tax lobbyist. After obtaining a PhD at King's College, Cambridge, Bracewell-Milnes advised the Federation of British Industries, the business lobby group which merged into the Confederation of British Industry (CBI) in 1965.[138] First as head of the CBI's economic division and from 1968 as its economic director, he campaigned vigorously against the 'various taxes levied on capital and investment income'.[139] In 1973, the staunch monetarist was forced to resign from his post after refusing to withdraw his radical suggestions on cutting capital taxation from the CBI's annual budget recommendation. Celebrated as a martyr, he joined the Mont Pelerin Society, the neoliberal think tank founded by Hayek. He became the New Right's key man on tax issues and popularized the claim that the British tax system was unfairly biased in favour of spending to the disadvantage of saving and investment.[140] This reputation within the neoliberal movement earned him an invitation by Conservative MPs David Howell and Peter Hordern to sit on their Wider Share Ownership Committee, which is not be confused with the lobby group, the Wider Share Ownership *Council*. In a series of publications Bracewell-Milnes set forth detailed steps towards a neoliberal tax regime and introduced the idea of tapering out the Capital Gains Tax to Howell's policy taskforce.[141] More broadly, he stressed that private ownership, both in terms of equity capital and housing, was 'the Conservative Party's most powerful weapon' that 'has scarcely been exploited at all'.[142]

Peter Hordern was the 'City man' on the Conservative Party committee. A self-proclaimed 'Thatcherite before Thatcher', Hordern was known as a 'traditional

---

[136] D. Howell, Smaller Business Policy Document, 6 June 1977, HWLL 2/4/1/8.
[137] Evans, *Thatcher and Thatcherism*, p. 59. See also Vinen, *Thatcher's Britain*, pp. 82–83.
[138] Rollings, 'Cracks in the Post-War Keynesian Settlement?', pp. 652–653.
[139] 'Bias against investors condemned', *Financial Times*, 9 February 1967; 'CBI to carry out own investment allowances study', *The Times*, 17 December 1968; 'Boost to Britain's balance of payments', *The Times*, 28 October 1969.
[140] Rollings, 'Cracks in the Post-War Keynesian Settlement?', pp. 654–656; 'Economic director is asked to leave CBI', *The Times*, 23 January 1973.
[141] Wider Share Ownership Group, Draft Discussion Document on Capital Taxes, 3 March 1977, HWLL 2/4/1/11.
[142] Barry Bracewell-Milnes, Ownership and taxation, WSOC meeting [i.e. Howell's policy group], 30 September 1976, THCR 2/6/1/36.

monetarist' and a 'sustained opponent of public service bureaucrats'.[143] He became a member of the London Stock Exchange in 1954 and was one of the few stockbrokers in the Commons when elected MP for Horsham in 1964.[144] Other committee members were the entrepreneur and later Tory MP, Nigel Vinson, who was also the founder director of the CPS, as well as George Copeman, Deputy Chairman of WSOC and restless advocate of employee share schemes.[145] Besides incentivizing private stock market investment, these members were also concerned about the 'increasing share of the Stock Market taken up by the institutions'—by 1975 institutional shareholdings had overtaken their private counterparts—and sought ways of reversing this trend to the benefit of individual investors.[146] As Howell reported to the party leadership in July 1975, the group set out to seek ways of 'de-institutionalising savings in order to put the private investor in a better position vis-a-vis the pension funds and insurance companies'.[147] In this regard, the group suggested abolishing the unequal tax treatment of direct investment as opposed to contractual savings and investments via pension schemes or insurances—an idea also put forward at that time by many stockbroking firms looking to attract private clients' business.[148] These tax breaks dated back to Gladstonian times and were seen as 'a powerful incentive for people to abandon direct investment in the stock market'—but unlike the investment income surcharge and in spite of serious consideration they were not abolished by the Thatcher government.[149]

The internal policy debate over capital taxation and wider share ownership could not disguise a clash of two Thatcherite dogmas. The Howell–Hordern groups' stated aim was to 'help people become more self reliant [sic], thrifty and genuinely independent'. There was, however, a tension between creating the desired change among people's attitudes towards spending and saving on the one hand and the prime Conservative objective of tackling paternalist attitudes in the state apparatus on the other hand. The committee paid lip service to the

---

[143] See Hordern's undated autobiographical sketch, available at http://www.aahorsham.co.uk/con tent/peterhordern. Accessed 7 April 2016; and his entry in Andrew Roth, *Parliamentary Profiles* (London: Parliamentary Services Ltd, 1983), pp. 379–380.

[144] 'HORDERN, Rt Hon. Sir Peter (Maudslay)', *Who's Who 2016*.

[145] Minutes of the Second Meeting of the Wider Share Ownership Committee, 24 November 1975, LSE, WSOC, Box 9. The Committee's first meeting on 21 October was not minuted.

[146] Peter Hordern, Memorandum to the Wider Share Ownership Committee, 18 April 1978, LSE, WSOC, Box 12. In 1975, individuals held 37.5% of UK listed shares while insurance companies held 15.9%, pension funds 16.8%, unit trusts 4.1%, and 'other financial institutions' 10.5% (total 47.3%). See the table on beneficial ownership of UK shares 1963–1997 in Office for National Statistics, *Share Ownership*, p. 8.

[147] D. Howell, Policy Group on Taxation: Chairman's Interim Report to the Shadow Cabinet, 23 July 1975, HWLL 2/4/1/1.

[148] See the discussion in Chapter 6. On Conservative considerations in this regard see Daunton, 'Creating a Dynamic Society', pp. 37–39.

[149] Quote after J. Plender and P. Wallace, *The Square Mile: A Guide to the New City of London* (London: Hutchinson Business, 1986), p. 68; on Gladstone's 1853 budget that brought tax relief for life insurance premiums see Daunton, *Trusting Leviathan*, pp. 99–100.

Thatcherite creed of widening individual 'choice' in the market. But its primary concern was a 'fundamental point' that Hordern stressed in a report about the committee's work to the Shadow Chancellor, Geoffrey Howe. This point helps understand measures like the sharp increase of value added tax from 8 per cent to 15 per cent, which the Thatcher government introduced in 1979 as an early measure to curb consumption:

> Some would say, rather than complicating life still further [ ... ] let the taxpayer choose whether he should invest or spend, as, after all, it is his money which we are considering. However, this is not the view of the group. [ ... ] There seems to us to be a strong case for pressing a positive bias towards savings rather than personal consumption.[150]

More broadly, this correspondence highlights the ambiguous character of Thatcherite individualism or, more bluntly, the fact that 'there was no coherent or fixed Thatcherite concept of the individual'.[151] The findings on wider share ownership support the argument that Thatcherite policies had no predefined understanding of individuals as 'capitalists or consumers', whether individuals were 'rational or irrational', or whether incentives should turn them into 'risk-taking entrepreneurs or prudent savers'.[152]

The committee's more immediate impact on Conservative policy is demonstrated in the 1977 policy paper, *The Right Approach*, authored by leading Tory strategists Geoffrey Howe, Keith Joseph, James Prior—and David Howell. Written in the light of growing economic unrest and the International Monetary Fund (IMF) crisis which saw the Callaghan government borrowing US$3.9 billion in exchange for budget cuts, the opposition quasi-manifesto was the blueprint for some of Thatcher's later economic policies. Besides its main concern, tackling inflation, it argued that the 'dearth of private risk capital [ ... ] is at the root of many of the small business sector's problems'.[153] The pamphlet called for a comprehensive reform of capital taxes in favour of the private investor to 'see the habit of personal capital cumulation [ ... ] much more deeply ingrained in our society'.[154] Hence, we can take *The Right Approach* as evidence for a genuine concern among Tory policymakers about the growing institutionalization of equity markets and the dominance of passive over active investment.

---

[150] P. Hordern to G. Howe, 22 June 1978, LSE, WSOC, Box 13.
[151] A. Davies, J. Freeman, and H. Pemberton, '"Everyman a Capitalist" or "Free to Choose": Exploring the Tensions within Thatcherite Individualism', *The Historical Journal* (2018), pp. 477–501.
[152] Davies et al., '"Everyman a Capitalist" or "Free to Choose"', pp. 477–501.
[153] G. Howe, *The Right Approach to the Economy: Outline of an Economic Strategy for the Next Conservative Government* (London: Conservative Central Office, 1977), p. 31.
[154] Howe, *The Right Approach to the Economy*, p. 34.

[O]ccupational pension rights and savings through life assurance schemes already offer the majority of households in Britain the chance during working life to acquire a proper stake (albeit at one remove) in the ownership of the wealth of the community. But we would like to promote more direct form of personal ownership as well.[155]

The new Conservative remedy against both private capital monopolization and state collectivism was a radical economic individualism that entailed the firm belief that small businesses revitalized by private risk capital were to be the engine of an economic recovery. However, *The Right Approach* did not include specific arrangements for denationalization, bearing further witness to the gulf between this policy and the task of widening share ownership.[156]

The wider share ownership movement could celebrate an unexpected success even before the Conservatives returned to power in May 1979. In order to pass the 1978 budget, James Callaghan's minority Labour government was compelled to make concessions to the Liberal Party. The Liberals made tax benefits for employee share schemes a condition of their support for the bill, a policy for which they drew on the WSOC for advice, in particular on George Copeman's expertise in this field.[157] After the passing of the Act, which included Approved Profit-Sharing, the Treasury acknowledged that Copeman's advice was 'taken fully into account in the preparation of the consultative document on profit sharing'.[158] Copeman's suggestions, in turn, were based on an internal green paper by the Howell Committee, highlighting the irony of this 'landmark shift towards share incentives'[159]—at the behest of the Liberal Party and based on policies predominantly designed by Tories, a Labour government introduced the first active encouragement of wider share ownership of the post-war years.

### Incentivizing Private Investment in Government

This cross-party consensus on share incentives paved the way for further steps taken from 1979 onwards. Now, Thatcher and Howe led a government that no longer regarded wider share ownership as impracticable, too risky, and potentially unpopular, but as a key policy for reshaping economy and society. Just as in 1970, the aim of building a capital-owning democracy loomed large in the Conservative

---

[155] Howe, *The Right Approach to the Economy*, p. 34.
[156] Stevens, 'The Evolution of Privatisation as an Electoral Policy, c. 1970–90', p, 54.
[157] Minutes of the Meeting of the Industrial Sub-Committee, 19 May 1978; Minutes of the Meeting of the Executive Committee, 14 June 1978, LSE, WSOC, Box 3.
[158] J. Barnett to G. Copeman, 4 October 1978, LSE, WSOC, Box 9.
[159] Munro, 'The Fiscal Politics of Savings and Share Ownership in Britain, 1970–1980', p. 771.

Party's 1979 manifesto.[160] This time, however, staunchly monetarist ministers were determined to go ahead with implementing these policies. The earliest strategies on economic policy of the newly elected government envisaged incentives for widening share ownership, particularly investment in small businesses as an important policy of supply-side economics. These sources also testify to Thatcher's new style of politics and her cabinet's ambition to involve the 'Government's friends in the press, the IEA and selected businessmen' when communicating its economic strategy to the electorate.[161]

Naturally, David Howell and Keith Joseph, Secretary of State for Industry in Thatcher's first cabinet, were particularly active in putting forward 'specific ideas' about how the government could achieve a 'really wide spread of the ownership of industry'.[162] Branding the 'polarisation of the stock market' as an impediment to emerging companies' growth, Joseph proposed substantial '[t]ax relief for individuals investing in small firm's equity'.[163] As ways of achieving this, Thatcher's most trusted adviser suggested they should 'redress [the] tax balance as between direct personal and institutional investment' and 'eliminate [the] distinction between earned and unearned income'—but only the latter became effective in 1984.[164] Howe's 1979 budget, passed only weeks after the election, addressed this issue straight away by raising the threshold for the investment income surcharge to '£5,000 for everyone; the rate above that level will remain at 15 per cent'.[165] Howe's successor, Nigel Lawson, abolished the investment income surcharge completely in his 1984 budget, effectively ending the Fabian tax discrimination against 'unearned' income that had been governing the British tax system since 1907. While Howe's step reduced the tax burden for smaller investors in particular, the complete abolishment of the surcharge, which became effective in 1985, was criticized as a tax gift to large financial institutions.[166] Lawson's 1984 budget also halved stamp duty on share transactions in order 'to contribute further to the creation of a property-owning and share-owning democracy, in which more decisions are made by individuals rather than by institutions'.[167] Further

---

[160] Green, *Thatcher*, p. 97.

[161] Cabinet Meeting at 10 Downing Street to Discuss John Hoskyns' Paper on Government Strategy, 18 June 1979, TNA, PREM 19/25, Economic Policy (Strategy).

[162] D. Howell to G. Howe, 1 August 1979, TNA, PREM 19/25.

[163] Acceleration of Enterprise: Note by the Secretary of State for Industry (Keith Joseph), 29 June 1979, TNA, PREM 19/25.

[164] K. Joseph to M. Thatcher, 25 June 1979, TNA, PREM 19/25; Munro, 'The Fiscal Politics of Savings and Share Ownership in Britain, 1970–1980'.

[165] Geoffrey Howe, Budget Speech 1979, MTF 109497; on the budget see Vinen, *Thatcher's Britain*, pp. 108–114.

[166] 'Opposition attack capital gains tax changes', *The Times*, 9 May 1985. On the end of the Fabian consensus see Munro, 'The Fiscal Politics of Savings and Share Ownership in Britain, 1970–1980', p. 765.

[167] N. Lawson, Budget Speech, 13 March 1984, MTF 109501. Stamp duty had first been raised to 2% by Labour in 1947, halved by the Conservatives in 1961 and redoubled in 1974 by the Labour Chancellor Dennis Healey.

legislations that bore the hallmarks of Howell's and Joseph's economic individualism were the Business Start-Up scheme of March 1981, which was further
developed into the Business Expansion Scheme by Howe in his 1983 budget.[168]
The Finance Acts of 1980 and 1984—with the Savings-related Share Option Plan
and Approved Share Options respectively—built on the tax breaks for employee
share schemes first introduced in 1978. Internally as well as in public, these
policies were motivated by the perception that the 'private investor has declined
in importance as a source of finance for small firms'.[169] In his Commons speech
on the Business Start-Up Scheme, Howe laid out the underlying logic of the
legislation as follows:

> One of the biggest problems faced by people thinking of starting their own
> business is the difficulty of attracting sufficient risk capital to finance it during
> its critical early years. [ ... ] The individual private investor has for many years
> had little encouragement to help fill that gap in the capital market. [ ... ] I am,
> therefore, introducing an entirely new tax incentive to attract individual investors
> to back new enterprises.[170]

It would be difficult to assess to what extent the new tax incentives on equity
investment actually encouraged private individuals to enter the stock market,
especially since these policies soon came to be flanked by privatization, first
gradually, then on a large scale. However, if Howe and Lawson did lure private
investors into the stock market, they did not come to the rescue of SMEs. As Ewen
Green has pointed out, 'in spite of their avowed intention to foster the interests
and growth of small business, the policies of the administrations of the 1980s did
not wholly favour small enterprise [ ... ] during Thatcher's premiership more
small businesses went bankrupt each year than were created and survived'.[171]

Thatcher's first government took small, incremental steps of denationalizing,
starting with the public sale of British Aerospace in 1981. Cable and Wireless,
Amersham International, and Associated British Ports were further minor companies which went on sale before the landslide election victory in June 1983.[172]
After the successful flotation of British Telecom in November 1984, which turned
1.5 million Britons into shareholders, privatization became one of Thatcherism's
most dynamic policies. The social and cultural ramifications of this will be
examined in more detail in Chapter 6. In many ways, privatization marked a
departure from long-term efforts to encourage wider share ownership and to

---

[168] Daunton, 'Creating a Dynamic Society', p. 45.
[169] Acceleration of Enterprise: Note by the Secretary of State for Industry (Keith Joseph), 29 June
1979, TNA, PREM 19/25.
[170] *HC Deb* 1000, 10 March 1981 cc. 781–782.        [171] Green, *Thatcher*, p. 73.
[172] For the first four years of privatization see Parker, *The Official History of Privatisation*, I,
pp. 113–165.

disperse market power. Denationalization was originally designed to cut back state expenditure, widen consumer choice, raise short-term revenue, and weaken the unions. Only later it became linked to wider share ownership after the first flotations attracted sufficient buyers. Once Tory ministers could boast an enormous rise in shareholder numbers, privatization seemed a much more spectacular method for widening share ownership than devising complex incentives for funnelling small investors' capital into start-up businesses, or even educating the public about the complexities of the stock market. Privatization also meant a formidable business opportunity for large investment banks which, by government request, designed the public flotations of state giants, often merely turning public into private monopolies.[173] Thatcher's right-hand man in the privatization process was John Moore. Having worked as a retail stockbroker in Chicago, the Financial Secretary to the Treasury seemed the perfect candidate to 'build upon our property-owning democracy and to establish a people's capital market' in Britain.[174] Already in the run-up to the Telecom flotation, however, Moore made clear the priorities of privatization. When challenged by Kenneth Baker to allot a larger amount of shares to small investors, Moore replied that 'it would not be right to subordinate our objective of maximizing proceeds to our objective of wider share ownership'.[175]

Did 'popular capitalism' 'fail' in Britain because Thatcherism merely served 'the interests and control of large financial institutions', as suggested by Amy Edwards?[176] The Thatcher administrations did indeed show an early commitment to financial deregulation and abolished exchange controls in October 1979.[177] However, there is no evidence that the City, much less the Stock Exchange, had any significant influence on government policy at that stage—quite the contrary. The Thatcherite reading that the anti-industrial spirit of Britain's established elites had caused the erosion of bourgeois, capitalist values, extended to the City of London. Richard Vinen points out that '[d]isdain for the City was especially marked amongst those ministers who had actually worked in it', like John Nott and Cecil Parkinson.[178] Keith Joseph urged the cabinet early on to '[e]ncourage (by speeches and contacts) the city [sic] institutions to look beyond the end of their noses' and 'to make clear that the Government expects the City generally to

---

[173] Kynaston, *The City of London*, IV, pp. 590–592, 659–660.

[174] 'British Telecom: All capitalists now', *The Economist*, 27 October 1984, p. 34. This quote was taken from a speech Moore had given at the opening of the WSOC's forum on Employee Share Schemes, held at the Institute of Directors. HM Treasury's Press Office, 'A People's Capital Market', 3 October 2014, LSE, WSOC, Box 12.

[175] Parker, *The Official History of Privatisation*, I, p. 299.

[176] Edwards, "Manufacturing Capitalists', p. 101.

[177] Michie, *The London Stock Exchange*, p. 500; E. Green, 'The Conservatives and the City', in R. Michie and P. Williamson (eds), *The British Government and the City of London in the Twentieth Century* (Cambridge: Cambridge University Press, 2004), p. 172.

[178] Vinen, *Thatcher's Britain*, p. 182.

bestir itself'.[179] The Conservative government was furthermore unwilling to suspend the referral of the Stock Exchange rulebook to the Restrictive Practices Court. Callaghan's outgoing Labour administration had enacted the referral in January 1979 in a late attempt to reform the Stock Exchange along more competitive lines.[180] Conservative ministers 'were not inclined to stop this prosecution' until the Stock Exchange bowed to several measures of reform laid down in a 1983 agreement between its Chairman, Nicholas Goodison, and Parkinson, which paved the way for the sweeping Big Bang deregulations of 27 October 1986.[181]

In retrospect, Thatcherism and the City appear as a 'love story (of sorts)',[182] but this was by no means predetermined. City–government relations improved after Nigel Lawson's appointment as Chancellor in 1983, not least because the former City editor of the *Sunday Telegraph* had much more intimate knowledge of the City and its affairs than his predecessor, Howe. Nevertheless, the Conservative government did not carry out a detailed plan of 'making the City the engine of the British economy' and recent source-based scholarship suggests thinking of Big Bang as 'an accident that had major consequences few of which were expected'.[183] Certainly, the shift towards institutional dominance was more marked than the growth in individual share ownership. We should not, however, draw simplistic conclusions of causality, and historians of Thatcherism have to subject the gap between the intentions of Tory policymakers and the outcome of their actions to the same rigorous scrutiny scholars apply to other periods.[184] Examining the 'failures' of popular capitalism does not unveil a 'Thatcherite–City' power bloc. Instead they demonstrate the restraints of modern democratic governments in shaping society and therefore the limits of the 'individual resurgence' desired by Thatcherites, especially against the backdrop of rapidly unfolding financialization on a global scale.[185] The institutionalization of stock markets may have been enhanced, but was not caused by Thatcherite policy of deregulation. It was, in fact, a global trend, exacerbated in Britain by age-old tax benefits for pension funds and life insurance companies.[186]

---

[179] Strategy—Proposals by Ministers, Economic Policy Strategy, 3 July 1979, TNA PREM 19/25.

[180] On the RPC see Michie, *The London Stock Exchange*, pp. 483–487.

[181] Quote after Vinen, *Thatcher's Britain*, p. 182; on the run-up to Big Bang see Michie, *The London Stock Exchange*, pp. 486–544 and more recently C. Bellringer and R. Michie, 'Big Bang in the City of London: An Intentional Revolution or an Accident?', *Financial History Review* 21 (2014), pp. 111–137.

[182] Kynaston, *The City of London*, IV, p. 581.

[183] Bellringer and Michie, 'Big Bang in the City of London', 132.

[184] R. Koselleck, 'Über die Theoriebedürftigkeit der Geschichtswissenschaft', in R. Koselleck, *Zeitschichten: Studien zur Historik*, 3rd edn (Frankfurt: Suhrkamp, 2013), pp. 310–314.

[185] Under the heading 'Education of the Public', Thatcher's Secretary of State for the Environment, Michael Heseltine, envisaged 'Draw[ing] up and orchestrat[ing] a continuing programme to articulate the profound nature of the individual resurgence we are seeking to create'. Strategy—Proposals by Ministers, Economic Policy Strategy, 3 July 1979, TNA PREM 19/25.

[186] Munro, 'The Fiscal Politics of Savings and Share Ownership in Britain, 1970–1980', p. 775.

A more complex picture emerges if we put Britain's quest for popular capitalism into perspective. By contrast with the United States, for example, the investment habit was certainly less entrenched in British society. On Wall Street, the New York Stock Exchange had partnered with fiscally conservative politicians and embarked on a mutual campaign in the interwar period to spread equity ownership as widely as possible among social classes. Shareholder numbers rose substantially during the interwar and post-WWII period, and equity ownership remains widely spread among American households to this day.[187] British observers during the 1980s, who wished to see share ownership become more engrained, often idolized the 'American ethic' of retail investment and speculation:

> On one particular point the critics of the system are perfectly correct. The City does thrive on speculation. [...] But even the Stock Exchange tries to play down the element of speculation in their market. This is simply silly, for it reinforces the view that investment and speculation mean separate things and encourages the belief that there is something inherently wrong with the concept and practice of speculation. But the whole American ethic is built upon the concept of speculation; those who are prepared to take risks in the hope of an eventual reward are society's idols.[188]

Compared to Continental European counterparts, however, the impact of Thatcher's popular capitalism comes more to the fore. Privatization became an export hit after the collapse of the Soviet Union, and former Thatcherite ministers served as advisors on privatization programmes in the newly formed Eastern European states.[189] In Ukraine, Slovakia, or the Czech Republic, however, the outcome of privatization was not popular capitalism, but an even more dramatic monopolization of capital in private hands.[190] Thatcherites like Howell and Lewis liked to reference Western Germany's experiences with 'people's shares' [Volksaktien] in the late 1950s and early 1960s. But the privatization of public companies like Volkswagen never had the effect of sustainably raising public acceptance for stocks and shares. If anything, Conservative ministers in the 1980s could have learned from the Volkswagen flotations that there was a trade-off between ensuring the political success of privatization by inviting as many buyers as possible, and achieving the desired behaviour of investors becoming

---

[187] Fraser, *Every Man a Speculator*.

[188] S. Rose, *Fair Shares: A Layman's Guide to Buying and Selling Stocks and Shares* (London: Comet, 1986), pp. 8–9

[189] J. Redwood, *The Democratic Revolutions: Popular Capitalism in Eastern Europe* (London: Centre for Policy Studies, 1990).

[190] P. Ther, *Die neue Ordnung auf dem alten Kontinent: Eine Geschichte des neoliberalen Europa* (Berlin: Suhrkamp, 2014), pp. 101, 161.

long-term shareholders. A vast number of small applicants in the Wolfsburg car manufacturer bought the heavily subsidized shares merely to cash in on a profit in early trading, causing critics to accuse the Christian Democratic government of Konrad Adenauer to have given the German public an 'education in specula-tion'.[191] We shall see later how stagging became a marked pattern during the Conservatives' privatizations agenda of the 1980s.

What the comparison with post-war Germany's experiments with privatization reveal is the extent to which the declinist assessment of British society lacking the entrepreneurial spirit of its European competitors was largely inaccurate. Thatcher and her allies were concerned with having to create a popular capitalism, but found that to a considerable extent, the required appetite for investment, risk-taking, and in fact speculation was already present. More broadly, these diverging experiences show that the extent of popular share ownership depends less on the policy design of stock market flotations or tax incentives, but largely on the nuances of national stock market cultures. These in turn are shaped by deeper historical experiences, economic mentalities, social structure, political intent, and the relationship between government and the financial sector. British politics, as this chapter has demonstrated, had come to regard private share ownership as economically and socially desirable by the late 1970s. In the 1950s and 1960s, the political establishment and Whitehall civil servants did not view it as the govern-ment's responsibility to widen share ownership. In the second half of the 1970s, neoliberal Tories in opposition, together with like-minded journalists and entre-preneurs, advocated individual stock market engagement as a key component of a free-market revival. Eventually, although the private investor had been witnessing relative decline in the stock market for decades, the 1980s saw the idea of the shareholding individual became a strong component of modern citizenship. But before we examine how the investing public reacted to the large privatization issues of the Thatcher years, we will turn to the severe economic turmoil of the 1970s that prompted significant rethinking on the acceptance of private profits in Britain's economic life.

---

[191] 'Auf dem Schleuderbrett', *Der Spiegel*, 19 April 1961; see also E. Hausteiner, 'Eine Aktie, ein Volk: Die Werbekampagne während des Wirtschaftswunders' in H. Münkler and J. Hacke (eds), *Wege in die neue Bundesrepublik: Politische Mythen und kollektive Selbstbilder nach 1989* (Frankfurt am Main: Campus, 2009), pp. 199–212.

# 5

# The Profit Motive

## Inflation and Retail Investment in the 1970s

During the 1970s, all western industrial nations were exposed to enormous economic and social pressures. The political responses to these challenges sooner or later brought down the corporatist economic settlements that had been established across Europe after WWII and in the US during the interwar period. The exceptional economic growth of the post-war decades came to an end and in the 1970s inflation and unemployment rates not seen since the 1930s created financial weather marked by uncertainty and volatility.[1] The stage was set for fundamental structural changes in the world's financial markets when, in 1971, the US government of Richard Nixon suspended the post-war monetary system of Bretton Woods. This abolition of a fixed currency exchange system in favour of a market-based financial order paved the way for the formation of a new global economic regime. Under monikers such as financialization, the 'rise of the trader', or the 'shock of the global', scholars today widely agree that the liberalization and globalization of financial markets after the end of Bretton Woods was the most lasting legacy of the tumultuous 1970s.[2] The decade saw finance become the fastest growing sector in industrialized economies, and as a result of this development, '"short termism" and speculation [...] reached dimensions that could not have been imagined in the 1920s and 1930s'.[3] The variety of financial securities that were exchanged across national borders grew enormously as trading desks at global investment banks sold 'increasingly complex strategies of risk management, insurance, hedging, and speculation'.[4] More often than not, they fuelled the very uncertainty and volatility they claimed to mitigate. At the same time, the economic mainstream in media, politics, and academia began to move away from the corporatist Keynesian orthodoxies that underpinned the social

---

[1] For a concise overview of socioeconomic, political, and intellectual trends culminating in the 1970s see M. Buggeln, M. Daunton, and A. Nützenadel, 'The Political Economy of Public Finance since the 1970s: Questioning the Leviathan', in M. Buggeln, M. Daunton, and A. Nützenadel (eds), *The Political Economy of Public Finance: Taxation, State Spending and Debt since the 1970s* (Cambridge: Cambridge University Press, 2017), pp. 1–31.

[2] N. Ferguson, 'Introduction', in N. Ferguson and C. S. Maier (eds), *The Shock of the Global: The 1970s in Persepective* (Cambridge, MA: Belknap Press of Harvard University Press, 2010), pp. 1–21; Kay, *Other People's Money*.

[3] J. Kocka, 'Writing the History of Capitalism', *Bulletin of the German Historical Institute (Washington, DC)* 47 (2010), p. 21.

[4] S. Strange, *Casino Capitalism* (Manchester: Manchester University Press, 1986), p. 119.

*Playing the Market: Retail Investment and Speculation in Twentieth-Century Britain*. Kieran Heinemann, Oxford University Press (2021). © Kieran Heinemann. DOI: 10.1093/oso/9780198864257.003.0006

democratic order.[5] Politicians re-embraced traditional tenets of laissez-faire capitalism, which certain intellectuals and journalists had been promoting as the ultimate solution for economic, political and social problems.[6] 'The market', in Daniel T. Rodger's words, became 'a metaphor for society as a whole'.[7] By 1980, the Anglo-Saxon world had elected right-wing political leaders—Ronald Reagan and Margaret Thatcher—whose market-driven policy agenda sooner or later spilt over to Continental Europe and the globe.[8]

Britain emerged as a new role model for a dynamic, service-driven, and globalized market economy after the collapse of the Soviet Union in 1989–90. This stood in stark contrast to Britain's perception at the outset of the 1970s. Politicians and economists across the continent feared to catch the 'English disease' from the 'sick man of Europe'.[9] These debates heightened the sense that Britain was experiencing a time of 'major economic crisis' and made the alarmist declinism of the Conservative opposition seem more convincing.[10] The list of Britain's economic deficiencies was indeed long. With an annual average of 2.3 per cent, UK GDP growth between 1970 and 1979 was lower than that of the US, the Federal Republic of Germany, France, and Italy. During the same time period, only the US and Italy had higher unemployment rates than Britain, where an average unemployment rate of 5.6 per cent between 1974 and 1980, coupled with severe industrial unrest, was deemed a fatal deviation from post-war levels. Arguably the most striking feature of 1970s Britain were its inflation rates, the highest out of all western economies with an average change of 12.4 per cent per annum in its Retail Price Index (Italy 12.2 per cent, France 8.8 per cent, US 7per cent, and FRG 4.9 per cent). This made a particular impact given that Britain—unlike other European societies—had never experienced inflation on a comparable scale before (Figure 5.1).

The story of Britain's stock market during this period has been rooted deeply in this narrative of decline. Investors small and large exited the market on a large scale after or in anticipation of the great bear market that followed the collapse of Bretton Woods. Ravaged by inflation, retail investors were wary of coming back, and those who did, or had remained, increasingly felt the squeeze of the institutional investors, whose continued growth led to a revolution of the investment process during the 1970s. This chapter offers a more refined understanding of how

---

[5] Burgin, 'Age of Certainty'.

[6] The literature on this transformation has grown enormously in the past decade. For Britain see Jackson, 'The Think-Tank Archipelago'; Rollings, 'Cracks in the Post-War Keynesian Settlement?'; Cockett, *Thinking the Unthinkable*.

[7] D. T. Rodgers, *Age of Fracture* (Cambridge, MA: Belknap Press of Harvard University Press, 2011), p. 75.

[8] D. Harvey, *A Brief History of Neoliberalism* (Oxford: Oxford University Press, 2011).

[9] 'Curing the sick man of Europe', *The Times*, 30 December 1969. By that time 'English disease' became shorthand for Britain's fatal combination of industrial unrest and stagflation.

[10] Harrison, *Finding a Role?*, pp. 296–300.

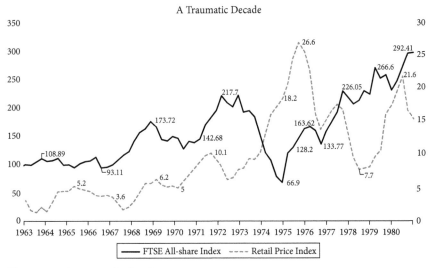

**Figure 5.1** A traumatic decade
*Source*: FTSE Russell.

small investors and speculators dealt with the challenges of inflation, volatility, and market uncertainty by tracing their activity into markets that have not been studied closely before. But inflation was more than a powerful economic driver that determined market behaviour. If we consider inflation as an unprecedented individual as well collective historical experience, we can identify a fundamental shift in attitudes towards the profit motive among ordinary savers and investors, a shift that eventually made them more receptive to the market populism of Margaret Thatcher's Conservative Party.

## 'The Financial Equivalent of the Great War'

The 1970s were a traumatic decade for investors across the globe, and in Britain the 1973–4 bear market was the most severe market collapse of the twentieth century. The crash, like any serious financial crisis was all the worse because it was preceded by a prolonged period of optimism and exuberance about markets. As we have seen, the 1950s and 1960s were strong decades for equities, and at first the momentum continued into another bull market from 1971–72—the decade's last one, which set the height of the fall. In the words of stockbroker and stock market chronicler John Littlewood: 'This bull market has been as good a party as any could remember. [ ... ] At moments like this, a bull market almost enters into a conspiracy with itself, fuelled by excitement and greed.'[11] A vivid example of how

---

[11] Littlewood, *The Stock Market*, p. 188.

this euphoria could translate into everyday life is given by an anecdote the 16-year old Ms Norgate from Halifax cared to share in a letter to the *Financial Times*. The teenager approached the highbrow paper with unwarranted self-deprecation, stating that 'as a mere female [she] could never hope to comprehend the intricacies of the stock market'. She told the paper about her father, who had developed an obsession with the stock market and an unwise attachment to the shares he bought—a habit that had come to disrupt the Norgates' family life. For instance, Mr Norgate had recently acquired a large stock in Northern Songs, The Beatles's music company, prompting him to buy every single record of the band from Liverpool. For his daughter this had the benefit of acquiring a record collection which was 'the envy of many of my friends'. But then he plunged into shares of a big TV company shortly afterwards, and as a result the television set was 'rarely switched off' at the Norgates's home. Showing a rather acute understanding of the stock market, the daughter dreaded to 'think what would happen if he bought shares in a brewery'. In the end 'however', Ms Norgate concluded, 'the stock market definitely helps to brighten our lives' and she hoped that her letter would 'show you the stock market is not solely a place of men, long faces and over-drafts'.[12] The letter prompted a response from a Mr Mason from Birmingham who rejoiced in her anecdote, endorsing the 'popular national pastime of stock market gambling and the great pleasure it gives to the Norgates and innumerable other families'.[13]

From May 1972, however, long faces and overdrafts came to haunt the British stock market. Between then and December 1974 the Financial Times All-Share Index lost 73 per cent of its value, making 1974 a worse year than 1929. One small investor described the period as so traumatic that 'there is as a result a wariness about the investor, a lack of the same debonair poise akin to that of a climber who has suffered a severe fall or a racing driver who has been badly injured. He will continue to climb or to race but the effects of the trauma will always be with him; so with the investor who experienced 1974'.[14] In even more dramatic terms, the London stockbrokers Rowe & Pitman wrote in their monthly client circular that 'this bear market is the financial equivalent of the Great War'.[15] Until this day, Britain's investment community references the 1970s as the ultimate warning sign. Especially after the 2016 Brexit referendum, rarely a week went by without a pro-business commentator or analyst warning against a 'return to the 1970s'.[16] Even though much of this talk may have been overblown and was intended to

---

[12] 'Letters to the Editors: Stock market joys', *The Financial Times*, 31 July 1971.
[13] 'Letters to the Editor: Horses for bourses', *The Financial Times*, 7 August 1971.
[14] Medomsley, *Opportunities for the Small Investor*, pp. 31–32.
[15] Kynaston, *The City of London*, IV, p. 510.
[16] For a selection of a few more recent articles see 'The brutal global stockmarket crash that hit Britain hardest', *MoneyWeek*, 15 September 2017; 'Britain's 1970s retreat', *The Economist*, 15 November 2017; John Plender, 'We must heed warnings from the 1970s bear market', *The Financial Times*, 25 April 2018; by the same author 'Why markets need to heed the lessons from the 1970s', *The Financial Times*, 24 July 2019.

warn against the radical left policies of then Labour leader Jeremy Corbyn, there are some uncanny parallels. Like the double-digit inflation of the 1970s, the quantitative easing of central banks after 2008 'impoverish[ed] average pensioners and savers in deposit-like products'.[17] Donald Trump's presidency, Brexit, and the global rise of populism are reminiscent of 1970s geopolitical uncertainty, making political risk a serious investment factor then as well as today. Last but not least, in both the 1973 slump and the 2007/08 global financial crash, the property sector played a prominent role.

In Britain, the crisis had been fuelled by the 'Barber boom', the Heath government's expansionary 'dash for growth' policies named after the Conservative Chancellor, Anthony Barber. Upon taking office in July 1970, Barber sought to facilitate lasting growth by relaxing controls on bank lending and on hire purchase, causing households to take out loans and to spend more on housing and consumer goods. At first, investors small and large joined the party, and sent house prices and property shares soaring, not least because they felt encouraged by asset strippers like Jim Slater who personified the bullish climate of the time. As more and more borrowers sought to mount the property ladder, or remortgaged in order to buy bigger homes, house prices more than doubled between 1972 and 1975, and continued to rise for the rest of the decade.[18] In autumn 1973, however, the decision by OPEC nations to raise the price of oil and, shortly afterwards, to cut output, forced the British government to raise interest rates—as opposed to cutting rates, which would have been the conventional method of tackling an economic downturn. The resulting increase in corporate borrowing costs sent UK share prices sharply lower and the ensuing bear market that engulfed global stock markets hit Britain disproportionately hard. Over the decade, the annualized return of the FT All Share Index was 4.47 per cent. But with an average retail price increase of 12.4 per cent per year, this meant that investors could no longer regard equities as an effective protection from inflation.

How did Britain's investors play the bear market? Many conventional buy-and-hold investors took a bad hit. As we shall see, those relying on their investments for retirement planning, in particular, quite often faced existential difficulties. More active investors, on the other hand, continued their search for yield—either in the stock market or elsewhere—and there is evidence of highly creative investment strategies. In November 1974, the *Investors' Chronicle* observed that 'the only certainty nowadays is volatility',[19] in light of the ways in which small punters moved in out and out of equities trying to profit from the enormous price fluctuations that became characteristic of the decade. Some claimed that '[w]ithout speculation in some form it is impossible to substantially improve

---

[17] 'Markets should beware the clock ticking back to the 1970s', *The Financial Times,* 7 June 2019.

[18] Gleeson, *People and Their Money,* pp. 113–123.

[19] Kynaston, *The City of London,* IV, p. 424.

ones [sic] financial position' and that if 'you never speculate, you will never accumulate'.[20] Certain techniques of stock picking were promoted as being equally applicable to shares as to 'quick action gambles like horses or roulette'.[21] After the FT All Share Index had slightly recovered in 1975, *The Guardian* pointed out the 'paradox of rising gambling during a time of personal cash shortage and general economic disarray'. The newspaper mused

> Whatever the Freudian principles behind this curious fact of economic life, its symptoms are by no means in evidence exclusively in betting establishments such as turf accountants and dog tracks. It is making presence felt in that den of equity and fixed-interest, the stock market.[22]

The gilt-edged or government bond market, usually a safe haven for investors in times of market turmoil, did not offer any retreat during the 1970s. At the end of 1974, Consols—UK Treasury bonds that had no maturity date—were yielding a staggering 16.7 per cent and never in the decade fell into single-digit territory.[23] Hypothetically, investors were able to lock in a guaranteed return of 16.7 per cent until 2014, when Chancellor George Osborne redeemed the last of these perpetual bonds. But with the retail price index at times reaching 26.6 in the mid-1970s, gilts rarely outperformed inflation, and an investment opportunity unheard of at a time when US$13 trillion worth of global debt was yielding below zero, was then shunned for good reasons.[24] As a result, the 1970s became the first decade of the century—after the period of 1910–19—in which both Britain and the US 'saw negative inflation-adjusted returns on both stocks and bonds'.[25]

The dire outlook prompted some investors to venture into more speculative areas of the bond market: defaulted debt issued by fallen regimes known as 'busted bonds'. This market first became popular in the late 1950s, when defaulted government bonds of Soviet satellite states that had been issued at a time when the City of London was still the financial nod of a global empire became an object of mass speculation. In order to fund large infrastructure projects, countries like Hungary, Romania, Ukraine, or the Baltic States had issued sterling-denominated bonds, but after coming under Soviet influence, had ceased to service their debt.[26] However, after Stalin's death in 1953, when the Soviet Block sought reintegration

[20] J. P. Hodgson, *Speculation for Gain* (Southwick: Herdcroft, 1979), p. 1.

[21] Hodgson, *Speculation for Gain*, p. 1.

[22] 'Survival tips for amateurs in the Market', *The Guardian*, 27 December 1975.

[23] UK Debt Management Office, available at https://www.dmo.gov.uk/media/2164/consolsyields.xls. Accessed 29 January 2020.

[24] As of 30 January 2020, the amount of global debt with negative yields stood at 13.1 trillion. Source: Bloomberg Barclays Index for Global Aggregate Negative Yielding Debt Market Value in USD.

[25] For a table of economic indices for 1960–80 see Ferguson, 'Introduction', pp. 10–11.

[26] Gifford and Stevens, *Making Money on the Stock Exchange*, p. 34 mention that 'one of the securities on the London Stock Exchange is called City of Kieff Municipal Electric Trams, 1914.'

into the world economy, leaders on both sides of the Iron Curtain entered trade talks, as part of which a future settlement of outstanding debt was negotiated. In anticipation of settlement, punters started to buy these bonds, which were trading at enormous discounts. Throughout the 1960s, City editors like Margot Naylor (*Observer*) or Patrick Sergeant (*Daily Mail*) would tip their favourite Baltic, Romanian, and Hungarian bonds that jobbers on the London Stock Exchange were quoting at around £5–£8 per £100 notional.[27] Within a few years, settlement on some of these securities seemed imminent and they soared up to 17per cent–18 per cent. Eventually bondholders reaped enormous profits when the Baltics in 1967 and Hungary in 1968 reached settlement terms with the Council of Foreign Bondholders.[28]

Far more than the stock market, the government bond market was affected by political and geostrategic developments, which made distressed debt a market for wagering bets on the direction of the Cold War and of decolonization. This became apparent when 'busted bonds' in Africa and the Far East staged a return in the 1970s. During the Rhodesian Bush War (1964–79), the white supremacist government of Ian Smith, which had unilaterally declared independence, defaulted on its sterling-denominated debt in response to British economic sanctions. Throughout the brutal conflict, at the end of which Robert Mugabe became president of the newly formed Zimbabwe, the market in busted Rhodesian bonds remained extremely volatile and attracted speculators large and small. More prominently, in 1973 Communist China applied for membership of the World Bank and the IMF. The Chinese government was keen to tap London's vibrant capital market, but the Bank of England made clear that it would only grant access if a settlement agreement was found for the outstanding 61 million sterling-denominated bonds that Imperial China had issued between 1898 and 1925. Again, *The Observer* tipped defaulted Chinese government bonds as 'fascinating gambles' that had the advantage of dealing at very small increments of £50, which made the market accessible to the small punter.[29] Between 1971 and 1973 they doubled in price from 2per cent to 4 per cent of their nominal value and throughout the decade the market in these bonds continued to rise and remained very active. Investors who held on until 1984 could have sold the bonds between 17 per cent and 23 per cent depending on the issue, taking home a profit of up to 575 per cent.[30] By that time, the Chinese government still had not settled the debt, but its continued endeavour to access the London market was enough to drive up prices. Eventually Britain and China struck a deal in 1987 as part of which British

---

[27] 'Buys in busted bonds', *The Observer*, 27 September 1964.
[28] 'See what Kosygin started', *Daily Mail*, 14 February 1967; 'Hungarian External Sterling Debt', *The Financial Times*, 25 October 1968.
[29] 'Honourable Chinese bond', *The Observer*, 18 April 1971; 'Busted yes, but not inscrutable', *The Observer*, 30 September 1973.
[30] 'Glory days back for busted bonds', *The Observer*, 2 December 1984.

holders of Imperial bonds were compensated with £21mwhile American investors even today push for a settlement agreement with China amid the ongoing trade war between the two superpowers.[31]

While inflation prompted investors with an appetite for risk-taking into speculative areas of the stock and bond market, it also led to a significant reallocation of funds from financial into physical assets. An oft-cited development of the decade is the explosion of the housing market: the average house price more than quadrupled from £3,920 in January 1970 to £18,542 in December 1979, far outpacing inflation.[32] This trend played into the hands of the building societies, who had already become a major player in the mortgage market—mainly because they faced no competition from banks, who were not allowed to issue mortgages. The savings held by building societies increased from £2.9m in 1970 to £22m in 1975, and enabled more and more lower- to middle-income savers to climb the property ladder.[33] The property boom was mirrored in the stock market, where commercial property was one of the few sectors that posted inflation-beating returns.[34] But property was not the only physical asset that attracted investor interest. Precious metals such as gold and silver did spectacularly well, but so did works of art, antique furniture, and old wine as collectors increasingly faced competition from investors and speculators. In an ironic investment review of the decade, the *FT*'s financial editor Richard Lambert, fantasized about the 1,400 per cent profit he would have made by 1979 if in 1970 he had sold £3,000 worth of equities, and reinvested the money in a small piece of agricultural land, Victorian stamps, ten crates of 1945 Bordeaux red wine, three sovereign gold coins, ten barrels of Nigerian crude oil, and an eighteenth-century shotgun.[35] Art, antiques, and collectibles are a prime example of small investors' and speculators' search for yield moving from financial markets into a physical market during the 1970s. The decade saw a boom in collectibles, dealings in which became known as 'alternative investment'. The term became one of the financial buzzwords of the decade, and was popularized by Robin Duthy, a former City investment analyst turned art dealer. Duthy rose to fame on the art collector scene for applying methods of financial analysis and stock valuation to Chinese ceramics, coins, diamonds, and firearms.[36] One particularly volatile of these alternative investments was to collect ancient bond and share certificates, a hobby that gained popularity as 'scripophily' in the early 1970s. Ironically, while investors sold real financial securities on a

---

[31] 'China's path cleared to London markets', *Financial Times*, 6 June 1987; 'American creditors say China should honour pre-Communist debts', *The Economist*, 27 September 2018.

[32] Bloomberg Terminal, UK House Price Index, Average Price for All Dwellings (UKLHUK Index <GO>). Accessed 7 January 2020.

[33] Harrison, *Seeking a Role*, p. 319.     [34] Littlewood, *The Stock Market*, p. 185.

[35] 'Best buys of the decade: the chances you missed', *The Financial Times*, 29 December 1979.

[36] R. Duthy, *Alternative Investment: A Guide to Opportunity in the Collectibles Market* (London: Joseph, 1978); R. Duthy, *The Successful Investor: A Guide to Art, Gold, Wine, Antiques and other Growth Markets* (London: Collins, 1986).

large scale, the value of physical remnants of defaulted bonds and shares of bygone companies suddenly increased. 'Scripophily'—a neologism of the Ancient Greek word for affection and the word scrip, which was commonly used for a share certificate—developed into a considerable market for retail speculation in the second half of the decade. This collector's market was as colourful as the ancient bond and share certificates of fallen empires or bankrupt companies that had been gathering dust rather than interest in the holders' drawers or attics. Scripophily had its origins in Frankfurt, when two German bankers, as part of their PhD theses in 1970, catalogued issues of Tsarist Russian railway bonds and Imperial Chinese government bonds.[37] But how did the subject of a quaint art and economic history research project, carried out by two German bankers, turn into a hobby that captured the imagination of British stockbrokers, collectors, and small investors?

Market conditions alone cannot explain why during the second half of the end of the decade, scripophily developed into a speculative frenzy that was unprecedented even in a country where trading in collectibles had long been a national obsession.[38] In 1979, certain bond certificates of sterling-denominated Russian and Chinese issues eventually came to be auctioned off for five-figure sums at the prestigious London auction houses Christie's and Sotheby's.[39] They realized these prices because they were a physical reminder of the British Empire and its former financial prowess at a time when Britain had become obsessed with debates over its decline as a global economic and political power. The real economic decline of the time caused shares to be sold, but it was the exaggerated sentiment of declinism that fuelled imperial nostalgia and caused some of that money to be reinvested in a market for historical memorabilia of a glorified past. Up until today, bonds of Imperial China and Tsarist Russia have remained among some of the most sought-after collector's items. But in the 1970s the collector's interest was further enhanced by investors' interest in 'busted' Chinese government bonds, which had rekindled with Mao Zedong's ambition to reintegrate the People's Republic into the world economy. In the words of Ulrich Drumm, one of the founding fathers of scripophily, 'it cannot be ruled out that these securities will one day be redeemed, so that their current holders have some prospect of repayment, however remote'. It was exactly this combination of collector's value and the prospect of settlement agreements resulting in windfall profits for the holder that made 'old securities interesting from a speculative point of view.'[40] Over time, certificates of securities as diverse and controversial as US Confederate States bonds or Ethiopian Railway shares also attracted enormous collector's

---

[37] U. Drumm and A. W. Henseler, *Old Securities* (Dortmund: Harenberg, 1978).
[38] Egginton, 'In Quest of the Antique'.
[39] 'Under the hammer', *Daily Mail*, 26 September 1979.
[40] Drumm and Henseler, *Old Securities*, p. 71.

interest.[41] Many observers expected scripophily to vanish as quickly as it gained popularity when prices collapsed in late 1979. However, the burst of the bubble did not spell of the end of scripophily because dealing in scrips other than the Russian and Chinese classics had steadied by then: in 1980 the *FT* noted 'the generally healthy state of scripophily'.[42] Overall, seeing the small investor resurface in niche markets like distressed debt or nostalgic collectibles highlights again the necessity of a broader conception of who and what constituted the investing public. Thinking of the market in this more comprehensive fashion allows for a more nuanced understanding of how cultural as well as economic factors influenced investor behaviour.

Coming back to the stock market, contemporaries noted that many of Britain's small investors did reasonably well in anticipating the bear market and—perhaps heeding Patrick Sergeant's famous advice in 1973 to 'weed out shares'—liquidated their equity holdings in a timely fashion.[43] Writing during the aftermath of the crash, the erstwhile business editor of *The Observer*, and founder of *Management Today*, Robert Heller, cited contemporary studies according to which 'individuals in Britain alone offloaded the staggering sum of £6500 millions' worth of securities' in the year leading up to the 1973 slump.[44] The private investors' wave of selling ahead of the crisis had the side effect of aggravating the dominance of institutional investors over UK equity markets that had begun in the previous two decades. Pension funds, insurance companies, and unit trusts held just over 20 per cent of listed equity at the beginning of the 1970s, but by the end of the decade they owned more than half of UK shares. Overall, the unit trust industry almost tripled its assets under management from £1.41 billion in 1970 to £3.94 billion in 1980, in spite of wild fluctuations throughout the decade.[45]

The continued growth of institutional investors caused many stockbrokers to rethink their notoriously nonchalant rule-of-thumb approach to the matter of investment advice in which boozy lunches with family or school connections were more often the source of buy and sell recommendations than thorough research or number crunching. As more and more money was managed by professional investment managers, the securities business and the advice behind it came to be organized more professionally and along more scientific or at least analytical lines. For some time, there had been two schools of thought in this field. Fundamental analysis or 'value investing', an approach pioneered by the British-born American investor Benjamin Graham, sought to determine a share's intrinsic value by analysing a company's earnings, assets and liabilities, cash flows, and so on. Technical analysis, also known as 'chartism', on the other hand, was the

---

[41] R. Hendy, *Collecting Old Bonds and Shares* (London: Stanley Gibbons Publications, 1978). Hendy was a stockjobber turned broker on the London Stock Exchange and widely considered Britain's leading expert in scripophily.

[42] 'The age of scripophily', *The Financial Times*, 2 August 1980.     [43] See Chapter 3.

[44] Heller, *The Naked Investor*, p. 8.     [45] Gleeson, *People and their Money*, pp. 121–122.

study of predicting market movements based solely on historical price movements; in Britain, as we have seen in Chapter 2, Alec Ellinger was considered the 'don of chartism'.[46] Continuing a trend that began in the late 1950s, many firms stepped up their efforts during the 1970s to hire qualified statisticians, mathematicians, and actuaries as financial analysts.[47] This 'revolution of investment analysis' created a new cultural divide between London stockbrokers. On the one side were traditionalists such as Cazenove & Co. whose business model relied largely on 'whom they knew' and whose partners encouraged their employees to trust their flair and intuition and to 'enjoy the whole fascinating affair'.[48] Their best investment advice was sourced from personal contacts and friendships with company chairmen who shared company earnings or other sensitive information ahead of publication over a City lunch or in other private, socially exclusive settings—a practice that by any modern standard would be classified as insider dealing. On the other side, meritocratic firms like Phillips & Drew served clients based on 'what they knew' about markets, industries, companies, and economic trends. These firms drew heavily on the burgeoning academic discipline of financial economics and would harness the power of computers for their stock-pricing efforts. The research department of Phillips & Drew was considered a market leader, and was a far cry from some of the old rule-of-thumb City firms where an academic background in any quantitative subject was treated with suspicion.[49]

Revealingly, it was firms like Cazenove who protested most vehemently against the decade's ever louder calls to outlaw or effectively regulate against insider trading. In the United States, the practice had been outlawed in the 1930s and the rules enforced by the Securities and Exchange Commission. The London Stock Exchange, however, managed to uphold the century-old convention of self-regulation in this regard until the 1980 Companies Act classified insider dealing as a criminal offence. But even before that, the practice had already come under increased scrutiny during the takeover booms of the late 1950s and 1960s. Even free-market advocates like Harold Wincott argued that insider dealing was poison for the financial sector and undermined the City's credibility among the wider society. These efforts resulted in the establishment of the City Takeover Panel in 1968, and throughout the 1970s the topic of insider dealing remained '*the* test issue of City ethics' in the public mind.[50] Because insider dealing distorted markets, advocates of the meritocratic school supported measures against it in

[46] Rowlatt and Davenport, *The Handbook of Saving and Investment*, p. 121.
[47] Jenkins, *The Stock Exchange Story*, pp. 175–176.
[48] Kynaston, *The City of London*, IV, p. 170.
[49] For Phillips & Drew see Rowlatt and Davenport, *The Handbook of Saving and Investment*, p. 122, and Michie, *The London Stock Exchange*, p. 591; for the discipline of financial economics see D. MacKenzie, *An Engine, Not a Camera: How Financial Models Shape Markets* (Cambridge, MA: MIT Press, 2006).
[50] Kynaston, *The City of London*, IV, pp. 172–175.

order to create a level playing field in which they believed their investment analysis would result in a competitive edge. There was furthermore correlation between insider trading and fixed commissions. As Stuart Banner has shown, 'when the commissions stockbrokers charged their customer were fixed by the exchange, the brokers could not compete on price, so one common way of competing was by offering tips to their customers'.[51] The New York Stock Exchange abandoned fixed commission in 1975, which encouraged competition on price and service, and gave a further boost to discount brokers that targeted the retail market. In London, for the time being, commissions remained fixed.

But with the ascent of investment analysis a debate arose about whether the new scientific methods were actually yielding better investment results. Traditionalists held that flair, instinct, and experience would persevere over computer-based financial models. The only thing that can be said with certainty was that the new scientific approach was there to stay, and that eventually both sides of the divide were challenged fundamentally by new theories from economics departments, particularly from US universities.[52] After studying large datasets of stock prices, a growing number of economists reached the conclusion that the disagreement between fundamentalists and chartists over whether investment was an art or a science, was beside the point. A growing number of scholars became convinced that stock prices moved at random and that it was impossible to predict future market movements. The works of these economists came to be known as the Efficient Market Hypothesis (EMS) or, in more popular terms, as the Random Walk Hypothesis. The Chicago School economist Eugene Fama was arguably the most prominent proponent of this theory, which earned him the Nobel Memorial Prize in Economic Sciences in 2013. The EMS has been challenged and revised many times over subsequent decades, and because of its complexity it continues to be often misunderstood or deliberately misinterpreted.[53] Essentially, it can be broken down to the belief that no investor—whether chartist or fundamentalist, arm-chair speculator, or professional investment manager—can outguess the market in the long run, which is why it caused an outrage in an industry that claimed to know better.

What were the implications of these trends for private investors during the 1970s? For one, if they subscribed to the Efficient Market Hypothesis, they could feel more comfortable pitting their judgement against that of the professionals—especially since they were competing less against a web of inside information and more against an army of PC-savvy investment analysts whose efforts were

---

[51] Banner, *Speculation*, p. 272.
[52] British proponents include Ryan, *Theory of Portfolio Selection*; for a contemporary overview of the debate see P. Slovic, 'Psychological Study of Human Judgment: Implications for Investment Decision Making', *The Journal of Finance* 27 (1972), pp. 779–799.
[53] 'As the efficient market hypothesis turns 50, it is time to bin it', *The Financial Times*, 1 January 2020.

cancelling each other out and leading to shares being traded 'near their intrinsic value most of the time'.[54] These investors found a prominent advocate in Robert Heller, the financial author and entrepreneur. He was convinced that 'the amateur investor, "on the hard and brutal record of fact, has no need to feel at either a practical or a psychological disadvantage against the pros"' as long as he or she heeded one warning: 'any hopeful soul who rests his policy on substantially beating the norm is moving into the realms of the higher unreason.'[55] The impact of institutionalization and professionalization, as will be illustrated, was felt even more keenly in the client–broker relationship. Brokers were increasingly shifting their focus away from the private investor and towards large deals with institutions, from whom they could charge hefty fees due to fixed commissions. The decade's rapid technological advance and the rise of electronic trading technology also meant that securities dealing lost its personal and intimate touch. This applied to the trading floor of the new Stock Exchange building, opened in 1972, which its future chairman, Nicholas Goodison, described as 'rather clinical' and 'having much less sense of atmosphere'.[56] It also applied to the relationship between brokers and their clients, where the decline in face-to-face interactions and increase in transactions undermined one of the most important ingredients of the financial sector: trust.[57]

The professionalization and scientification of investment was ultimately down to the rise of institutional investors, especially pension funds and life insurance companies. By the second half of the 1970s, the concentration of corporate power in the hands of a new class of investment managers that went along with this development began to attract political attention, particularly from the left. The Labour Party accused the 'institutions' of 'misallocat[ing]' capital in such a way that was deeply harmful to the industrial base of the domestic economy'.[58] The institutionalization of equities markets became a hotly contested subject in the debate over Britain's perceived economic and financial decline that reached escalation point towards the end of the decade.

## 'Does this country need the small investor any longer?' Writing Letters to the Wilson Committee

We have seen in previous chapters that a key tenet of declinism was that Britain, more than any other industrialized economy, had long been suffering from a poor

[54] Rowlatt and Davenport, *The Handbook of Saving and Investment*, p. 152.
[55] Heller, *The Naked Investor*, pp. 156, 16.     [56] Kynaston, *The City of London*, IV, p. 418.
[57] Kay, *Other People's Money*, pp. 14–26.
[58] Davies, *The City of London and Social Democracy*, p. 27.

relationship between its domestic industry and the financial sector.[59] Although shared by some right-wing critics, this age-old critique of British finance being governed by a 'gentlemanly', anti-industrial elite was most prominent on the left wing of the Labour Party and the trade unions, now represented by the increasingly radical Tony Benn. Essentially, the financial sector stood accused of depriving British industry of capital in favour of higher-yielding investments abroad. Whether it was Ethiopian and Russian railways at the turn of the century or the Eurobond market in the post-war decades, both were considered to come at the expense of factories in Lancashire or the Midlands. The City's counter-argument was that state intervention and trade unions' collective bargaining had crippled Britain's international competitiveness, thereby causing foreign as well as domestic financiers to invest outside of Britain. But we have seen that even free-market liberals and Conservatives subscribed to the view that deep-seated anti-industrial attitudes prevailed in the City and that these were responsible for the persistence of restrictive practices that were harmful to the wider economy.[60] The solution they advocated was to expose the financial sector to international competition as opposed to the far left's nationalization plans.

The controversy over a potential nexus between anti-industrial attitudes in the City and poor manufacturing performance reached something of a climax at the Labour Party conference in Blackpool in October 1976, half a year after Harold Wilson had resigned as Labour prime minister and been succeeded by James Callaghan. By then, those within the Labour leadership who sought to encourage 'industrial investment without the necessity of nationalization, [had been] able to gain a more public airing of their views'.[61] But they were struggling to turn ideas into legislation—not least because the conference passed a motion on 'Banking and Finance', initiated by Benn, which envisaged 'widespread nationalization of the financial sector'.[62] In order to find a compromise with the party left's endeavours, Callaghan appointed his predecessor to chair a 'Committee to Review the Functioning of Financial Institutions', which soon became known as the Wilson Committee. Tasked with establishing whether British finance was starving out domestic industry, the committee gathered evidence from City institutions like banks, stockbrokers, and clearing houses as well as from large industrial companies, unions, lobby groups, and SMEs. However, the committee eventually failed to make an impact on Britain's financial landscape since the political climate had

---

[59] 'The early 1970s saw a general preoccupation with an apparent institutional and cultural divide between the City and domestic industry.' Davies, *The City of London and Social Democracy*, p. 57.

[60] On earlier variants of this prolonged dispute see E. H. H. Green, 'Rentiers versus Producers? The Political Economy of the Bimetallic Controversy, c. 1880–1898', *English Historical Review* 103 (1988), pp. 588–612.

[61] Davies, *The City of London and Social Democracy*, p. 71.

[62] Davies, *The City of London and Social Democracy*, p. 71.

shifted dramatically by 1980, when it published its 'largely anodyne majority report'.[63]

What is more relevant for the purpose of this chapter is that the committee also invited members of the public to provide testimony of their experiences with financial institutions: between 1976 and 1980 the committee received letters from 258 small savers and investors who offered their take on Britain's economic condition. These letters are a rare window into popular perceptions of the cultural divide between the City and industry. They allow us to build a lively picture of how ordinary savers and investors navigated through a decade of economic turmoil. These sources also reveal the diverse and often ambivalent attitudes that existed towards the financial sector in Britain at that time. On the one hand, the letters bear witness to a deep-rooted scepticism towards the City of London. Financial institutions, the Stock Exchange in particular, were viewed as being aloof from the rest of society and a moral objection against speculative profit-seeking is palpable in many of the testimonies. On the other hand, the letters also bring to light a tangible discontent with the post-war economic settlement. Letter writers bemoan rising inflation and the lack of incentives for saving and for private investors to provide risk capital for British industry. We should not mistake the letters addressed to the Wilson Committee for an accurate depiction of popular attitudes at that time. But a close reading of these testimonies in contrast with other sources allows us to uncover the continued existence of what previously has been described as 'genuine investment': the notion that stock market investment was a key aspect of industrial capitalism, which relied on responsible citizens exercising 'bourgeois' virtues of thrift and deferred gratification. Making sense of these ambiguities in the realm of personal finance during the 1970s allows us to better understand the appeal of Thatcherism, because from 1975, Britain's first female Leader of the Opposition publicly personified the economic virtues attached to the concept of 'genuine investment'.

If one public persona epitomized the very opposite of these economic virtues, it was Harold Wilson's. Throughout the post-war decades, Harold Wilson had been an anathema for many hard-money advocates, a factor likely to have prompted middle-class investors and thrifty working-class savers to vent their anger in protest letters. Wilson had a negative image with fiscally conservative voters not just since he had presided over the controversial devaluation in 1967, during which he famously promised that 'it would not effect [sic] the £ in the pocket or prices in the stores' as one letter reminded him.[64] Wilson's public image was that of a socialist technocrat who attacked 'passive and functionless shareholders' who,

---

[63] J. Tomlinson, 'British Industrial Policy', in R. Coopey and N. W. C. Woodward (eds), *Britain in the 1970s: The Troubled Economy* (London: UCL Press, 1996), pp. 177–178. For a similar assessment of the Wilson Committee as ineffective see Michie, *The London Stock Exchange*, pp. 539–541.

[64] Quote from [N/A] to Sir Harold Wilson, 14 March 1977, TNA, BS 9/26. On the ramifications of devaluation for the post-war settlement see S. Newton, 'The Sterling Devaluation of 1967, the

in his opinion, were 'becoming more and more avid for quick gains'.[65] There was, however, a lesser-known side to Wilson, namely that of a moderate and indeed pragmatic politician, who was actually very well connected and respected in the City of London. For instance Siegmund Warburg, the German financier and architect of the first hostile takeover in 1959, 'became one of Harold Wilson's most trusted confidants on economic questions'.[66] During Wilson's first term (1964–70) they convened together in 'regular meetings, about which other Cabinet members knew little' and in 1966 the prime minister knighted Warburg for his services.[67] In 1976, this personal, clandestine affinity towards the City became immediately apparent to the newly appointed staff of the Wilson Committee. One of the first things Wilson did after commencing work was to instruct his personal assistant to forward to him 'any letters that arrived from well known [sic] people' in the City, meaning that he probably never read those from less illustrious members of the public.[68] While being the public image of a political effort to reign in the power of the financial sector, he maintained close personal relationships with leading City figures, for example when going out for lunch at the offices of the leading stockbroking firm de Zoete & Bevan or the merchant bank Kleinwort & Benson.[69]

Retired financial professionals, accountants, university lecturers, directors, and employees of SMEs, farmers, manual workers, shopkeepers, and strike participants; various private individuals followed the Wilson Committee's appeal to the public to provide evidence. Wilson left most of the correspondence to his secretary, the highly rated civil servant Brian Hudson, who dealt with letters diligently, normally replying within a few days.[70] While the social backgrounds of letter writers were diverse, most of them had reached retiring age and were far more likely to be male than female. Hudson and his staff received queries from savers and investors who reported instances of alleged abuse or neglect by the hands of banks and stockbrokers. Other letters came in from citizens offering more or less specific policy suggestions, mostly based on experiences involving their own personal finances. And then there were those correspondents whose sweeping allegations of corruption and criminal activity in the City amounted to mere

International Economy and Post-War Social Democracy', *English Historical Review* CXXV (2010), pp. 912–945.

[65] *HC Deb* 608, cc. 34–36, 29 June 1959.

[66] N. Ferguson, *High Financier: The Lives and Time of Siegmund Warburg* (London: Allen Lane, 2010), p. xv; on the takeover, known as the Aluminium War, see Kynaston, *The City of London*, IV, pp. 107–115.

[67] Ferguson, *High Financier*, p. xv. On Warburg's knighthood see pp. 282–283.

[68] Eve to Sir Harold Wilson, 23 December 1976, TNA, BS 9/33.

[69] A. Steel to Sir Harold Wilson, 28 July 1978, TNA, BS 9/29; J. P. MacArthur to Sir H, 13 December 1977, TNA, BS 9/28.

[70] Anticipating a trend of the Thatcher years, Hudson left the civil service half-way through the Committee's work 'for a career in the City' with the Norwegian Bank, DNB. 'Shining star who opted for a job in the City', *The Times*, 10 October 1978.

conspiracy theories. The reasons for writing were manifold, but the letters' common denominator was a deep-seated frustration with inflation.

Given Wilson's public image as a City critic, many correspondents welcomed the elder statesman's endeavour to, in their words, 'clean up the City' or to 'remove undesirable practices' in the financial sector.[71] Ron Riley was a former bricklayer, foreman, and retired shop steward who reminded Wilson in his letter that 'it was through your good offices that I received a Grant to further my "mature" education at Enfield College, Middlesex Polytechnic'. Riley was now involved in a strike at a power station construction site on the Isle of Grain and assured his political idol that a 'great number of workers are more than pleased you are going to look into the city [sic] and its financial workings. [ ... ] Many ordinary hard working people want to know how the speculators get away with things, whilst pretending to be patriotic?'[72]

While the key role it played in the global Eurodollar market helped the City of London to reassert some international significance during the 1960s, an 'obdurate culture of secrecy and lack of accountability' continued to govern the Square Mile throughout the 1970s.[73] Even members of the Stock Exchange acknowledged that their House 'still remain[ed] something of a mystery to the bulk of the population'.[74] W. T. Thorneycroft from Cornwall lamented in his letter to Wilson that 'the stock exchange is seen as a "casino"; shares are by and large bought and sold for financial profit, not for any desire to influence the management of a company'.[75] Paul Thompson from Watford sided unequivocally with the Labour left's interpretation of manufacturing decline by invoking images of 'the working population of this country—the true primary producers of wealth' on the one hand and of the City of London as 'a conclave where non-productive administrators dominate by stealth and guile' on the other.[76] In line with this, others wished to see curtailed speculative practices like short selling and futures dealing, which were seen as 'harmful to the national interest'.[77] Among the letters, we even find remnants of the century-old religious aversion to financial speculation as a perversion of ownership, which Chapter 2 revealed to have lingered throughout the post-war decades. John A. Kemp, a Cornish 'retired farmer aged 75 years with no axe to grind' condemned the very principle of limited liability as a violation of

---

[71] Fred Riches to Sir Harold Wilson, 4 October 1976; A. G. Buckley to Sir Harold Wilson, 14 October 1976, The National Archives, Committee to Review the Functioning of Financial Institutions (Wilson Committee), Miscellaneous Letters from the Public (henceforth: TNA), BS 9/25.

[72] Ron Riley to Sir Harold Wilson 15 October 1976, TNA, BS 9/25. For the strike see 'Strike over hours hits power station', *The Guardian*, 5 May 1978.

[73] Quote after D. Kynaston, *The City of London*, IV, p. 427.

[74] Berman, *The Stock Exchange*, p. 1. The author had been a member of the London Stock Exchange Council since 1963.

[75] Dr W. T. Thorneycroft to Brian Hudson, Secretary of the Wilson Committee, TNA, BS 9/24.

[76] F. P. Thomson to Sir Harold Wilson, 6 January 1978, TNA, BS 9/28.

[77] J. Lloyd Owen to James Callaghan [forwarded to Wilson Committee], 29 October 1976. Lloyd Owen averred that '[s]hort selling by Jobbers should be banned', TNA, BS 9/25.

Christian ethics and cited at length a section from Trevelyan's *Social History of England* in support of his view.

> This country predominatly [sic] professes the Christain [sic] faith and its laws in general are based on the Christian ethic. The Limited Liability Companies Acts (1855–1948) [ ... ] have created a new class, or tribe, in the social order, the shareholder, and a larger gap between employees and owners has been created than has ever existed before in this country.[78]

It is difficult to establish the exact root cause of these antipathies towards the financial industry. We have surveyed political, social, religious, and cultural rejections of financial capitalism that had different trajectories and coexisted throughout the twentieth century. The City's club-like character reinforced these reservations since most Britons never came into direct touch with its inhabitants. In some cases, however, a negative image of the City was indeed based on specific experiences with its institutions, instances of which some letter writers provided very rich details. One particularly well-documented and revealing example was that of Dr Gwendoline Ayers from East Sussex. Dr Ayers was a 68-year-old 'retired research worker' who during WWII had been 'sentenced [ ... ] to two years' imprisonment for misdemeanours under the Official Secrets Act' and in 1971 published her PhD thesis in sociology on *England's First State Hospitals*.[79] She had conducted her research under the guidance of Richard Titmuss, who was on 'the Fabian wing of the Labour Party' and had pioneered post-war welfare policy as professor at the London School of Economics.[80] This connection allows us to assume that Dr Ayers must have been supportive of Britain's post-war social democracy. We can also count her as a member of the academic middle class, who were 'more likely than average citizens to own financial assets' and for whom, in financial terms, 'the seventies were the worst decade of the twentieth century aside from 1910 to 1919'.[81] She complained to the Wilson Committee about the

---

[78] John A. Kemp to Brian Hudson, Secretary of the Wilson Committee, 23 March 1977, TNA BS 9/24. Kemp cites the following passage: 'Such larg [sic] impersonal manipulation of capital and industry greatly increased the numbers and importance of shareholders as a class, an element in the national life representing irresponsible wealth detached from the land and the duties of the landowner and almost equally detached from the responsible management of business [ ... ] The shareholder, as such, had no knowledge of the lives, thoughts or needs of the [workmen] employed by the company in which he held shares, and his influence on the relations of capital [and] labour was not good.' Original in G. M. Trevelyan, *English Social History*, new illustrated edition with an Introduction by Asa Briggs (London: Longman, 1978), p. 510.

[79] Quote from *The Daily Telegraph*, 17 September 1943; G. M. Ayers, *England's First State Hospitals and the Metropolitan Asylums Board, 1867–1930* (London: Wellcome Institute of the History of Medicine, 1971).

[80] Quote from A. H. Halsey, 'Titmuss, Richard Morris (1907–1973)', *ODNB*.

[81] Ferguson, 'Introduction', pp. 10–11. Ferguson discusses the example of the historian A. J. P. Taylor whose investment portfolio suffered a loss of more than half its value after the stock market crash in 1973.

'mismanagement from stockbrokers' she had experienced two years previously.[82] What Dr Ayers's brokers, the large City firm Messel & Co., had done was to give her the unsolicited investment advice to sell her shares in British Petroleum, which in October 1974 were worth £1,300. The brokers suggested that she switch her holdings to the Burmah Oil Company and Dr Ayers followed the advice. However, only two months later Burmah went bust and the Bank of England had to rescue the company, while BP shares soared due to the loss of a competitor.[83]

Dr Ayers made clear to the committee that she had bought the shares in order to supplement her 'inflation-eroded savings'. Now this loss 'deprived [her] of the regular dividends from BP on which [she] relied to pay [her] fuel bills'. Was Dr Ayers a victim of insider trading, which was basically what she accused her stockbrokers of? This is extremely unlikely, because insider deals normally happen on a much larger scale. And in the exchange of letters that extended between Dr Ayers, the Wilson Committee, and the Board of Trade over the following ten months, she was told that she had no chances of claiming redress, because brokers were perfectly allowed to give unsolicited advice to existing clients.[84] Most likely, Dr Ayers's case does not testify to insider trading, which was still rife, but increasingly under the microscope in the City of the 1970s. Instead it highlights a broader structural shift in British stock markets and echoed wider complaints about the 'declining standards of service'[85] provided by stockbrokers. In the 1970s, many City firms encouraged clients to shift their holdings more frequently. The reason for this common practice was simple. Brokers lived off commission and as the lucrative business moved towards the large institutional investors, many smaller firms like Messel struggled in an increasingly competitive market, prompting them to find ways of increasing turnover. As one commentator observed in 1976, when the average holding period of stock listed on the FTSE had declined to two years from eight years in 1966:

> The people who man, run and serve the exchanges make their livings, not out of the success of their customers, but out of the volume of the trade. They have a built-in incentive to oversell, and thus to overkill geese and golden eggs alike.[86]

---

[82] G. M Ayers to Sir Harold Wilson, 23 October 1976, BS 9/24.

[83] 'Burmah Oil Holders Set up Committee', *Financial Times*, 25 January 1975.

[84] T. Lennon, Assistant Secretary to G. M. Ayers, 23 December 1977, BS 9/24. After conversing with the Board of Trade Lennon explained to Dr Ayers that 'control over the activities of Members of the Stock Exchange is a self-regulatory not a statutory matter. Stockbrokers are therefore bound by the extensive Rules and Regulations laid down by the Council of the Stock Exchange. These rules inter alia forbid unsolicited approaches to non-clients, but not the giving of advice, solicited or unsolicited, to existing clients'.

[85] 'Stock Exchange must review role of small investor', *The Daily Telegraph*, 25 October 1976.

[86] Heller, *The Naked Investor*, p. 18. On the rapid decline in the FTSE average holding period see Business, Innovation and Skills Committee of the House of Commons, *The Kay Review of UK Equity*

In addition, Dr Ayers's experience with a firm of London stockbrokers highlights again the personal character of the broker–client relationships in the Old City. Brokers who did not know their clients personally were far more inclined to give bad advice for the sake of increased turnover, which added to the growing discontent with the City of London among less privileged members of the public.

Harbouring reservations towards high finance, however, was not necessarily tantamount to subscribing to the view that the City was to blame for Britain's decline as a manufacturing power or to endorsing Labour's nationalization proposals. When looking at the collection of letters as a whole, outspoken Labour supporters were even outnumbered by people of presumably upper working- or lower middle-class backgrounds who offered a more nuanced take on Britain's economic and cultural divisions based on their personal financial experiences. One such example is a letter by a pensioner from the West Midlands by the name of R. D. Taylor. Like many others, he was wary of financial conduct in the Square Mile and aware that 'the Man in the Street is very suspicious of "The City" [ . . . ] and would be horrified to become a shareholder with all the stigma attached to that lowest form of parasite on the society'. But Mr Taylor was convinced that this perception needed to change as he explicitly blamed a lack of incentives for ordinary people to invest in domestic industry for Britain's economic misery. Mr Taylor's evidence is worth quoting at length as it is the lament of a veteran investor who joined Britain's investing public during WWI.

> I was brought up by frugal parents who continually saved for the family better-ment, and I have continued to do the same, cycling to work and by thrift to save for my country, for the future and for retirement. Small savings have been placed with the Post Office, Building Societies, National Savings Institutions proper-gandised [sic] investments of War Loan, Savings Bonds, Save as you Earn Schemes etc and also Investing in Industry seen as providing them with funds for employment, manufacture, and in return expecting a fair return [sic]. I have always endeavoured to follow the interests of the Company and its employees, without trying to 'gamble on the Stock Exchange' and without dabbling in profit taking/speculating on Takeover bids etc or endangering the industry concerned or its employees.[87]

What resurfaces in Mr Taylor's testimony is the delicate, hazy, and highly contested line between what was to be regarded as legitimate investment and condemnable speculation. Like the self-styled 'genuine investors' who felt offended by speculating stags during the post-war period, Taylor imagined the

*Markets and Long-Term Decision Making: Third Report of Session 2013–14*, p. 7, available at https://www.publications.parliament.uk/pa/cm201314/cmselect/cmbis/603/603.pdf. Accessed 19 June 2017.
[87] R. D. Taylor to Sir Harold Wilson, 9 February 1977, TNA, BS 9/18.

stock market not merely as a place for trading financial securities. Instead the Stock Exchange could claim legitimacy when acting as a national institution that mediated between domestic industry and the small saver or investor. In a similar fashion, Dr Ayers had relied on shares of BP, the most renowned national oil company to pay her fuel bills—and not on shares of a steel, manufacturing or textile company. This testifies to a still prevalent notion of investment being motivated by a sense of reliance, trust, and identification with national companies. Investors like Dr Ayers and Mr Taylor shunned speculation on price differences and, as share*holders* championed responsibility towards business and employees.

But Mr Taylor felt that successive governments had not rewarded his decade-long exercise in financial patriotism. He was now embittered with the post-war compromise between capital and labour, stating that '[i]n these difficult times those of us who have saved up are continually exhorted to help those less fortunate, but I regret I am now becoming sadly disillusioned with the system'. For Taylor, dividends and yields were not unearned income, but 'fair returns' and he suggested that one way of incentivizing private industrial investment would be to abolish the penal tax treatment of investment income—something, as we have seen, free-market liberals had long demanded and the Thatcher government eventually delivered in 1984.[88] Mr Taylor's testimony reflects a coexistence of idiosyncratic attitudes towards the profit-motive and financial practices. A visceral distaste for speculative finance was coupled with a clear moral compass of how profits could and should be earned in a market economy. The view that in Britain it rarely paid to put up capital for business was shared by many others who wrote to the Wilson Committee. One unidentifiable letter writer from Dulwich, London accused that Labour's taxation of capital had 'created a situation whereby many small investors such as myself are being legally robbed blind'.[89] Other correspondents concurred and urged Wilson to 'look into the plight of the small investor', wondering whether 'this country [does] not need the small investor any longer'[90] or went on to elaborate that

The morals to be drawn from this are inescapable. If we want more wealth, people must work harder and/or invest more. To encourage investment we could make it safer and/or more profitable. We could, for instance, reduce or abolish the tax on dividends.[91]

Statements like this need to be read against a narrow and a broader context. More specifically they expressed growing concerns among members of the

---

[88] Munro, 'The Fiscal Politics of Savings and Share Ownership in Britain, 1970–1980'. See also the discussion in Chapter 4.
[89] [N/A] to Sir Harold Wilson, 14 March 1977, TNA, BS 9/26.
[90] Arthur Wagg to Sir Harold Wilson, 6 January 1977, BS 9/25.
[91] [N/A] to Sir Harold Wilson, 13 June 1977, TNA, BS 9/26.

public—shared by financial journalists and indeed Stock Exchange firms—over the private investor's increasingly precarious situation. Leading stockbroking firms urged Wilson to acknowledge that the private investor and small speculator had an important role to play in the stock market, especially when it came to providing the risk capital necessary for SMEs to get off the ground. The blue-blooded brokers of Cazenove argued in their evidence that 'the demise of the private investor and the contraction in the Stock Exchange are factors which will need to be reversed if recovery on the financial front is to be sought'.[92] According to the research department of brokers Parsons & Co. the high volatility charac-teristic of the 1970s was 'symptomatic of a market dominated by the professional investor without the counterweight of small speculators'.[93] In order to upgrade the private investor against the institutions, many stockbroking firms suggested abolishing the tax breaks that pension funds and insurance companies enjoyed over individuals holding equity.[94] Whether it was broking firms, banks, or the unit trust industry, the Wilson Committee was flooded with corporate appeals to advise a major overhaul of capital taxation in its report.[95] The financial press, however, still held the City as partly responsible for the small investor's demise. Engaging in the debate over the specific functions of the private investor in the market, the *Daily Telegraph* argued that the Stock Exchange must make commis-sions more flexible in order to encourage the 'stabilising influence of the small investor, who is often buying when the institutions, who make the market, are selling, and vice versa'.[96]

## Inflation, Thrift, and Market Populism

We have seen that many letters expressed a longing for monetary stability by savers and investors who were deeply troubled by 1970s inflation rates. Much of the unrest of Mr Taylor, for instance, sprang from the fact that his 'hard earned savings [were] whistling away [and] reducing in value so fast with the high rate of inflation that they are only to be considered if proofed against it'.[97] F. C. Deeley from Northampton, who had been running a small business since 1948, 'believe [d] all Governments should really make a super effort to reduce inflation down to

---

[92] Cazenove & Co., The Market for New Industrial Capital, Evidence to Wilson Committee, 23 March 1977, TNA, BS 9/117.
[93] Parsons & Co., Evidence for Submission to Wilson Committee on the Subject of Finance for Industry, April 1977, TNA, BS 9/117.
[94] See the detailed discussion on these tax breaks and Thatcherite considerations to abolish them in Chapter 4.
[95] For further evidence in this regard see Davies, *The City of London and Social Democracy*, pp. 138–139.
[96] 'Stock Exchange must review role of small investor', *The Daily Telegraph*, 25 October 1976.
[97] R. D. Taylor to Sir Harold Wilson, 9 February 1977, TNA, BS 9/18.

at most 4 per cent then and only then will real confidence return so that business will expand'.[98] But it was not just middle-class investors and savers who raised concerns over inflation. They were also brought forward by manual workers such as Richard Holden from Lancashire, who defiantly introduced himself to Wilson as 'one of the old fashioned people who saved a part of my salary each month for a lifetime to supplement retirement pension after 40 years in industry'. With inflation at a staggering 16 per cent, Holden accused Labour's economic policy of penalizing thrift and encouraging frivolous spending:

> This may suit the people who constantly resort to 'access cards' [Access was a credit card company launched in 1972] and hire purchase but is most unfair and no incentive to small savers. Surely this policy is all wrong and encourages people to squander their money instead of providing for their retirement.[99]

The Wilson letters allow us to closely scrutinize an ongoing struggle over economic cultures and values in the second half of twentieth-century Britain. Thrift as a defining middle-class virtue continued to hold sway over members of the investing public, which is mirrored in other sources such as a 1978 investment guide by hobby investor Jack Medomsley:

> Thrift is a universal characteristic but more special to the middle class because it is an assurance of independence at a later stage in life, an independence from too many hand-outs from the State.[100]

As Niall Ferguson has noted, however, 'Victorian thriftiness was the worst possible strategy for surviving the seventies'. Quite the opposite, as the working-class saver Richard Holden from Lancashire lamented, the 1970s were an excellent decade for the consumer, who had little problems paying off credit card or hire-purchase debt with the staggering wage increases that resulted from double-digit inflation. An economic climate that incentivized spending over saving and deferring gratification partly explains the appeal of such alarmist interventions like Patrick Hutber's *The Decline and Fall of the Middle Class*.[101] The insight we can gain from the Wilson letters is that for many savers and investors the conclusion from this experience was to re-embrace the profit motive. And we can trace this reappraisal into other areas of public debate at that time. At the same time as Harold Wilson presided over the Committee to Review the Functioning of Financial Institutions, we can carve out a shift in public attitudes that ran counter

---

[98] F. C. Deeley to Sir Harold Wilson, 14 August 1977, TNA, BS 9/27.
[99] Richard Holden to Sir Harold Wilson, 18 July 1977, TNA, BS 9/27.
[100] Medomsley, *Opportunities for the Small Investor*, p. 8.
[101] Ferguson, 'Introduction', p. 10; Hutber, *The Decline and Fall of the Middle Class, and How it Can Fight Back*.

to his 1960s vision of 'a Britain whose motivation is not private profit and the aggrandizement of personal fortunes but national effort and national purpose'.[102] In the second half of the 1970s, the public suspicion towards individual as well as corporate profit-seeking we had known from the post-war decades began to wane, and increasingly came under attack from free-market proponents in the media and the Conservative opposition party. Even James Callaghan's famous 1976 Labour Party conference speech in Blackpool—which is often dubbed the birth moment of monetarism in Britain—paid lip service to this change. Besides famously telling his party that 'you could [no longer] spend your way out of a recession', the Prime Minister and party leader stated:

> When I say they [industry] must have sufficient funds, I mean they must be able to earn a surplus and that is a euphemism for saying they must be able to make a profit. (Applause) Whether you call it a surplus or a profit, it is necessary for a healthy industrial system, whether it operates in a socialist economy, a mixed economy or a capitalist economy.[103]

As discussed, the 1978 budget was an early, yet minor political appreciation of this shift towards creating incentives for equity investment. By then, large parts of the quality and popular press had detected a change in public attitudes towards profits and deliberately sought to undermine what they regarded as post-war restrictions on making money in the public psyche. The cartoonist and *Daily Telegraph* columnist Bernard Hollowood, previously editor of the satire magazine *Punch*, was at the forefront of bringing about and chronicling this transformation. He charted the shift in financial mores as follows:

> Like sex—everybody did it, but NEVER talked about it. Money talk was taboo. Today, money, again like sex, screams at you from every poster, TV screen and newspaper headline. We have an insatiable appetite for it. Like love, it is very serious and very funny.[104]

When he celebrated in his weekly column that 'profit is no longer a dirty word', he joined in on a wider debate that recast economic language in Britain.[105] The same year, Barclays Bank launched an advertising campaign that explained 'why profit isn't a dirty word' at the company—though it did feel the need to stress that its

---

[102] Harold Wilson and the Labour Party, *The New Britain: Labours Plan*, Selected Speeches 1964 (Harmondsworth, 1964), p. 12.

[103] Speech available at http://www.britishpoliticalspeech.org/speech-archive.htm?speech=174. Accessed 16 June 2017. On the speech's reception see chap. 5, *Evolution of British Monetarism*, in Davies, *The City of London and Social Democracy*, pp. 181–214; also Cockett, *Thinking the Unthinkable*, pp. 185–187.

[104] Hollowood, *Funny Money*, p. 1.

[105] B. Hollowood, 'Profit is no longer a dirty word', *Daily Telegraph*, 17 July 1976.

profits derived 'not from speculation'. Pushing the slogan in the popular press, the leading *Daily Mail* columnist, Andrew Alexander, urged his readers to no longer 'apologise for the one word that can make us all smile again'.[106] And the *Guardian* commented that Margaret Thatcher, eager to reconcile her party with the profit motive, had 'set out to take one of the dirty words of postwar British politics to the cleaners'.[107] In a widely noted speech she condemned the 'constant attempt to make us ashamed of profit', pleading to 'rehabilitate the idea of profit as something necessary and praiseworthy in our economic system'.[108]

Towards the late 1970s, conservatives, liberals, and even parts of the Labour Party seemed to rally behind a reappraisal of the profit motive. This apparent unity, however, glossed over many of the fissures behind the new consensus, which would become apparent in the 1980s as a result of deindustrialization and the rise of the service sector, financial services in particular. It is therefore worthwhile to scrutinize the nuances and different trajectories that to some extent were already shaping contemporaries' horizon of expectations.[109] Arguably, most of those who agreed that a new attitude towards profits was needed also subscribed to Thatcher's mantra that Britain's decline would be reversed by strengthening its manufacturing base. When she was Leader of the Opposition, Thatcher's rhetoric was heavily geared towards manufacturing. She declared that 'the flourishing society' she envisaged for Britain 'can only develop if more of our most able young people decide to work in private enterprise and especially in manufacturing industry'.[110] However, this rejuvenation of industrial capitalism that Thatcher and her followers had intended, was somewhat at odds with the financial capitalism championed by corporate raiders like Jim Slater, who took pride in dealing 'with any one thing other than money' and whose cheerleaders in the financial press held 'foolish the present fashion that damns people who make money but praises those who make things'.[111]

---

[106] A. Alexander, 'Why apologise for the one word that can make us all smile again?', *Daily Mail*, 15 March 1977.

[107] 'Profit without honour on Left', *The Guardian*, 5 May 1976.

[108] M. Thatcher, Speech to Junior Carlton Club Political Council, 4 May 1976, Margaret Thatcher Foundation website, document 103017. For the reception of this speech see 'Profit not dirty word says Mrs Thatcher', *Daily Mail*, 5 May 1976; 'Thatcher Defence of Profit', *Daily Telegraph*, 5 May 1976, 'Mrs Thatcher sees way for industry to flourish', *The Times*, 5 May 1976. On the wider trajectory of this shift in the late 1970s see Cockett, *Thinking the Unthinkable*, pp. 243–286.

[109] On expectation as 'the future made present' see Reinhart Koselleck's chapter ' "Space of Experience" and "Horizon of Expectation": Two Historical Categories', in R. Koselleck (ed.), *Futures Past: On the Semantics of Historical Time*. Translated and with an Introduction by Keith Tribe (New York: Columbia University Press, 2005), p. 259.

[110] M. Thatcher, Speech to Melton Conservatives, 22 May 1976, Margaret Thatcher Foundation website, available at www.margaretthatcher.org/document/103032 (hereafter MTF 103032). Accessed 19 December 2020.

[111] P. Sergeant, 'Jim Slater must stop this disastrous bid', *Daily Mail*, 18 June 1973. See Chapter 3 for the context of the previous quote.

The swashbuckling element of Britain's stock market culture had gained head-way in public perception during the 1960s and increasingly did so during the 1970s. Just as much as the 1970s were traumatic for British savers and investors, the decade was crucial for popularizing the belief that the stock market had an important role to play in Britain's economy and society. In order for that to happen, it was widely agreed that the Stock Exchange had to be forced to change—and change it did with the 'Big Bang' reforms of 1986. Nobody could know that the decade would herald the acquisitive, short-term, and speculative approach to finance that dominated the 1980s, and which stood in stark contrast to the Thatcherite insistence on purportedly bourgeois values of thrift, hard work, and deferred gratification or the notion of 'genuine investment'. In May 1979, Britain elected a prime minister who had repeatedly claimed that a return to economic freedom and monetary stability would make 'Britain great again'. Thatcher had been using this trope—eerily resembling the political language of post-Brexit Britain—since her first General Election Address in 1950, where she made clear at outset her 'earnest desire to make Great Britain great again'.[112] The experiences that ordinary savers and investors described to the Wilson Committee urge us to consider the contribution of Margaret Thatcher's market populism—preaching thrift, hard work, and sound money—to her ascent to power. Eventually the Conservative Party under Thatcher turned out to be successful at selling 'a more optimistic future to a weary electorate', a future that was promised to be governed by 'individual choice, free of the constraints of state control, which would lead to a dynamic, enterprising society'.[113] In truly populist fashion, this vision of the future drew heavily on images of a better past ('Victorian values') and of Imperial grandeur ('Make Britain great again'). As part of this market populism, the likes of Thatcher, Howe, and Lawson promoted an individualism that skilfully tapped into a growing distrust of those at the top—be they City financiers or Whitehall mandarins—combined with a sense that markets were quintessentially democratic and therefore always on the side of the 'little fellow', the 'man in the street', or the 'ordinary chap'.[114]

However, Britain also voted for a prime minister whose Methodist upbringing by her father Alfred Roberts had shaped her moral universe to the extent that she inherited an ingrained distrust of the stock market and speculative finance.[115]

---

[112] M. Thatcher, 1950 General Election Address, 3 February 1950, MTF 100858. In a 1976 article for *The Sun*, Thatcher wrote 'I believe that Britain can be great again. But that it will never be great again until it is free again.' M. Thatcher, Article for the *The Sun* ('The Hand in Your Pocket'), 13 September 1976, MTF 102838. Making Britain great again was in fact a popular battle cry in the late 1970s and early 1980s invoked by tabloid journalists, the political right, and business representatives.

[113] M. Daunton, 'Questioning Leviathan: Restructuring the State in Britain since 1970', *East Asian Journal of British History* 5 (2016), p. 48.

[114] On the concept of market populism see Frank, *One Market under God*; McKnight, 'The Sunday Times and Andrew Neil, pp. 754–768.

[115] J. Campbell, 'Roberts, Alfred (1892–1970)', *ODNB*.

Thatcher was convinced that capitalism was the economic system most suited for putting Christian ethics into practice and she did not shy away from publicly justifying social inequality as God given. In 1981, for instance, she reckoned that Britain may 'have lost the idea that is inherent in Christ's parable of the talents. The steward who simply did not use the resources entrusted to him was roundly condemned. The two who used them to produce more wealth were congratulated and given more.'[116] Furthermore, one of her closest advisers, speechwriter Alfred Sherman, was convinced that the 'de-Christianisation of social and political thought' in Britain had contributed to its decline—a statement that is even more remarkable when read against the background of Sherman's Jewish origin and Communist past.[117] However, Thatcher's moral nexus between capitalism and Christianity was difficult to square with the realm of finance. Her biographer, John Campbell, has noted that Thatcher 'did not really approve of the Stock Exchange, believing at heart that wealth should be earned by making and selling real goods and services, not by gambling and speculation'.[118] Having railed against speculators in Parliament in the 1960s, she admitted privately in 1981 that 'her father disapproved of the Stock Market, which he considered "a form of gambling"'.[119] But although she kept a 'psychological distance from the City' throughout her career, she did more than any other politician to facilitate the expansion of financial markets during the 1980s.[120] Campbell pinned down this discrepancy between Thatcher's conservative values and the outcome of her policies as follows:

> The central paradox of Thatcherism is that Mrs Thatcher presided over and celebrated a culture of rampant materialism—'fun, greed and money'—fundamentally at odds with her own values which were essentially conservative, old-fashioned and puritanical.[121]

We will see that the Protestant foundation of Margaret Thatcher's ideal of a share-owning democracy was fundamentally at odds with the acquisitive stock market culture that was to characterize the 1980s. In order to make sense of this

---

[116] M. Thatcher, Speech at St Lawrence Jewry, 4 March 1981, MTF 104587. Thatcher employed the parable of the talents throughout her career. See, for instance, Speech to American Chamber of Commerce, 20 October 1976, MTF 103115; Speech to Conservative Central Council, 23 March 1985, MTF 106000.

[117] Quote after Grimley, 'Thatcherism, Morality and Religion', p. 85.

[118] J. Campbell, *Margaret Thatcher: The Iron Lady* (London: Jonathan Cape, 2003), vol. II, p. 248.

[119] J. Campbell, *Margaret Thatcher: The Grocer's Daughter* (London: Jonathan Cape, 2000), vol. I, p. 30; see also Vinen, *Thatcher's Britain*, p. 182.

[120] Harrison, *Finding a Role?*, p. 342.

[121] Campbell, *Margaret Thatcher*, II, p. 250. See also Grimley, 'Thatcherism, Morality and Religion', p. 93.

ambiguity, we need to challenge the conception of 'modern capitalism' as a rational undertaking devoid of 'irrational speculation' and pay closer attention to the emotional economy of the stock market. This will allow us to gain a better understanding of the social and cultural implications of the Conservative Party's 'popular capitalism' and to focus on some of the unintended consequences of privatization, deregulation and demutualization.

# 6

# Popular Capitalism? Privatization and Demutualization in the 1980s and 1990s

In a TV interview with the weekly current affairs programme *This Week* on 10 December 1987, less than two months after global stock markets had crashed on Black Monday, the Conservative Prime Minister Margaret Thatcher faced some pressing questions about her government's agenda to establish a popular capitalism in Britain that had made millions of investment newcomers enter the stock market. Jonathan Dimblebly, Thames Television's quick-witted interviewer, challenged Thatcher on her decision of having gone ahead with the second stage of selling the government's stake in British Petroleum only two weeks after the UK stock market had lost a quarter of its value: 'What about the 270,000 [small investors] who bought at the offer price which was way above the market price?' Surely now, after thousands of new investors had burnt their fingers, her key political slogans 'sound[s] rather tattered—popular capitalism'. Thatcher naturally disagreed—'Not at all! Not at all!'—and went on to explain that the millions of retail investors she had created by privatizing national industries like British Telecom and British Gas had not entered the market for short-term gains, but were in it for the long run:

> The small investor buys not really to sell the next day, the next week, the next month, the next year. Most of them buy to put it, as we would say, in the bottom drawer, to give an investment for the future and yes it will.[1]

The idealized image of the conservative private investor who saw share ownership as an exercise in economic enfranchisement and long-term wealth creation was a cornerstone of Thatcher's rhetoric. The Prime Minister, who had once famously stated that '[e]conomics are the method; the object is to change the heart and soul'[2] of the British people, was confident that her policies of widening share ownership were an expression of her often cited Victorian values, a connection she made clear in a 1985 speech: 'But there is another purpose behind privatization: Wider share ownership. It should be as natural for people to own shares as to own their home or to own a car. [ ... ] All of this helps to build a more robust and more

---

[1] M. Thatcher, TV Interview for Thames TV This Week, 10 December 1987, MTF 106993.
[2] M. Thatcher, Interview for *Sunday Times*, 1 May 1981, MTF 104475.

*Playing the Market: Retail Investment and Speculation in Twentieth-Century Britain*. Kieran Heinemann, Oxford University Press (2021). © Kieran Heinemann. DOI: 10.1093/oso/9780198864257.003.0007

responsible society. The strength of our policies is that they are founded on the basic instincts of our people. An instinct: for ownership, for thrift, for honest work, for fair rewards, and for helping others.'[3]

In the eleven years of being Prime Minister, Margaret Thatcher pursued two flagship policies that aimed to establish Britain as a share-owning democracy. First, the privatization of state assets in heavily advertised stock market flotations encouraged small investors to buy shares at knock-down prices, and thereby benefit financially from Thatcher's effort to 'roll back the frontiers of the state'. Second, her administrations introduced comprehensive measures of financial deregulation, most notably the abolition of restrictive practices on the London Stock Exchange in 1986, commonly known as the Big Bang. In the same year, Parliament passed the Building Societies Act, a piece of deregulation that scholars have paid much less attention to, and which unfolded its full dynamic under Thatcher's successors, the Conservative John Major, and the Labour Prime Minister Tony Blair. So far, scholars of popular capitalism have focused on the series of events between 1979 and 1990, when the privatization of forty state assets generated £33 billion of revenue for the Treasury, and left Britain with more shareholders than trade union members (11m).[4] While Thatcher certainly did much to coin the term, we have seen that the concept and the term itself predate her time in office. Similarly, the exclusive focus on the Thatcher years has led scholars to overlook popular engagements with financial markets that took place after her premiership, but that were an immediate result of her policies.

This chapter seeks to enrich our understanding of popular capitalism by bringing the 1990s into the picture, in particular the demutualization of the building societies, which resulted from the 1986 Building Societies Act. Between 1989 and 2000, ten of Britain's largest building societies shed their mutual status and converted into publicly listed banks, a process that generated windfall profits for depositors whose savings accounts were converted into shares. The idealized small investors that Thatcher portrayed in the 1987 TV interview and elsewhere *did* exist to some extent, but they tell only one side of the story. As this chapter will demonstrate, a significant amount of investors did not buy shares in British Telecom or British Gas in order to put them 'in the bottom drawer', but to sell them for a quick profit in early trading. Britain's investing public stagged the flotations of nationalized industries in an even more aggressive manner than the stags of the post-war years operated in the new issue market. During the 1990s, demutualization saw a continuation of this trend in speculation for short-term profits as an immediate result of Thatcher's politics of privatization and deregulation.

---

[3] Margaret Thatcher, Speech to Conservative Trade Unionists Conference, 30 November 1985, MTF 106185.

[4] *A Nation of Shareholders: Report of the CBI Wider Share Ownership Task Force* (London: CBI, 1990).

The chapter will focus on the tension between two ideas of capitalism that were at stake throughout the decades. On the one hand, Thatcher's moral universe made her identify capitalism with a Puritan emphasis on thrift, hard work, and asceticism and at the same time harbour reservations towards speculative finance. This mentality was strikingly congruent with Max Weber's concept of modern capitalism as an economic system rooted not in 'irrational speculation',[5] but sober calculation and the taming of emotions—an analytical framework that, as we will see, has left its mark on scholarship. Previous chapters, on the other hand, have highlighted that the supposed rationality of stock market activity was constantly accompanied, if not undermined, by its constitutive opposites of a certain gambling spirit and emotions. In particular, we have traced how a more quixotic approach to investment—epitomized by traders like Jim Slater—had been gaining traction since the 1960s and creating tensions with traditional notions of 'genuine investment'. As Thatcher liberalized financial markets during her premiership, millions of Britons took advantage of the ample opportunities that opened up during the 1980s and 1990s to indulge in the swashbuckling element of financial capitalism, which stood in contrast to the moralizing rhetoric that Thatcher's Conservatives used to instigate this agenda.

Paradoxically, deregulated financial markets were left to amplify emotional exuberance at the same time that academics and politics came to regard markets as inherently rational and self-regulating. We need to understand this 'irrational' side of Britain's late twentieth-century capitalism as an unintended, yet fundamental aspect of its legacy, which has been blurred by explicitly and implicitly Weberian assumptions of academics and politicians about the nature of capitalism. As millions of people 'stagged' privatization issues in the 1980s and speculated on short-term profits during the demutualization of building societies in the 1990s, popular capitalism was less an enfranchisement 'in the economic life of the nation'[6], and more an expressive culture of self-referential speculation, personal enrichment, and stock market gambling.

## Privatization or 'the Next Best Thing to Buying £10 Notes for a Fiver'

Unhappy that previous Conservative governments merely followed an approach of 'passive encouragement', Margaret Thatcher's three administrations between

---

[5] M. Weber, *The Protestant Ethic and the Spirit of Capitalism*, translated by Talcott Parsons, with an introduction by Anthony Giddens, Routledge Classics (London: Routledge, 2001 [1905]), p. 37.

[6] M. Thatcher, Speech to Conservative Party Conference, 10 October 1986, MTF 106498. Full quote: 'The great political reform of the last century was to enable more and more people to have a vote. Now the great Tory reform of this century is to enable more and more people to own property. Popular capitalism is nothing less than a crusade to enfranchise the many in the economic life of the nation. We Conservatives are returning power to the people.' See also Francis, 'A Crusade to Enfranchise the Many'.

1979 and 1990 adopted an activist stance to making Britain a property- and share-owning democracy. The interwar trope of a property-owning democracy and its inclusive language was first applied to the privatization of council houses and only later to the stock market flotations of large public industries. The 1980 Housing Act laid the groundwork for Thatcher's 'Right to Buy' policy, which allowed tenants of council houses to buy their homes at favourable prices, with sales already peaking in 1982, when 174,697 council flats and houses became owner-occupied over the course of the year.[7] Throughout the decade, Conservatives paid a lot of lip-service to building an 'enterprise society'. But their actual policies were mostly geared towards expanding property ownership among lower- and middle-income groups, which was seen to have the added benefit of creating long-term electoral advantages.[8] Partly as a result, owning property, more than working or running a business, became the most significant wealth factor over the course of the decade. As David Edgerton has pointed out, the 'profoundly unproductive' politics of property the Conservative pioneered in the 1980s meant that middle-class homeowners, subsidized by enormous tax relief on mortgage interest, 'made money simply by sitting in the right sort of homes'.[9] While the privatization of housing drew public attention from the beginning, the public flotations of nation-alized industries, beginning in 1981 with British Aerospace, happened more quietly and with smaller state assets being privatized. Unlike Thatcher visiting tenants who made use of her 'Right to Buy' policy, the first stock market flotations of nationalized industries did not catch much media attention, but were a matter discussed in the City and money pages of tabloids and broadsheets. This changed in 1984 with the flotation of British Telecom and reached a first peak in 1986, when British Gas was privatized—the same year that sweeping deregulations sent shockwaves across Britain's financial sector.

Much of the scholarship on Thatcherism and the theme of wider share or property ownership is occupied with the question of whether historians should regard 1980s popular capitalism as a failure or a success. Scholars now widely agree that privatization did not entrench share ownership in society as deeply as the grandiose rhetoric of Tory ministers claimed. Several accounts point out that the growth in shareholder numbers did not reverse the trend towards concentra-tion of equity capital in hands of large institutional investors who owned 75 per cent of UK listed stock by 1989.[10] Surveys conducted during the privatization programme already revealed that only around 16 per cent of those who had bought shares of privatized industries went on to build a diversified portfolio

[7] A. Beckett, 'The right to buy: the housing crisis that Thatcher built', *The Guardian*, 26 August 2015.

[8] Stevens, 'The Evolution of Privatisation as an Electoral Policy, c. 1970–90'.

[9] Edgerton, *The Rise and Fall of the British Nation*, p. 464.

[10] A. Edwards, '"Manufacturing Capitalists"', p. 116; Parker, *The Official History of Privatisation*, I, pp. 430–431.

including shares of other public companies.[11] Geographically, private share ownership continued to be 'disproportionately concentrated in the south-eastern region of the country' after the 1980s.[12] The regional distribution reflected the continued predominance of investment among middle-class households, which the first surveys into Britain's shareholder population had already observed in the post-war decades. Although a third of the new investors were manual workers, the average investor by the end of the decade continued to be 'male, married, middle-age, relatively affluent, and living in the south-east of England'.[13]

The City of London underwent dramatic changes in October 1986, when the deregulations known as Big Bang became effective, which abolished fixed dealing commissions on the London Stock Exchange as well as the century-old single capacity rule that strictly separated brokers and jobbers. From now on, brokers could deal on their own book and jobbers were allowed to deal directly with the public without having to go through a broker. This very quickly led to the formation of so-called broker–dealers, in the process of which longstanding jobbing and brokerage firms were bought by large banks, primarily US investment banks, who as a result of Big Bang, were no longer facing any membership restrictions at the Stock Exchange. Since the owner of a security and the facilitator of a deal could now be one and the same person, a potentially significant conflict of interest emerged, which would often come at the expense of the less informed investor. Studies suggest that flexible commissions resulted in an increase of dealing costs for small transactions and did very little to improve service for less affluent investors.[14] Finally, and perhaps most revealingly, very few investors held on to their shares in privatized companies. Reliable estimates show that 'the average percentage of the original shareholders who still retained their shares in privatised companies by 1989 was estimated to be around 40 per cent'.[15] In other words, more than half of the 'investors' who bought shares in a privatization issue sold their shares for a quick profit and the flotations of nationalized industries were targeted by stags on an enormous scale. Based on this, scholars have concluded that '[a]ttempts by Government to build on the success of privatisation issues in attracting small investors [...] generally failed'[16] or that '[p]opular capitalism was never, in fact, that popular [...] because [...] the distribution of shares was not as spectacular as it looked'.[17] And according to Amy Edwards,

---

[11] P. Grout, 'The Wider Share Ownership Programme', *Fiscal Studies* 8 (1987), pp. 59–74; see also the survey in 'Educating the new capitalists', *The Independent*, 18 February 1988.

[12] 'Here [in the Southeast], some 28 per cent of households own shares directly [...]. In contrast, in Northern parts of Britain only 16 per cent of households own shares.' R. L. Martin, *The Geography of Private Shareholding: Mapping Popular Capitalism in Britain* (Swindon: Economic and Social Research Council, 1999), p. 9.

[13] Harrison, *Finding a Role?*, pp. 538–539.

[14] Edwards, '"Manufacturing Capitalists"', pp. 115–122.

[15] Parker, *The Official History of Privatisation*, I, p. 432.

[16] Parker, *The Official History of Privatisation*, I, p. 432.      [17] Vinen, *Thatcher's Britain*, p. 200.

'Thatcherism [...] failed to endow the individual with a meaningful role in a "property-owning democracy"'.[18] She adds that 'Thatcherism it appeared was about financial capitalism not consumer capitalism and so it failed to create cultural change'.[19]

These are all valid assessments if one juxtaposes the outcome of privatization and Conservative efforts of creating a property-owning democracy with the intentions and the rhetoric of policymakers. However, the binary of whether privatization succeeded or failed, whether popular capitalism was indeed popular or unpopular, does carry with it some normative assumptions about the concept of capitalism, which makes it difficult to gain a historical understanding of this polarized period. Even though Margaret Thatcher's vision of popular capitalism was not realized, we should not regard the large-scale stagging of public flotations as well as the culture of self-enrichment and entertainment that accompanied them, as evidence that capitalism was not 'popularized' in Britain. Instead, seen in the wider context of the twentieth century, these phenomena allow us to better understand a significant departure from previously held notions of share *ownership* towards a more short-term, acquisitive approach to stock market investment that was characteristic of the period's financial capitalism.

| <ul>Company and date of flotation</ul> | <ul>Initial share register → later [PB1]date</ul> |
|---|---|
| British Aerospace (February 1981) | 158,000 → 27,000 in February 1982 |
| Cable and Wireless (November 1981) | 150,000 → 26,000 in November 1982 |
| Amersham International (February 1982) | 62,000 → 10,000 one month after flotation |
| Jaguar (July 1984) | 125,000 → 49,000 by May 1985 |
| British Airways (February 1987) | 1,200,000 → 450,000 three months after flotation |

**Figure 6.1** Share register development of privatized industries
Source: D. Parker, *Official History of Privatisation, I, The Formative Years 1970–1987* (London, Routledge, 2009), p. 432; see also the table in 'A nation taking stock', *The Times*, 11 September 1987.

---

[18] Edwards, '"Manufacturing Capitalists"', p. 104.
[19] Edwards, '"Manufacturing Capitalists"', p. 122.

When the flotation of British Telecom in November 1984 attracted 2 million retail investors, Britain entered something of a collective share fever and *The Economist* reasoned that 'personal investors might stage a comeback'.[20] In light of this popularity, Conservative ministers geared up their rhetoric on privatization, wider share ownership, and their commitment to making Britain a property-owning democracy.[21] In a public speech, Margaret Thatcher treated the ownership of financial securities in the same way as the ownership of privatized council houses. Whether shareholder or house owner, '[a]s a property owner you understand your own responsibility and you respect the responsibilities and duties of others'.[22] Of course, political constraints made the practicalities of each privatization issue more complex and the goal of Thatcher's idealized small investor more difficult to realize. Each flotation marked a trade-off between '[s]etting a correct share price on flotation so as to attract a sufficiently large number of applications for shares, but without the opportunity for large "stagging" gains, would continue to prove a challenge during all of the government's privatization flotations'.[23] Over time, the government considered and experimented with several types of flotations. They ranged from Milton Friedman's suggestion of a free but equal dispersion of equity capital among voters, over tender issues, in which the share price was left to market forces, to flotations with a fixed price. The Friedman option was dismissed early on by Geoffrey Howe, Chancellor in Thatcher's first cabinet 1979–83, on educational grounds:

> A giant scheme of this nature would, of course, introduce many people to the idea of share ownership for the first time. But one is bound to have doubts whether shares doled out free to all would represent any effective lesson in the responsibility of ownership.[24]

Tenders placated free-market purists like Nicholas Ridley, but proved to be risky and the tender of Britoil in 1982—overseen by Nigel Lawson as Energy Secretary—flopped because it did not attract sufficient investor interest.[25] Hence, Thatcherite ministers, in close consultation with investment banks like Kleinwort Benson or Warburg, resorted to the pragmatic option of fixing the initial share price in the following flotations deliberately below the anticipated

[20] 'The people's capitalism: Personal investors might stage a come-back', *The Economist*, 14 July 1984.

[21] For a detailed temporary account of the BT sale see Newman, *The Selling of British Telecom.*

[22] M. Thatcher, Speech to Scottish Party Conference, 10 May 1985, MTF 106046.

[23] Parker, *The Official History of Privatisation*, I, p. 134.

[24] G. Howe to M. Thatcher, 1 July 1980, Proposal for a national investment trust to promote wider property ownership: report by Leo Pliatzky, MTF, PREM 19/191, ECONOMIC POLICY, Proposal for a national investment trust to promote wider property ownership: report by Leo Pliatzky, July 1980.

[25] '70pc of shares unsold: Government snubbed on Britoil sale', *The Times*, 20 November 1982; 'No deal for Nigel', *The Economist*, 15 January 1983.

market price in order to attract investors and to guarantee the political success of the privatization programme. The predicament was that if stock market operators knew that the company was deliberately undervalued for political reasons, early buyers could quickly offload their shares and make a profit in early days trading.

Figure 6.1 shows the extent to which issues of national industries attracted stags, the 'stock market beast who makes a habit of applying for shares in companies which are being floated on the market for the first time'.[26] Financial journalists, otherwise highly supportive of the Conservative government's free-market agenda, were quick to question the long-term benefits of this procedure for the quest of widening share ownership in Britain. The veteran *Sunday Times* City editor, Graham Searjeant, commented that 'small investor became a euphemism for thousands of ordinary newspaper readers who can spot a no-loss speculation joining thousands of professional stags who rush round collecting application forms in bulging briefcases. Few will hold the shares more than a week'.[27] Some investors complained that the government was not teaching the public a lesson about capitalism, but was actually suspending the very mechanisms of the free market it had been preaching so vehemently by giving the 'impression that it is easy to make a quick killing with shares, but it should be remembered that these situations are the exception, not the rule'.[28] Looking back at the 'stagging bonanza' that accompanied the flotation of Amersham International in 1982—the third nationalized industry to be sold after British Aerospace and Cable & Wireless—Searjeant voiced scepticism:

Genuine mass participation would require a much more imaginative approach. Today's residual active small shareholders are, by and large, not pink-nosed rabbits inhabiting a vanishing habitat and waiting for kindly ministers to set up financial nature reserves. They survived in a hostile environment by natural selection, by learning to be more like speculators.[29]

Note, however, that Searjeant did not condemn per se the practice of stagging, which he described as the 'joys of making a quick profit'. Instead he expressed scepticism that the government policies could bring about a long-term change in ownership patterns. Attitudes towards short-term capital gains still varied across media outlets. The *Daily Mirror,* the Labour-leaning mass daily, was one of the few to raise concerns over the amount of stags targeting privatization issues. The paper's austere City editor Robert Head criticized how the Amersham issues

[26] W. Kay, *A-Z Guide to Money* (London: Constable, 1983), p. 224.

[27] 'The joys of making a quick profit', *The Sunday Times*, 21 February 1982.

[28] J. T. Stafford, *The Share-Owner's Guide: How to Invest Profitably and Safely in Shares* (Cambridge: Woodhead-Faulkner, 1987), p. 3.

[29] 'The wit to woo small investors', *The Sunday Times*, 2 May 1982; P. Shearlock, 'Stags sniff a bonanza on Amersham's offer', *The Sunday Times*, 14 February 1982.

witnessed 'a flood of applications by speculators who put in for more shares than they wanted, to re-sell them immediately and pocket an instant profit'.[30] But Head still promoted a type of market populism that was surprisingly similar with that of Margaret Thatcher and at odds with the *Mirror*'s general approach to polemicize against the Conservative government. Head presented to his readers the prospect of being active members in a market society, explaining to them that 'only the market—which means millions of people like you and me' can influence share prices.[31] When British Telecom went private he welcomed his readers 'to a world of fun and adventure, risk and reward'. In truly populist fashion, and invoking a language steeped in 1970s declinism that sounds eerily familiar to observers of twentyfirst-century politics, he was convinced that the 'courage to take risks is one of the things that could make Britain great again'.[32] All this earned him praise from the Chairman of the London Stock Exchange, Nicholas Goodison, who lauded how 'excellent [it is] that commentary on stocks and shares can now be found in the pages of the *Daily Mirror*'—even though this had been the case since 1960.[33] However, Head remained sceptical of the speculative side of stock market finance, urging his readership not to dabble in stock trading and to 'hold on to a good number: don't sell those Telecom shares'.[34] In other words, the City editor of the largest Labour-leaning tabloid newspaper wished to see the mass arrival of the same type of long-term small investor as desired by Margaret Thatcher.

At the *Daily Mail*, on the other hand, stagging privatization issues was advertised as a national sport. Its dandy City editor, Patrick Sergeant was an uncanny mirror image of his rival Robert Head. Sergeant was an old confidante of Mrs Thatcher and walked in and out of Downing Street on a regular basis, but cheered his readers on to cash in on a quick profit.

> Charge your pens, get out your cheque books, bully your bank managers and stampede today for what looks like the stag of the year—tomorrow's offer of the 50 million shares in Amersham International at 142p each.[35]

In an article that captured first images of 1980s popular capitalism *avant la lettre*, the paper had celebrated the Cable and Wireless sell-off in a similar fashion, describing how 'City gents joined housewives and businessmen yesterday in a

---

[30] R. Head, 'New big state sell-off is slammed', *Daily Mirror*, 26 February 1982, p. 21. On Robert Head's place in financial journalism see Porter, '"City slickers" in Perspective'; 'Capitalism goes pop', *The Guardian*, 24 August 1987; 'Robert Head: Obituary', *The Times*, 19 February 2009.

[31] R. Head, 'Propping up the pound', *Daily Mirror*, 30 November 1982.

[32] R. Head, 'Are Telecom's shares a good number for YOU?', *Daily Mirror*, 20 November 1984; 'TELECOMANIA!: Investors ring up big profits', *Daily Mirror*, 4 December 1984.

[33] N. Goodison, *Shares for All: Steps towards a Share-Owning Society* (London: Centre for Policy Studies, 1986), pp. 9–10.

[34] R. Head, 'Hold on to a good number: Don't sell those Telecom shares', *Daily Mirror*, 11 December 1984.

[35] P. Sergeant, '£1½ billion joins the Amersham stampede', *Daily Mail*, 19 February 1982.

scramble to buy shares in the denationalised Cable and Wireless communications company'.[36] Anticipating the sale of Britoil, which turned out to be a flop, even the otherwise sober Christopher Fildes, declared that '[p]atriotism, pride, the sight of a soaring oil price, the likelihood of a stag's profit, and, beyond that, the jolly gamble on where BP shares will be by February, when the second payment must be made.... All point the same way'.[37]

These voices suggest to rethink the conventional chronology of the Thatcher period according to which 'quite suddenly the City became glamorous' after Big Bang had ushered in a new culture of yuppie extravagance, greed and speculative money-making in October 1986.[38] The early privatizations attracted a great number of private investors and short-term speculators even without government-backed advertising, which demonstrates retail investors' willingness to re-enter the stock market after the ordeal of the 1970s, if they felt the conditions were right for a comeback. Stagging was a marked pattern in early privatizations and the financial press encouraged punters to cash in on quick profits, with hardly any concerns being raised within the investing public (Figure 6.1). All this points towards the dissemination of a new stock market culture, in which, according to one 1981 guide, investors 'must treat company shares as pieces of paper, and form no other relationship with them other than that they are a means of making a profit'.[39]

If the *Daily Mail* more generally helped promote this culture of self-referential speculation, then its deputy City editor, Michael Walters was particularly bold about his opposition to conventional notions of share ownership that attached responsibility or identity to the company behind a share. In the run-up to the privatization of British Gas, which the government advertised with its notorious 'Tell Sid' TV, billboard and newspaper campaigns, Walters represented the pinnacle of short-termism in the investment community:

> Reach for your cheque book Sid. It's time to send for your British Gas shares. [ ... ]
> For myself, I like the notion of a quick, easy profit in early trading. Many will want to hold on, but I would prefer a few pounds in my pocket before election uncertainties hit the market.[40]

Throughout the 1980s, Walters authored several popular investment guides that candidly encouraged a culture of self-enrichment, speculation and individual profit-seeking. He educated the enlarged investing public about the stock market

---

[36] J. Hamshire, 'Scramble in the City', *Daily Mail*, 31 October 1981; see also P. Sergeant, 'Even in chinese [sic], C&W is stag of the year', *Daily Mail*, 22 October 1981.
[37] C. Fildes, 'Britoil-cheap to us, but pricey in the City', *Daily Mail*, 17 November 1982.
[38] Campbell, *Margaret Thatcher*, II, p. 244.
[39] B. J. Millard, *Stocks and Shares Simplified: A Guide for the Smaller Investor*, 2nd edn (London: Heyden, 1986 [1981]), p. 71.
[40] M. Walters, 'Time for Sid to turn on to Gas', *Daily Mail*, 28 November 1986.

in a language that would have been inconceivable in the investment literature of the 1950s or 1960s. It was much closer to the gimmickry of an interwar bucket shop operator than to Margaret Thatcher's rhetoric of Victorian values. According to Walters '[t]he whole business of investment comes preciously close to being a highly sophisticated form of gambling'[41] or was 'like playing Monopoly with real money'.[42] Stagging flotations of privatized industries was advertised as 'the next best thing to buying £10 notes for a fiver'[43] and in regards to hostile takeovers, investors were given the following advice:

> If you are a share trader, forget the debate about whether or not [takeover] bids are good for Britain, good for industry or serve the consumer well. What matters is the chance of quick, fat profits. [ ... ] Never mind the industrial strategy; enjoy the thrill of a soaring share price.[44]

As shared notions of investment and speculation became increasingly detached from economic and social contexts, commentators the resemblance between stock market activity and gambling front and centre again. Not every author was as cynical as Walters, but the investment community did speak more openly about this subject. Unlike in previous decades, a growing number of investment guides were now authored by women, one stating that 'serious investors would probably deny that investing in the stock market was akin to gambling, but there is almost always some element of chance and it is certainly a place where fortunes can be lost or won'.[45] Gambling analogies became more candid: 'The stock market game is, like most games, between two sides, which in this case are on the one hand the buyers, and on the other hand, the sellers'.[46]

We can trace this development on several levels and it became apparent even in privatization issues that came under less pressure from stags such as the flotation of British Gas on 8 December 1986. On that day, at 'the new stock exchange building in Manchester, 100 people crowded into the foyer to see the start of dealings'. Ann Green, the general manager of the Stock Exchange's northern unit, afterwards described the bizarre events that had unfolded: 'They were cheering when the price went up and booing when it went down. It was just like a bookie's office.'[47] We know that very few of the new shareholders turned up to companies' annual general meeting to assert their legal influence on companies like British Gas and others which they were legally entitled to do as shareholders.[48] Instead, a

---

[41] M. Walters, *How to Make a Killing in New Issues* (London: Sidgwick & Jackson, 1988), p. 7.

[42] Walters, *How to Make a Killing in the Share Jungle*, p. 4.

[43] Walters, *How to Make a Killing in the Share Jungle*, p. iv.

[44] Walters, *How to Make a Killing in the Share Jungle*, p. 72.

[45] Stafford, *The Share-Owner's Guide*, p. 13.      [46] Millard, *Stocks and Shares Simplified*, p. 1.

[47] 'The Big Year of the Small Shareholder', *The Sunday Times*, 21 December 1986.

[48] On the more or less complete lack of shareholder activism see S. Rose, *The Shareholder: The Truth about Wider Share Ownership* (London: Mercury, 1989).

group of punters quite literally turned the local stock exchange into a gambling den. Part of the culture change that had swept the City was to carry a more relaxed attitude towards public criticism in this regard. While post-war chairmen of the London Stock Exchange had to spent a significant amount of their time defending 'the house' against accusations of gambling, Nicholas Goodison, chairman from 1976–86, publicly went on the offensive in this matter. He viewed a certain gambling instinct as part of the national character, and he now wished to leverage this for economic purposes. In a speech to the Centre for Policy Studies, the think tank Margaret Thatcher had founded with Keith Joseph, he contended:

> We need to change attitudes toward risk. I have heard it said that the real cause for the decline in private share ownership [prior to 1980] is that the British people are more 'risk averse' than others. I doubt it. Certainly the experience of the bookies and the pools promoters suggests otherwise.[49]

The new City's more relaxed attitude became even more evident in the public reception of Caryl Churchill's sharply satirical theatre play *Serious Money*, which premiered at the London Royal Court Theatre in March 1987, only five months after Big Bang.[50] On stage, *Serious Money* turned the post-Big Bang City, more precisely the London International Finance Futures Exchange (LIFFE), into an obscene casino where yuppie traders—now female as well as male—indulged in unfettered commercial gambling.[51] The gist of the play is encapsulated in the scene when the main protagonist Scylla, a young LIFFE trader, is challenged by her father—a City gent in pin-stripes and with a bowler hat, clearly representing the old City—to explain the essence of her business: 'It's like playing a cross between roulette and space invaders.'[52] The reaction of the yuppies villainized in this manner was highly revelatory. Instead of being outraged, the City's new generation of derivative traders embraced and celebrated the depiction of *Serious Money* and on several occasions the Royal Court Theatre was sold out because investment banks had bought all the tickets for work parties.[53] The late Ewen Green recalls how the 'chorus of City brokers singing "five more glorious years" in celebration of the 1983 Conservative election victory in Carol [sic] Churchill's musical *Serious Money* is one of the author's abiding memories of the 1980s, as is his witnessing actual brokers singing the very same song in a City

---

[49] Goodison, *Shares for All*, p. 13.

[50] For a selection of reviews see 'Vigorous drama of a new elite', *The Times*, 30 March 1987; 'Trading futures', *TLS*, 3 April 1987; 'Power and the woman', *The Guardian*, 9 April 1987; 'Big Bang is hit on the knocker', *The Observer*, 5 April 1987.

[51] See also the vivid account in D. Kynaston, *LIFFE: A Market and its Makers* (Cambridge: Granta Editions, 1997).

[52] C. Churchill, *Serious Money* (London, New York, NY: Methuen in association with the Royal Court Theatre, 1987), p. 49.

[53] Vinen, *Thatcher's Britain*, pp. 185–186.

wine bar on the evening after the Conservatives' 1987 victory'.[54] The cult embracing of the play largely nullified its satirical bite and under-scored how deeply the culture it portrayed had captured large parts of the City in the public sphere.

## Popular Capitalism—Failure or Success?

More than any other decade, the 1980s cemented a political as well as an academic belief in the supremacy of free markets over government intervention in the economy. The day after the 1987 general election, City brokers and traders could be found drinking champagne at lunch hour, celebrating the stock market's surge resulting from the Thatcher government's re-election and invoking Harold Macmillan's famous post-war dictum that 'we've never had it so good'.[55] Before the return of the market in western politics, economists had done much to foster the notion that markets are per se efficient, self-regulating, and governed by rational decision making. Beginning in the 1950s and gaining traction after the collapse of Bretton Woods, increasingly complex mathematical models were devised not only to analyse, but to reshape stock, commodity, and derivative markets.[56] Perhaps most surprisingly, the idea that markets were inherently rational, efficient, and self-regulating triumphed 'amid so much real-world market imperfection'.[57] One such imperfection occurred on 19 October 1987, when global security markets suddenly collapsed. The crash, known as Black Monday, meant that by the end of the month the Financial Times Stock Exchange 100 Index (FTSE) had lost 26.45 per cent of its value—the biggest daily downturn since 1929.[58] The ensuing debate over who was to blame for the crash is revealing. In France, 'amateur speculators were quickly identified as the source of market confusion and condemned, not only for erratic speculation, but for "contagious mimicry"'.[59] In Britain, amateur investors, speculators, or gamblers had been blamed in similar fashion for causing financial crashes in the previous two centuries. This time, however, they were exempted from any questions of guilt, highlighting both their diminished potential to move an institutionalized equity market as well as the extent of which the New City had shed the Old City's paternalist anxiety towards small speculators. Whether or not the 'man in the

---

[54] Green, 'The Conservatives and the City', p. 172.

[55] 'Yuppies in City BBC Election 1987', available at https://www.youtube.com/watch?v=CpRYHkXTB6I&t=204s. Accessed 24 July 2017; trader invoking Macmillan at 2:57.

[56] On this 'performativity' of financial theory see especially MacKenzie, *An Engine, Not a Camera*.

[57] Rodgers, *Age of Fracture*, p. 43.

[58] 'Share rout in London and Wall Street beats 1929 crash', *The Guardian*, 20 October 1987. The crash turned out to be not as dramatic as 1929. Charles Kindleberger argues that '[t]he stock market's troubles of October 1987 cleared up brilliantly as the monetary authorities rapidly increased bank liquidity to forestall any shortage of credit'. Kindleberger, *Manias, Panics, and Crashes*, p. 102.

[59] Stäheli, *Spectacular Speculation*, p. 55.

street' should play the market was no longer a matter of moral or economic concern. The Conservative privatization architect and former stockbroker John Moore in 1992 shared an anecdote of a 'senior City figure', whose concerns about the government's wider share ownership proposals in retrospect seemed outdated to him: 'But John, he said in a shocked voice, we don't want all those kind of people owning shares, do we?' When markets crashed in 1987, instead of small speculators, inexperienced City yuppies and their seemingly irrational, panicking behaviour bore the brunt of accusations:

> The movements are also thought to be exaggerated by the Yuppie mentality which is rife in the City and seems to know no moderation. The new generation of City dealers have never experienced a bear market—they were too young to remember the horrors of the early 70s. Having been advocates of 'buy, buy, buy' they have now been scared into 'sell, sell, sell.'[60]

Faced with such behavioural patterns one could ask, with Joseph Vogl, 'whether what is taking place in the arenas of the international finance economy is the efficient interaction of rational actors or a spectacle of the purest irrationality'.[61] However, it might be more helpful not to think of rationality as the opposite of emotionality and to highlight instead the ways in which perceptions of both aspects fluctuated or remained stable over time in financial markets.[62] If we look at political debates and academic theories of financial markets over the course of the twentieth century it stands out how far both have oscillated towards both extremes. The global stock market crash of 1929 and the following Great Depression led observers to challenge the school of neoclassical economics, which was the discipline's intellectual gold standard at that time and provided a theoretical justification of nineteenth-century laissez-faire capitalism. This move away from traditional economic liberalism is most commonly associated with the theories of John Maynard Keynes. The Cambridge economist and prodigiously successful investor viewed financial markets as inherently unstable and prone to irrational outbursts—a scepticism that was shared by the policymakers behind the corporatist economic settlement of the post-war period. As neoclassical economic theory successfully pushed Keynesian orthodoxy back to the margins during the

---

[60] 'World-Aid For Wall Street', *Daily Mail*, 21 October 1987; see also 'Market starts a painful recovery', *Daily Mirror*, 22 October 1987: 'City Yuppies also came under attack yesterday for panicking investors.' *The Economist* commented that '[t]he fathers of today's yuppies everywhere should urge their shell-shocked offspring to study the grown-up story of Slater Walker Securities, which was the darling of London markets between 1968 and 1973, right past the eve of when it was bound to crash'. 'When the bull turned', *The Economist*, 24 October 1987.

[61] J. Vogl, *The Specter of Capital* (Stanford, CA: Stanford University Press, 2015), p. ix.

[62] U. Frevert, 'Passions, Preferences, and Animal Spirits: How Does Homo Oeconomicus Cope with Emotions?', in F. Biess and D. M. Gross (eds), *Science and Emotions after 1945: A Transatlantic Perspective* (Chicago, IL: Chicago University Press, 2014), p. 312.

1970s, the latter's insistence on animal spirits, 'whim', 'sentiment', and 'chance' as driving forces of the financial world was also jettisoned.[63] Policies and financial models came to be based on 'homo economicus', the assumption that market participants acted rationally, pursued their self-interest, and sought to maximize utility.[64] In many ways, economic theory came full circle after 2007/8, when the global financial meltdown prompted an international resurgence of Keynes's theorem of 'animal spirits', most visibly in the newly prominent behavioural economics.[65] Economists of all sorts, including Harold Wincott's successor at the *Financial Times*, Martin Wolf, challenged neoclassical dogmas and reincorporated Keynesian thought into the academic mainstream.

What is astonishing against this backdrop of fluctuating sentiment in high politics and the ivory towers of Anglo-Saxon universities, is that popular understandings of finance hardly changed over the same period of time. Here the stock market continued to be seen as a sphere in which prudent and rational behaviour is constantly balanced with irrational and overbearing elements. Britain's investment community had long stressed the emotional economy of the stock market. The sight of frantic yuppies on a trading floor, for instance, would probably not have surprised Francis Hirst, the interwar editor of *The Economist* and advocate of democratic capitalism, who had warned that people 'think and act in mobs; and the speculative fever always rages in an atmosphere of high prices'.[66] During the post-war period, there was widespread awareness about the 'exuberance of emotions' and '"crowd psychology" in the investment world' and in this context, authors often cited Charles Mackay's 1841 essay on *Extraordinary Popular Delusions and the Madness of Crowds*, in which many of these aspects were famously laid out by the Scottish journalist.[67] The stock market's ability to amplify

---

[63] H. Berghoff, 'Rationalität und Irrationalität auf Finanzmärkten', in G. Budde (ed.), *Kapitalismus: Historische Annäherungen* (Göttingen: Vandenhoeck & Ruprecht, 2011), pp. 73–96. On 'new histories' of capitalism that stress the importance of animal spirits see K. Lipartito, 'Reassembling the Economic: New Departures in Historical Materialism', *American Historical Review* 121 (2016), p. 117.

[64] To be sure, this narrative is complicated by the fact that economists outside the academic mainstream continued to uphold Keynesian scepticism towards finance, Hyman Minsky and Robert Shiller being the most prominent among them. See for instance, H. P. Minsky, *John Maynard Keynes* (London: Macmillan, 1976); R. J. Shiller, *Irrational Exuberance* (Princeton, NJ: Princeton University Press, 2000). However, the fact that they were seen as outsiders supports the argument.

[65] R. Skidelsky, *Keynes: The Return of the Master* (London: Allen Lane, 2009). Martin Wolf, Harold Wincott's heir at the *FT*, commented that 'Keynes offers us the best way to think about the crisis', *The Financial Times*, 24 December 2008; see also 'Stunning reversal of economic orthodoxy', *The Financial Times*, 30 December 2008. As part of this resurgence, the late Hyman Minsky's post-Keynesianism was rediscovered and his works were published in new editions. Robert Shiller won the Nobel Memorial Prize in Economic Sciences in 2013.

[66] Hirst, *The Stock Exchange*, p. 165.

[67] The 'exuberance of emotions' is stressed by Naish, *The Complete Guide to Personal Investment*, p. 123; for '"crowd psychology" in the investment world' see E. James, *Sound Principles for the Small Investor* (London: Staples and Staples, 1942), p. 21. On Mackay's 'throw' see P. M. Logan, 'The Popularity of "Popular Delusions": Charles Mackay and Victorian Popular Culture', *Cultural Critique* 54 (2003), pp. 213–241. C. Mackay, *Extraordinary Popular Delusions and the Madness of Crowds* (London: Allen & Unwin, 1973).

human emotions caused observers to believe that 'in private life their character-
istics may be prudence, intelligence and courage, but as average investors on the
Stock Exchange they become greedy, fearful and stupid'.[68] More balanced commentators would describe investment as a 'deliberate activity involving rational
thought', which nevertheless, 'like all mental processes [included] an emotional
quality'.[69] Hence, in popular financial discourse, investment was viewed as 'an art
rather than an exact science'[70] and the stock market conceived of as an 'emotional,
gossipy place, given to rumours, panics and wildly mystifying fluctuations'.[71] Even
after the rise of rational economic man, financial commentators were sceptical
about the scientification of investment activity and the consequences of this trend.
After the 1987 crash, Gordon Cummings, the stock market sage who in 1937 had
testified against share pushers to the Bodkin Committee, criticized that decisions
over millions of pounds had been delegated to computers 'at the expense of the
good old non-scientific guide of instinct'.[72] And even a former member of the
London Stock Exchange, who advised small speculators on how to make profits in
highly risky option markets, warned that 'successful investment in equities is not,
never has been and never will be a wholly rational activity; nor is it easy, no matter
what the so-called experts imply!'[73]

The question of rational and emotional elements in financial capitalism bears
on how we should assess the failures, successes, or wider implications of
Thatcherite efforts to wed the British people to the stock market. Since the emergence of the first modern securities markets, gambling had been a core element of
financial capitalism and has remained so ever since in various guises.[74] During the
first half of the nineteenth century, stagging had come to be regarded as a
sophisticated form of speculation that closely resembles outright forms of
betting due to its dependence on chance, short time horizons, and the high level
of risk involved.[75] In post-war Britain, as Chapter 2 has shown, stagging became a
popular, yet controversial, form of mass participation in the stock market. Against
this backdrop and given that millions of 'investors' rediscovered this practice
during the 1980s, how expedient is it to view Thatcher's agenda of popular
capitalism as either failed or unpopular? Some conclusions can be drawn from a
1994 study on the sociological impact of *Privatization and Popular Capitalism* by
Peter Saunders and Colin Harris, a study that set the tone of the academic debate.

[68] Taylor, *Investment*, p. 65.    [69] Barrada, *How to Succeed as an Investor*, p. 18.
[70] Barrada, *How to Succeed as an Investor*, p. 10.
[71] N. Whetnall, *How the Stock Exchange Works*, 1st edn (Reading: Flame Books, 1979), p. 62.
[72] Cummings, *Investor's Guide to the Stock Market*, p. v.
[73] G. Chamberlain, *Trading in Options: An Investor's Guide to Making High Profits in the Traded Options Market*, 3rd edn (Cambridge: Woodhead-Faulkner, 1990), p. iii.
[74] A. Murphy, *The Origins of English Financial Markets: Investment and Speculation before the South Sea Bubble* (Cambridge: Cambridge University Press, 2009), pp. 33–36.
[75] Robb, *White-Collar Crime in Modern England*, pp. 39–40.

The study was written because 'virtually no sociological research has been carried out to assess and evaluate' 1980s popular capitalism and had the following agenda:

> The crucial link between ownership of shares and changed values and behaviour is simply assumed, yet it rests on an extremely crude materialist premise which few sociologists would uncritically endorse, and it completely ignores the question of what share ownership means to the people involved.[76]

Saunders and Harris subscribed to the view that capitalism is characterized by 'the collapse of bourgeois culture' and shared the Thatcherite assessment that anti-industrial spirits had caused Britain's long-term national decline. They argued that '[Martin] Wiener's fear that the British antipathy towards profit-making may be too entrenched to be reversed [was] well grounded'.[77] Against this backdrop, the sociologists analysed the investment behaviour of a sample of 828 employees who had bought shares in privatized companies in 1989 and 1991.[78] They set out to explore whether their respondents came closest to the ideal type of a 'passive investor or saver', of a 'gambler'—a term they applied to stags who sought short-term gains—or, last but not least, whether they could be classified as 'true capitalist', 'rational risk-taking investors'.[79] Applying this method, they concluded that 'the great privatization crusade has turned out to be much ado about nothing'.[80] Because the majority of their sample did not fall into the latter group, but instead indulged in a 'casino mentality', they concluded that Britain had not become a more capitalist country.

Remarkably, the study's definition of the 'rational, risk-taking investor' was derived directly from Max Weber's renowned study of the *Protestant Ethic*, according to which 'the true spirit of capitalism entails the search for ever renewed profits rather than for windfall gains'.[81] Max Weber famously argued that modern capitalism as an economic system is not only based on contractual labour, free markets, and private property, but intrinsically driven by bourgeois virtues like rational calculation, prudence, deferred gratification, and worldly asceticism. The *Protestant Ethic* is a sweeping exploration of the historical conditions of capitalism and scholars like Talcott Parsons, who translated Weber's writings, and Richard Tawney, who prefaced and edited the British edition, have done much to popularize Weber's ideas in Anglo-Saxon academia.[82] But even historians who view his

---

[76] P. Saunders and C. Harris, *Privatization and Popular Capitalism* (Buckingham, PA: Open University Press, 1994), p. 27.

[77] Saunders and Harris, *Privatization and Popular Capitalism*, pp. 138–142.

[78] Saunders and Harris, *Privatization and Popular Capitalism*, p. 164.

[79] Saunders and Harris, *Privatization and Popular Capitalism*, p. 154.

[80] Saunders and Harris, *Privatization and Popular Capitalism*, p. 162.

[81] Saunders and Harris, *Privatization and Popular Capitalism*, p. 154.

[82] U. Gerhardt, 'Much More than a Mere Translation: Talcott Parsons's Translation into English of Max Weber's "Die protestantische Ethik und der Geist des Kapitalismus": An Essay in Intellectual

analyses as 'among the best that have ever been written about capitalism' acknowledge that the core argument of the *Protestant Ethic* is inaccurate.[83] The intellectual historian Peter Ghosh concurred that 'Weberian capitalism was conceptually thin and problematic' for many reasons.[84] Besides the slim empirical evidence, another factor for this assessment is Weber's skewed juxtaposition between 'modern rational capitalism' and traditional 'adventurous capitalism'.[85] The former was allegedly based solely on 'formal, calculative rationality' and sober profit seeking while the latter lacked 'rational structures of law and of administration' and was driven by 'irrational speculation', an aspect which, according to Weber, modern societies would overcome.[86] However, just as Weber's conception of modern capitalism was flawed by a lopsided reading of nineteenth-century Britain and America,[87] Thatcherite understandings of capitalism were distorted by an obsession with decline being linked to the alleged demise of bourgeois, middle-class, or Victorian values. To be sure, this is not to suggest that the German sociologist had any direct influence on the likes of Thatcher, Joseph, Howe, or Lawson. But the similarities are glaringly obvious. Both Weberian and Thatcherite notions of capitalism stressed the cultural significance (*Kulturbedeutung*) of capitalism, exaggerated the system's dependence on deferred gratification, and overemphasized the close link between Protestant religion and the capitalist 'spirit'.

The problem is that if we apply Weber's concept of modern capitalism as an analytical framework for measuring investment behaviour during the flotation of state assets in 1980s Britain and beyond, we are effectively subscribing to an understanding of capitalism matching that of Mrs Thatcher, who preached hard work, solid book-keeping, and thrift as cardinal economic values. Ironically, it is Weber's less renowned adversary, Werner Sombart, who allows us to overcome some of the shortcomings in Weber's—and Thatcher's—conception of modern capitalism and its historical driving forces.[88] Sombart acknowledged the contribution of Protestant temperance to capitalist expansion, but contended that '[n]o

---

History', *The Canadian Journal of Sociology* 32 (2007), pp. 41–62; Weber, *The Protestant Ethic and the Spirit of Capitalism*.

[83] Quote after Kocka, *Capitalism*, p. 14.

[84] Ghosh, *Max Weber and the Protestant Ethic*, p. 75. Although Weber had written on European Stock Exchanges and 'tried hard to assimilate them to a generalized model of capitalist activity [ ... ] he could not conceal that naked (and wholly "irrational') financial speculation, bereft of any real economic function, reached 'the highest degree of its development in stock exchange trading'".

[85] Weber, *The Protestant Ethic and the Spirit of Capitalism*, p. 111.

[86] Kocka, *Capitalism*, p. 13; Weber, *The Protestant Ethic and the Spirit of Capitalism*, pp. xxxviii, 37.

[87] G. Roth, 'Weber the Would-Be Englishman: Anglophilia and Family History', in H. Lehmann and G. Roth (eds), *Weber's Protestant Ethic: Origins, Evidence, Contexts* (Washington, DC: Cambridge University Press; German Historical Institute, 1995), pp. 83–121.

[88] H. Lehmann, 'The Rise of Capitalism: Weber versus Sombart', in H. Lehmann and G. Roth (eds), *Weber's Protestant Ethic, Origins, Evidence, Contexts* (Washington, DC: Cambridge University Press; German Historical Institute, 1995), pp. 195–208.

less significant has been the contribution of Hazard [*Spielwut*] in the history of the capitalist spirit'.[89] For Sombart, the speculator was an essentially capitalist agent:

> He sees visions of giant undertakings; his pulse beats quickly like a person's in a fever. [ … ] He awakes mighty instincts, and contrives to make them subservient to his ends. Above all, he tickles the gaming propensities, utilizing them to his advantage. In short, there is no speculative undertaking on any large scale without stock-exchange gambling. The gamble is the soul of the business, or the flame that glows right through it.[90]

If we acknowledge the swashbuckling, emotive, and playful side of financial capitalism, without denying its rational and prudent elements, Thatcherite popular capitalism also appears in a new light. As an analysis of the letters to the Wilson Committee has shown, Thatcher's economic moralism *did* appeal to some savers and investors who had lived through the 1970s. And capitalism does rely, to some extent, on rational planning and deferred gratification. But the large privatizations, the Big Bang, and the stock market crash of 1987 illustrate that the system derives much of its energy—and destructive character—from chance, emotions, and an element of gambling. In this way, the 1980s experience was a far cry from the 1970s expectations of financial conservatives. On the other hand, it is the whimsical side of the stock market and its continuing affinity to gambling that explains much of the criticism it continues to draw as well as its unabated appeal to masses of small investors, speculators, stags, punters, and gamblers.

If measured by Thatcherite intentions, popular capitalism can be viewed as failed. Conservative policies of the 1980s did not reverse the institutionalization of stock markets, did little to disperse share ownership beyond traditional class barriers, and, in spite of Thatcher's market populist rhetoric, they did not compel the financial sector to significantly improve services for less affluent clients. When considering Thatcher's stated aim to reverse the decline of Britain's manufacturing power, it must be said that neither the government nor the new small investors came to the rescue of domestic industry and small enterprises, as Chapter 5 has already discussed. The 1980s and, as we will see, the 1990s witnessed less of a return than a marked departure from the self-styled middle-class virtues of thrift, prudence, and readiness to defer gratification. For one thing, the idea of Britain's middle classes as a value system defined by these virtues had largely been a politically motivated construct in the first place. For another thing, the financialization of western economies led the short-termism that governed capital markets to gradually spill over into social and cultural spheres. Britain's experience of runaway inflation during the 1970s had heralded a cultural shift in attitudes

---

[89] Sombart, *The Quintessence of Capitalism*, p. 45. 'Gambling fever' would be a more accurate translation of the original term, *Spielwut*.
[90] Sombart, *The Quintessence of Capitalism*, pp. 91–92.

towards the profit motive and made the New Right's reading of industrial decline seem plausible and convincing. But the larger structural changes and the prag-matic policy design of the privatizations of state assets in the 1980s assured that more people indulged in stagging issues for short-term profits instead of becoming long-term investors in British business.

Again, putting Britain's case into a comparative context can prove insightful. In the 1990s, which the next section will turn to in more detail, Britain came to be seen as a role model that led the rest of Europe the way into the new economy of the twenty-first century. After decades of European countries worrying about catching the 'English disease', the service-driven British economy of the 1990s had come to be seen as a pioneer again. Britain was no longer debating its decline, and had passed on the buck of being the 'sick man of Europe' to Germany, the country that Thatcherites had long idolized for its social market economy. The continent's largest economy was still struggling with the economic aftermath of its reunification in 1990, and many on the political right believed that in order to cure its economic ills, Germany would have to become more like Britain. And so in 1996, late into his 16-year reign, the Christian Democratic Chancellor Helmut Kohl launched the country's second experiment with privatization in a bid to emulate the British Telecom experience. In the 1980s, more and more Germans had come to invest their disposable incomes in bonds, but the stock market was still deemed as unsuitable for ordinary people, which the German central bank explained with households' 'distinctive need for security'.[91] The government intended to change that by selling its stake in the state-owned Deutsche Telekom with preferential treatment given to applications by small investors. Between 1996 and 2000, the government spent millions of Deutsche Mark on advertising campaigns that were aimed at first-time investors—here the Christian Democrats very much followed the script of 'Tell Sid' campaigns that preceded the British Gas flotation.[92] In the run-up to the entire undertaking, German com-mentators expected the German economy to be revolutionized along Anglo-Saxon lines. The official journal of the Frankfurt Stock Exchange pointed out that

Unlike the Americans, who are inclined to gamble (one could frame this posi-tively as risk-taking), and the English, whose gambling spirit could be called legendary, the German mentality is simply more oriented towards security and predictability than towards profit and growth.[93]

[91] Quote after Deutsche Bundesbank, 'Die Aktie als Finanzierungs- und Anlageinstrument', *Monatsbericht der Deutschen Bank* 49 (1997), p. 36. See also M. Kutzner, *Marktwirtschaft schreiben: Das Wirtschaftsressort der Frankfurter Allgemeinen Zeitung 1949 bis 1992* (Tübingen: Mohr Siebeck, 2019), p. 293.
[92] S. Müller, *Der Börsengang der Telekom*, (München: Hampp, 1998).
[93] M. Dunzendorfer, 'Der Lackmustest', *Zeitschrift für das gesamte Kreditwesen* 49 (1996), pp. 1084–1090.

The first two Telekom issues, in fact, were a great success. At first it seemed as if, after the 1960s privatization of Volkswagen, Germany's second state-administered attempt to change the notoriously low risk appetite of its investing public was to have the desired effect. Together with technology companies large and small across the globe, the Telekom share price went through the roof. The internet allowed retail investors to place orders and follow real-time price movements from home. However, after a short share fever in Germany during the late 1990s, the third and final flotation ended in a dramatic flood of lawsuits in 2000, because the company's board were discovered to have overvalued its property holdings.[94] The following year, the Telekom stock came under further pressure due to the bursting of the dot-com bubble, the global stock market crash caused by over-speculation in shares of technology, and newly-founded internet companies. Telekom's share price never recovered, and once again the German public experienced a financial trauma that 'reinforced Germans' reluctance to invest in equities'.[95] To be sure, across the globe, investors large and small burnt their fingers in the dot-com bubble. But in Germany the crash occurred in sync with the collapse of a national giant, which reinforced deeply held suspicions of the stock market and financial risk-taking—an aspect bemoaned by German advocates of wider share ownership to this day.[96]

In light of the wider context of this book, Thatcher's popular capitalism then seems less of a break with British stock market culture of the twentieth century and more a continuation of previous trends. Popular capitalism was certainly not the big revolution of the decade that Conservative politicians until very recently claimed it to be, and scholars have rightfully pointed out that the short-term effect of political efforts to widen share ownership at that time has been overestimated.[97] But at the same time we should be wary of viewing popular capitalism as the grandiose failure it is depicted as in the recent historiography. Instead, scrutinizing the diverse changes in the investing public in a wider chronological context allows us to better understand how a more self-referential, speculative, and buccaneering type of financial capitalism gained a foothold in British society during the 1980s and found further modes of expression in the following decade.

[94] '20 Jahre Telekom-Börsengang', *Der Tagesspiegel*, 18 November 2016.
[95] 'Court favours investors in Deutsche Telekom IPO dispute', *Financial Times*, 11 December 2014.
[96] For lagging shareholder numbers in Germany from a historical perspective see the diagram in the 2016 survey *Aktionärszahlen des Deutschen Aktieninstituts*, available at https://www.dai.de/files/dai_usercontent/dokumente/studien/2016-02-09%20DAI%20Aktionaerszahlen%202015%20Web.pdf. Accessed 10 April 2016.
[97] See for instance the speech by former Prime Minister David Cameron, at the Davos forum on 19 January 2012, in which he singled out popular capitalism as the single greatest achievement of the Thatcher period and a role model for the 21st century. Full speech available at https://www.newstatesman.com/uk-politics/2012/01/economy-capitalism-market. Accessed 26 February 2021.

## The Decade of the Carpetbagger: Building Societies Demutualizing in the 1990s

If any remnants of 'Victorian values' of thrift and self-help were to be found in Britain's financial system of the late twentieth century, it was in the building societies. With roots in the eighteenth century, the building societies movement took its modern shape in the mid-Victorian era. Together with other friendly societies and mutual improvement societies they originated as a collectivist response to industrial capitalism, and enabled 'aspiring artisans and small trades-men' to save towards owner-occupation.[98] Samuel Smiles, the Scottish author of *Self-Help* (1859), the bible of mid-Victorian liberalism that was an important source of inspiration to Margaret Thatcher, spent a lot of time in these mutual societies, which he regarded as an 'idyll of self-help'.[99] By the mid-twentieth century the 'mutuals', as the building societies were now known, had come to dominate the British mortgage market because banks were not allowed to enter this market. Building societies, on the other hand, were not allowed to offer traditional banking services, and throughout 1960 and 1970s, they originated over 90 per cent of British mortgages. The mutuals did not compete with each other, meaning that wherever a borrower went, the rate was always the same. By 1980, Britain's 100 societies counted 30 million individual members and the movement was dominated by a handful of societies that tended to be named after the town or region in which they were established, such as Halifax, Leeds Permanent, National & Provincial, Northern Rock, Woolwich, Birmingham Midshires or Bradford & Bingley (B&B). Every mutual was a member of the Buildings Society Association, an umbrella organization that gave the movement a national voice. Besides local expertise and community embeddedness, the economic benefits of mutuality were considered to be low interest rates for borrowers because directors were not accountable to shareholders, hence did not have to pay dividends, and could plough back profits into servicing their members.

Over time, however, criticism arose that the mutuals, particularly the large societies, had become bloated and unresponsive to members' needs. In addition, the Big Four banks—Lloyds, Barclays, NatWest, and Midland—complained that they were banned from the lucrative business of selling mortgages and pushed for entry into the housing market. The Thatcher government, with its dislike of fixed prices and what it regarded as 'competition-curbing equality ideas', strove for greater competition. In 1986, the government accommodated the banks' calls to put away with the age-old 'who-does-what divides between activities', and passed

---

[98] G. R. Searle, *A New England?: Peace and War, 1886–1918* (Oxford: Oxford University Press, 2004), p. 188.
[99] R. J. Morris, 'Samuel Smiles and the Genesis of Self-Help: The Retreat to a Petit Bourgeois Utopia', *Historical Journal* 24 (1981); on Thatcher and Smiles see D. Cannadine, *Margaret Thatcher: A Life and Legacy* (Oxford: Oxford University Press, 2017), p. 3.

the 1986 Building Societies Act, the decade's most important piece of financial deregulation besides the Big Bang.[100] The Act abolished the restriction in services that building societies and banks could offer, based on the argument that diversification of both banks and building societies would offer better customer service. Now any financial institution could enter the mortgage market, a move that paved the way for the securitization of mortgage debt and the proliferation of the complex mortgage-linked financial derivatives that fuelled the subprime mortgage crisis in 2007–08.[101] On the other side, building societies were free to offer current accounts, insurance services, exchange currencies, and—after a review of the act in 1988—even to provide stockbroking services. Perhaps tinged by her traditional instincts, Margaret Thatcher herself was a 'little concerned about building societies owning stockbrokers', an episode that highlights again the tension between two variants of capitalism at play here. On the one side, and very much fighting a rearguard action at that time, was a movement that combined collectivist elements with mid-Victorian ideas of self-help and thrift—exactly those 'Victorian values of the Samuel Smiles variety', to borrow Nigel Lawson's words, that were widely considered a key ingredient of Thatcherism.[102] On the other side, and firmly on the rise, was a deregulated, 'everything goes' finance capitalism that removed any controls or restrictions that were deemed to curb competitiveness and choice, regardless of whether they had served originally to encourage behaviour in line with the former type of capitalism. Thatcher eventually signed off on the proposal after being convinced that this would 'give a welcome boost to wider shareownership [sic]', and under the condition that building societies were precluded from acting as market makers on the Stock Exchange.[103]

The most momentous consequence of the 1986 Act, however, was that it gave building societies the opportunity to shed their mutual status and to become banks by floating on the stock market—provided their members voted for this democratically.[104] In 1989, the Abbey National building society was the first mutual to venture into this new territory and to list its shares on the London Stock Exchange.[105] In the following eleven years, nine more building societies voted to go public or to be taken over by a bank, creating a share bonanza that once again increased the number of shareholders, but also attracted short-term speculators who bought and sold quickly. Engineered by the last Thatcher

---

[100] Quotes after M. Reid, *All-Change in the City: The Revolution in Britain's Financial Sector* (Basingstoke: Palgrave Macmillan, 1988), p. 4; on the 1986 Act see also Harrison, *Seeking a Role*, p. 345.

[101] 'Mortgage bonds make their debut', *The Financial Times*, 21 January 1987.

[102] Lawson, *Memoirs of a Tory Radical*, p. 64.

[103] Paul Gray (Private Secretary for Economic Affairs to Margaret Thatcher), to Guy Westhead (HMRC), 25 January 1988; Westhead to Gray, 26 January 1988, TNA, PREM 19/3802, 'Organization and Structure of Building Societies'.

[104] C. Davis, *Finance for Housing: An Introduction* (Bristol: Policy Press, 2013), pp. 96–97.

[105] M. Reid, *Abbey National Conversion to PLC: The Inside Story of Abbey National's Conversion and Flotation* (London: Pencorp Books, 1991).

administration, and presided over by her successors John Major and Tony Blair, demutualization was a prime example of Thatcherite policy favouring consumer choice, competition, and abolition of controls over the promotion of cardinal capitalist virtues it self-confidently promoted as Victorian values. Demutualization spelt a fundamental shift in the balance of power in personal finance that entailed an extent of popular mass speculation emblematic of the period's short-termism that favoured quick gains over long-term economic wellbeing. In other words, the legacy of Thatcher's policies was to further undermine those capitalist virtues—thrift and deferred gratification—it claimed to rejuvenate in the first place.

The little explored history of demutualization during the 1990s is inextricably linked to the bizarre and erratic persona of Michael Hardern. Hardern was a freelance butler who from the mid-1990s made frequent headlines with his obsessive quest to force Britain's building societies into conversion. Born in 1957 and raised on the Isles of Scilly, an archipelago off the South West Coast of England, Hardern took a degree in mathematics at the University of Bristol and, after failing to make a career in finance in the 1980s, began to freelance as a butler. He first rose to minor notoriety as leader of a group of shareholder rebels in the Isles of Scilly Steamship Company who unsuccessfully attempted to elect him as director at the 1995 annual general meeting.[106] The same year had seen increased speculation over the future of the building society movement, and a widespread expectation that more and more mutuals were to follow the example of Abbey, leading the *FT* to predict towards the year end that 'those who have a spare few hundred pounds could do a lot worse than play the building society market'.[107] Inspired by these developments, Hardern then resurfaced in 1996 as founder of Members for Conversion, his vehicle for forcing building societies to hold members' votes over their mutuality status. If members were to vote in favour of a stock market flotation, they stood to reap windfall profits from their accounts being converted into shares. Hardern himself publicly bragged to have opened accounts with fifty-two building societies and, seeking constant media attention, he soon became known as the 'self-styled king of carpetbaggers'. The derogatory term carpetbagger became shorthand for small speculators who opened a building society account not in order to save towards a mortgage, but with the sole hope that the society would go public and therefore convert the savings account into shares. It had its origins in 'the aftermath of the American civil war when politicians from the victorious North went to the South in order to profit from its defeat'.[108] The speculative element arose from the fact that nobody could be

[106] 'Isle of Scilly shareholders steam ahead for coup', *The Guardian*, 18 September 1995; 'Scilly attempt hits the rocks', *The Guardian*, 21 September 1995.

[107] 'Are mutuals friendless?', *The Financial Times*, 11 November 1995.

[108] 'All the way to a bank?', *The Financial Times*, 16 January 1999. 'The word "carpetbagging" dates from the aftermath of the American civil war when politicians from the victorious North went to the South in order to profit from its defeat.'

certain which mutual was going to go public next. Often, in the case of Northern Rock for instance, a board member's statement in favour of mutuality could be revoked several weeks later with a call for a members' vote. In such times, local branches of building societies who were rumoured to go public would be besieged by armies of these speculators. Carpet-bagging came to be the decade's most popular and controversial form of mass speculation.

The year 1997 was going to be the year of Tony Blair becoming the first Labour prime minister in eighteen years, of the first Harry Potter novel being published, and of Britain winning the Eurovision Song Contest. It was also going to be the year of the carpetbagger. With Halifax, Woolwich, Alliance & Leicester, Northern Rock, and Bristol & West some of the biggest mutuals were scheduled to hold conversion votes, and in each case the board had publicly spoken out in favour of going public. The future of the entire movement seemed at stake and some City analysts predicted: 'Mutuality was a 20th-century phenomenon. We won't see it in the 21st.'[109] Vulture funds were set up, some with Conservative MPs on their board, whose investment strategy was to raid building societies or to bet on their going public.[110] In March, for instance, carpetbaggers opened over 7,000 speculative accounts with the relatively small Birmingham Midshires, resulting in 'a monthly inflow record of £125m' and causing major disruption to its branch network.[111] Annual data published by the Building Societies Association gives an insight into the national scale of the speculation. In the first half of the 1990s, annual net receipts of all building societies were an average of £3.2 billion. In 1995, receipts had already doubled to £6.7 billion and in 1997, they rose to a record £12.5 billion—a number that was only surpassed at the height of the property bubble in 2007.[112]

Britain's largest building society by members and balance sheet was Halifax. Its flotation in June resulted in the largest ever single intake of investors in Britain with more than 7 million people having their savings accounts turned into shares. Customers with a minimum balance of £100 were given an equivalent of 200 shares, which on the first day of stock exchange trading were worth £1,469. Even more profitable for small speculators was the conversion of Northern Rock in October, where the conversion rate turned out to be a staggering £100 to £2,300. The flotation was considered to be particularly significant because one in three

---

[109] 'Speculators still abound', *The Financial Times*, 29 January 1997.

[110] The member for Wokingham, John Redwood, was on the board of the Scottish fund Murray Financial, which had a £30.5m takeover bid rejected from the members of Leek United, leaving 'in tatters the Edinburgh-based company's dreams of buying up a string of smaller societies and developing them into an internet bank.' 'Leek United rejects Murray's mint', *The Guardian*, 4 December 1999.

[111] In July, the board closed its doors to new applicants. 'Carpetbaggers stampede building societies', *The Guardian*, 19 July 1997.

[112] For 2007 the BSA reported £16bn. 'Net receipts and changes in deposit balances' available at https://www.bsa.org.uk/statistics/savings. Accessed 8 January 2020.

households in the North-East was involved in the conversion, thereby breaking the trend of the average middle-class investor from the South East who had been the main participant in the 1980s privatization issues.[113] In the ten years following its flotation, Northern Rock became heavily involved in the market for mortgage-backed securities. The outcome was disastrous. With billions worth of toxic mortgage bonds on its balance sheet, the lender had to apply for liquidity support from the Bank of England in September 2007. The news triggered a run on Northern Rock branches—the first bank run in Britain in 150 years—and eventually led to the lender's collapse, which in the City of London marked the prelude to the financial meltdown of 2008.[114]

Halifax and Northern Rock had been enormous flotations. But the most anticipated day in the mutual sector's calendar was 24 July 1997, the day members of the Nationwide building society were scheduled to vote over its future status. The vote was widely regarded as a referendum the over the future of the entire movement, and it was Michael Hardern who had filed a formal petition for the largest remaining mutual to hold the vote.[115] He and two other Members for Conversion ran to be elected as Nationwide board members with the slogan 'Vote for us and get £1,000'.[116] Opponents of demutualization pointed out that Nationwide consistently topped lender rankings for offering the best value to customers when it came to low interest rates and service. But the bizarre events that unfolded in the run up to the decision day might explain even better why Michael Hardern remained to be seen as the public face of carpet-bagging and the bane of the building societies movement, but never actually succeeded in bringing down a large mutual. On 20 June, exactly two weeks after publicly launching his campaign, he called in a hastily arranged press conference in a greasy-spoon cafeteria near Russell Square, Central London and declared that he did not want Nationwide to end its mutual status after all. 'I was wrong. I made a mistake.' he explained, but stated that he would nevertheless continue to stand for board election and did not abandon his hopes for a free windfall. But instead of converting savings deposits into tradeable shares, Hardern went on to reason, Nationwide should pay out profits by issuing short-term debt and by expanding its services into 'selling coffee, used cars and maybe Internet terminals'.[117] Hardern later denied that he had changed his mind about seeking conversion—in fact, he tried again two more times. But his credibility was not helped by press reports a week later that the London police had to evict him from Nationwide's

---

[113] 'Northern Rock flotation produces £2,300 windfalls', *The Financial Times*, 2 October 1997.
[114] Kay, *Other People's Money*, pp. 89–91.    [115] 'Judgment day', *The Economist*, 19 July 1997.
[116] 'Butler who's king of the carpetbaggers', *The Observer*, 8 June 1997.
[117] 'Nationwide rebel makes U-turn', *The Guardian*, 20 June 1997.

Holborn branch following 'aggressive behaviour by Mr Hardern towards a senior manager who refused to advance him £3m at 15 minutes' notice.'[118]

Hardern ended up losing the vote. Five incumbent Nationwide board members, who were in favour of mutuality, 'gained 70 per cent of the vote after a postal ballot in which 1.3 million of Nationwide's 3.5million members took part'. Supporters celebrated the outcome as a vote for mutuality across the country and as a 'rejection of short-term greed'.[119] Even *The Economist*, not known as an ardent supporter of mutuality, commented that 'building societies still have a strong business case. They have proved stable and competitive on service.'[120] The same day, Hardern—carrying an Iranian carpet bag at the annual general meeting—announced that he would seek election again in the next year and he came tantalizingly close when he lost by 33,000 votes in 1998 with 50.8 per cent. Generally, 1998 can be seen as the year of push-backs for the carpetbaggers. In March, several regulations became effective that made the practice not impracticable but more expensive and difficult. Minimum thresholds for opening accounts were raised to £1,000, and the requirement for conversion votes was raised from 20 per cent to 50 per cent of members. However, the newly elected Labour government was hardly intent on reigning in the free market, in spite of some Labour backbenchers condemning carpet-bagging as 'asset-stripping [and] legalized theft from future generations'.[121] Gordon Brown, the Chancellor and future Prime Minister, blocked tougher regulations such as the 'two-year rule', in which members would have to be with the society for two years in order to qualify for a payout.[122]

The following year started with fresh momentum for the carpetbaggers. In January 1999, members of Birmingham & Midshires voted to accept a £750m takeover bid by Halifax, and Michael Hardern announced a new campaign of targeting seven of the largest remaining building societies: Britannia, Yorkshire, Coventry, Portman, Chelsea, Leeds & Holbeck, and Skipton.[123] In another PR stunt he was seen donning baronial robes outside the Houses of Parliament and calling for each member of a post-conversion Britannia to be given a seat in the House of Lords. At the same time, Hardern continued to make negative headlines, for instance when 'he was caught rifling through the Prince of Wales's private letters while buttling at a function at Highgrove'.[124] He did not succeed in

---

[118] Mr Hardern said that 'he wanted the £3m to bid for the manuscript The Song Of Solomon, auctioned by Sotheby's that day'. 'Police eject Nationwide carpetbagger', *The Daily Telegraph*, 27 June 1997.

[119] 'Nationwide rebels defeated', *The Financial Times*, 24 July 1997.

[120] 'Blood on the high streets', *The Economist*, 7 June 1997.

[121] Davis, *Finance for Housing*, p. 98.

[122] 'Breathing space after a hectic year', *The Financial Times*, 10 March 1998.

[123] 'Building societies prepare to do battle with mutual enemy', *The Financial Times*, 4 January 1999; 'All the way to a bank?', *The Financial Times*, 16 January 1999; 'Carpetbagger targets seven more building societies', *The Financial Times*, 2 January 1999.

[124] 'Ballot or bottle?', *The Guardian*, 3 April 1999.

converting any of the above mutuals as it had become apparent that his publicity stunts may have been enough to attract media attention, but would never convince sufficient members to vote for him as a chairman, even if it entailed a large windfall.[125] Hardern caused the last major public outrage when in April 1999 he suddenly dropped out of the Britannia board vote, thereby coercing the society into spending £1m on printing and sending out new ballot papers to members without Hardern's name on them.[126]

By that time, Hardern—now with his image as a 'social vandal', 'oddball', and 'crackpot' firmly established—had to yield the rank of 'carpetbagger in chief' to a much quieter, yet more successful campaigner by the name of Stephen Major. It was Major who eventually brought down B&B, then Britain's second largest remaining building society. A self-employed plumber and self-proclaimed hobby investor from Belfast, he started playing the building societies market in 1997, reaping windfalls in the flotations of Woolwich and Alliance & Leicester. Allegedly angered by the decision of B&B's board that year to hold a vote over its status that did not even give members the option to vote for a flotation, he launched his own campaign for conversion. Throughout the campaign, Major pursued a strategy contrary in style to Hardern's by largely avoiding the press and generally shunning the limelight. His quiet success and the fact that he made no missteps throughout the heavily contested campaign prompted rumours that he may have had help from City insiders 'such as a rival bank or a potential bidder'. These rumours were never confirmed to be true and the reason for Major's success was arguably much more mundane. As he explained in an interview with the *Daily Telegraph* after the B&B vote in April, he knew enough about the market himself: 'I know most people expect plumbers to read the *Sun* or the *Mirror*, [b]ut I have always preferred reading the *Financial Times*. It might sound a bit off, but I have dabbled in the stockmarket for years. I guess you could call it a bit of a hobby.'[127]

On 26 April, a majority of B&B's 2.5 million members voted in favour of conversion, marking the first time that building society members had defied their board's wishes on this crucial question. Later it was found that the narrow decision of ending 149 years of mutuality may have been avoided if B&B had not refused to introduce effective measures against carpet-bagging like most mutuals had previously, thereby becoming an easy target for carpetbaggers in the run up to the vote.[128] In many ways, Stephen Major's success also marked the end of the demutualization wave. No major building society has converted since, and the plumber's attempt to convert Nationwide, the third and final attempt after

---

[125] S. Hoopes, 'The Credibility Factor in Elections: Evidence from Britain's Nationwide Building Society's Vote Against Conversion', *Public Choice* 107 (2001), pp. 115–133.
[126] 'Carpetbagger drops out of Britannia board vote', *The Daily Telegraph*, 18 April 1999.
[127] 'How a plumber fixed the float', *The Daily Telegraph*, 2 May 1999.
[128] 'Carpetbaggers found the door left open', *The Financial Times*, 27 November 1999.

Hardern had not succeeded in 1998, failed in 2001 when he withdrew from the board's election campaign.[129]

What is the legacy of demutualization for Britain's financial landscape? The subprime mortgage crisis of 2007–08 exposed the poor state of the British banking sector, including those lenders that used to be building societies. As John Kay points out, 'all but one of the major societies had either collapsed or been absorbed into a large financial conglomerate'.[130] The exception was Nationwide, which remains the world's largest building society with 15m members. Northern Rock failed as described and B&B was nationalized in 2008. Alliance & Leicester and Halifax, after merging with the Bank of Scotland in 2001, both had to be rescued by the government in 2008. There is widespread agreement that this chain of disasters contributed to the housing crisis that the UK is suffering from up until today, which makes it extremely difficult for young or lower-income households to find affordable homes. In this sense, the speculative profits that baby-booming carpetbaggers enjoyed in the 1990s came at the expense of the following generation of millennials who are struggling to climb the housing ladder.

The large-scale flotations first of state assets during the 1980s and later of building societies, as well as the deregulatory agenda of successive governments meant that the UK stock market grew enormously in size and influence. After WWI heralded the end of the 'heyday of Victorian and Edwardian investor capitalism', Britain in the late twentieth century once again became 'one of the most substantially stock exchange-driven economies in the world'.[131] The UK's stock market capitalization as per cent of GDP rose from an all-time low of 6.37 per cent in 1980 to 175.63 per cent in 1999, putting Britain far ahead of its European peers.[132] For most of the 1980s and 1990s it even exceeded the United States, before in both countries the bursting of the dot-com bubble brought the ratio down to 100 per cent, where it stands again at the time of writing. As the twentieth century drew to a close, free-market proponents like John Littlewood, the stockbroker turned historian, lauded the fact that as a result of Thatcherism, 'the pioneering spirit of the old British Empire is alive and well' again.[133] On the other side, critical voices, like that of another former stockbroker, Will Hutton, argued 'that the weakness of the British economy, particularly the level and character of investment, originates in the financial system'.[134] The critics will have felt vindicated by the crash of 2007/08, but remain frustrated with Britain's overdependence on financial services. In the words of John Kay: 'A country can be

[129] 'Plumber pulls plug on Nationwide fight', *The Financial Times*, 10 January 2001.

[130] Kay, *Other People's Money*, p. 151.

[131] Hannah, 'London as the Global Market for Corporate Securities before 1914', p. 149.

[132] Data available from the World Bank's online database, https://data.worldbank.org/. Accessed 12 April 2020.

[133] Littlewood, *The Stock Market*, p. 432.

[134] W. Hutton, *The State We're In* (London: Vintage, 1996), p. xxvii.

prosperous only if it has a well-functioning financial system, but that does not imply that the larger the financial system a country has, the more prosperous it is likely to be. It is possible to have too much of a good thing.'[135]

What do Hardern, Major, and the popularity of carpet-bagging tell us about Britain's market culture and attitudinal shifts in this period? We could easily dismiss Michael Hardern, as many contemporaries did, as a freak who sought to test the boundaries of English eccentricity, a social phenomenon that receives unbroken attention in British public life up until today.[136] After all, Hardern eventually did not accomplish any of the ambitious goals he had set out. But this verdict overlooks the scale of the phenomena that he publicly represented like nobody else. The nine building societies that demutualized in the relatively short time period between 1994 and 2000 enabled more than 12 million members—many of them, of course, holding accounts with more than one society—to participate in a shared bonanza worth more than £20bn.[137] Neither does brushing Hardern aside give an answer to the question of why he was able to garner media attention with his campaign in the first place. Hardern, and later Major, captured the public imagination not least because traditional restraints surrounding profits made from financial securities, which had waned slowly and privately during the interwar and post-war years, had now begun to collapse in public. In their own different ways they played their part in actively bringing about this collapse.

[135] Kay, *Other People's Money*, p. 2.
[136] 'Boris Johnson and the dark art of shamble chic', *The Financial Times*, 20 June 2019.
[137] 'If you convert you have to pay dividends', *The Financial Times*, 20 July 2002.

# Conclusion

## The Covid-19 Pandemic and the Return of the Small Investor

When the Covid-19 pandemic broke in February 2020, there were already signs that the small investor may have been staging a global comeback in the financial markets. Online brokerages first in the US and soon in many other countries had made it possible for anyone with a bank account to buy and sell shares free of commission, and conveniently from a smartphone app. But when lockdowns forced millions of people to stay at home, and online betting was suspended due to cancellation of sports events, the gambling spirit was quickly channelled into the stock market. Aided by fiscal stimulus packages and low interest rates a new generation of 'have-a-go investors' with plenty of time on their hands began seeking their luck and thrills in the stock market. The trend was largely driven out of the US, but in Europe, Britain's investing public was leading the way. In 2020, a record 400,000 new trading accounts were opened in the UK, with investors getting younger on average, and surveys suggesting that globally, the number of accounts had tripled since 2019. Some retail brokerages saw their customer base grow by 30 to 40 per cent, and trading volumes in stocks and shares had more than doubled in the 12 months since the outbreak of the Covid-19 pandemic. Proponents extolled—once again—the 'democratization of investing', while critics—once again—feared that gullible newcomers and bored gamblers would mistake the stock market for a casino and either disrupt the efficient allocation of capital or inflict heavy losses on themselves, or both. MPs from across the political divide called for stricter regulation, demanding that 'smaller traders need protecting from the big gamblers of Wall Street', and warning that 'some people are going to be ruined by this. Experts know to get out early: it's the novices who lose it all'.[1]

As the pandemic wore on, the new crowds of small investors, amateur speculators, and day traders grew so fast that it became a force to be reckoned with in equity markets that had long been dominated by the big institutional investors. Estimates assumed that '20 per cent of the trading volume in the UK and US in

---

[1] 'Calls Mount to Protect Novice Investors From GameStop Craze', *The Daily Telegraph*, 1 February 2021.

*Playing the Market: Retail Investment and Speculation in Twentieth-Century Britain.* Kieran Heinemann, Oxford University Press (2021). © Kieran Heinemann. DOI: 10.1093/oso/9780198864257.003.0008

2020 came from the retail investors'.[2] And even more crucially, the stuck-at-home investors began to organize themselves, most prominently in the subreddit WallStreetBets (WSB), an online forum dedicated to investment ideas on the social media website Reddit. Here, in a language as colourful as vulgar, the predominantly male members discussed aggressive trading strategies for so called 'meme stocks': volatile shares of hyped companies whose sentiment is often driven by a 'fear of missing out' (FOMO) and whose buyers often justify their investment decisions with the hashtag YOLO ('You Only Live Once'). They gradually built up positions in certain stocks, and many of the widely followed Reddit users actually had a professional finance background, explaining the level of analytical sophistication of some strategies. More and more, the WSB Redditors concerted their actions, and seemed to channel the populist, anti-establishment sentiment that since the financial crisis had been shaking up global politics into predatory trading strategies. Specifically, they encouraged each other, and the rapidly growing number of newcomers, to buy shares of certain distressed companies that hedge funds—investment firms with a high risk appetite, and an elitist self-image—had been betting against over the course of 2020. Several hedge funds had 'shorted' companies that were negatively affected by Coronavirus lockdowns such as the high-street video-game retailer GameStop (GME) or the American Multi-Cinema chain (AMC). A hedge fund would sell borrowed stock in these names in the hope that the fund could buy them back at a lower price at a later date—and expect to pocket the difference in price after returning them to the lender. Some hedge funds, most prominently the Wall Street firm Melvin Capital, had borrowed and sold so much GME that they risked incurring significant—and theoretically unlimited—losses if the share price were to move up and not down. What some of the more market-savvy Redditors had come to realize was that more GME shares had been sold short than actually existed. That turned their attention to the options market, where they could add significant leverage to their bets by buying derivatives that granted the holder the right but not the obligation to buy a stock at a predetermined price.

The showdown between the crowd of day traders and the professionals culminated during a few days in late January 2021, when the stock ticker GME became shorthand for what many saw as a financial revolution. The Redditors, or 'degenerates' as they liked to call themselves, succeeded in bringing about a short squeeze of GME shares, which drove up the price of $17 in early January to a temporary all-time high of $469 on 28 January 2021. By then, hedge funds had already scrambled to close their short position by frantically seeking to buy back

[2] Quote after 'Reddit investors' real power is over Wall Street's future behavior', *The Financial Times*, 29 January 2021; for UK data on retail investment see 'Hargreaves CEO Plays Down Mania as Younger Investors Pile In', *Bloomberg*, 1 February 2021; 'Stuck-at-Home U.K. Investors Pour Cash Into AJ Bell Platform', *Bloomberg*, 21 January 2021.

the stock—thereby adding to the price rise—and suffered heavy losses.[3] Melvin Capital, for instance, lost $4.1bn on its bet against GME, wiping off 53 per cent of the fund's value. During these days in late January 2021, the global world of finance seemed to have been turned on its head. Nigel Farage, the architect of Brexit and former commodities trader, proclaimed that small investors were waging 'war against the establishment'. Anthony Scaramucci, the hedge fund founder who was President Donald Trump's Director of Communications for ten days in July 2017, tweeted that we were 'witnessing the French revolution of finance'. And the Marxist philosopher Zlavoj Žižek argued in *The Spectator* that 'the very centre of global capitalism is beginning to fall apart' since the day traders' nihilism had opened up 'a class war transposed into a conflict among stock investors and dealers themselves'.[4] The revolution, however, was short-lived. Within days, GME lost over 80 per cent of its value—leaving those retail punters who had joined the party late suffering enormous losses. Other 'meme-stocks' quickly followed GME on its way down, and early stories of day traders having earned millions were soon superseded by news of students, nurses, and janitors having lost large amounts of money in what looked like an illegal 'pump and dump' scheme.[5] It became clear, as the *Wall Street Journal* pointed out, that the GME saga 'was not some "amateur traders vs. Wall Street fat cats" fantasy', and the idea that retail investors could permanently take on the financial establishment, and correct the politically polarizing levels of wealth inequality in the US and Britain by waging massively leveraged bets against hedge funds was quickly debunked as naive.[6] As one prescient observer put it: 'Waging war against Big Finance by becoming a day trader is like waging war against the casino industry by becoming a gambling addict.'[7]

Yet financial observers across the board expected the breathtaking surge in retail investing to be a lasting trend. The *Financial Times* reckons that the events

---

[3] A short squeeze is a market situation in which a trader who had bet against a stock by selling it short has to deal with a sudden and steep increase in price. Short sellers are forced to buy the stock in order to cut their losses. In the case of GME, and other meme stocks that hedge funds had shorted, retail traders made use of the options market in order to drive up the share price. If thousands of investors buy a stock's call options (the right to buy a stock at a certain price) this drives up the price and causes the sellers of the options—normally banks or other large financial institutions—to start buying the stock as well in order to hedge their position in the options market, thereby further driving up the share price. A short seller looking to buy a desperately needed share in this kind of environment is bound to lose a lot of money.

[4] N. Farage, 'The GameStop Saga Proves Populism is Here to Stay', *Newsweek*, 30 January (accessed 23 February 2021); Scaramucci repeated this phrase on Bloomberg Television on 28 January 2021; S. Žižek, 'The capitalist nihilism of WallStreetBets', *The Spectator*, 1 February 2021.

[5] In a pump and dump scheme, investors conspire to pump up the price of a financial security by spreading false information about its value in order to attract buyers on which to offload the holdings at an inflated price. Since the Redditors did not, strictly speaking, spread misinformation about stocks like GME, but instead stated that they wanted to inflict financial damage on hedge funds, it is at the time of writing still under investigation whether any of the activity was illegal.

[6] 'A Stock-Trading Dupe Is Born Every Minute', *Wall Street Journal*, 21 February 2021.

[7] 'The GameStop Story You Think You Know Is Wrong', *The Atlantic*, 3 February 2021.

of January 2021 could prove 'symbolic of a new era of greater retail influence over stock markets'.[8] They will certainly pose regulatory challenges to the market infrastructure for years to come. The GameStop saga, and the trends that culminated in it, offer an opportunity to hold a sharp and topical mirror against the historical findings of this book, which in turn may inform future debates about the meaning of retail investing. Some aspects of the retail stock market frenzy that followed the outbreak of the Covid-19 pandemic, like the amplifying role of social media, are unique and novel. But in the wider context of this book, other issues that were at stake in 2021—the antagonism between alleged amateurs and professionals or concerns over the 'gamification of investing'—are in many ways a resurgence of deep historical legacies.

Today's observers who argue for or are expecting the democratization of investing, intervene in a debate that has shaped British politics, society, and finance recurrently over the past 100 years. First pinned down in an essay by the editor of the *Financial News* in 1919, we have traced how the idea shaped Conservative political thought and, eventually, government policy under Thatcher in the 1980s. An interesting parallel between the social expansion of investing during the interwar years and today is the regulatory uncertainty surrounding the actions of the new investors and their financial intermediaries. In the aftermath of the GME frenzy, the Financial Conduct Authority (FCA), Britain's market regulator, issued a statement that it was investigating potential market manipulation and insider trading by high-profile day traders who used social media platforms like Twitter to whip up support for their efforts to drive up share prices. Similarly, there is concern that the business model of zero-commission broking poses a threat to market stability. Chapter 1 demonstrated how a regulatory intervention in the retail market affected Britain's financial landscape for decades to follow, and we can therefore expect the response of today's regulators to have wide-ranging consequences for the future direction of retail investing. As we have seen, 1930s policymakers dealt with a far less regulated environment and were focused on the market fringes, where outside brokers and bucket shops catered for the investment newcomers the official exchanges had turned away. These intermediaries exploited the uncertainty around the stockbroker profession and appealed to novices by proactively marketing investment services as accessible, affordable, and entertaining—an approach not dissimilar to that of modern stockbroking apps. The fact that some of the more gullible members of the investing public were fleeced by financial fraudsters prompted the Board of Trade to draft new regulatory measures in the late 1930s. In these deliberations, the City of London's financial establishment successfully muddled the distinction between criminal and legitimate operators leading scholars to overlook the extent to which the

---

[8] 'Is a new era of retail trading emerging after GameStop saga?', *The Financial Times*, 8 February 2021.

Stock Exchange stamped out unwanted competition in the guise of investor protection. The British response protected investors from fraudulent share pushers and company promoters, but hampered the development of a US-style retail market. If we draw a parallel back to today's situation, we see regulators facing similar trade-offs between investor protection, free-market access, and competition. Like their 1930s counterparts, they also find themselves having to navigate a political climate characterized by staunch anti-finance sentiment on the one side, and the vested interests of the financial industry on the other.

The interwar experience also highlighted the importance of the financial press as a pioneer of popular capitalism in Britain, and this book was mindful of the crucial role the media played in layering the different levels of access to information in financial markets. Whether in broadsheet or tabloid formats, financial journalists sought to advertise the stock market to a wider audience, but also to educate investment newcomers about the risks involved. Britain's financial press quickly became as diverse as the investment audience it sought to address, and different newspapers reflected not only the socioeconomic differences of their readers, but also the different moral connotations attached to investment and speculation. However, it took the profession a couple of decades to come of age, and financial journalists continued to come under the suspicion of participating in insider trading at the cost of their readers. Jim Slater's *Sunday Telegraph* share-tipping column 'Capitalist' was a post-war reminder that influential journalists or columnists could move the market to their own or someone else's benefit by creating self-fulfilling prophecies. Today, we see this potential amplified on an unprecedented scale by social media. On the one hand, financial markets are more strictly regulated than the City of the early 1960s in which Jim Slater operated. On the other hand, it continues to be just as challenging, if not more, for regulators in the twenty-first century to identify influencers and to reconstruct causalities in an environment increasingly driven by social media's ability to mobilize crowds and to channel emotions into investment decisions. Market participants and decision makers increasingly see social media as a 'new risk to the effective functioning of markets as it has to politics, exposing the limitations of politicians and regulators to manage viral campaigns'. Chapter 3 highlighted the extent to which the market populism of City journalists anticipated the Thatcherite language of profit, risk-taking and free-market capitalism. Then, free-market capitalism politically was on the rise, and seemed particularly appealing to middle-class savers and investors ravaged by inflation. However, in the more polarized political climate after the financial crash of 2008, which exacerbated already existing social inequalities, financial capitalism was deeply unpopular. This may partly explain why in social media investing was increasingly couched in hedonistic, even nihilistic terms: trading stocks appealed from an entertainment point of view, but needed to be disassociated from and believed to be pursued in opposition to the financial establishment. It will remain to be seen whether YOLO, FOMO, and meme-investing will cede as quickly as it appeared, or whether this mentality will leave a lasting impact on market culture and contribute towards an even more short-term orientated, exuberant, and masculine investment culture. We should not, however, regard the nihilism on display in social media by a new generation of amateur speculators as simply a product of disillusioned and bored Millennials. Instead, as Zizek has accurately observed, to a large degree this is a 'nihilism immanent to the stock exchange itself, a nihilism already at work' in the financial industry.

Historically, for the most part, stock markets had been dominated by individual, mostly wealthy investors. Only during the second half of the twentieth century did they develop into institutionalized, and more professionalized markets. This growing dominance especially of pension funds and life insurance companies over equity markets was one of the most impactful structural changes in Britain's financial landscape during that time—a trend that many financial historians of this period have been occupied with. Consequently, scholars have downplayed the simultaneous gradual expansion in absolute numbers of private investors that went hand in hand with their relative decline, and the simultaneous waning of traditional reservations towards investment and speculation. This attitudinal shift—which ran counter to the state-centred political economy of the post-war settlement—began in the private sphere during the 1950s and 1960s and gained public visibility during the troublesome 1970s. This is not to suggest that reservations and antipathy towards stock market investment ceased to exist among those who did not participate in the market, or who were involved only indirectly through their pensions or life insurances. We have seen how even among members of the investing public, traditional notions of share ownership that eschewed speculation—fashioned as 'genuine investment'—continued to hold sway. What emerged from my narrative is a far more diverse understanding of Britain's investing public that corrects our prevailing image of the ordinary private investor as passive, risk-averse, and primarily interested in long-term income for retirement planning. If we listen to what small investors have to say about their experiences in the stock market when given room to speak on their own terms, different stories emerge from those conveyed by contemporary surveys or speeches by politicians. It then becomes clear that investment was not only regarded as a 'very serious business'. For many, the 'stock market game' had become a popular and socially acceptable hobby, because it promised thrills of risk and reward similar to gambling. In that regard, the 'gamification of investment' that observers are debating today is not a new social trend per se, but an age-old phenomenon that has become acceptable over time, and which has been escalated by new technologies.

By tracing these developments throughout the twentieth century, I have identified during the 1970s and 1980s a significant departure from previously held notions of 'genuine investment' towards a more speculative, individualistic, and gamified paradigm of investment. In the late 1970s, Margaret Thatcher's market populism and moralizing rhetoric of thrift, hard work, and sound money appealed to savers and investors hit by inflation. But the powerful trend of financialization—abetted by the sweeping financial deregulations the Conservatives presided over in the following decade—meant that Thatcher's appeal to Victorian values went largely unanswered. Instead, when the heavily advertised give-away flotations offered the British public a subsidized entry into the capitalist class, the majority 'stagged' the issues for quick profits rather than becoming enfranchised citizens of a nation of shareholders. The post-Big Bang City, the culture of self-enrichment, and the stock market crash of 1987 reminded the investing public that capitalism may rely on thrift and deferred gratification, but was equally driven by emotional exuberance, 'animal spirits', and a certain gambling spirit. I have also attempted to move beyond the binary question of whether Thatcher's popular capitalism failed or succeeded. There is indeed strong evidence that the investment habit did not climb down the social ladder or spread geographically beyond the South East of England as far as Conservative policymakers had eventually hoped for. But on the other hand, their expectations of the stock market being able to absorb a company like British Telecom—and thereby their assessment of the wider investing public's willingness and ability to exploit an investment opportunity—were also proven wrong. My narrative was less driven by the question of how successfully the Conservative Party's popular capitalism promoted investment in stocks and shares. Instead it highlighted the extent to which Britain already had an active and sophisticated core investing public, whose members in the words of the *Sunday Times* City Editor, Graham Searjeant, had learned in previous decades 'to be more like speculators'.

The intended regional and social impact of privatization on attitudes towards investment is debatable, in spite of its architects' intentions and millions of pounds spent on advertising, such as the 'Tell Sid' campaign during the 1986 flotation of British Gas. On the contrary, the unintended impact of the demutualization of the building societies on attitudes towards speculation, was considerable. When Thatcher, as an elder stateswoman, spoke of 'achieving our dream of everyman a capitalist', she probably did not envisage a Northern Irish plumber with a knack for investing almost singlehandedly bringing down a Victorian institution of financial self-help for the benefit of self-enrichment.[9] Because building societies were embedded in their local communities and dispersed across Britain, their conversions brought financial speculation into regions where opposition towards the workings of finance were historically much more pronounced than in the affluent South East of England. In particular, the stock market flotations of mutuals such as Halifax or Northern Rock resulted in windfall profits

---

[9] M. Thatcher, Speech in Sao Paolo ('Challenges of the 21st Century'), 16 March 1994, MTF 108330.

for millions of carpetbaggers in the deindustrializing North, constituencies where Labour politicians once used to garner support by railing against the Stock Exchange as a rich man's casino. But such was the belief in the free market by New Labour, which presided over the majority of conversions, that hardly any measures were taken to curb the practice of carpet-bagging, or to rethink the concept of demutualization altogether.

It is worth contextualizing the twentieth-century development of investment and speculation into mass activities in a wider time frame. If we look back at the eighteenth century, stock market activity as a whole was widely viewed as an immoral and harmful form of gambling. Only in the second half of the nineteenth century did dealing in financial securities come to be regarded as a legitimate economic activity—provided it was carried out by informed professionals. In politics and finance, however, a paternalist anxiety about the small investor— who could quickly turn into an amateur speculator—persisted well into the postwar decades. Whereas Wall Street displayed confidence that investment newcomers could be educated or disciplined into economic citizens, the City of London remained far more sceptical about this prospect and feared that unbridled speculation by uninformed and destitute investors could disrupt the market and bring the financial industry into disrepute. Before Thatcher, this paternalist mindset was shared by most politicians and civil servants. Besides, incentives for investing were deemed difficult to square with the priorities of the mixed economy; and on all sides the experience of the 1929 stock market crash provided further arguments for seeking to channel retail funds into investment vehicles like unit trusts, which were managed by professionals. However, the institutionalization of British equities markets from the 1950s gradually assuaged City concerns about retail speculation. As pension funds, life insurance companies, and unit trusts did come to own an increasing share of corporate equity, the transactions of small investors and speculators less and less had a significant impact on price movements. With the growth of the institutions, the market became more competitive for the private investor, and the City's warnings against too much amateur involvement in the market grew quieter. After the 1980s privatizations, at the latest, the City was no longer concerned about the small speculator. This experience, coupled with Thatcherite individualism and market populism, put an end to the financial paternalism that had guided many decision makers in the old, club-like City, in the Treasury, and the civil service. The new, more meritocratic and competitive City had come to terms with the small investor or speculator, and the speculative frenzies during the privatization issues or the demutualization of the building societies made for good business during the 1980s and 1990s. The legal scholar Stuart Banner has noted that historically for stock market elites, 'the danger of letting the non-affluent speculate was not just that they might bankrupt themselves, but that they would harm the respectable, by causing "sudden fluctuations in values" that could not be foreseen even by the steady merchant'.[10] The reason why in 2021 the concerted actions of the Reddit traders horrified the financial establishment was that they shattered the widely held conviction that retail investors—or 'dumb money' as finance professionals liked to refer to them— could not move markets. Now that it became clear that retail activity organized via social media could have a dramatic impact on markets, calls by institutionalized finance for stricter regulation of retail activity have grown louder again, and we may once more see a significant shift in financial professionals' attitudes towards investment and speculation by amateurs.

In order to understand how Britain developed a lively culture of engaging with the markets, this book has drawn frequent comparisons with the US and mainland Europe, in particular Germany. Factors that contributed to the American culture of popular finance—Wall Street's aggressive marketing strategies, surging standards of living in the post-war decades, and a culture that promoted financial risk-taking and speculation—have been explored by a substantial body of scholarship. By means of comparison, twentieth-century Britain has been portrayed as lagging behind the American investment culture as a result of lower disposable incomes, the City of London losing its eminent status to Wall Street, and the unequal tax treatment of investment income in Britain. When compared with Europe, however, Britain stands out as the most stock-exchange driven economy of the continent, both historically and today. Germany, on the other hand, with its corporatist 'social market economy', decentralized banking system, and idolization of saving, is widely considered the historic counter-model to Britain.[11] Yet this was not a linear or straightforward story. In the late 1950s and early 1960s, more than twenty years before the first privatizations under Thatcher, Germany's Christian Democrats embarked on an experiment in people's capitalism by selling shares in Volkswagen and other state-owned industries to the public. At the same time, Whitehall mandarins and senior policymakers advised successive Conservative governments against actively encouraging equity ownership. Ironically, the German attempt to rekindle the investment habit among lower- and middle-income households went largely unanswered, while in Britain, middle- and, to some extent, working-class savers did not need government encouragement to invest their rising disposable incomes in the booming post-war stock market.

---

[10] Banner, *Speculation*, p. 78. Anyone who has ever played poker against someone playing the game for the first time knows how these turn-of-the-century stock market professionals must have felt. At the poker table, it is also impossible to read a beginner's uninformed actions, making it painstakingly difficult to bet against them.

[11] In the early twenty-first century some German commentators went as far as describing the competitive differences between the Anglo-Saxon and the German models as a 'culture struggle': see W. Abelshauser, *Kulturkampf: der deutsche Weg in die Neue Wirtschaft und die amerikanische Herausforderung* (Berlin: Kulturverlag Kadmos, 2003).

But the German public's aversion towards stocks and shares—and Britain's risk appetite in comparison—are not exclusively a result of different socioeconomic models. We need to bear in mind that at the beginning of the twentieth century, the Berliner Börse had become an important European securities market, which was far less plutocratic than the London Stock Exchange, and which had a high level of retail participation. Many reasons for why Britain and Germany subsequently took such different trajectories can be found in the diametrically opposed experiences both countries made during and after World War I with war bonds. As we have seen, Britain and the United States had an overall positive experience with their governments tapping into private savings in an effort to finance the war economy, and many bond holders later developed an interest in stocks and shares. German owners of war bonds, on the other hand, had their investments wiped out by inflation. This trauma resulted in hostility towards speculators, profiteers, and financiers, which was often fuelled by antisemitism, and which proved to be a heavy burden for the fragile democracy of the Weimar Republic. By implication, Germany developed a strong preference for financial security and monetary stability, which was felt even more keenly after the devastations of World War II. In that regard, war bonds really were an all-in bet on the outcome of the war, and the winners carried away a broad-based acceptance of the benefits of financial securities for generations to come.

In the history of modern capitalism, no institution occupies a place as ambivalent and polarizing as the stock market. Opinions, emotions, attitudes as well as economic and political thought oscillate between adulation and exaltation on the one side, and outright hostility on the other. This book was written with the conviction that the history of capitalism should not only be written top-down with ordinary people being imagined passively as consumers or employees. Writing the history of financial capitalism from below meant to foreground the active participants in the market: investors, speculators, punters, stags, and carpetbaggers. Regardless of our own normative position, we should not underestimate the extent to which their activities have legitimized capitalism in Britain. And we need to acknowledge that historically, the affinity between gambling and financial practices has not just been a source of criticism, but a means of mobilizing mass participation. The GME frenzy and the migration of millions of betters from the gambling public to the investing public during Coronavirus lockdowns again made this clear in a forceful way. The affinity between speculation and gambling has been, and will be, an elementary driving force of financial capitalism—for better or worse.

But the recent surge in retail activity also raises the question whether the power and influence that small investors have proven they can garner collectively could be leveraged for purposes more sustainable and constructive than hurting hedge funds. Activist small investors might one day organize taking action against excessive corporate pay, against a lack of women on a company's board, or a business' poor environmental record. Before the outbreak of the pandemic and the events that followed, we witnessed the emergence of a global debate over the sustainability of capitalism. In the United States, members of the Business Roundtable (BRT)—a lobby group of 181 chief executive officers including the likes of Tim Cook (Apple), Jeff Bezos (Amazon), and Jamie Dimon (JPMorgan)— signed a declaration that pledged to redefine the purpose of corporations to promote 'an economy that serves all Americans', and not just the interests of shareholders.[12] The year before, Larry Fink, the Chief Executive of the world's largest investment firm, BlackRock, had already lectured the CEOs of companies in his vast portfolio that in order 'to prosper over time, every company must not only deliver financial performance, but also show how it makes a positive contri- bution to society'.[13] For decades, the BRT and the vast majority of corporate America had upheld the dogma of shareholder primacy or shareholder value maximization, according to which a company's sole indicator of success was the extent to which it increased the returns of its investors. Or, in the words of Milton Friedman, who pinned down this dogma in an essay in 1970: 'There is one and only one social responsibility of business: to use its resources and engage in activities designed to increase its profits.'[14] In Britain, the *Financial Times* took the BRT's lead and declared it was 'time for a reset' of capitalism.[15] In order for the system to save itself, these bastions of Anglo-Saxon capitalism declared in unison, business leaders would have to tackle climate change, reduce the grotesque levels of wealth inequality, and generate '*long-term* value for shareholders, who provide the capital that allows companies to invest, grow and innovate'.[16]

In many ways, these twenty-first-century calls for a 'responsible' or 'stakeholder capitalism' echo debates over the morality of capitalism during the post-war decades when the Church of England became one of the country's biggest institutional investors and so-called 'genuine investors' voiced their discontent with increased speculation in the stock market. The Church Commissioners and genuine investors did not reject capitalism per se and believed in the benefits of private enterprise. But they rejected the paradigm of shares as a mere 'means of making a profit', and subjected companies to certain ethical standards. They believed that investors had a responsibility towards a business and its employees, just like corporations had a responsibility towards the community in which it was

---

[12] Website of the Business Roundtable, Business Roundtable Redefines the Purpose of a Corporation to Promote 'An Economy That Serves All Americans', 19 August 2019, available at https://www. businessroundtable.org/business-roundtable-redefines-the-purpose-of-a-corporation-to-promote-an- economy-that-serves-all-americans. Accessed 12 April 2020.

[13] 'BlackRock's Message: Contribute to Society, or Risk Losing Our Support', *New York Times*, 16 January 2018.

[14] M. Friedman, 'The Social Responsibility of Business is to Increase its Profits', *The New York Times Magazine*, 13 September 1970.

[15] Front page of the *Financial Times*, 18 September 2019.

[16] Website of the Business Roundtable [see n. 12 for URL]; emphasis added.

embedded. Surveys taken before the outbreak of the pandemic indicated that this belief was increasingly shared again by millennial investors, 85 per cent of whom were interested in sustainable investing in 2019—an investment priority some-what at odds with 'meme investing'.[17] It is worth noting that while Millennials have had to bear the brunt of the devastating legacy of the Great Recession, only a minority of them were investors at that time. The vast majority have yet to experience a prolonged market downturn in their investment careers, the Coronavirus Crash having been a very short-lived bear market. At the time of writing, many observers and historians are convinced that we are experiencing the late phase of a stock market bubble.[18] Sooner or later, there will be a market correction, and we shall then have a better sense of whether that experience will set up Millennials to become more responsible, sustainable, and activist investors.

[17] MSCI ESG Research LLC, *Swipe to invest: the story behind millennials and ESG*, available at https://www.msci.com/documents/10199/07e7a7d3-59c3-4d0b-b0b5-029e8fd3974b.   Accessed   12 April 2020.

[18] N. Ferguson, 'GameStop, Robinhood and the Return of the Wind Trade', *Bloomberg News*, 7 February 2021, available at https://www.bloomberg.com/opinion/articles/2021-02-07/niall-ferguson-gamestop-robinhood-reddit-and-the-wind-trade. Accessed 21 February 2021.

# Bibliography

## Archival Sources

British Library
Terence Rattigan Papers
  Correspondence with stockbroker, Western Manuscripts, Add MS 74537, 1957–68

Churchill Archive Centre
The papers of Sir Winston Churchill, Chartwell Papers
  CHAR 12/9/54; 80–82; 85–87
David Howell papers
  HWLL 2/4/1/1; 8; 10; 11; 17
The papers of Baroness Thatcher LG, OM, FRS
  THCR 2/6/1/36

Franciscan Library, University of Buckingham
  Harold Wincott papers

Guildhall Library
Collection Stock Exchange, London, General Purpose Committee Minutes
  MS 14600/116; 117; 123

London School of Economics Library
  Wider Share Ownership Council Collection
  William Piercy papers

Margaret Thatcher Foundation Website
The National Archives, Kew
Treasury Solicitor and HM Procurator General's Department
  TS 58/3, Bank Rate Tribunal, Transcripts of Proceedings, Days 9–12
Foreign Office
  FO 1109/321, Conservative Policy Committee on Share Ownership, 1958–59
Prime Minister's Office
  PREM 11/2669, Discussions on wider ownership of shares in industry, 1959
  PREM 19/25, Economic strategy, 1979
  PREM 19/191
  PREM 19/3802
Treasury
  T 277/802, Committee on Wider Ownership of Shares in Industry, 1958
  T 233/1851, Committee on Wider Ownership of Shares in Industry, 1959–60
  T 306/42, Committee to Review National Savings, 1971–72
  T 326/88, Investment of Small Savings in Industry, 1960–62

T 326/285, Investment of Small Savings in Industry, 1962–64

T 326/505, Investment of Small Savings in Industry, 1964–66

T 326/917, Investment of Small Savings in Industry, 1966–69

T326/1275, Equity-linked version of SAYE, 18 September 1970

T326/1605 Memorandum on Wider Share Ownership Council proposals for an equity-linked contractual savings scheme, 10 May 1972

Committee to Review the Functioning of Financial Institutions (Wilson Committee)

BS 9/18, Evidence files

BS 9/24, Letters from the public: suggestions to the committee, 1976 Oct 7–1980 Apr 24

BS 9/25, Miscellaneous letters from the public, 1976 Oct 4–1977 Sept 14

BS 9/26, Miscellaneous letters from the public, 1977 Jan 28–Nov 28

BS 9/27, Miscellaneous letters from the public, 1977 July 1–Nov 17

BS 9/28, Miscellaneous letters from the public, 1977 Nov 15–1978 Dec 8

BS 9/29, Miscellaneous letters from the public, 1978 June 9–Sept 29

BS 9/33, Evidence to Sir Harold Wilson, 23 December 1976.

BS 9/117, Evidence received from individuals, 1976 Nov 15–1978 Apr 5

Board of Trade: Departmental Committee on Share-Pushing (Bodkin Committee)

BT 55/104, Papers

BT 55/108, Evidence and Correspondence. Individual Files of various Witnesses, 2

BT 55/109, Evidence and Correspondence. Individual Files of various Witnesses, 3

BT 55/110, Evidence and Correspondence. Individual Files of various Witnesses, 4

BT 55/111, Evidence and Correspondence. Individual Files of various Witnesses, 5

# Printed primary sources

Newspapers and periodicals

*The Atlantic Bloomberg News*

*Daily Express*

*Daily Mail*

*Daily Mirror*

*The Daily Telegraph*

*The Economist*

*The Financial News*

*The Financial Times*

*The Financial Review of Reviews*

*Fiscal Studies*

*The Guardian*

*The Independent*

*Investors' Chronicle*

*Moneyweek*

*The New York Times*

*The News Chronicle*

*Newsweek*

*The Observer*

*The Spectator*

*Der Spiegal*

*The Stock Exchange Journal*

*The Sunday Telegraph*
*The Sunday Times*
*Der Tagesspiegel*
*The Times*
*The Times Literary Supplement*
*Wall Street Journal*

## Parliamentary Debates (Hansard)

Books, articles, pamphlets

Acton Society Trust, *Wider Shareholding* (London: The Society, 1959).

Armstrong, F. E., *The Book of the Stock Exchange: A Comprehensive Guide to the Theory and Practice of Stock and Share Transactions and to the Business of the Members of London and Provincial Stock Exchanges*, 5th edn (London: Pitman, 1957).

Astley, H. J. D., 'The Morality of Investment', *The Financial Review of Reviews* 13 (1918), 243–260.

Ayers, G. M., *England's First State Hospitals and the Metropolitan Asylums Board, 1867–1930* (London: Wellcome Institute of the History of Medicine, 1971).

Bareau, P., *The Future of the Sterling System* (London: The Institute of Economic Affairs, 1958).

Bareau, P., 'Financial Journalism', in R. C. Bennett-England (ed.), *Inside Journalism* (London: Owen, 1967), pp. 153–161.

Barrada, B. H., *How to Succeed as an Investor* (London: Newnes, 1966).

Berman, H. D., *The Stock Exchange: An Introduction for Investors*, 5th edn (London: Pitman Publishing, 1966).

*A Better Tomorrow: The Conservative Programme for the Next 5 Years* (London: Conservative Central Office, 1970).

Bohrer, K. H., *Ein bißchen Lust am Untergang: Englische Ansichten* (München: Carl Hanser, 1979).

The Bond & Share Society, *The Scripophily Handbook: An Introduction to the Collecting of Old Bonds and Shares* (Croydon: The Society, 1986).

Business, Innovation and Skills Committee of the House of Commons, *The Kay Review of UK Equity Markets and Long-Term Decision Making: Third Report of Session 2013–14*, available at https://www.publications.parliament.uk/pa/cm201314/cmselect/cmbis/603/603.pdf. Accessed 19 December 2020.

Chamberlain, G., *Trading in Options: An Investor's Guide to Making High Profits in the Traded Options Market*, 3rd edn (Cambridge: Woodhead-Faulkner, 1990).

Churchill, C., *Serious Money* (London, New York, NY: Methuen in association with the Royal Court Theatre, 1987).

Clark, A., *Bargains at Special Prices* (London: New Authors, 1960).

Cobbett, D., *Before the Big Bang: Tales of the Old Stock Exchange* (Horndean, Portsmouth, Hants: Milestone Publications, 1986).

Cobbett, W., *Rural Rides in the Counties of Surrey, Kent, Sussex* (London: W. Cobbett, 1830).

Crow, D., *A Man of Push and Go: The Life of George Macaulay Booth* (London: R. Hart-Davis, 1965).

Crump, A., *The Theory of Stock Exchange Speculation*, 2nd edn (London: Longmans, Green, and Co, 1874).

Cummings, G., *The Complete Guide to Investment*, 1st edn (Harmondsworth: Penguin, 1963).

Cummings, G., 'Who are the Shareholders?', *The Stock Exchange Journal* 11 (1966), 4–5.

Cummings, G., *Investor's Guide to the Stock Market*, 5th edn, repr. with amendments (London: Financial Times Business Information, 1988).

Dahrendorf, R., *On Britain* (London: University of Chicago Press, 1982).

Davenport, N., *Memoirs of a City Radical* (London: Weidenfeld and Nicolson, 1974).

Deutsche Bundesbank, 'Die Aktie als Finanzierungs – und Anlageinstrument', *Monatsbericht der Deutschen Bank* 49 (1997), pp. 27–41.

Drumm, U. and Henseler, A. W., *Old Securities* (Dortmund: Harenberg, 1978).

Duguid, C., *The Stock Exchange*, 5th edn (London: Methuen and Co, 1926).

Duncan, W. W., *Duncan on Investment and Speculation in Stocks and Shares*, 2nd edn (London: E. Wilson, 1894).

Dunzendorfer, M., 'Der Lackmustest', *Zeitschrift für das gesamte Kreditwesen* 49 (1996), 1084–1090.

Duthy, R., *Alternative Investment: A Guide to Opportunity in the Collectibles Market* (London: Joseph, 1978).

Duthy, R., *The Successful Investor: A Guide to Art, Gold, Wine, Antiques and other Growth Markets* (London: Collins, 1986).

Ellinger, A. G., *The Art of Investment*, 1st edn (London: Bowes and Bowes, 1955).

Ferris, P., *The City* (London: Penguin, 1960).

Giffen, R., *Stock Exchange Securities: An Essay on the General Causes of Fluctuations in their Price* (London: George Bell and Sons, 1877).

Gifford, C. and Stevens, J. A., *Making Money on the Stock Exchange: A Beginner's Guide to Investment Policy*, 2nd edn (London: Macgibbon & Kee, 1960).

Gleeson, A., *People and Their Money: 50 Years of Private Investment* (Norwich: Fletcher & Son, 1981).

Goodison, N., *Shares for All: Steps towards a Share-Owning Society* (London: Centre for Policy Studies, 1986).

Grout, P., 'The Wider Share Ownership Programme', *Fiscal Studies* 8 (1987), 59–74.

Harold Wilson and the Labour Party, *The New Britain: Labours Plan*, Selected Speeches 1964 (London: Harmondsworth, 1964).

Harris, R., 'Foreword: Harold Wincott – Doyen of Financial Journalism', in G. E. Wood (ed.), *Explorations in Economic Liberalism: The Wincott Lectures* (Basingstoke: Macmillan, 1996).

Hayek, F. A., *The Road of Serfdom* (Chicago, IL: The University of Chicago Press, 1944).

Heath, A. and Garrett, G., *The Extension of Popular Capitalism* (Glasgow: University of Strathclyde, 1989).

Heller, R., *The Naked Investor: Cautions for Dealing with the Stock Market* (London: Weidenfeld and Nicolson, 1976).

Hendy, R., *Collecting Old Bonds and Shares* (London: Stanley Gibbons Publications, 1978).

Hirst, F. W., *The Stock Exchange: A Short Study of Investment and Speculation*, 4th edn (London: Williams and Norgate, 1948).

Hobson, J. A., *The Evolution of Modern Capitalism: A Study of Machine Production*, new and rev. edn (London: The Walter Scott Publishing Co. 1926 [1896]).

Hobson, O., *How the City Works*, 4th edn (London: Dickens Press, 1954).

Hodgson, J. P., *Speculation for Gain* (Southwick: Herdcroft, 1979).

Hollowood, B., *Funny Money* (London: Macdonald and Jane's, 1975).

Holmes, B. G., *In Love With Life: A Pioneer Career Woman's Story* (London: Hollis & Carter, 1944).

Howe, G., *The Right Approach to the Economy: Outline of an Economic Strategy for the Next Conservative Government* (London: Conservative, 1977).

Hutber, P., *The Decline and Fall of the Middle Class, and How it Can Fight Back* (London: Associated Business Programmes, 1976).

Hutton, G., 'All Capitalists Now', in R. Harris (ed.), *Radical Reaction: Essays in Competition and Affluence* (London: The Institute of Economic Affairs, 1961), pp. 29–62.

*The Industrial Charter: A Statement of Conservative Industrial Policy* (London: Conservative and Unionist Central Office, 1947).

Investors' Chronicle, *Beginners, Please*, 2nd edn (London: Eyre & Spottiswoode, 1960).

James, E., *Sound Principles for the Small Investor* (London: Staples and Staples, 1942).

Jenkins, A., *The Stock Exchange Story* (London: Heinemann, 1973).

Jordan, H. W., 'Profit-Sharing and Co-Partnership', *The Financial Review of Reviews* June (1920), 166–186.

Kay, W., *A-Z Guide to Money* (London: Constable, 1983).

Kellett, R., *Taxes for Today* (London: Conservative Political Centre on behalf of the Bow Group, 1958).

Kellett, R., *City Page* (London: Newman Neame Take Home Books, 1962).

Kellett, R., *Ordinary Shares for Ordinary Savers*, Hobart papers (London: The Institute of Economic Affairs, 1962), vol. 16.

Kellett, R., *Money on Your Mind: A Simple Guide to Successful Share-Buying*, Corgi Books (Transworld, 1964).

Kellett, R., *The Merchant Banking Arena: With Case Studies* (London: St. Martin's Press, 1967).

Keynes, J. M., *The General Theory of Employment, Interest and Money* (London: Macmillan, 1961 [1936]).

Labour Party, *Your Personal Guide to the Future Labour Offers You* (London, 1959).

Lawson, N., *Memoirs of a Tory Radical* (New York: Biteback Publishing, 2011).

Lewis, R., *Industry and the Property Owning Democracy* (London: Bow Group, 1954).

Lewis, R., *A Bonfire of Restrictions* (London: Conservative Political Centre, 1965).

Lewis, R., 'How to Denationalise', in R. Boyson (ed.), *Goodbye to Nationalisation* (London: Churchill Press, 1971), pp. 80–93.

Lewis, R., *Margaret Thatcher: A Personal and Political Biography* (London, Boston: Routledge and K. Paul, 1975).

Liberal Party of Great Britain, *Britain's Industrial Future: Being the Report of the Liberal Industrial Inquiry* (London: E. Benn, 1928).

London Stock Exchange, *How Does Britain Save? A summary of the results of a survey conducted for the London Stock Exchange by the British Market Research Bureau Limited* (London, 1966).

Low, T., *Everyman a Capitalist: Some Proposals for the Small Saver in Industry* (London: Conservative Political Centre, 1959).

Mackay, C., *Extraordinary Popular Delusions and the Madness of Crowds* (London: Allen & Unwin, 1973).

McKnight, G., *The Fortunemakers* (London: Michael Joseph, 1972).

Macmillan, H., *Macmillan Diaries: The Cabinet Years 1950–1957*, Edited and with an Introduction by Peter Catterall (London: Macmillan, 2003).

Medomsley, J., *Opportunities for the Small Investor* (Durham: MEL Publications, 1978).

Millard, B. J., *Stocks and Shares Simplified: A Guide for the Small Investor*, 2nd edn (London: Heyden, 1986 [1981]).

Minsky, H. P., *John Maynard Keynes* (London: Macmillan, 1976).

Morgan, E. V. and Thomas, W. A., *The Stock Exchange: Its History and Functions* (London: Elek Books, 1962).

Moseley, S. A., *Money-Making in Stocks and Shares: A Popular Guide for Investors and Speculators* (London: Sir Isaac Pitman & Sons, 1927).

Moseley, S. A., *The Small Investor's Guide*, 2nd edn (London: Sir Isaac Pitman & Sons, 1930).

Moyle, J., *The Pattern of Ordinary Share Ownership 1957–1970* (Cambridge: Cambridge University Press, 1971).

Muller, H. S., *Scientific Speculation*, The 'Money-Maker' Manuals for Investors (London: The Office of the Money-Maker, 1901).

Naish, P. J., *The Complete Guide to Personal Investment* (London: C. Tinling, 1962).

*A Nation of Shareholders: Report of the CBI Wider Share Ownership Task Force* (London: CBI, 1990).

Naylor, G., *Sharing the Profits: An Inquiry into the Habits, Attitudes and Problems of Employees' Shareholding Schemes*, with an introduction by Nancy Seear and George Copeman. Foreword by Lord Shawcross and Maurice Macmillan (London: Garnstone Press, 1968).

Office for National Statistics, *Share Ownership: A Report on the Ownership of Shares at 31st December 1997* (London: The Stationery Office, 1997).

*Owning Capital: Proposals of a study group formed by the Political Council of the Junior Carlton Club* (London: Conservative Political Centre, 1963).

Parkinson, H., *The A B C of Stocks and Shares: A Handbook for the Investor* (London: Longmans, Green and Co., 1925).

Parkinson, H., *The Small Investor* (London: Blackie & Son, 1930).

Parkinson, H., *Ownership of Industry* (London: Eyre & Spottiswoode, 1951).

Plender, J. and Wallace, P., *The Square Mile: A Guide to the New City of London* (London: Hutchinson Business, 1986).

Powell, E., *Letters to a Small Investor: A Straightforward & Non-Technical Introduction to the Science of Investment* (London: The Financial News, 1916).

Powell, E., 'Democratisation of Investment', *The Financial Review of Reviews* 14 (1919), 243–258.

Powell, E., *The Evolution of the Money Market, 1385–1915: An Historical and Analytical Study of the Rise and Development of Finance as a Centralised, Co-ordinated Force* (London: Frank Cass & Co., 1966).

Powell, J. E., *Saving in a Free Society* (London: The Institute of Economic Affairs, 1960).

*The Private Diaries of Sydney Moseley* (London: Max Parrish, 1960).

Proudhon, P.-J., *Manuel du Spéculateur à la Bourse*, 4th edn (Paris: Librairie de Garnier Frères, 1857).

Public Relations Department of the London Stock Exchange, *A Career on the London Stock Exchange* (London: London Stock Exchange, 1963).

Raw, C., *Slater Walker: An Investigation of a Financial Phenomenon* (London: Deutsch, 1977).

Reader, W. J., *A House in the City: A Study of the City and of the Stock Exchange Based on the Records of Foster & Braithwaite, 1825–1975* (London: Batsford, 1979).

Redwood, J., *The Democratic Revolutions: Popular Capitalism in Eastern Europe* (London: Centre for Policy Studies, 1990).

Research Services Limited, *Savings and Attitudes to Share Owning* (London: Wider Share Ownership Committee, 1962).

Revell, J. and Moyle, J., *The Owners of Quoted Ordinary Shares: A Survey for 1963* (London: Chapman and Hall for the Department of Applied Economics, University of Cambridge, 1966), vol. 7.

Rose, S., *Fair Shares: A Layman's Guide to Buying and Selling Stocks and Shares* (London: Comet, 1986).

Rose, S., *The Shareholder: The Truth about Wider Share Ownership* (London: Mercury, 1989).

Rowlatt, J. and Davenport, D., *The Handbook of Saving and Investment* (London: Arthur Barker, 1965).

Rowlatt, J. and Davenport, D., *Guide to Saving and Investment*, rev. edn (Newton Abbot: David & Charles, 1971).

Ryan, T. M., *Theory of Portfolio Selection* (Basingstoke: Macmillan, 1978).

Saleeby, C., 'The Nemesis of Speculation', *The Financial Review of Reviews* 14 (1919), 20–41.

Saunders, P. and Harris, C., *Privatization and Popular Capitalism* (Buckingham, Philadelphia, PA: Open University Press, 1994).

Sergeant, P., *Money Matters* (London: Bancroft, 1967).

Sergeant, P., 'Tip for Tap in the City', in A. Ewart and V. Leonard (eds), *100 Years of Fleet Street: As Seen through the Eyes of the Press Club* (London: Press Club, 1982), p. 66.

Shiller, R. J., *Irrational Exuberance* (Princeton, NJ: Princeton University Press, 2000).

Simmery, F., *The Poor Man's Guide to the Stock Exchange* (London: Labour Research Department, 1959).

Skelton, N., 'Constructive Conservatism IV: Democracy Stabilized', *The Spectator*, 18 May 1923.

Slovic, P., 'Psychological Study of Human Judgment: Implications for Investment Decision Making', *The Journal of Finance* 27 (1972), 779–799.

Smith, A., *The Money Game* (London: Michael Joseph, 1968).

Sombart, Werner, *The Quintessence of Capitalism: A Study of the History and Psychology of the Modern Business Man*, translated and edited by M. Epstein (London: T. Fisher Unwin, 1915).

Spiegelberg, R., *The City: Power without Accountability* (London: Blond & Briggs, 1973).

Stafford, J. T., *The Share-Owner's Guide: How to Invest Profitably and Safely in Shares* (Cambridge: Woodhead-Faulkner, 1987).

Taylor, R., *Investment* (London: Collins, 1963).

Thatcher, M., *The Downing Street Years, 1979–1991* (London: HarperCollins, 1993).

Thrower, A. H., *How to Invest for Profit in Stocks and Shares: A Guide for the Small Investor* (Preston: Thomas, 1961).

Trevelyan, G. M., *English Social History*, new illustrated edition with an Introduction by Asa Briggs (London: Longman, 1978).

Vernon, R. A., Middleton, M., and Harper, D. G., *Who Owns the Blue Chips? A Study of Shareholding in a Leading Company* (Epping: Gower Press, 1973).

Wallace, C., *The Investor's Pocket Book* (London: Evans Bros, 1955).

Walters, M., *How to Make a Killing in the Share Jungle*, 3rd edn (London: Sidgwick & Jackson, 1987).

Walters, M., *How to Make a Killing in New Issues* (London: Sidgwick & Jackson, 1988).

Warren, H., *The Modern Bucket Shop: A description of the wiles of the 'outside' stockbroker or dealer, of the manner in which he runs his gambling den, of the London gutter Press which assists him, and of the shearing of the lambs* (London: Everett, 1906).

Warren, H., *Dr Taylor of London Wall: Prince of Bucket-Shop Swindlers, An Account of the Greatest Bucket-Shop Fraud the World has Ever Known* (London: Robert Sutton, 1908).

Warren, J. P., *Pounds, Shillings and Sense: A Guide for the New Investor* (Sensible Investments Publications, 1959).

Warren, M., *Investment for the Ordinary Man* (London: Macgibbon & Kee, 1958).

Warren, M., 'Number One, Millbank, and the Market', *The Stock Exchange Journal* 6 (1961).

Weber, M., *Die Börse: Innerer Zweck und äussere Organisation der Börsen*, Göttinger Arbeiterbibliothek (Göttingen: Vandenhoeck und Ruprecht, 1894), Bd. 1, Heft 2–3.

Weber, M., *The Protestant Ethic and the Spirit of Capitalism*, translated by T. Parsons, with a foreword by R. Tawney (London: G. Allen & Unwin, 1930).

Weber, M., 'Stock and Commodity Exchanges [Die Börse (1894)]', translated by Steven Lestition, *Theory and Society* 29 (2000), 305–338.

Weber, M., *The Protestant Ethic and the Spirit of Capitalism*, translated by Talcott Parsons, with an Introduction by Anthony Giddens, Routledge Classics (London: Routledge, 2001 [1915]).

Westropp, E., *Invest £100: A Guide to Investment*, 4th edn (London: Oldbourne, 1964).

Whetnall, N., *How the Stock Exchange Works*, 1st edn (Reading: Flame Books, 1979).

Whitehouse, B., *Investing Your Money* (London: Foyle, 1961).

*Why Britain Needs a Social Market Economy: With a Foreword by Sir Keith Joseph* (London: Centre for Policy Studies, 1975).

Wider Share Ownership Council, *Growth in a Responsible Society* (London, 1961).

Wider Share Ownership Council, *The Shareholder's Rights and Responsibilities* (London, 1963).

Wilson, H. and the Labour Party, *The New Britain: Labour's Plan*, Selected Speeches 1964 (Harmondsworth, 1964).

Wincott, H., *The Stock Exchange* (London: S. Low, Marston, 1947).

Wincott, H., *The Business of Capitalism: A Selection of Unconventional Essays on Economic Problems of the 1960s* (London: The Institute of Economic Affairs, 1968).

Withers, H., *Hints About Investments* (London: Eveleigh Nash & Grayson, 1926).

Withers, H., *Stocks and Shares*, 4th edn (London: J. Murray, 1948).

# Printed Secondary Works

Abelshauser, W., *Kulturkampf: der deutsche Weg in die Neue Wirtschaft und die amerikanische Herausforderung* (Berlin: Kulturverlag Kadmos, 2003).

Abelshauser, W., *Deutsche Wirtschaftsgeschichte: Von 1945 bis zur Gegenwart*, 2nd edn (München: Beck, 2011).

Aitken, R., 'Capital at Its Fringes', *New Political Economy* 11 (2006), 479–498.

Aitken, R., *Performing Capital: Toward a Cultural Economy of Popular and Global Finance* (New York: Palgrave Macmillan, 2007).

Arditti, M., 'Rattigan, Sir Terence Mervyn (1911–1977)', *Oxford Dictionary of National Biography (ODNB)* (Oxford: Oxford University Press, online edn, January 2008).

Avrahampour, Y., '"Cult of Equity": Actuaries and the Transformation of Pension Fund Investing, 1948–1960', *Business History Review* (2015), 281–304.

Banner, Stuart, *Speculation: A History of the Fine Line between Gambling and Investing* (New York, Oxford: Oxford University Press, 2017).

Barber, B. M. and Odean, T., 'Trading Is Hazardous to Your Wealth: The Common Stock Investment Performance of Individual Investors', *The Journal of Finance* 55 (2000), 773–806.

Barber, B. M., and T. Odean, 'Boys will be Boys: Gender, Overconfidence, and Common Stock Investment', *The Quarterly Journal of Economics* 116 (2001), pp. 261–292.

Barber, B. M. and Odean, T., 'The Behavior of Individual Investors', in G. M. Constantinides, M. Harris and R. M. Stulz (eds), *Handbook of Economics and Finance* (Amsterdam: Elsevier, 2013), pp. 1533–1570.

Barber, B. M., Odean, T., and Zhu, N., Do retail trades move markets? *Review of Financial Studies* 22 (2009), 151–186.

Beckert, S., *Empire of Cotton: A New History of Global Capitalism* (London: Allen Lane, 2014).

Beckert, S., Burgin, A., Hudson, P. J., Hyman, L., Lamoreaux, N., Marler, S. et al., 'Interchange: The History of Capitalism', *Journal of American History* 101 (2014), 503–536.

Bellringer, C. and Michie, R., 'Big Bang in the City of London: An Intentional Revolution or an Accident?', *Financial History Review* 21 (2014), 111–137.

Berghoff, H. 'Rationalität und Irrationalität auf Finanzmärkten', in G. Budde (ed.), *Kapitalismus: Historische Annäherungen* (Göttingen: Vandenhoeck & Ruprecht, 2011), pp. 73–96.

Bingham, A., *Gender, Modernity, and the Popular Press in Inter-War Britain* (Oxford: Oxford University Press, 2004).

Bingham, A., *Family Newspapers? Sex, Private Life, and the British Popular Press 1918–1978* (Oxford: Oxford University Press, 2009).

Bingham, A. and Conboy, M., *Tabloid Century: The Popular Press in Britain, 1896 to the Present* (Oxford: Peter Lang AG, 2015).

Blaazer, D., '"Devalued and Dejected Britons": The Pound in Public Discourse in the Mid-1960s', *History Workshop Journal* 47 (1999).

Black, L., *The Political Culture of the Left in Affluent Britain, 1951–64: Old Labour, New Britain?* (Basingstoke: Palgrave Macmillan, 2003).

Black, L. and Pemberton, H., 'Introduction: The Uses and (Abuses) of Affluence', in L. Black and H. Pemberton (eds), *An Affluent Society? Britain's Post-War 'Golden Age' Revisited* (Aldershot: Ashgate, 2004), pp. 1–13.

Black, L. and Pemberton, H., 'Introduction: The Benighted Decade? Reassessing the 1970s', in L. Black and H. Pemberton (eds), *Reassessing 1970s Britain* (Manchester: Manchester University Press, 2013).

Bradley, K., 'Rational Recreation in the Age of Affluence: The Cafe and Working-Class Youth in London, c.1939–1965', in E. D. Rappaport, S. T. Dawson, and M. J. Crowley (eds), *Consuming Behaviours: Identity, Politics and Pleasure in Twentieth-century Britain* (London: Bloomsbury Academic, 2015), pp. 71–86.

Brandes, S., '"Free to Choose": Die Popularisierung des Neoliberalismus in Milton Friedmans Fernsehserie (1980/90)', *Zeithistorische Forschungen* 12 (2015), 526–533.

Bristow, E., 'Profit-Sharing, Socialism and Labour Unrest', in K. D. Brown (ed.), *Essays in Anti-Labour History: Responses to the Rise of Labour in Britain* (London: Macmillan Press, 1974), pp. 262–289.

Buchner, M., *Die Spielregeln der Börse: Institutionen, Kultur und die Grundlagen des Wertpapierhandels in Berlin und London, ca. 1860–1914* (Tübingen: Mohr Siebeck, 2019).

Buggeln, M., Daunton, M., and Nützenadel, A. (eds), *The Political Economy of Public Finance: Taxation, State Spending and Debt since the 1970s* (Cambridge: Cambridge University Press, 2017).

Buggeln, M., Daunton, M., and Nützenadel, A., 'The Political Economy of Public Finance since the 1970s: Questioning the Leviathan', in M. Buggeln, M. Daunton, and A. Nützenadel (eds), *The Political Economy of Public Finance: Taxation, State Spending and Debt since the 1970s* (Cambridge: Cambridge University Press, 2017), pp. 1–31.

Burgin, A., 'Age of Certainty: Galbraith, Friedman, and the Public Life of Economic Ideas', *History of Political Economy* 45 (2014), 191–219.

Campbell, J., *Margaret Thatcher: The Grocer's Daughter* (London: Jonathan Cape, 2000), vol. I.

Campbell, J., 'Roberts, Alfred (1892–1970)', *Oxford Dictionary of National Biography (ODNB)* (Oxford: Oxford University Press,).

Campbell, J., *Margaret Thatcher: The Iron Lady* (London: Jonathan Cape, 2003), vol. II.

Cannadine, D., *Margaret Thatcher: A Life and Legacy* (Oxford: Oxford University Press, 2017).

Chambers, D., 'Gentlemanly Capitalism Revisited: A Case Study of the Underpricing of Initial Public Offerings on the London Stock Exchange, 1946–86', *Economic History Review* 62 (2009), 31–56.

Chancellor, E., *Devil Take the Hindmost: A History of Financial Speculation* (London: Plume, 1999).

Chandler, A., *The Church of England in the Twentieth Century: The Church Commissioners and the Politics of Reform, 1948–1998* (Woodbridge: Boydell Press, 2009).

Clapson, M., *A Bit of a Flutter: Popular Gambling in England, c.1820–1961* (Manchester: Manchester University Press, 1992).

Clarke, P., *Keynes: The Twentieth Century's Most Influential Economist* (London: Bloomsbury, 2009).

Cockett, R., *Thinking the Unthinkable: Think Tanks and the Economic Counter Revolution 1931–1983* (London: Fontana, 1995).

Collins, M. 'The Fall of the English Gentleman: The National Character in Decline, c. 1918–1970', *Historical Research* 75 (2002), 90–111.

Cowing, C. B., *Populists, Plungers, and Progressives: A Social History of Stock and Commodity Speculation* (Princeton, NJ: Princeton University Press, 1965).

Crafts, N., 'The Golden Age of Economic Growth in Western Europe, 1950–1973', *Economic History Review* 48 (1995), 429–447.

Crouch, C., 'Privatised Keynesianism: An Unacknowledged Policy Regime', *The British Journal of Politics & International Relations* 11 (2009), 382–399.

Dardi, M. and Gallegati, M., 'Alfred Marshall on Speculation', *History of Political Economy* 24 (1992), 571–594.

Daunton, M., '"Gentlemanly Capitalism" and British Industry 1820–1914', *Past and Present* 122 (1989), 119–158.

Daunton, M., 'Financial Elites and British Society, 1880–1950', in Y. Cassis (ed.), *Finance and Financiers in European History 1880–1960* (Cambridge: Cambridge University Press, 1991), pp. 121–146.

Daunton, M., *Trusting Leviathan: The Politics of Taxation in Britain, 1793–1914* (Cambridge: Cambridge University Press, 2001).

Daunton, M., *Just Taxes: The Politics of Taxation in Britain, 1914–1979* (Cambridge: Cambridge University Press, 2002).

Daunton, M., 'Afterword', in N. Henry and C. Schmitt (eds), *Victorian Investments: New Perspectives on Finance and Culture* (Bloomington, IN: Indiana University Press, 2009), pp. 202–219.

Daunton, M., 'Questioning Leviathan: Restructuring the State in Britain since 1970', *East Asian Journal of British History* 5 (2016), 29–50.

Daunton, M., 'Creating a Dynamic Society: The Tax Reforms of the Thatcher Government', in M. Buggeln, M. Daunton and A. Nützenadel (eds), *The Political Economy of Public Finance: Taxation, State Spending and Debt since the 1970s* (Cambridge: Cambridge University Press, 2017), pp. 32–56.

Daunton, M. and Hilton, M. (eds), *The Politics of Consumption: Material Culture and Citizenship in Europe and America*(Oxford: Berg, 2001).

Davenport-Hines, 'Aspinall, John Victor (1926–2000)', *Oxford Dictionary of National Biography (ODNB )* (Oxford: Oxford University Press, 2004).

Davenport-Hines, R. 'Lowson, Sir Denys Colquhoun Flowerdew, first baronet (1906–1975)', *Oxford Dictionary of National Biography (ODNB)* (Oxford: Oxford University Press, 2004).

Davies, A., '"Right to Buy": The Development of a Conservative Housing Policy, 1945–1980', *Contemporary British History* 27 (2013), 421–444.

Davies, A., *The City of London and Social Democracy: The Political Economy of Finance in Britain, 1959–1979* (Oxford: Oxford University Press, 2017).

Davies, A., Freeman, J. and Pemberton, H., '"Everyman a Capitalist" or "Free to Choose": Exploring the Tensions within Thatcherite Individualism', *The Historical Journal* 61 (2018), 477–501.

Davis, A., *Public Relations Democracy: Public Relations, Politics and Mass Media in Britain* (Manchester: Manchester University Press, 2002).

Davis, C. *Finance for Housing: An Introduction* (Bristol: Policy Press, 2013).

de Goede, M., 'Mastering "Lady Credit"', *International Feminist Journal of Politics* 2 (2000), 58–81.

de Goede, M., *Virtue, Fortune, and Faith: A Genealogy of Finance*, Borderlines (Minneapolis, MN: University of Minnesota Press, 2005).

Dell, E., 'Lever, (Norman) Harold, Baron Lever of Manchester (1914–1995)', *Oxford Dictionary of National Biography (ODNB)* (Oxford: Oxford University Press, . . . ).

Doering-Manteuffel, A. and Raphael, L., *Nach dem Boom: Perspektiven auf die Zeitgeschichte seit 1970*, 3rd edn (Göttingen: Vandenhoeck & Ruprecht, 2012).

Dorey, P., *British Conservatism and Trade Unionism, 1945–1964* (Aldershot: Ashgate, 2009).

Edgerton, D., *The Rise and Fall of the British Nation: A Twentieth-Century History* (London: Allen Lane, 2018).

Edwards, A., '"Manufacturing Capitalists": The Wider Share Ownership Council and the Problem of "Popular Capitalism", 1958–92', *Twentieth Century British History* 27 (2016), 100–123.

Edwards, A., '"Financial Consumerism": citizenship, consumerism and capital ownership in the 1980s', *Contemporary British History* 31 (2017), 210–229.

Egginton, H., 'In Quest of the Antique: The Bazaar, Exchange and Mart and the Democratization of Collecting, c. 1926–1942', *Twentieth Century British History* 28 (2016), 159–185.

Engel, A., 'Vom verdorbenen Spieler zum verdienstvollen Spekulanten: Ökonomisches Denken über Börsenspekulation im 19. Jahrhundert', *Jahrbuch für Wirtschaftsgeschichte* 54 (2013), 49–70.

Engel, A., 'Spiel', in C. Dejung and M. Dommann (eds), Auf der Suche nach der Ökonomie: Historische Annäherungen (Tübingen: Mohr Siebeck, 2014), pp. 263–285.

Engel, A., 'The Bang after the Boom: Understanding Financialization', Zeithistorische Forschungen/Studies in Contemporary History 12 (2015), 500–510.

Epstein, G. A., 'Introduction: Financialization and the World Economy', in G. A. Epstein (ed.), Financialization and the World Economy (Cheltenham: Edward Elgar, 2006), pp. 3–16.

Evans, E. J., Thatcher and Thatcherism, 3rd edn (London, New York: Routledge, 2013).

Fabian, A., Card Sharps, Dream Books, & Bucket Shops: Gambling in 19th-Century America (Ithaca, NY: Cornell University Press, 1990).

Ferguson, N., 'Siegmund Warburg, the City of London and the Financial Roots of European Integration', Business History 51 (2009), 364–382.

Ferguson, N., High Financier: The Lives and Time of Siegmund Warburg (London: Allen Lane, 2010).

Ferguson, N., 'Introduction', in N. Ferguson and C. S. Maier (eds), The Shock of the Global: The 1970s in Persepective (Cambridge, MA: Belknap Press of Harvard University Press, 2010), pp. 1–21.

Fine, B., and Saad-Filho, A., 'Thirteen Things You Need to Know About Neoliberalism', Critical Sociology 43 (2017), 685–706.

Fisher, J. and Bewsey, J., The Law of Investor Protection (London: Sweet & Maxwell, 2003).

Fong, W. M., The Lottery Mindset: Investors, Gambling and the Stock Market (Basingstoke: Palgrave Macmillan, 2014).

Foote, G., The Republican Transformation of Modern British Politics (New York: Palgrave Macmillan, 2006).

Foroohar, Rana, Makers and Takers: How Wall Street Destroyed Main Street (New York: Crown Business, 2017).

Francis, M., 'A Crusade to Enfranchise the Many: Thatcherism and Property-Owning Democracy', Twentieth Century British History 23 (2012), 275–297.

Frank, T., One Market under God: Extreme Capitalism, Market Populism, and the End of Economic Democracy (London: Secker & Warburg, 2001).

Fraser, S., Every Man a Speculator: A History of Wall Street in American Life (New York: HarperCollins, 2005).

Fraser, S., Wall Street: A Cultural History (London: Faber and Faber, 2006).

Frevert, U., 'Gefühle und Kapitalismus', in G. Budde (ed.), Kapitalismus: Historische Annäherungen (Göttingen: Vandenhoeck & Ruprecht, 2011), pp. 50–72.

Frevert, U., 'Passions, Preferences, and Animal Spirits: How Does Homo Oeconomicus Cope with Emotions?', in F. Biess and D. M. Gross (eds), Science and Emotions after 1945: A Transatlantic Perspective (Chicago, IL: Chicago University Press, 2014), pp. 300–317.

Garnett, M., 'Walker, Peter Edward, Baron Walker of Worcester (1932–2010)', Oxford Dictionary of National Biography (ODNB) (Oxford: Oxford University Press, first published January 2014).

Gauci, P., Emporium of the World: The Merchants of London, 1660–1800 (London: Hambledon Continuum, 2007).

Geppert, D., Thatchers konservative Revolution: Der Richtungswandel der britischen Tories 1975–1979 (München: R. Oldenbourg Verlag, 2002).

Geppert, D., '"Englische Krankheit"? Margaret Thatchers Therapie für Großbritannien', in N. Frei and D. Süß (eds), Privatisierung: Idee und Praxis seit den 1970er Jahren, Jena

Center Geschichte des 20. Jahrhunderts—Band 12 (Göttingen: Wallstein Verlag, 2012), pp. 51–69.

Gerhardt, U., 'Much More than a Mere Translation: Talcott Parsons's Translation into English of Max Weber's "Die protestantische Ethik und der Geist des Kapitalismus": An Essay in Intellectual History', *The Canadian Journal of Sociology* 32 (2007), 41–62.

Ghosh, P., *Max Weber and the Protestant Ethic: Twin Histories* (Oxford: Oxford University Press, 2014).

Goux, J., 'Values and Speculations: The Stock Exchange Paradigm', *Cultural Values* 1 (1997), 159–177.

Green, E. H. H., 'The Conservative Party, the State and the Electorate, 1945–64', in J. Lawrence and M. Taylor (eds), *Party, State and Society: Electoral Behaviour in Modern Britain* (Aldershot: Scolar Press, 1997), pp. 176–200.

Green, E. H. H., 'Rentiers versus Producers? The Political Economy of the Bimetallic Controversy, c. 1880–1898', *English Historical Review* 103 (1988), 588–612.

Green, E. H. H., *Ideologies of Conservatism: Conservative Political Ideas in the Twentieth Century* (Oxford: Oxford University Press, 2002).

Green, E. H. H., 'The Conservatives and the City', in R. Michie and P. Williamson (eds), *The British Government and the City of London in the Twentieth Century* (Cambridge: Cambridge University Press, 2004), pp. 153–173.

Green, E. H. H., *Thatcher* (London, New York: Hodder Arnold, 2006).

Green, S., *The Passing of Protestant England: Secularisation and Social Change, c.1920–1960* (Cambridge, New York: Cambridge University Press, 2011).

Grimley, M., 'Thatcherism, Morality and Religion', in B. Jackson and R. Saunders (eds), *Making Thatcher's Britain* (Cambridge: Cambridge University Press, 2012), pp. 78–94.

Halsey, A. H., 'Titmuss, Richard Morris (1907–1973)', *Oxford Dictionary of National Biography (ODNB)* (Oxford: Oxford University Press, ).

Hampton, M., *Visions of the Press in Britain, 1850–1950* (Urbana, IL: University of Illinois Press, 2004).

Hannah, L., 'London as the Global Market for Corporate Securities before 1914', in Y. Cassis and L. Quennouëlle-Corre (eds), *Financial Centres and International Capital Flows in the Nineteenth and Twentieth Centuries* (Oxford: Oxford University Press, 2011), pp. 126–160.

Harrison, B., *Seeking a Role: The United Kingdom 1951–1970* (Oxford: Oxford University Press, 2009).

Harrison, B., *Finding a Role? The United Kingdom 1970–1990* (Oxford: Clarendon Press, 2011).

Harvey, D., *A Brief History of Neoliberalism* (Oxford: Oxford University Press, 2011).

Hausteiner, E. 'Eine Aktie, ein Volk: Die Werbekampagne während des Wirtschaftswunders' in H. Münkler and J. Hacke (eds), *Wege in die neue Bundesrepublik: Politische Mythen und kollektive Selbstbilder nach 1989* (Frankfurt am Main: Campus, 2009), pp. 199–212.

Higgins, D. M., 'British Manufacturing Financial Performance,1950–79: Implications for the Productivity Debate and the Post-War Consensus', *Business History* 45 (2003), 52–71.

Hilton, B., *The Age of Atonement: The Influence of Evangelicalism on Social and Economic Thought, 1785–1865* (Oxford: Clarendon Press, 1991).

Hochfelder, D., '"Where the Common People Could Speculate": The Ticker, Bucket Shops, and the Origins of Popular Participation in Financial Markets, 1880-1920', *The Journal of American History* 93 (2006), 335–358.

Hollow, M., 'A Nation of Investors or a Procession of Fools? Reevaluating the Behavior of Britain's Shareholding Population through the Prism of the Interwar Sharepushing Crime Wave', *Enterprise and Society* 20 (2019), 132–158.

Hoopes, S., 'The Credibility Factor in Elections: Evidence from Britain's Nationwide Building Society's Vote against Conversion', *Public Choice* 107 (2001), 115–133.

Howell, D., *A New Style of Government: A Conservative View of the Tasks of Administrative, Financial and Parliamentary Reform Facing an Incoming Government* (London: Conservative Political Centre, 1970),

Huizinga, J., *Homo Ludens: A Study of the Play Element in Culture* (London: Routledge & Kegan Paul, 1949).

Humphries, C., 'Bodkin, Sir Archibald Henry (1862–1957)', *Oxford Dictionary of National Biography (ODNB)* (Oxford: Oxford University Press,),

Hutton, W., *The State We're In* (London: Vintage, 1996).

Itzkowitz, D. C., 'Fair Enterprise or Extravagant Speculation: Investment, Speculation, and Gambling in Victorian England', in N. Henry and C. Schmitt (eds), *Victorian Investments: New Perspectives on Finance and Culture* (Bloomington, IN: Indiana University Press, 2009), pp. 98–119.

Jackson, B., 'Revisionism Reconsidered: "Property-Owning Democracy" and Egalitarian Strategy in Post-War Britain', *Twentieth Century British History* 16 (2005), 416–440.

Jackson, B., 'Property-Owning Democracy: A Short History', in M. O'Neill and T. Williamson (eds), *Property-Owning Democracy: Rawls and Beyond* (Hoboken, NJ: Wiley-Blackwell, 2012), pp. 33–52.

Jackson, B., 'The Think-Tank Archipelago: Thatcherism and Neo-Liberalism', in B. Jackson and R. Saunders (eds), *Making Thatcher's Britain* (Cambridge: Cambridge University Press, 2012), pp. 43–61.

James, H., 'Finance Capitalism', in J. Kocka and M. van der Linden (eds), *Capitalism: The Reemergence of a Historical Concept* (London, New York: Bloomsbury Academic, 2016), pp. 133–164.

Jarvis, M., *Conservative Governments, Morality and Social Change in Affluent Britain, 1957–64* (Manchester: Manchester University Press, 2005).

Jeffery, T. and McClelland, K.,'A World Fit to Live in: The *Daily Mail* and the Middle Classes 1918–1939', in J. Curran, A. Smith, and P. Wingate (eds), Impacts and Influences: Essays on Media Power in the Twentieth Century (London, New York: Methuen, 1987).

Jeremy, D. J., *Capitalists and Christians: Business Leaders and the Churches in Britain, 1900–1960* (Oxford: Oxford University Press, 1990).

Johnson, P., *Saving and Spending: The Working-Class Economy in Britain, 1870–1939* (Oxford: Clarendon Press, 1985).

Johnson, P., *Making the Market: Victorian Origins of Corporate Capitalism*, Cambridge Studies in Economic History (Cambridge: Cambridge University Press, 2010).

Johnson, P., 'In Pursuit of Prudence: Speculation, Risk, and Class in Victorian Britain', in C. Griffiths (ed.), *Classes, Cultures, and Politics: Essays on British History for Ross McKibbin* (Oxford: Oxford University Press, 2011), pp. 59–69.

Jovanovic, F., 'The Construction of the Canonical History of Financial Economics', *History of Political Economy* 40 (2008), 213–242.

Kay, J., *Other People's Money: Masters of the Universe or Servants of the People?* (London: Profile Books, 2015).

Keegan, W., *Nine Crises: Fifty Years of Covering the British Economy from Devaluation to Brexit* (London: Biteback Publishing, 2018).

Kindleberger, C., *Manias, Panics, and Crashes: A History of Financial Crises*, 5th edn (Hoboken, NJ: John Wiley & Sons, 2005).

Knight, P., 'Animal spirits', in P. Crosthwaite, P. Knight and N. Marsh (eds), *Show Me the Money: The Image of Finance, 1700 to the Present* (Manchester: Manchester University Press, 2014), pp. 65–99.

Knight, P., *Reading the Market: Genres of Financial Capitalism in Gilded Age America* (Baltimore, MD: Johns Hopkins University Press, 2016).

Kocka, J., 'Writing the History of Capitalism', *Bulletin of the German Historical Institute Washington* 47 (2010), 7–24.

Kocka, J., *Capitalism: A Short History*, Translated by Jeremiah Riemer (Princeton, NJ: Princeton University Press, 2016).

Kocka, J., 'Introduction', in J. Kocka and M. van der Linden (eds), *Capitalism: The Reemergence of a Historical Concept* (London, New York: Bloomsbury Academic, 2016), pp. 1–10.

Koselleck, R., '"Space of Experience" and "Horizon of Expectation": Two Historical Categories', in R. Koselleck (ed.), *Futures Past: On the Semantics of Historical Time*. Translated and with an Introduction by Keith Tribe (New York: Columbia University Press, 2005), pp. 255–275.

Koselleck, R., 'Über die Theoriebedürftigkeit der Geschichtswissenschaft', in R. Koselleck, *Zeitschichten: Studien zur Historik*, 3rd edn (Frankfurt: Suhrkamp, 2013), pp. 298–316.

Krippner, G. R., *Capitalizing on Crisis: The Political Origins of the Rise of Finance* (Cambridge, MA.: Harvard University Press, 2011).

Kutzner, M., *Marktwirtschaft schreiben: Das Wirtschaftsressort der Frankfurter Allgemeinen Zeitung 1949 bis 1992* (Tübingen: Mohr Siebeck, 2019).

Kynaston, D., *The Financial Times: A Centenary History* (London: Viking, 1988).

Kynaston, D., *Cazenove & Co: A History* (London: Batsford, 1991).

Kynaston, D., *The City of London: Golden Years, 1890–1914* (London: Pimlico, 1996), II.

Kynaston, D., *LIFFE: A Market and its Makers* (Cambridge: Granta Editions, 1997).

Kynaston, D., *The City of London: Illusions of Gold 1914–1945* (London: Pimlico, 2000), III.

Kynaston, D., *The City of London: A Club No More 1945–2000* (London: Pimlico, 2001), IV.

Kynaston, D., *Till Times Last Sand: A History of the Bank of England 1694–2013* (London: Bloomsbury, 2017).

Lawrence, J., '"Paternalism, Class and the British Path to Modernity"', in S. Gunn and J. Vernon (eds), *The Peculiarities of Liberal Modernity in Imperial Britain* (Berkeley, CA: University of California Press, 2011), pp. 147–164.

Lawrence, J., 'Class, "Affluence" and the Study of Everyday Life in Britain, c. 1930–1964', *Cultural and Social History* 10 (2013), 273–299.

Lawrence, J., 'Social-Science Encounters and the Negotiation of Difference in Early 1960s England', *History Workshop Journal* 77 (2014), 215–239.

Lawrence, J. and Sutcliffe-Braithwaite, F., 'Margaret Thatcher and the Decline of Class Politics', in B. Jackson and R. Saunders (eds), *Making Thatcher's Britain* (Cambridge: Cambridge University Press, 2012), pp. 132–147.

Lehmann, H., 'The Rise of Capitalism: Weber versus Sombart', in H. Lehmann and G. Roth (eds), *Weber's Protestant Ethic: Origins, Evidence, Contexts* (Washington, DC: Cambridge University Press; German Historical Institute, 1995), pp. 195–208.

Lipartito, K., 'Connecting the Cultural and the Material in Business History', *Enterprise and Society* 14 (2013), 686–704.

Lipartito, K., 'Reassembling the Economic: New Departures in Historical Materialism', *American Historical Review* 121 (2016), 101–139.

Littlewood, J., *The Stock Market: 50 Years of Capitalism at Work* (London, San Francisco, CA: Financial Times, Pitman Publishing, 1998).

Logan, P. M., 'The Popularity of "Popular Delusions": Charles Mackay and Victorian Popular Culture', *Cultural Critique* 54 (2003), 213–241.

Loussouarn, C., 'Spread Betting and the City of London', in R. Cassidy, A. Pisac and C. Loussouarn (eds), *Qualitative Research in Gambling: Exploring the Production and Consumption of Risk* (New York, London: Routledge, 2013), pp. 233–249.

Lowe, R., *The Official History of the British Civil Service: Reforming the Civil Service, Volume I: The Fulton Years, 1966–81* (London, New York: Routledge, 2011).

Luhmann, N., *The Reality of the Mass Media* (Stanford, CA: Stanford University Press, 2000).

Lutz, M., 'Mennonite Entrepreneurship in the United States: Adapting to the Industrial Economy in the Late 19th Century', *Entreprises et Histoire* 81 (2015), 29–42.

McClymont, G., 'Socialism, Puritanism, Hedonism: The Parliamentary Labour Party's Attitude to Gambling, 1923–31', *Twentieth Century British History* 19 (2008), 288–313.

MacKenzie, D., *An Engine, Not a Camera: How Financial Models Shape Markets* (Cambridge, MA, London: MIT Press, 2006).

McKnight, D., 'The Sunday Times and Andrew Neil: The Cultivation of Market Populism', *Journalism Studies* 10 (2009), 754–768.

Maier, C. S., '"Malaise": The Crisis of Capitalism in the 1970s', in N. Ferguson and C. S. Maier (eds), *The Shock of the Global: The 1970s in Persepective* (Cambridge, MA: Belknap Press of Harvard University Press, 2010), pp. 25–48.

Mandler, P., 'The Problem with Cultural History', *Cultural and Social History* 1 (2004), 94–117.

Marcuzzo, M. C., Sanfilippo, E., and Fantacci, L., 'Speculation in Commodities: Keynes' "Practical Acquaintance" with Futures Markets', *Journal of the History of Economic Thought* 32 (2010), 397–418.

Marsh, N., *Money, Speculation and Finance in Contemporary British Fiction* (London: Continuum, 2007).

Martin, R. L., *The Geography of Private Shareholding: Mapping Popular Capitalism in Britain* (Swindon: Economic and Social Research Council, 1999).

Matthews, D., 'The British Experience of Profit-Sharing', *Economic History Review* 42 (1989), 439–464.

Mazower, M., *Dark Continent: Europe's Twentieth Century* (London: Penguin, 1999).

Michie, R., *The London and New York Stock Exchanges 1850–1914* (London: Allen & Unwin, 1987).

Michie, R., 'The Stock Exchange and the British Economy, 1870–1939', in J. J. van Helten and Y. Cassis (eds), *Capitalism in a Mature Economy: Financial Institutions, Capital Exports and British Industry, 1870–1939* (Aldershot: Edward Elgar, 1990), pp. 95–114.

Michie, R., *The City of London: Continuity and Change since 1850* (London: Macmillan, 1991).

Michie, R., *The London Stock Exchange: A History* (Oxford: Oxford University Press, 2001).

Michie, R., 'The City of London and the British Government: The Changing Relationship', in R. Michie and P. Williamson (eds), *The British Government and the City of London in the Twentieth Century* (Cambridge: Cambridge University Press, 2004), pp. 31–55.

Michie, R., 'Gamblers, Fools, Victims, or Wizards? The British Investor in the Public Mind, 1850–1930', in D. R. Green (ed.), *Men, Women, and Money: Perspectives on Gender, Wealth and Investment 1850–1930* (Oxford: Oxford University Press, 2011), pp. 156–183.

Michie, R., 'Financial Capitalism', in L. Neal and J. G. Williamson (eds), *The Spread of Capitalism: From 1848 to the Present*, The Cambridge History of Capitalism (Cambridge: Cambridge University Press, 2014), pp. 230–263.

Middleton, S., '"Affluence" and the Left in Britain, c.1958–1974', *English Historical Review* 129 (2014), 107–138.

Morris, R. J., 'Samuel Smiles and the Genesis of Self-Help: the Retreat to a Petit Bourgeois Utopia', *Historical Journal* 24 (1981).

Müller, S., *Der Börsengang der Telekom* (München: Hampp, 1998).

Müller, T. B. and Tooze, A., 'Demokratie nach dem Ersten Weltkrieg', in T. B. Müller and A. Tooze (eds), *Normalität und Fragilität: Demokratie nach dem Ersten Weltkrieg* (Hamburg: Hamburger Institut für Sozialforschung, 2016), pp. 9–36.

Munro, C., 'The Fiscal Politics of Savings and Share Ownership in Britain, 1970–1980', *The Historical Journal* 55 (2012), 757–778.

Murphy, A., *The Origins of English Financial Markets: Investment and Speculation before the South Sea Bubble* (Cambridge: Cambridge University Press, 2009).

Needham, D., *Monetary Policy from Devaluation to Thatcher, 1967–1982* (Basingstoke: Palgrave Macmillan, 2014).

Needham, D., '"Goodbye, Great Britain"? The Press, the Treasury, and the 1976 IMF Crisis', in S. Schifferes and R. Roberts (eds), *The Media and Financial Crises: Comparative and Historical Perspectives* (London, New York: Routledge, 2015), pp. 261–276.

Newman, K., *Financial Marketing and Communications* (Eastbourne: Holt, Rinehart and Winston, 1984).

Newman, K., *The Selling of British Telecom* (New York: St. Martin's Press, 1986).

Newton, S., 'The Sterling Devaluation of 1967, the International Economy and Post-War Social Democracy', *English Historical Review* CXXV (2010), 912–945.

Nixon, S., *Hard Sell: Advertising, Affluence and Transatlantic Relations, c. 1951–69* (Manchester: Manchester University Press, 2013).

Ortolano, G., *The Two Cultures Controversy: Science, Literature and Cultural Politics in Postwar Britain* (Cambridge: Cambridge University Press, 2009).

Ott, J. C., '"The Free and Open People's Market": Political Ideology and Retail Brokerage at the New York Stock Exchange, 1913–1933', *Journal of American History* 96 (2009), 44–71.

Ott, J. C., *When Wall Street Met Main Street: The Quest for an Investors' Democracy* (Cambridge, MA: Harvard University Press, 2011).

Parker, D., *The Official History of Privatisation: The Formative Years 1970–1987* (London: Routledge, 2009), vol. I.

Parker, D., *The Official History of Privatisation: Popular Capitalism, 1987–1997* (London: Routledge, 2012), vol. II.

Parsons, W., *The Power of the Financial Press: Journalism and Economic Opinion in Britain and America* (New Brunswick, NJ: Rutgers University Press, 1989).

Plehwe, D., 'Introduction', in P. Mirowski and D. Plehwe (eds), *The Road from Mont Pèlerin: The Making of the Neoliberal Thought Collective* (Cambridge, MA.: Harvard University Press, 2009), pp. 1–44.

Porter, D., '"A Trusted Guide of the Investing Public": Harry Marks and the Financial News 1884–1916', *Business History* 28 (1986), 1–17.

Porter, D., 'City Editors and the Modern Investing Public: Establishing the Integrity of the New Financial Journalism in Late Nineteenth-Century London', *Media History* 4 (1998), 49–60.

Porter, D., '"Where There's a Tip There's a Tap": The Popular Press and the Investing Public, 1900–60', in P. Catterall and C. Seymour-Ure (eds), *Northcliffe's Legacy: Aspects of the British Popular Press* (London: Macmillan, 2000), pp. 71–96.

Porter, D., '"City Slickers" in Perspective: The Daily Mirror, its Readers and their Money, 1960–2000', *Media History* 9 (2003), 137–152.

Porter, D., 'Marks, Harry Hananel (1855–1916)', *Oxford Dictionary of National Biography (ODNB)* (Oxford: Oxford University Press, 2004).

Porter, D., '"Speciousness is the Bucketeer's Watchword and Outrageous Effrontery his Capital": Financial Bucket Shops in the City of London, c.1880–1939', in J. Benson and L. Ugolini (eds), *Cultures of Selling: Perspectives on Consumption and Society since 1700* (Aldershot, England, Burlington, VT: Ashgate, 2006), pp. 103–125.

Porter, D., 'Withers, Hartley (1867–1950)', *Oxford Dictionary of National Biography (ODNB)* (Oxford: Oxford University Press, online edn, Oct 2006).

Pottle, M., 'Carr, Sir Arthur Strettell Comyns (1882–1965)', *Oxford Dictionary of National Biography (ODNB)* (Oxford: Oxford University Press,, 2004).

Preda, A., 'The Rise of the Popular Investor: Financial Knowledge and Investing in England and France, 1840–1880', *The Sociological Quarterly* 42 (2001), 205–232.

Preda, A., *Framing Finance: The Boundaries of Markets and Modern Capitalism* (Chicago, IL: The University of Chicago Press, 2009).

Ramsden, J., *The Winds of Change: Macmillan to Heath, 1957–1975* (London, New York: Longman, 1996).

Raven, J., 'British History and the Enterprise Culture', *Past and Present* 123 (1989), 178–204.

Reid, M., *All-Change in the City: The Revolution in Britain's Financial Sector* (Basingstoke: Palgrave Macmillan, 1988).

Reid, M., *Abbey National Conversion to PLC: The Inside Story of Abbey National's Conversion and Flotation* (London: Pencorp Books, 1991)

Robb, G., *White-Collar Crime in Modern England: Financial Fraud and Business Morality, 1845–1929* (Cambridge: Cambridge University Press, 1992).

Rodgers, D. T., *Age of Fracture* (Cambridge, MA: Belknap Press of Harvard University Press, 2011).

Rodwell, G., 'Dr Caleb Williams Saleeby: The Complete Eugenicist', *History of Education* 26 (1997), 23–40.

Roesler, K., *Die Finanzpolitik des Deutschen Reiches im Ersten Weltkrieg* (Berlin: Duncker & Humblot, 2017).

Rollings, N., 'Cracks in the Post-War Keynesian Settlement? The Role of Organised Business in Britain in the Rise of Neoliberalism before Margaret Thatcher', *Twentieth Century British History* 24 (2013), 637–659.

Roodhouse, M., *Black Market Britain, 1939–1955* (Oxford: Oxford University Press, 2013).

Roth, G., 'Weber the Would-Be Englishman: Anglophilia and Family History', in H. Lehmann and G. Roth (eds), *Weber's Protestant Ethic: Origins, Evidence, Contexts* (Washington, D.C.: Cambridge University Press; German Historical Institute, 1995), pp. 83–121.

Rutterford, J., 'The Evidence for "Democratization" of Share Ownership in Great Britain in the Early Twentieth Century', in D. R. Green and J. Rutterford (eds), *Men, Women, and Money: Perspectives on Gender, Wealth, and Investment 1850–1930* (Oxford, New York: Oxford University Press, 2011), pp. 184–206.

Rutterford, J. and Maltby, J., '"She Possessed Her Own Fortune": Women Investors from the Late Nineteenth Century to the Early Twentieth Century', *Business History* 48 (2006), 220–253.

Rutterford, J. and Sotiropoulos, D. P., 'The Rise of the Small Investor in the US and the UK, 1895 to 1970', *Enterprise and Society* 18(3) (2017), 485–535.

Rutterford, J., Green, D. R., Owens, A. and Maltby, J., 'Who Comprised the Nation of shareholders? Gender and Investment in Great Britain, c. 1870–1935', *The Economic History Review* 64 (2011), 157–187.

Saunders, R., '"Crisis? What Crisis?": Thatcherism and the Seventies', in B. Jackson and R. Saunders (eds), *Making Thatcher's Britain* (Cambridge: Cambridge University Press, 2012), pp. 25–42.

Savage, M. and Majima, S., 'Contesting Affluence: An Introduction', *Contemporary British History* 22 (2008), 445–455.

Sayers, R. S., *The Bank of England, 1891–1944* (Cambridge: Cambridge University Press, 1986).

Schofield, C., *Enoch Powell and the Making of Postcolonial Britain* (Cambridge: Cambridge University Press, 2013).

Searle, G. R., *Corruption in British Politics: 1895–1930* (Oxford: Oxford University Press, 1987).

Searle, G. R., *Morality and the Market in Victorian Britain* (Oxford: Oxford University Press, 1998).

Searle, G. R., *A New England? Peace and War, 1886–1918* (Oxford: Oxford University Press, 2004).

Searle, G. R., 'Saleeby, Caleb Williams Elijah (1878–1940)', in H. C. G. Matthew and B. Harrison (eds), *The Oxford Dictionary of National Biography (ONDB)* (Oxford: Oxford University Press, 2004).

Sell, G., *Liberal Revival: Jo Grimond and the Politics of British Liberalism 1956–1967*, University of London PhD thesis (1996).

Sewell, W. H., 'A Strange Career: The Historical Study of Economic Life', *History and Theory* 49 (2010), 146–166.

Seymour-Ure, C., 'Northcliffe's Legacy', in P. Catterall and C. Seymour-Ure (eds), *Northcliffe's Legacy: Aspects of the British Popular Press* (London: Macmillan, 2000), pp. 9–25.

Shepherd, J., *Crisis? What Crisis? The Callaghan Government and the British 'Winter of Discontent'* (Manchester: Manchester University Press, 2013).

Skidelsky, R., *Keynes: The Return of the Master* (London: Allen Lane, 2009).

Slinn, J., 'Braithwaite, Sir John Bevan (1884–1973)', *Oxford Dictionary of National Biography (ODNB)* (Oxford: Oxford University Press, 2004).

Slinn, J.,'Serocold, Claude Pearce (1875–1959)', *Oxford Dictionary of National Biography (ODNB)* (Oxford: Oxford University Press, 2004).

Slobodian, Q., *Globalists: The End of Empire and the Birth of Neoliberalism* (Cambridge, MA: Harvard University Press, 2018).

Stäheli, U., *Spectacular Speculation: Thrills, the Economy, and Popular Discourse* (Stanford, CA: Stanford University Press, 2013).

Stedman Jones, D., *Masters of the Universe: A History of Neoliberalism* (Princeton, NJ: Princeton University Press, 2012).

Stevens, R., 'The Evolution of Privatisation as an Electoral Policy, c. 1970–90', *Contemporary British History* 18 (2004), 47–75.

Strachan, H., *Financing the First World War* (Oxford: Oxford University Press, 2004).

Strange, S., *Casino Capitalism* (Manchester: Manchester University Press, 1986).

Süß, D., 'En Route to a Post-Industrial Society? Western German Contemporary History Writing on the 1970s and 1980s', *Contemporary European History* 18 (2009), 521–529.

Sutcliffe-Braithwaite, F., 'Neo-Liberalism and Morality in the Making of Thatcherite Social Policy', *The Historical Journal* 55 (2012), 497–520.

Swinson, C., *Regulation of the London Stock Exchange. Share Trading, Fraud and Reform 1914–1945* (Oxford: Routledge, 2018).

Swinson, C., *Share Trading, Fraud and the Crash of 1929. A Biography of Clarence Hatry* (Oxford: Routledge, 2019).

Taylor, J., *Creating Capitalism: Joint-Stock Enterprise in British Politics and Culture, 1800–1870* (London: Royal Historical Society, 2006).

Taylor, J., 'Watchdogs or Apologists? Financial Journalism and Company Fraud in Early Victorian Britain', *Historical Research* 85 (2012), 632–650.

Thaler, Richard H., *Misbehaving: The Making of Behavioural Economics* (London: Penguin, 2016).

Theakston, K., 'Armstrong, William, Baron Armstrong of Sanderstead (1915–1980)', *Oxford Dictionary of National Biography (ODNB)* (Oxford: Oxford University Press,).

Ther, P., *Die neue Ordnung auf dem alten Kontinent: Eine Geschichte des neoliberalen Europa* (Berlin: Suhrkamp, 2014).

Thomas, W. A., *The Provincial Stock Exchanges* (London: Cass, 1973).

Thorpe, D. R., *Eden: The Life and Times of Anthony Eden*, First Earl of Avon, 1897–1977 (London: Chatto & Windus, 2003).

Thorpe, D. R., 'Eden, (Robert) Anthony, first earl of Avon (1897–1977)', in H. C. G. Matthew and B. Harrison (eds), *The Oxford Dictionary of National Biography (ONDB)* (Oxford: Oxford University Press, 2004).

Tomes, J., 'Bareau, Paul Louis Jean (1901–2000)', *The Oxford Dictionary of National Biography (ODNB)* (Oxford: Oxford University Press,).

Tomlinson, J., 'British Industrial Policy', in R. Coopey and N. W. C. Woodward (eds), *Britain in the 1970s: The Troubled Economy* (London: UCL Press, 1996), pp. 163–191.

Tomlinson, J., '"Liberty with Order": Conservative Economic Policy, 1951–1964', in M. Francis and I. Zweiniger-Bargielowska (eds), *The Conservatives and British Society, 1880–1990* (Cardiff: University of Wales Press, 1996), pp. 274–288.

Tomlinson, J., 'Labour Party and the City 1945–1970', in R. Michie and P. Williamson (eds), *The British Government and the City of London in the Twentieth Century* (Cambridge: Cambridge University Press, 2004), pp. 174–192.

Tomlinson, J., 'Managing the Economy, Managing the People: Britain c. 1931-70', *Economic History Review* 58 (2005), 555–585.

Tomlinson, J., 'Thrice Denied: "Declinism" as a Recurrent Theme in British History in the Long Twentieth Century', *Twentieth Century British History* 20 (2009), 227–251.

Tomlinson, J., 'Thatcher, Monetarism and the Politics of Inflation', in B. Jackson and R. Saunders (eds), *Making Thatcher's Britain* (Cambridge: Cambridge University Press, 2012), pp. 62–77.

Tomlinson, J., 'The Politics of Declinism', in L. Black and H. Pemberton (eds), *Reassessing 1970s Britain* (Manchester: Manchester University Press, 2013), pp. 41–60.

Tomlinson, J., 'British Government and Popular Understanding of Inflation in the Mid-1970s', *Economic History Review* 67 (2014), 750–768.

Torrance, D., *Noel Skelton and the Property-Owning Democracy* (London: Biteback, 2010).

Traflet, J. M., *A Nation of Small Shareholders: Marketing Wall Street after World War II* (Baltimore, MD: Johns Hopkins University Press, 2013).

Tunstall, J., *Newspaper Power: The New National Press in Britain* (Oxford: Clarendon Press; Oxford University Press, 1996).

Ure, J., 'Clark, Alan Kenneth (1928–1999)', *Oxford Dictionary of National Biography (ODNB)* (Oxford: Oxford University Press, online edn, Oct 2006).

Ure, J., 'Low, Austin Richard William [Toby], first Baron Aldington (1914–2000)', *Oxford Dictionary of National Biography (ODNB)* (Oxford: Oxford University Press,, .).

Vinen, R., *Thatcher's Britain: The Politics and Social Upheaval of the 1980s* (London: Simon & Schuster, 2009).

Vogl, J., *The Specter of Capital* (Stanford, CA: Stanford University Press, 2015).

Wennerlind, C., *Casualties of Credit: The English Financial Revolution, 1620–1720* (Cambridge, MA, London: Harvard University Press, 2011).

Whipple, A., 'Revisiting the "Rivers of Blood" Controversy: Letters to Enoch Powell', *Journal of British Studies* 48 (2009), 717–735.

White, S., '"Revolutionary liberalism"? The Philosophy and Politics of Ownership in the Post-War Liberal Party', *British Politics* 4 (2009), 164–187.

Whiting, R., *The Labour Party and Taxation: Party Identity and Political Purpose in Twentieth-Century Britain* (Cambridge: Cambridge University Press, 2001).

Whiting, R., 'The City and Democratic Capitalism', in R. Michie and P. Williamson (eds), *The British Government and the City of London in the Twentieth Century* (Cambridge: Cambridge University Press, 2004), pp. 96–114.

Williamson, A., *Conservative Economic Policymaking and the Birth of Thatcherism, 1964–1979*, Palgrave Studies in the History of Finance (Basingstoke: Palgrave Macmillan, 2015).

Williamson, P., 'Skelton, (Archibald) Noel (1880–1935)', *Oxford Dictionary of National Biography (ODNB)* (Oxford: Oxford University Press).

Woolven, R., 'Eve, (Arthur) Malcolm Trustram, first Baron Silsoe (1894–1976)', *Oxford Dictionary of National Biography (ODNB)* (Oxford: Oxford University Press, . . . ).

Wormell, J., *The Management of The National Debt of The United Kingdom* (London: Routledge, 2000).

Wright, A. M., *The Threadbare Plea: The Hatry Crash of 1929* (Independently published, 2018).

# Index

·